# MAKING SENSE OF THE
# INDUSTRIAL REVOLUTION

MANCHESTER
UNIVERSITY PRESS

# MAKING SENSE OF THE INDUSTRIAL REVOLUTION

Steven King and Geoffrey Timmins

MANCHESTER
UNIVERSITY PRESS
Manchester and New York
*distributed exclusively in the USA by Palgrave*

Copyright © Steven King and Geoffrey Timmins 2001

The right of Steven King and Geoffrey Timmins to be identified as the
authors of this work has been asserted by them in accordance with the
Copyright, Designs and Patents Act 1988

*Published by Manchester University Press*
Oxford Road, Manchester M13 9NR, UK
*and* Room 400, 175 Fifth Avenue, New York, NY 10010, USA
http://www.manchesteruniversitypress.co.uk

*Distributed exclusively in the USA by*
Palgrave, 175 Fifth Avenue, New York, NY 10010, USA

*Distributed exclusively in Canada by*
UBC Press, University of British Columbia, 2029 West Mall,
Vancouver, BC, Canada V6T 1Z2

*British Library Cataloguing-in-Publication Data*
A catalogue record for this book is available from the British Library

*Library of Congress Cataloging-in-Publication Data applied for*

ISBN   0 7190 5021 9   *hardback*
0 7190 5022 7   *paperback*

First published 2001

08   07   06   05   04   03   02   01      10  9  8  7  6  5  4  3  2  1

Typeset by Carnegie Publishing, Lancaster
Printed in Great Britain by Biddles Ltd, Guildford and King's Lynn

FOR MARGARET HANLY

# CONTENTS

vii

*Contents*

# FIGURES

# Figures

# TABLES

# ACKNOWLEDGEMENTS

This book has been long in the making and overdue in the delivery. We owe our thanks to Vanessa Graham for sticking by the project through its up and downs and to the production team at Manchester University Press. A number of our colleagues have been kind enough to give up their time in order to read draft chapters or just to discuss ideas. They include Anne Digby, John Stewart and Matthew Craske at Oxford Brookes, and Keith Vernon and Henry French at Central Lancashire and to them we offer our thanks. The chapters on demography, the family and agriculture are underpinned by research papers given at the University of Trier and the University of Salzburg and in England at Cambridge, Oxford Brookes and the 1999 Economic History Society conference at St Catherine's college Oxford. The participants in these seminars saved us from error, as did the anonymous referee for Manchester University Press, to whom we express particular thanks. Steven King would also like to thank Professor Dr Dietrich Ebeling from the University of Trier, who arranged a visiting professorship for him at Trier and allowed him the time to write much of his part of the manuscript out of which this book emerged. Joint writing of our book has, perhaps unusually in the history of such enterprises, been a great pleasure. We owe thanks to our respective partners for putting up with the protracted drafting and redrafting and long telephone calls. We also perhaps owe thanks to the M6 Services where we met several times to exchange documents or talk about the project!

# INTRODUCTION

This book arises from our experience in teaching undergraduate courses on the Industrial Revolution. We have frequently found that students attending these courses have difficulty in understanding the more specialised journal literature we ask them to read, especially – and not surprisingly – that based upon econometric techniques. Additionally we have found that they sometimes struggle with contributions in the standard textbooks, the usual problem being that too high a level of conceptual understanding and background knowledge is expected of them. This is especially the case with the growing number of our students who have not previously studied social and economic history to any appreciable extent. To make this point is not to argue that those writing such material do not, as a rule, communicate effectively with an undergraduate audience, but it is to suggest that a significant problem exists with which we need to grapple if we are to capture and enthuse a new generation of economic and social historians.

Against this backdrop, we set out to help students *make sense* of the Industrial Revolution. We have several interlocking objectives:

1 To explain the key concepts, both technical and theoretical, which underpin the issues that we explore. The emphasis on this aspect of our work varies according to the subject matter under consideration, but each chapter begins with a conceptual overview which tries to set up the key issues, to explore problems of terminology, approach or sources and, where appropriate, to tell some real life stories as a way of locating and understanding the key everyday experiences of the Industrial Revolution. In these endeavours we are not claiming or aiming to be exhaustive; we

1

have tried to ensure that consideration of conceptual issues does not dominate the text, since our prime purpose is to engage with historical debates. We have not sought to explain the mathematical techniques employed by econometric historians, for instance, let alone to explore aspects of economic or sociological theory in any depth. Such issues are considered by others.

2 Not to try and do too much. We have not sought to produce a shallow overview of Industrial Revolution historiography, seeking to range across every issue which historians have addressed, as some texts have attempted to do. Rather, we have confined our attention to selected themes which we consider fundamental in seeking to understand the continuities and changes of the Industrial Revolution period. In terms of the economic infrastructure, we engage with the finance of agricultural and industrial development, the nature of marketing, technological innovation and the development of the rural economy. In terms of wider institutional, cultural and social variables, we engage with issues such as demography, the form and function of the family, the changing dynamics of the household economy, and continuity and change in the fabric of the built environment. Naturally, we could have chosen a variety of other themes which are either not considered here or at least not considered directly. We could have looked at issues such as the nature of skill and the work process, class and class consciousness, religion, urbanisation, poverty and welfare, the changing role of the state and legal systems, or even the relationship between industrialisation, urbanisation and crime. These topics are missing or are indirectly addressed in part because they have their own comprehensive literature, in part because of space constraints and in part because we wanted to deal with the basic building blocks of the Industrial Revolution and to understand the effect of industrialisation on some of the most immediate and central institutions of everyday life such as the family. The fact that a potentially long list of themes is addressed only tangentially here should not be read as a reflection of our view as to their importance.

3 To help students engage with primary source material. Our research and publishing activity is focused on the Industrial Revolution period. In the course of this research, we inevitably unearth material which is not of direct use to us with regard to work in

hand, but which nonetheless informs other important themes relating to the period. We can make use of such material in our teaching, but writing a general book on the Industrial Revolution period provides the opportunity to disseminate it more widely. And since the book addresses some of the themes tied up with our own specialist interests, there is scope to incorporate our unpublished research findings as well. By adding a research dimension in this way we have been able to intersperse the review of historiographical debates with considerable amounts of primary material and we hope that the way we have used it will lead students to appreciate more fully how historians evaluate the reliability of their evidence and how they achieve historical interpretation. Crucially, too, we have attempted where appropriate to demonstrate how investigation based upon primary evidence can be used to question interpretations of the past made by historians. Our hope in deploying this approach is that students will not only feel more confident about making informed criticism of the existing literature, but that they will be encouraged to conduct their own research on the Industrial Revolution through dissertation work. In short, we believe that part of the process of *making sense of the Industrial Revolution* is gaining an appreciation of primary evidence and what it can and cannot show, and in this we go beyond the confines of many other textbooks from which the primary source has been largely or completely relegated.

4 To consider the social and economic developments of the Industrial Revolution period not only from a national perspective but also from a regional one. The value of such a perspective has long been recognised and has been urged as a way forward in recent literature in order to counter a perceived overemphasis on national perspectives and aggregate discussion. In taking up this challenge we seek to reassess the notion of an Industrial Revolution by considering the balancing of continuity and change in different English regions and the nature of regional interaction. Even if it is not always seamlessly done, the individual chapters are all underpinned by an essentially regional perspective, and in consciously taking this line we are again trying to step beyond the confines of the conventional textbook.

5 To enhance student understanding of the Industrial Revolution

by viewing it, where appropriate, from the micro-perspective – from the perspective of the individuals, families, firms and communities that experienced continuity and change in their cultural, economic, social and institutional environment. This is by no means a new approach. As we will see in the next chapter, looking at what contemporaries thought and said has a long history, and a sophisticated historical literature stemming from the 1960s has emphasised the need to try and understand some aspects of the Industrial Revolution with reference to the everyday lives and life-cycles of real individuals. However, relatively little material from this school of thought – led by scholars such as Samuel or Thompson – makes it into modern Industrial Revolution textbooks, where the odd reference is often the only concession to ordinary lives that students are likely to see. We offer something slightly different. We frequently use stories of individual lives to organise and focus the arguments in the text, though these are not always elegantly incorporated into discussion of the drier aspects of the economic infrastructure. In adopting this approach we hope that we have made a textbook that is interesting to read, a matter of no little significance given the need to motivate students and to demonstrate to them the fascination that economic and social history can hold. But there is also a wider purpose, for we want to show students that insights obtained at the level of individuals or groups can lead us to make effective challenges to historiographical generalisations as well as to raise questions that lead to fresh lines of investigation. This contention is not new; it has come to dominate approaches to many branches of social history, most notably writing on poverty and welfare. Nor should the approach be taken too far. We must guard against the idea that the experiences of individuals are necessarily representative and against reading more into the evidence than it can actually tell us. Yet, to depict continuity and change only in national and regional terms, as so many textbooks have tended to do, seems to us to overlook opportunities for extending analysis in potentially fruitful directions.

Realising these objectives has been no easy matter and we have had to grapple with three thorny issues as a precursor to our more detailed discussion. First, the issue of spatial focus. Ideally, this would have been a book dealing with the British Industrial Revolution.

However, the mushrooming of recent writing on the Scottish economy and society has begun to suggest very clearly that Scotland had its own development trajectory which is worthy of a history in its own right. More limited writing for Wales suggests that the same may be true here as well. Given the space constraints of this book it would not have been possible to do justice to all three of the mainland countries. Rather than simply adding odd references about Scottish and Welsh experiences to what is otherwise a story of the English Industrial Revolution (as so many textbooks have done) we take a purely English focus here.

The second problematic issue is one of periodisation. A long and winding historiography has advanced a range of different dates for the 'Industrial Revolution'. Some commentators see the Industrial Revolution starting or continuing after 1850. Others see the Industrial Revolution starting well before 1700, and a whole range of periodisations between 1700 and 1850 have been advanced over almost one hundred years of writing. The nature of this debate has been dealt with by other scholars whose work is detailed in our bibliography and we do not propose to review it here. Yet this *is* an important issue. It is now well established that where historians set their chronological goalposts will dictate the degree of change they see, and it is important that we are clear at the outset about the logic of our own periodisation. Thus, in this volume we talk about the Industrial Revolution occurring over a long 150-year period between 1700 and 1850. There are a number of reasons for adopting these dates. On the one hand we feel that too much energy has been devoted to dating precisely a range of experiences that by their very regional and individual nature cannot be so treated. On the other hand our extensive engagement with contemporary narratives over a collective forty years of historical work suggests to us that in this 150-year period we can locate the onset of changes which appeared to contemporaries as more significant than any which had gone before. There is thus a sense in which our periodisation predisposes us to the underlying message of this volume, that there *was* an Industrial Revolution, but this bias is at least acknowledged here.

The final issue with which we must grapple before launching into more detailed analysis follows on from the last. That is understanding the significance of the balancing of continuity and change that can be observed for any arbitrarily defined period. Many of the trends and experiences of the Industrial Revolution period as we have defined it here were not unique and because of this historians have to ask themselves rhetorical questions in order to pin down the point at which changes in the economic or social situation become a matter of order rather than simply degree. What was more significant, the introduction of the turnip in the seventeenth century or its rapid spread in the eighteenth century? Which was more significant, the development of the cotton factory or the application of intensive hand techniques in the new luxury trades of eighteenth- and nine-teenth-century England? If partnerships as a form of industrial organisation double their importance during the eighteenth century but they do so from a low base, is this *significant and revolutionary* or not? The chapters which follow continually engage with the issue of what marks significant change and in doing so they adopt two key yardsticks – the intensity of regional experiences and, where appropriate and possible, the likely cumulative impact of continuity and change on the lives and life-cycles of ordinary historical individuals. Ultimately, however, it is the chapters collectively that must provide the foundation for judging the significance of change, and we return to this issue once again in the Conclusion.

The text which follows is divided into three main parts. The first deals with how contemporaries and historians have perceived the notion of the Industrial Revolution. We suggest that there was a widely held view amongst contemporaries that, irrespective of whether or not they approved, theirs was a society undergoing substantial change. They felt that 'something was happening' much as the Internet gives modern society a feeling of cumulative and fundamental change. We contrast these perceptions with the long-running historiographical debate over the nature of the Industrial Revolution, highlighting the problem of measuring the continuities and changes that were played out on the ground and suggesting that understanding this debate is partly a matter of understanding the regionality of development (on which we have a whole chapter) and in part a function of under-standing the constraints to development that might make even slow growth rates revolutionary. We argue that while wide-ranging changes were put in place both before and after the time period covered by this book, there was a substantial and widely felt ratcheting up of change during the eighteenth and early nineteenth century which, when compared implicitly to what was possible or what might have been expected, merits the title 'Industrial Revolution'.

Part II deals with aspects of the development of the English economic infrastructure. We deal with investment and technological change, both themes which feature strongly in the historiography of the Industrial Revolution and which are linked to abstract measures such as economic growth. There is also a chapter dealing with the nature of domestic demand in both its abstract sense and in the context of the marketing techniques and problems of individuals and firms. The section ends with a chapter on agricultural development, in which we consider and reconsider the long-running debate on the nature and timing of an 'agricultural revolution'. In each of these chapters, and in Part II as a whole, we have tried to identify key changes and to locate them in a temporal and spatial sense in a process of untangling what was and was not significant about the Industrial Revolution period as we have defined it for our book. Methodologically, our approach has been to move from the particular to the general and back again as we seek to demonstrate that the one perspective informs the other and that, if we are to make sense of the Industrial Revolution, we need to take both into account.

Part III focuses on some of the issues that we feel would have lain at the core of everyday experience of the Industrial Revolution. A chapter dealing with recent research on the extent of population growth and family formation sets the scene. It is followed by chapters concerned with family form and function and the household economy. The final chapter assesses the impact of population growth and intensifying regional industrialisation on the physical environment, particularly housing, drawing on evidence from field investigations. As we have suggested already, these are not the only features of everyday life that the historiography considers important. Nor is it always easy, as we have again suggested, to mesh individual, regional and national perspectives in order to assess what it was that constituted 'revolutionary' change in the period under the microscope here. In demography, for instance, some historical demographers would argue that the fertility decline of the late nineteenth century was more revolutionary than the ratcheting up of population growth after 1750. However, these issues have been chosen because they seem to us to be fundamental to an understanding of the impact of the Industrial Revolution on everyday life.

What we will argue in the following chapters is that the interlocking and overlapping changes of the period 1700–1850 considered together do merit the title of 'Industrial Revolution'. Changes in some variables will be seen to be faster and more fundamental than changes in other variables, but our key contention is that cumulative change became visible and immediate to large sections of the ordinary population during this period in a way that it had not done before and, arguably, would not do again in the rest of the nineteenth century.

# PART I

# CONCEPTUALISING THE INDUSTRIAL REVOLUTION

# CHAPTER ONE

# PERCEPTIONS OF THE INDUSTRIAL REVOLUTION

## The contemporary perception

Contemporaries have bequeathed us a great deal of (admittedly disjointed) commentary on how they viewed the social, economic and cultural changes that confronted them in the period 1700–1850. Their remarks appear in both published and manuscript sources, including diaries, letters, social surveys, essays and autobiographies, and, for the most part, they were made by British citizens, though overseas visitors also contributed. Such commentary is both useful and problematic for students of the Industrial Revolution. Native or foreign, contemporary commentators were overwhelmingly male. They sometimes based their observations on first-hand enquiry, thereby achieving a degree of objectivity, but at other times they did little more than rehearse their own strongly held opinions or those of others. They reported alike the circumstances they found unpalatable and those they viewed with favour. Not all that they wrote was intended to enter the public domain, though later publication has ensured that much of it has. The range of social and economic matters they addressed was wide, embracing such long-standing concerns as how best to deal with poverty, as well as new concerns over the social impact of the factory system. However, as will become apparent below, contemporary commentary is disproportionately focused on certain regions and economic sectors, so it is all too easy to obtain an unbalanced perspective. Even if this were not the case, a further feature of contemporary commentary is that it was overwhelmingly either a retrospect on the nature of development or a more immediate observation of maturing industrial society. Relatively few contemporaries recorded their thoughts on areas and industries in the first throes of development or change. Sources and perspectives from literature and art history can offer us complementary perspectives on contemporary views of the continuities and changes of the period 1700–1850 as a way of balancing out our other sources, but unfortunately there is not the space here to pursue these lines of enquiry. Students of the Industrial Revolution must thus think carefully about *both* what contemporaries say and what they do not.

With these caveats in mind, the first part of the chapter considers extracts from a selection of writings to demonstrate the strong conviction amongst contemporaries that England was experiencing unprecedented change during the Industrial Revolution period. We have concentrated on industrial and commercial growth, the expansion of towns and the rise in population, all of them matters which particularly excited contemporary interest, though of course there are many other indicators that we could have chosen. In the second part of the chapter we move to a consideration of the way in which historians have perceived the contemporary view of change and how they have sought to modify it. We will trace the fragmentation of 'Industrial Revolution history' into sub-disciplines such as historical geography, gender history and historical sociology, and try to make sense of the numerous competing and conflicting approaches to understanding the Industrial Revolution that emerged in the last two decades of the twentieth century in particular. Let us start, then, with the contemporary view, noting the comments of Patrick Colquhoun who was particularly impressed with the pace at which industry was developing. In 1814 he observed:

> It is impossible to contemplate the progress of manufactures in Great Britain within the last thirty years without wonder and astonishment. Its rapidity, particularly since the commencement of the French Revolutionary war, exceeds all credibility. The improvement of the steam engines, but above all the facilities offered to the great branches of the woollen and cotton manufactures by ingenious machinery, invigorated by capital and skill, are beyond all calculation. [1]

This is of course a *British* perspective, but the theme of profound change within the textile industries associated with technological change was one that particularly captured the interest of overseas contemporaries as well. Leon Faucher, a German visitor to England in the 1840s, suggested that:

> It is not more than seventy or eighty years since, that a few humble Mechanics, in Lanarkshire [Lancashire], distinguished by anything scarcely more than mechanical ingenuity and perseverance of character,

succeeded in forming a few, but important mechanical combinations, the effect of which has been to revolutionise the whole of British society, and to influence, in a marked degree, the progress of civilisation in every quarter of the globe.[2]

That he does not define what he meant by 'revolutionise' and that, even if he had, he would still have exaggerated the impact that technological change alone could bring (a theme to which we return later) is not the point at issue. Important for our purposes is his belief that revolutionary change had indeed occurred.

As the last extract begins to suggest, it was the prodigious development of the *cotton* textile industry that particularly impressed contemporaries. Thus, writing in 1828, William Radcliffe, a cotton manufacturer from Mellor in Derbyshire, suggested:

> From the year 1770 to 1788, a complete change has gradually been effected in the spinning of yarns – that of wool had disappeared altogether, and that of linen was also nearly gone, – cotton, cotton, cotton, was become the almost universal material for employment.[3]

Radcliffe based his view on the changes that were taking place in Mellor, but he considered that they applied 'generally to every other sub-division of the manufacturing districts, and to most of them on a much larger scale'.[4]

To demonstrate how impressed contemporaries were with the extent to which cotton manufacturing grew, they adduced some remarkable statistics. For instance, in 1824, the publisher and writer Edward Baines, could observe:

> At the commencement of the reign of George III, and for several years afterwards, the annual value of cotton manufactures of this kingdom did not exceed £200,000; at present it is estimated that they amount yearly to from thirty to forty million sterling, of which amount there is exported, including cotton yarn, to the value of twenty millions.[5]

So strong was this growth, he observed, that the industry could be ranked in no less a position than first in the world. Moreover, since the industry was concentrated in Lancashire, it represented 'a phenomenon in growth such as has never been exhibited within the same period in any other county in England'.[6] This theme of 'concentration' is taken up in the next chapter. Meanwhile, we may note too that Baines was moved to describe the progress made by the woollen cloth industry as 'astonishing', the West Riding output rising from a little over two million pieces between 1772 and 1781 to more than 4.5 million pieces between 1812 and 1821.[7]

Such development inevitably led contemporaries to reflect on the ways in which textile workers were affected and to what extent their way of life was altered. Foremost amongst those who argued for a revolutionary impact was Frederick Engels, who believed that:

> The history of the proletariat in England begins with the second half of the last century, with the invention of the steam-engine and of machinery for working cotton. These inventions gave rise, as is well known, to an industrial revolution, a revolution which altered the whole civil society; one, the historical importance of which is only now beginning to be recognised.[8]

To justify this stance, Engels sought to demonstrate how the replacement of traditional spinning wheels – which spun only a single thread – by the multi-spindle jenny, created a labour proletariat. He painted an idealised picture of families engaged in domestic textile production before the jenny. Living in the countryside, wives and daughters did the spinning whilst the fathers wove. Crucially, however, these families usually rented a small piece of land and even if the weaver did not cultivate this land well, its possession meant that he 'was no proletarian, he had his stake in the country, he was permanently settled, and stood one step higher in society than the English workman of today'. With the adoption of the jenny, however, a surplus of yarn was created, with the result that the demand for weavers, and hence the wages they could earn, increased. In these circumstances, the weaver

> gradually abandoned his farming, and gave his whole time to weaving ... By degrees the class of farming weavers wholly disappeared, and was merged in the newly arising class of weavers who lived wholly upon wages, had no property whatever, not even the pretended property of a holding, and so became working-men, proletarians.[9]

Nor, according to the same line of thought, was the position of the proletariat in the textile sector improved by the rise of factory production. Indeed, factory workers were seen by Engels as slaves:

> Owing to the extensive use of machinery and to division of labour, the work of the proletarians has lost all individual character, and, consequently, all charm for the workman. He becomes an appendage of the machine.[10]

Other commentators also took the view that textile factories brought fundamental change for those who worked in them, though not necessarily of an adverse nature. For instance, Richard Guest, an early historian of the cotton industry, suggested that its growth

> introduced great changes into the manners and habits of the people. The operative workmen being thrown together in great numbers, had their faculties sharpened and improved by constant communication. Conversation wandered over a variety of topics not before essayed; the questions of Peace and War, which interested them importantly, inasmuch as they might produce a rise or fall of wages, became highly interesting, and this brought them into the vast field of politics and discussions on the character of their Government, and the men who composed it. They took a greater interest in the defeats and victories of their Country's arms, and from being only a few degrees above their cattle in the scale of intellect, they became Political Citizens.[11]

One further point we should make about contemporary comment on the impact of the rapidly growing textile sector concerns the stimulus given to other industries. In the case of the Manchester area, for instance, John Aiken observed in 1795 that:

> The prodigious extension of the several branches of the Manchester manufacturers has likewise greatly increased the business of several trades and manufactures connected with or dependent upon them. The making of paper at mills in the vicinity has been brought to great perfection, and now includes all kinds, from the strongest parcelling paper to the finest writing sorts, and that on which banker's bills are printed. To the ironmongers shops, which are greatly increased of late, are generally annexed smithies, where many articles are made, even to nails. A considerable iron foundry is established in Salford, in which are cast most of the articles wanted in Manchester and its neighbourhood, consisting chiefly of large cast wheels for the cotton machines; cylinders, boilers, and pipes for steam engines; cast ovens and grates of all sizes.[12]

Of course, contemporary commentary on both the positive and the negative nature of industrial change was not confined to the textile industries, the northwest or the nineteenth century. By the early eighteenth century the development of the coal industry in the northeast had been sufficiently vigorous to prompt contemporaries to lament the scarring of the landscape and the creation of a range of unstable mining-related jobs.[13] At the other end of the eighteenth century, Frederick Morton Eden in the 1790s wondered at the growth of Birmingham but also observed the profound influence of the trade fluctuations that accompanied the growth of industrial centres. He noted, 'The trade of this "Toy shop of Europe" as Mr Burke calls it, has suffered very considerably by the war, particularly in the article of buttons and buckles.'[14] Yet, he was also more positive about the effects of non-export industries. Of Monk Wearmouth in Durham he noted approvingly:

> Many ships are built on the shores of the Wear ... and there is now building a ship of 1200 tons burden ... Much window glass is made here. There are 2 potteries, several ironworks, and firestone and lime-stone quarries.[15]

We could go on utilising quotes in this way, but the key point for students of the Industrial Revolution is that in several areas and industrial sectors, contemporaries thought that something was happening. Moreover, in addition to identifying revolutionary changes in industry, contemporaries drew attention to accompanying changes in commerce, which they regarded as equally far-reaching during the early nineteenth century in particular. Those occurring in Manchester and Liverpool, two of the 'boom' towns of the Industrial Revolution period, particularly excited their interest. James Kay's survey of the working class in Manchester in 1832 concluded that:

> Visiting Manchester, the metropolis of the commercial system, a stranger regards with wonder the ingenuity and comprehensive capacity, which, in the short space of half a century, have here established the staple manufacture of this kingdom. He beholds with astonishment the establishments of its merchants – monuments of fertile genius and successful design; – the masses of capital which have been accumulated by those who crowd upon its mart, and the restless but sagacious spirit which has made every part of the known world the scene of their enterprise.[16]

As to the growth of Liverpool's commerce, the comments and statistics supplied by Edward Baines, writing in 1824, are revealing. He observed that the 'rapid rise of commerce, with its usual concomitants, wealth and population, constitute the grand characteristic of the town and port of Liverpool'. It was only about two centuries previously, he continued, that the place was described as 'the little creek of Liverpool' and was dependent on the port of Chester. The first half of the eighteenth century brought notable progress, however, and in 1760, 1,245 ships traded at the port, the dock duties payable reaching £2,330. Yet these figures were soon eclipsed and by 1820 the number of trading vessels at the port amounted to 7,276 and the dock duties to more than £805,000.[17]

Mention of Manchester and Liverpool serves as a reminder that contemporaries were also struck by the unprecedented rate at which urban areas were expanding. For instance, Joseph Kay, a barrister speaking to the Manchester Statistical Society in December 1852, right at the end of our period, drew attention to the rise of 'vast and populous' provincial cities and suggested that:

> *In no former era and under no former phase of national life, has anything at all similar been witnessed.* There have been great and crowded capitals in bygone ages and amongst other races, as at present, but the history of the centuries, which have passed away, tells us of no such agglomeration of people and wealth in *Provincial* Cities, as that which we now witness.[18]

To take a specific example of how impressed contemporaries were with the rapidity of urban growth, we can note the comments on Ashton-under-Lyne (near Manchester) made by the Revd Stephens in 1849. He suggested that:

> Within a narrow ring of what a few years ago was clay bed and Moorland, with a stretch of hill and a sweep of lovely dale, now swarm not less than a hundred thousand souls. Suddenly, as if by a spell of fairy or fiend, stray hamlet, scattered township and straggling parish have run together and have become one vast unbroken wilderness of mills and houses, a teeming town where the ceaseless whirl and rattle, clink and clank of groaning wheel and flying shuttle bespeak the presence of an industry unparalleled in its nature, its intensity and its duration.[19]

As with industry and commerce, contemporaries adduced telling statistics to highlight the unprecedented rate at with which towns were growing. And with regard to the larger towns, they pointed to certain parts as growing particularly fast. This was the case, for example with Chorlton-upon-Medlock, a township in southeast Manchester. According to figures provided by Edwin Butterworth, writing at the start of 1841, the township's population stood a little above 200 in the early 1770s, but had reached no less than 20,569 by 1831. 'Half a century ago', Butterworth remarked, 'this place was quite in the country, now the greater part of it in an exceedingly populous town.' He also cited the case of Everton, which comprised the northeast part of the borough of Liverpool. 'A few years ago', he pointed out, 'the place was a retired village, now it is an elegant suburb.' In

1801, the Everton population was 499, but by 1831 had reached 4,518.[20] Of course, urbanisation proceeded much faster in some areas than in others, but, as contemporary diarists show us so often, what was new about the early nineteenth century in particular was the degree to which there was a national awareness of the process of urban growth.

Contemporaries did not just comment on the scale of urban development. They were also concerned with the changing role of towns and cities and the expanding range of services and amenities that could be found in urban areas. To appreciate the type of new facilities that major towns acquired during the Industrial Revolution era, Edward Baines's comments on Sheffield are instructive. Baines maintained that a new era of the town's history opened during the mid-eighteenth century, heralded in 1742 by Thomas Bolsover's invention of Sheffield plate – a cheap substitute for silver plate made by fusing silver to the surface of copper. But it was much more than the introduction of additional industries that moved him to identify the new era.

> The flood of improvement and prosperity continued to flow freely through this age. In the year 1750, Mr. Joseph Broadbent first opened a direct trade with the Continent from Sheffield; and in the following year the river Don was made navigable to Tinsley, within three miles of the town, which greatly facilitated the export of merchandise. The first stage waggon which travelled from this neighbourhood was set up about the same time by Joshua Wright of Mansfield; and to add to the public accommodation, a stage coach was established from Sheffield to London, in the year 1760, by Mr. Samuel Glanville, of the Angel Inn. Five years after the first coffee-house in Sheffield was opened, by Mr. Holland, at the same inn; and in 1770, Mr. Roebuck opened a bank in the town, which was then a perfectly *unique* establishment in Sheffield, for the accommodation of its merchants and traders. In 1786, the first steam-engine grinding wheel was erected by Messrs. Proctors, on the east bank of the Sheaf, and the agency of water has since been in a great measure superseded in the large manufactories, by the use of that much more certain and efficient power – steam. Up to the year 1786, there was no newspaper existing in Sheffield ... but now there are no fewer than three weekly newspapers issued from the public press of Sheffield.[21]

It was both the extent and importance of additions made to Sheffield's business and public amenities during the second half of the eighteenth century that so impressed Baines. Each of the improvements he cites represented a first important step, but, taken together, they give a good deal of substance to his notion that a new era had emerged. And this is the more so when we bear in mind that each of the developments led to other, similar ones and that Baines was defining his new era only in terms of new developments and not in terms of extensions to existing facilities, such as places of worship and public buildings. On a lesser scale, urban development up and down the country heralded a new era in provision of facilities.

Naturally, not all contemporary comment relating to towns reveals a picture of progress. Writing in 1795, for instance, Sir Frederick Morton Eden noted of the Devon parish of Tiverton that there were

> 7,096 inhabitants, 5,343 of whom are in the town, the rest in the parish outside the town; but in the first decade of the eighteenth century it contained about 8,693, the reduction being due to the competition of Norwich stuffs and other woollen with the locally made serge.[22]

Of Frome in Somerset, he remarked that:

> The town is very ancient, and has been the seat of woollen manufacture for several centuries; yet the external appearance of the town does not indicate that wealth which is usually attendant on commerce. The houses are very different from the elegant dwellings that are to be found in the Yorkshire manufacturing towns ... The streets are narrow, unpaved and dirty.[23]

The West Country wool industry was evidently encountering severe competition from the expansion of wool manufacturing elsewhere, and this extract reminds us both that the massive growth in urban populations had a distinctly regional flavour and that the Industrial Revolution was partly a process within which regional industrial concentration was accentuated. We return to this theme in the next chapter.

Eden also drew attention to rural change, a factor which we have neglected thus far but analyse in depth in Part II. Thus, of Blandford in Dorset Eden remarked:

> The rapid rise of the Poor's Rate in this parish is generally attributed to the high price of provisions, the smallness of wages, and the consolidation of small farms, and the consequent depopulation of villages, which obliges small farmers to turn labourers or servants ... It is said that there are now only 2 farms in Durweston, about 3 miles from here, which contained about 30 small farms 20 years ago. And what is

more singular the town of Abbey Milton, which was formerly the central market of the county, is now a fish pond.[24]

Meanwhile, apart from noting the varying rates at which urban populations grew, and instances of rural depopulation, contemporaries also drew attention to the rapidity with which the national population was expanding. During the eighteenth century, before decennial census figures were compiled, contemporaries disagreed as to whether the English population was rising or falling. By 1800, however, Eden concluded that a rapid rise was taking place. Surveys of parish baptism and burial totals made during the 1790s revealed that the former were almost 50 per cent higher that the latter.[25] By the 1820s, Thomas Malthus, who had long been concerned about population growing faster than food supplies, was drawing conclusions about the rate of population growth that could scarcely have reassured him. Utilising evidence from the first three censuses of England and Wales, he calculated that there was an increase of 13.3 per cent between 1801 and 1811 and of 15.6 per cent between 1811 and 1821:

> making the rate of increase in the former period such as, if continued, would double the population in about 55 years, and in the latter, such as would double it in 48 years. Taking the whole 20 years together, the rate of increase would be such as, if continued, to double the population in about 51 years.

Such figures, he concluded, represented 'a most extraordinary rate of increase'.[26]

Equally impressed by the rate at which national population was growing were those responsible for compiling the 1851 census. They wrote:

> With all we now see around us it is difficult to place ourselves in the position of the people of 1751; and to understand either the simplicity of the means, or the greatness of the task which has since been achieved by the people of England and Scotland.

They were particularly taken with the thought that, as they put it, 'two more nations, each in number equal to the existing population', had been created during this period. And, in a decidedly anti-Malthusian stance, they argued that the achievement was all the more remarkable because it was accomplished with the wealth of the country increasing at a faster ratio than the population.[27]

The evidence presented in this section reveals that at least some of those living in England during the Industrial Revolution period as we have defined it believed they were experiencing an era of unprecedented social and economic change. It is impossible to know how widely their views were shared at the time and we must concede that change would be much more marked for some individuals and their families than for others and in some parts of the country than in others. Yet it is hard to believe that, even if they were sceptical about the degree of advantage arising, a great many contemporaries would not have taken the view that theirs was a society undergoing profound change and even that the degree of change was unprecedented. Certainly this was a view to which early historians of the Industrial Revolution were wedded, an issue to which we turn below.

## Historians' perceptions

The type of positive contemporary comments we have noted above also dominate the works of antiquarian historians who came in ever larger numbers to write local and regional histories after 1800. With an emphasis on narrative rather than analysis, the antiquarian historians reserved a special place for the period 1700 (more particularly 1750) to 1850. It was a period they characterised not in terms of an Industrial Revolution but in the language of 'economic upheaval', 'the age of the factory' or the 'grand age'. As with Eden, they were both commenting on what they saw, or what the records seemed to tell them, and adding to a national impression of 'something having happened'. The scale of their contribution is rarely appreciated. In the West Yorkshire industrial districts alone, it is estimated that 310 antiquarian histories were written between 1780 and 1880 with a probable circulation of well over 100,000. These were very significant purveyors of the notion of an Industrial Revolution.[28]

The first academic commentators on the Industrial Revolution gave a national emphasis to what had been conceived by contemporaries as a regional phenomenon. The Great Exhibition, the heroic inventors and great manufacturers became the symbols of a national Industrial Revolution that was seen to upset the whole basis of everyday life. To Arnold Toynbee, writing in 1884, the key characteristic lying behind an Industrial Revolution, which started around 1760, was 'the substitution of competition for the medieval regulations which had previously controlled the production and distribution of wealth'.[29]

Other early commentators used different yardsticks to characterise the Industrial Revolution. In particular the Hammonds and Webbs drew attention to the conundrum of the industrialisation process – increasing wealth and increasing poverty. Together, both processes were seen to create the backdrop of a fundamental change in the social fabric.[30] By contrast, Mantoux took a more traditional 'economic history' approach, acknowledging that a long series of changes underpinned the more fundamental developments of the last third of the eighteenth century. Yet he concluded: 'Even though, unlike political revolutions, it [the Industrial Revolution] did not alter the legal form of society, yet it modified its very nature.'[31]

Such categorical statements were not to hold sway for long and academic historians soon came to be embroiled in debate over the timing of fundamental economic change, and over questions of basic terminology and methodology – does the term 'revolution' overstate the speed of change and does the term 'industrial' constrain our thinking on a topic with a wide and interlinked train of cause and effect? Was the 'Industrial Revolution' an economic revolution, or should we throw our conceptual net rather wider? What variables should we use to investigate the eighteenth and nineteenth centuries and what yardsticks should we apply to establish whether the 'changes' we see were significant or not? How do we balance what can be measured against that which cannot? Not without good reason did Arthur Redford label the period 1760–1860 as 'the most controversial century in the economic history of England'.[32] He went on to suggest:

> The developments which took place in the reign of George III must therefore be regarded as the quickening of an age-long evolutionary process, rather than as a violent break with the past and a fresh beginning. The whole trend of modern research has been to show that the economic changes of the eighteenth century were less sudden, less dramatic, and less catastrophic than Toynbee and his disciples thought.[33]

About a hundred years after the term 'Industrial Revolution' had passed into common usage, therefore, academic historians were re-writing history. The 'modern research' to which Redford referred in 1931 was largely that of Clapham who did not use the term 'Industrial Revolution' in his book title and found nothing in the census data which underpinned his analysis to suggest that large sectors of the British workforce (or the way in which they did their jobs) had been revolutionised.[34] This perspective was to develop much further after Redford wrote. Clapham published more volumes of his *Economic history of Modern Britain*, and Herbert Heaton concluded that 'A revolution that continued for 150 years and had been in preparation for at least another 150 years may well seem to need a new label.'[35] Lipson suggested that the changes of the Industrial Revolution period represented just the most recent instance of 'a constant tide of progress and change, in which the old is blended almost imperceptibly with the new'.[36] There is, however, a subtle distinction to be made between those early commentators who thought that there was a discontinuity but no revolution, and those, like Lipson, who simply thought that there was no discontinuity. T. S. Ashton, for instance, felt that 'there is a danger of overlooking the essential fact of continuity' and suggested that we should stop trying to link 'Industrial Revolution' to a period in time. He nonetheless believed that something very significant happened in the seventy years after 1760. And he also suggested that the fundamental nature of this change could have been seen more clearly by historians had British entrepreneurs not been obliged to make all the mistakes that later entrepreneurs could avoid, had unproductive expenditure not been so frequent and had politicians been more purposeful.[37]

Commentators after Ashton were no less divided. Charles Wilson, writing in the mid-1960s, saw the roots of accelerated (but not revolutionary) growth in output firmly located in the 1660s under the aegis of state-sponsored trade growth.[38] Geoffrey Taylor likewise traced very considerable continuities in social variables (such as the experience of being poor) between the seventeenth and nineteenth centuries, but identified 'revolutionary change' after the 1840s.[39] Yet, even as the evolutionary view was consolidating its academic position, there were dissenting voices. Peter Mathias put forward the view that the Industrial Revolution 'marks one of the great watersheds in the history of human society'. He also suggested that the significance of numbers showing the speed of change 'is, again, a subjective criterion, and judged against a perspective of the whole sweep of history, the adjective revolutionary is surely appropriate?'[40] Rostow's 'stage theory' of economic growth was also challenging, linking the experience of leading industrial sectors like cotton with an upsurge in national investment (capital formation) during the late eighteenth century to generate an Industrial Revolution.[41] David Landes's renewed emphasis on the importance of technological change also reinforced notions of substantial change occurring in the eighteenth and nineteenth centuries, while Deane and Cole's initial attempt at assembling empirical evidence on the quantitative dimensions of the Industrial Revolution also tended in the same direction.[42] With Phyllis Deane's *The first Industrial Revolution*, the label itself was making a renewed foray into academic acceptability.[43] Attempts to specify the causes of the Industrial Revolution, as opposed to its impact or its identity, added to this renewed interest in the Industrial Revolution as an identifiable phenomenon.[44]

After Deane, the whole issue of an Industrial Revolution became more complicated. The tendency for history to split into a variety of notional, overlapping sub-disciplines switched attention from the Industrial Revolution as a phenomenon towards the constituent parts of the process. From the late 1960s and early 1970s it was possible to approach the 'Industrial Revolution' from the perspectives of business history, accountancy, historical geography, gender history, feminist history, social history, cultural history, economic history and a whole variety of other nooks and crannies within the discipline of 'history'. Such perspectives are very valuable and some of the classic historical texts, all of them dealing directly or indirectly with the Industrial Revolution, stem from this fragmentation.[45] Judging the Industrial Revolution thus became intricately tied up with a range of 'smaller' questions. These included the degree to which industrialisation excluded women from the formal paid labour market and created a class society; the extent to which it widened access to consumer goods and raised living standards; and how far it created a sub-strata of poor people.[46] The implications of these smaller questions for the way in which we should regard the Industrial Revolution itself are profound. The Industrial Revolution period can be seen to have coincided with an acceleration and intensification of some existing trends, for instance, in the scale and depth of poverty, and to have created a whole set of new experiences, such as exclusion of women from the workforce or the criminalisation of customary behaviour. The relatively few studies that appeared in the 1970s dealing with the wider sweep of the Industrial Revolution process helped to resurrect the notion of discontinuity.[47]

However, Claphamite emphasis on slow processes of evolution was never far below the surface, and the work of Crafts in 1985 constituted both a restatement of these broad themes and an apparent discontinuity in the historiography. Crudely put, Crafts revisited the national economic numbers offered by Deane and Cole and found them wanting. He suggested that such key indicators as growth of gross national product and industrial productivity had been substantially overstated for the classic Industrial Revolution period. The economy grew more slowly than previous historians had suggested and, by 1700, Britain was further advanced in terms of such key indicators as the proportion of the labour force engaged in industry than had ever been thought to be the case. These findings are significant, though they have been contested. We return to them shortly, but the really important point to note is that the work of Crafts, along with other early quantifiers such as Williamson, made discussion of the Industrial Revolution as a concept partly contingent upon the lessons to be drawn from national economic numbers, a concept which would not have been recognisable to contemporaries.[48]

Table 1.1 contrasts the different estimates of growth in per capita national income generated by Deane and Cole and by Crafts. The limited nature of the historical evidence which underpins national economic numbers of this type, and the range of assumptions that have to be employed in dealing with it, mean that there is scope for continual reinterpretation of the figures. Some of the complexities are covered in Part II when figures on national investment (capital formation) are discussed, and they are given more attention by a range of other commentators than is either possible or desirable here.[49] Such figures proved contentious in the 1980s and early 1990s, and they have been subject to revision and counter-revision. We do not propose to review this debate here or provide detailed tables of the different figures; the key point for students is that the broad perspective – that *national* income grew slowly during the Industrial Revolution – remained and remains largely unshaken. The changes in other, narrower, indicators which might throw light on the concept of the Industrial Revolution have been seen as equally unspectacular in a quantitative sense. Thus, table 1.2 gives some idea of the revisions and counter-revisions in the estimated annual growth rates of industrial production. If we were going to see a narrowly defined Industrial Revolution anywhere, then this is presumably where it should emerge. Yet, while these rates are respectable the estimates and revisions/counter-revisions suggest nothing like spectacular growth. Indeed, it has been argued that growth in agricultural productivity rather than industrial production is what drove the eighteenth-century economy forward, although even this conclusion has been questioned, as chapter seven will show. Productivity estimates relating to factors of production (labour and capital) provide an equally dense wet blanket to throw on notions of the Industrial Revolution as a spectacular national event, at least in so far as it can be measured by national numbers.

**Table 1.1** *Per capita national income growth rates (%) from different authors*

| Period | Deane and Cole | Crafts |
| --- | --- | --- |
| Early eighteenth century | 0.44 | 0.30 |
| Late eighteenth century | 0.52 | 0.17 |
| Early nineteenth century | 1.61 | 0.52 |
| Mid- to late nineteenth century | 1.98 | 1.98 |

*Source*: J. Mokyr, 'The new economic history and the Industrial Revolution', in Mokyr (ed.), *The British*, p. 9.

It is tempting to undertake a further elaboration of these figures and of the methods used to weight the contributions of various industrial sectors in the national experience, but in many respects this would be a diversion from the central task and central theme of our book. In any case, the important point is that in one sense the lessons to be drawn from tables 1.1 and 1.2 should not really surprise us. The magnitude of, and trends in, national numbers reflect what we have known for almost a century, that eighteenth- and nineteenth-century England had two economies – traditional and modern – with the former bigger by far than the latter. Of course, labels like this are inadequate and potentially misleading as Hudson and Berg point out in their now classic riposte to quantitative estimates of the sort we see in the two tables.[50] 'Traditional' did not mean slow-growing or technologically backward and 'modern' did not mean fast-growing and technologically forward, as we will see in Part II. Such labels also mask the essential regional dimension of the Industrial Revolution and the varying degree of change within and between industries. What they do offer, however, is an impression that a revolution in the structure of the economy took all of the 150 years covered by this book and longer. Against this backdrop we would not expect to see rapid change in the numbers reviewed above, however fast output growth in the cotton industry, however significant the accumulated impact of small changes in the 'traditional sector' and however significant movements such as a declining participation rate in the female labour force. National numbers thus provide one index of change, but not the only one.

**Table 1.2** *Annual percentage growth rates of industrial production*

| Period | Deane and Cole | Crafts | Harley | Jackson |
|---|---|---|---|---|
| Early eighteenth century | 0.74 | 0.70 | — | — |
| Late eighteenth century | 1.24 | 1.3 | 1.5 | 1.3 |
| Early nineteenth century | 4.4 | 2.8 | 3.0 | 2.9 |
| Mid- to late nineteenth century | 2.9 | — | — | — |

*Source*: N. F. R. Crafts and C. K. Harley, 'Output growth and the British Industrial Revolution: a restatement of the Crafts–Harley view', *Economic History Review*, 45 (1992) 703–30.

Other commentators have suggested the same thing. The contribution from Hudson and Berg represents one attempt to take a more holistic view, but there were others. Mokyr suggested that 'The Industrial Revolution was "revolutionary" because technological progress and the transformation of the economy were not ephemeral events.'[51] Moreover, he went on to talk of a whole range of aspects that made it 'more than an Industrial Revolution' – attitudes, class consciousness, family life, demographic behaviour.[52] Meanwhile, Landes noted the 'macroeconomic reconstruction and diminution of the industrial revolution', and particularly the diminution of the role afforded to technical change. But like Hudson and Berg he suggested that new numbers obscure as much as they reveal in a process of acknowledged 'selective unbalanced growth'.[53] He maintained that the national numbers

> build on a variety of theoretical assumptions, often unspecified, that shape [distort] reality to the needs of calculations; make generous use of proxies, interpolations, and extrapolations to fill in the spotty data; make drastic assumptions about the changing composition of the workforce and draw inferences therefrom about the changing composition of product; and combine data from different sources, assembled at different times for different purposes.[54]

To Landes 'the basis of wealth, hence power, had been transformed' and this was the basic if ultimately unquantifiable indicator that testified to an Industrial Revolution. We are not so scathing of national numbers. The work of Crafts, Harley and others is ingenious and well placed. At no point have these commentators sought to deny that what happened in England in particular was 'historically unique and internationally remarkable' nor that, in a wide sense, England experienced a fundamental transformation in the period covered by this book. Indeed, read imaginatively, work on national economic numbers should have been a call to arms to historians, obliging them to think in terms of what was and was not 'significant' about trends in abstract numbers; to generate yardsticks against which to measure 'change' that are historically accurate and would have been recognised by contemporaries; and to set a new agenda for looking at how regional economies fitted together to generate the sort of Industrial Revolution that we see played out in tables 1.1 and 1.2. It is hardly the fault of quantitative historians that others have not taken up their call to arms.

There is also a danger here of setting up straw figures to be subsequently blown down. The importance of the work of Crafts and others is that it propelled national numbers to the forefront of the debate over the English Industrial Revolution. Yet, this does not mean that writing on the social and cultural aspects of the industrialisation process had stopped. On the contrary, the 1980s and 1990s yielded a raft of new empirical and general studies on topics as varied as social protest, poverty and welfare, the family, the language of class and experience of life-cycle phases such as childhood. This literature is partially dealt with in Part III of our book and we do not have the space to rehearse it here too. The important point for students of the Industrial Revolution is that it is possible and desirable to locate the work of econometric historians within the framework of a wider literature which frequently identifies more radical social and cultural change.

It is also desirable, of course, to acknowledge that despite the energy devoted to discussion of national numbers, other deeply rooted approaches to the Industrial Revolution have continued to develop. Thus, while we suggested earlier that regional perspectives have not been forthcoming in the sorts of numbers that are desirable, regional studies of the metalware, brewing and other industries *have* been conducted and there has been a vibrant debate around the issue of whether 'regions' can be identified and what gave them their unity. These are themes to which we return in the next chapter. In addition, it is important to acknowledge that alternative theoretical approaches to industrialisation have also developed alongside the econometric approach. Most notably, historians have tried to flesh out the notion of an 'industrious revolution' as a process complementary to and partially substitutable for the Industrial Revolution. The concept of the 'industrious revolution' is perhaps more flexible than its older counterpart, identifying change as well as continuity as important and dealing less with strictly measurable criteria such as output and more with issues such as the nature of work organisation, product diversification, design, marketing, the pace of work, the nature of skill and the quality of products. In this model, toy makers, those who manufactured luxury goods, lace handworkers, mantua makers and a range of other neglected trades contribute as much to a sense of 'something happening' as do the cotton factories of the Midlands and northwest.[55] Once again, these are themes which wind through this book.

## Conclusion

If we are to move beyond Clark's well-worn phrase that the Industrial Revolution is a 'handy phrase for describing a period',[56] or Clapham's equally well-worn phrase that the Industrial Revolution reminds him of a 'thrice squeezed orange' but with 'an astonishing amount of juice in it',[57] we must take a newer and broader view. Unfortunately, historians have generally been much better at calling for this sort of thing than delivering it. Mokyr lists the wider variables that made an Industrial Revolution but does not explore them. Ashton warns that, 'the changes were not merely industrial, but also social and cultural', but then never examines them.[58] And notwithstanding Hudson and Berg's call for the writing of more regional histories – histories of areas that changed permanently, those that changed temporarily and those that hardly seem to have changed at all – the regionality of the Industrial Revolution did not attract great emphasis in the 1990s. There is thus a need to go back to the basics in the process of making sense of historiographical trends with regard to the Industrial Revolution.

Against this backdrop we could use David Cannadine's contention that historians are influenced in their focus, style and interpretation by their contemporary economic and social conditions, as a way of organising our thoughts. Doing so would allow us to divide the historiography into five or six distinct phases.[59] Alternatively, we might follow Joel Mokyr, who divides recent historiography into four strands of emphasis, focusing on social change, industrial organisation, the national economy and technology. Or we might want to locate the precise regional and source focus of the main contributors to the Industrial Revolution debate, on the basis that what the historian sees is at least partly a reflection of where and when they look and what exactly they look at. David Landes provides us with a useful alternative to this arduous task and to the other potential ways of making sense of the historiography. He suggests three central reasons for the pre-eminence of the quantifiers in the historiography of the 1980s and 1990s. First, because there are few 'historians' as opposed to economists writing about the Industrial Revolution now, we lose 'a sense of proportion and of knowledge of context'. Second, and related to this point, 'we are talking past one another', and finally, he suggests, 'Rhetoric and loose imagery are the enemies of understanding.' [60]

Of course, we have seen that econometric studies fit in with a long and rich history of diverse approaches to the Industrial Revolution. We have also suggested that even in the 1980s and 1990s alternative theoretical and empirical approaches to the industrialisation process were alive and well. Yet, Landes is absolutely right to suggest that historians of the Industrial Revolution have been talking past each other for very many years. In practice, there is no such thing as a historiography of *the* Industrial Revolution, merely historiographies of several Industrial Revolutions differently conceived and dated. Historians manufacture their own Industrial Revolution, and in this respect we are no different from anyone else. But we are at least transparent. Our Industrial Revolution springs from a series of questions that are played out in the chapters that follow. What was being revolutionised? How was it being revolutionised? Where did change take place and where did it not? How visible would change have been to contemporaries? How did change affect ordinary everyday lives? And by what yardsticks would contemporaries have judged 'their times'? The 'what' and the 'how' are the focus of Parts II and III. The 'where' is explored in the next chapter.

### Notes

1  P. Colquhoun, *A treatise on the wealth, power and resources of the British empire* (London, Cass, 1969 reprint), p. 68.

2  L. Faucher, *Manchester in 1844* (London, Cass, 1969 reprint) p. 6.

3  W. Radcliffe, *Origin of the new system of manufacture, commonly called powerloom weaving* (Stockport, Lomax, 1828), p. 61.

4  *Ibid.*

5  E. Baines, *History, directory and gazetteer of the county palatine of Lancaster, volume 1* (Newton Abbot, David and Charles, 1968 reprint), p. 112.

6  *Ibid.*, p. 118.

7  E. Baines, *History, directory and gazetteer of the county of York, volume 1* (Newton Abbot, David and Charles, 1969 reprint), p. 287.

8  F. Engels, *The condition of the working class in England in 1844* (London, CTR, 1991), p. 43.

9  *Ibid.*, p. 102.

10 *Ibid.*, p. 136.

11 R. Guest, *A compendious history of the cotton manufacture* (London, Cass, 1969 reprint), p. 231.

12 J. Aiken, *A description of the country from thirty to forty miles round Manchester* (Newton Abbot, David and Charles, 1968 reprint), p. 176.

13 K. Wrightson and D. Levine, *The making of an industrial society: Whickham 1560–1765* (Oxford, Oxford University Press, 1991).

14 F. M. Eden, *The state of the poor* (London, Cass, 1969 reprint), p. 92.

15 *Ibid.*, p. 276.

16 J. P. Kay, *The moral and physical condition of the working classes* (Manchester, Morton, 1832), pp. 76–7.

17 Baines, *History of York*, pp. 187–88.

18 J. Kay, *On the nature and training of children in England and Germany* (Manchester, Manchester Statistical Society, 1852), p. 6. Our italics.

19 Quoted in C. Aspin, *The first industrial society* (Preston, Carnegie, 1995), p. 128.

20 E. Butterworth, *A statistical sketch of the County Palatine of Lancaster* (Manchester, Lancashire and Cheshire Antiquarian Society, 1841), p. 65.

21 Baines, *History of York*, p. 287.

22 Eden, *The state*, pp. 358–9.

23 *Ibid.*, p. 302.

24 *Ibid.*, p. 177.

25 F. M. Eden, *An estimate of the number of inhabitants in Great Britain and Ireland* (London, Wright, 1800), pp. 50–2.

26 T. R. Malthus, *An essay on the principle of population* (London, Murray, 1826), pp. 441–5.

27 *Census of Great Britain, 1851, Population tables II: ages, civil condition, occupation and birth places of the people, volume 1.*

28 P. Hudson and S. King, *Industrialisation and everyday life* (forthcoming, 2001).

29 A. Toynbee, *The Industrial Revolution* (London, Green and Co., 1894), p. 85.

30 J. Hammond and B. Hammond, *The rise of modern industry* (London, Methuen, 1925), and S. Webb and B. Webb, *The history of trade unionism* (London, Green and Co., 1894).

31 P. Mantoux, *The Industrial Revolution in the eighteenth century: an outline of the beginnings of the modern factory system* (London, Cape, 1961), p. 476.

32 A. Redford, *The economic history of England 1760–1860* (London, Longman, 1931), p. vii.

33 *Ibid.*, p. 4.

34 J. H. Clapham, *An economic history of modern Britain, volume 1: the early railway age 1820–1850* (Cambridge, Cambridge University Press, 1930).

35 H. Heaton, 'Introduction', in R. M. Hartwell (ed.), *The causes of the Industrial Revolution in England* (London, Methuen, 1967), p. 35.

36 E. Lipson, *The economic history of England* (London, Longman, 1934), p. 12.

37 T. S. Ashton, *The Industrial Revolution 1760–1830* (Oxford, Oxford University Press, 1948), pp. 2, 114, 125–6 and 129.

38 C. Wilson, *England's apprenticeship 1603–1763* (London, Longman, 1965).

39 G. Taylor, *The social experience of the Industrial Revolution* (London, Longman, 1959).

40 P. Mathias, 'Preface', in Hartwell, *The causes*, pp. vii–ix.

41 W. W. Rostow, *The stages of economic growth* (Cambridge, Cambridge University Press, 1960).

42 D. Landes, *The unbound prometheus: technological change and industrial development in western Europe from 1750 to the present* (Cambridge, Cambridge University Press, 1968), and P. Deane and W. A. Cole, *British economic growth, 1688–1959* (Cambridge, Cambridge University Press, 1967).

43 P. Deane, *The first Industrial Revolution* (Cambridge, Cambridge University Press, 1965).

44 M. W. Flinn, *Origins of the Industrial Revolution* (London, Longman, 1966).

45 For the best-known examples, see E. P. Thompson, *The making of the English working class* (London, Penguin, 1968), A. J. Taylor (ed.), *The standard of living in Britain in the Industrial Revolution* (London, Methuen, 1975), and J. Scott and L. Tilly, *Women, work and the family* (New York, Academic Press, 1978).

46 See, for instance, B. Inglis, *Poverty and the Industrial Revolution* (London, Hodder, 1971), and J. Foster, *Class struggle and the Industrial Revolution: early industrial capitalism in three English towns* (London, Macmillan, 1974).

47  For instance R. M. Hartwell, *The Industrial Revolution and economic growth* (London, Methuen, 1956).

48  N. F. R. Crafts, *British economic growth during the Industrial Revolution* (Oxford, Clarendon, 1985).

49  See C. Knick-Harley, 'Reassessing the Industrial Revolution: a macro view', in J. Mokyr (ed.), *The British Industrial Revolution: an economic perspective* (Boulder, Col., Westview Press, 1993), P. Hudson, *The Industrial Revolution* (London, Arnold, 1992), and R. V. Jackson, 'Rates of industrial growth during the Industrial Revolution', *Economic History Review*, 45 (1992) 1–23.

50  P. Hudson and M. Berg 'Rehabilitating the industrial revolution', *Economic History Review*, 45 (1992) 24–50.

51  Mokyr, 'The new economic history and the Industrial Revolution', in Mokyr (ed.), *The British*, p. 4.

52  *Ibid.*, pp. 5–6.

53  D. Landes, 'The fable of the dead horse; or, the Industrial Revolution revisited', in Mokyr (ed.), *The British*, p. 142.

54  *Ibid.*, p. 150.

55  For more on the industrious revolution as a concept and practical research tool specifically in the English context, see M. Berg, *The age of manufactures: industry, innovation and work in Britain, 1700–1820* (London, Fontana, 1985).

56  G. N. Clark, *The idea of the Industrial Revolution* (Glasgow, Brent, 1953), pp. 32–3.

57  J. H. Clapham, 'The transference of the worsted industry from Norfolk to the West Riding', *Economic Journal*, 20 (1910) 195.

58  Ashton, *The Industrial*, p. 2.

59  D. Cannadine, 'The past and the present in the English Industrial Revolution, 1880–1980', *Past and Present*, 103 (1984) 149–58.

60  Landes, 'The fable', pp. 168–9.

CHAPTER TWO

# THE REGIONALITY
# OF ENGLISH ECONOMIC
# DEVELOPMENT

## Conceptual framework

Pat Hudson has suggested that the key feature of the post-1750 period was the emergence of 'distinct and internally integrated regions' which drove the industrialisation process forward and had far-reaching effects on work patterns, household economies and the nature of everyday life. In terms of the national economy, the turmoil which was associated with the emergence of specialist regions in industry, agriculture and commerce was a more significant indicator of 'Industrial Revolution' than aggregate growth rates.[1] She is not alone in this view. John Langton has likewise suggested that industrialisation broke down small-scale localism and created a situation in which people identified themselves as part of broad economic regions. Only the coming of railways at the very end of our period, he believes, brought fundamental inter-regional integration.[2] However, other commentators have been less convinced, either that we can identify the emergence of meaningful economic regions during the Industrial Revolution, or that, having done so, investigating the existence and development of such regions can really help us in our interpretation of the character of the 'Industrial Revolution' in an English context.[3] It is these two key issues that we want to address here.

As a starting point, it is important to understand that contemporaries thought they could identify distinctive regions in the English 'development' process. By the early eighteenth century Daniel Defoe had opened up to what we now call 'middle England' the first reliable overview of its English regional heritage.[4] He was followed by a whole series of travellers and commentators who traced and retraced the outlines of English regional development during the eighteenth and nineteenth centuries.[5] By 1800 the language of 'manufacturing districts', 'pastoral districts', 'arable districts' and 'commercial districts' was firmly entrenched in contemporary descriptions of the processes of economic change. As we saw in chapter one, regional surveys sold well, particularly those that explored the industrial or commercial prowess of towns or areas. There is thus at least a prima facie case for saying that whether we believe England to have grown rapidly or slowly during the Industrial Revolution we must not ignore the fact that contemporaries had little conception of 'England' as opposed to 'bits of England'. Viewed from the perspective of a southern market town, Lancashire may have seemed like a foreign country. Mr Oakes from Bury St Edmunds certainly thought so when his banking duties necessitated a trip to Manchester in 1803. He suggested that Manchester was a 'marvel' of modern progress, and watched in wonder as his carriage drove past the serried ranks of warehouses, factories and homes under construction. The noise and smoke played on his senses and he thought Lancashire was 'like a different country'.[6]

For Oakes, Lancashire and its cotton industry positively epitomised the processes of industrial and economic change. Robert Sharp, a schoolmaster from South Cave in the rural East Riding, was rather less positive about the impact of the cotton trade, noting on 11 December 1826 that:

> Last night I had to go down to the workhouse with a poor young woman to get her lodgings, she had neither shoes nor stockings, and was almost starved to death, she is one of the victims of the accursed cotton trade; there is scarcely a day but some of the Poor creatures who have been brought up in these abominable mills, are begging their bread; Happy would it have been for England if never a pound of the infernal *Fuzz* had ever found its way into this country. Had it not been for cotton we should not have been taxed as we are; when the country went mad, cotton was to do every thing; and indeed it has done every thing but make us prosperous and happy.[7]

Any student of the Industrial Revolution will be aware of the fallacy of this proposition; cotton was *the* key player in rising national income after 1750. However, this is not the point. What is important is that at this time of severe national depression the cotton trade was far removed by distance and experience from Robert Sharp. Like other industries it had become concentrated in a relatively small spatial area during the process of industrialisation, impinging on wider consciousness particularly at times of severe dislocation. We might make similar points about other industries; the most dynamic parts of the pottery industry came to be concentrated in the 'Staffordshire potteries', the hosiery industry came to be concentrated in the counties of the east and central Midlands, and the metalware trades came to be concentrated in and around Sheffield, Birmingham and Wolverhampton. English politicians and the reading public were periodically reminded of this gradually solidifying regional structure throughout the eighteenth and nineteenth centuries.

Other evidence supports the existence of a solidifying regional industrial structure with which contemporaries could identify. Thus, as the Napoleonic Wars raged in the 1790s, John Eales arrived back in his parish of settlement (the only place legally responsible for a person's relief under the poor law) at Colne in northeast Lancashire. He brought with him a certificate from a parish near Birmingham which stated that he had been removed from that parish and that he was working his passage home through the 'manufacturing districts'. The certificate was signed in each parish at which he stopped and found temporary work. By the time it was handed to the overseer of Colne, the certificate had been signed on twenty-six occasions. The certificate reveals that Eales had moved from Birmingham to Coventry, where he had worked briefly in the nascent ribbon trade. Thereafter he had moved through a number of industrial parishes in Nottinghamshire – where he undertook different sorts of weaving and labouring work – then into Staffordshire and finally back through six Lancashire textile townships before arriving in Colne.

The Colne overseer conducted an examination of Eales to establish the liability of the town to relieve him. At no point had he gained settlement elsewhere, so the overseer's examination turned to the history of the Eales family prior to removal from Birmingham. Born in Colne, Eales had served his weaving apprenticeship in the town, but had left at the age of twenty-three to seek work in the woollen industry of West Yorkshire. Unable to set up as an independent tradesman he moved to Nottinghamshire to work in the hosiery industry as a contract weaver, before eventually removing to Birmingham.[8] Eales could have taken many routes home, but with the sole exception of Leicestershire he had chosen to move through all of the significant *expanding* textile regions which drove the early phases of the English Industrial Revolution. His experience demonstrates that we *can* identify core economic regions, as Hudson and Langton have suggested and as contemporaries did.

This said, there are a number of conceptual and practical problems with imposing regional structures on the English landscape, and they need to be at least reviewed here. First, the Eales's life history does not accurately portray the spatial extent of 'the textile regions' during the Industrial Revolution. In practice, the central core of textile activity increasingly came to be associated with relatively small areas even within county boundaries. The cotton industry is a classic example. Contemporary travellers walking just a few miles north of Preston would have found themselves in some of the most productive fields that England had to offer. Walking directly south for eight miles or so would have brought them to the outskirts of the Lancashire coalfields. Had they gone east then they would have encountered the textile town of Blackburn, part of a 'textile district' which stretched in a broad dog leg from Preston, through Blackburn, south to towns such as Bolton and Bury and then to Manchester and its hinterland. Had the same travellers gone just a few miles to the southwest they would have entered the potato fields of the Lancashire wetlands. Industrial Lancashire, the powerhouse of the early Industrial Revolution, was thus crammed into a very limited spatial box indeed.[9]

Similar points could be made about the location of other industries. The 'Staffordshire' potteries in reality comprised just six towns – Burslem, Fenton, Longton, Hanley, Stoke and Tunstall – leaving much of Staffordshire in terms of area or population unconnected (at least directly) with the pottery industry. Similarly, the South Yorkshire metalware industry with its network of outworkers and large workshops was essentially concentrated in just thirty-one townships in and around Sheffield.[10] In short, when we talk about 'Industrial Revolution', what we often mean is intense change in a few quite small areas. And when we talk about abstract notions such as 'industrial development', 'the modernised sector', 'agrarian change' or 'commercial development' what we really mean is that certain areas changed rapidly, others changed slowly, and some did not change at all.[11]

A second difficulty follows on from the first when we shift our focus away from the textile regions explicitly. That is, the issue of how to define regions, whether they can be defined at all, and what gave them their identity, has tortured generations of English historians.[12] For instance, in considering the spatial dimensions of agriculture, do we classify areas according to topography, product or cultivation regime?[13] In the industrial sector, do we impose identifiable areas on the English landscape on the basis of product type, the way industry was organised, the penetration of industrial occupations within the overall occupational structure, or perhaps the nature of the labour market? The simple focus of an industry in a given area does not adequately define a region, as we have already seen in the case of Lancashire or Staffordshire, but more detailed analysis might require sources which do not exist.[14] Certainly Paul Laxton warns of the very considerable problems of evidence raised by all but the very roughest attempts to establish the spatial outlines of the English textile industries.[15]

Even if rough characterisations were acceptable, a third difficulty is that it is clear that industrial regions,[16] agricultural regions, cultural regions, administrative regions, religious regions and urban regions[17] did not conveniently superimpose upon one another, blurring the significance of regional structures for our assessment of the nature of the development process. Nor were regions stable over time; they grew and shrank in the face of a range of exogenous and endogenous factors such as technological change, the redrawing of administrative boundaries, the rate of population growth or the state of internal and international competition.

Cornwall provides a good example of these sorts of problems. 'Industrial' Cornwall defined by its mining was to be found in the west of the administratively defined county, but between the late eighteenth and mid-nineteenth centuries mining expanded eastward to bring the industrial and administrative region more into line. Occupational concentration here was more substantial than in most of the better-known industrial regions, such that 'the success of metal mining ... may have acted to crowd out other industries'.[18] Yet, the 'region' lacked a large urban centre to act as a unifying force and, according to Deacon, consistently lacked 'institutional shape' (institutions such as scientific and literary societies that helped to create a regional identity) and might best be labelled a 'proto-region'.

The regional development of the coalmining industry provides another example of the difficulties of pinning down the issue of regionality. Thus, the phenomenal increase in English coal output which can be traced between 1750 and 1850 was accompanied by the development of deep-mining coal regions in the Midlands, northeast and Lancashire. Yet in a period of continuously expanding demand more peripheral areas such as the West Riding and Westmorland were also able to develop their traditional mining industries. The 1787 census of Westmorland provides persuasive evidence that mining for coal was a mainstay occupation in some communities.[19]

The presence of peripheral producers does not make regional analysis impossible, but even where we look at the core mining regions themselves we obtain a picture of considerable fluidity in the spatial boundaries that we must apply. Mining exploration was undertaken either by landowners or by speculators renting land from landowners, and there was little systematic development of the mining industry in a given area. More importantly, mining was unpredictable – the life-cycle of pits was short and there was a constant flow of labour and resources between old and new mining areas within a locality and even between coalmining regions.

There is not the space here to review fully these and other conceptual and practical difficulties or to offer solutions to the regionality conundrum.[20] The key point is that what seemed a simple fact to some contemporaries – the regionality of industrial development – has become much less clear to modern historians. And if some commentators now come to see the value of 'regional' approaches in a whole variety of debates coalescing round the theme of 'Industrial Revolution', they are little nearer to reaching a consensus over what such an approach consists of, how it should be undertaken, and how it should be interpreted.[21] Our basic questions – can we identify a regionality to the Industrial Revolution, and if we can is regionality a useful tool for understanding the nature of the Industrial Revolution process? – thus still stand.

For these reasons, our aim in this chapter is not to offer a comprehensive overview of the regional dynamics of English economic development (a task which is at present impossible) but merely to emphasise the importance of spatial variation in making sense of the Industrial Revolution during the period 1700–1850. As a vehicle we will consider the regionality of textile proto-industry and factory industry. This focus should not, of course, lead students to place an undue emphasis on the textile industries.[22] Other industries – pottery, metalwares, straw plaiting, shoe making and brewing – had complex and important trajectories of regional growth and decline which differed in their exact detail from the experiences of the textile industries and which are an integral part of understanding the spatial dimensions of the Industrial Revolution. Such experiences will filter into the analysis as we proceed and we must read the general lessons from the story of the textile industries rather than concentrating on the specifics of their development.

## Proto-industrialisation

Most English communities on the eve of the Industrial Revolution had some basic framework of domestic production of textiles, metalware and other goods. While the 'ready made' garment trade was more important than historians allow, it is nonetheless true that families made a substantial portion of their own clothing, and may also have produced a surplus for market.[23] This was the cottage economy. Proto-industrialisation, a term coined only in 1972, was something very different.[24] In an English context it seems to have had several central characteristics.

1 It involved the production of textiles, metalware and other goods in a domestic economy for national and international markets.

2 Such production took place mainly in rural areas.

3 Production of industrial goods was systematic (rather than random as under the cottage economy system) and often engaged a substantial proportion of local households. It might be undertaken by men at slack times of the agricultural year, by women more regularly throughout the year, or by whole families throughout the year, and communities which took up systematic domestic production of this sort generally became progressively more dependent on the earning opportunities afforded by rural industry.

4 Production was organised in a variety of ways. At one end of the spectrum, production was generated within households that maintained a nominal or effective link to land via formal landholding or use of commons. This was a system of dual-occupation artisan production where the artisans themselves engaged in part or all of the production process, and often marketed their own finished goods. At the same time they or their families raised crops or animals. Dual-occupation production of this sort was to be found in the textile industries, metalwares, hatting and glovemaking, and was compatible with the employment of non-family labour in the form of journeymen. At the other end of the spectrum, production was based upon families working full-time in the industrial sector, and working with the tools and raw materials given out to them by merchants or middlemen. Such families took no part in the marketing process and often

worked on just one part of the production process such as weaving or spinning. This was the 'putting out' system, and these were proletarianised (landless, wage-earning) workers whose prosperity was dependent upon the whim of the market and the merchant.

Somewhere in the middle of the organisational spectrum we find a typology in which the majority of output was generated by households where some workers were fully engaged in industrial production, but worked with their own equipment, whilst other household members earned income by different means.[25] Where individual communities and families fell on this spectrum was dependent upon a range of factors such as the nature of industrial production (wool, cotton, ironware, worsteds, etc.), the quality of the product, the market for that product, the long term availability of land, and the nature of social and institutional structures in place at the outset of proto-industrial development. However, as a rule of thumb, the representative experience moves towards the proletarian end of the spectrum the further we get into the eighteenth century.

5 Proto-industrialisation was a labour-intensive system. It is tempting and romantic to be beguiled by a 'revolution' in cotton technology, but until well into the nineteenth century expanding industrial production in most industries meant employing more workers or employing the same workers more intensively.[26] As we will see later, continuing dependence on hand technology was a fundamental feature of the English industrialisation process.

6 Increased proto-industrial output at an aggregate level was accompanied by, and at least partially dependent upon, a process of regional concentration. This process created external economies (such as a skilled and flexible labour force and credit networks) in areas of proto-industrial growth and, through the mechanism of inter-regional competition, divested other parts of England of some of their traditional industrial pursuits. In terms of its impact on 'national indicators' such as productivity and growth rates, this process of regional concentration may have been by far the most important aspect of English proto-industrial development. Of course, there is some disagreement over the extent of regional concentration and the speed with which the advantages of external economies 'kicked in' to compromise

the viability of industrial activities elsewhere. Did distinctive regional concentration of proto-industry start to make an impact in the 1720s, the 1790s, the 1820s or the 1840s? This dispute arises partly from genuine problems – the lack of data or the fact that there have been relatively few recent studies of 'southern' proto-industrial areas – but also from a confusion between proto-industry on the one hand and the continuance in many areas of low-level domestic production for local and regional markets on the other. Nonetheless, in textiles and to some extent in metalwork, regional concentration was becoming clearly visible by 1700 and for some regional competitors on the periphery this meant rapid and terminal decline. Certainly by 1820, regional concentration was clearly apparent, and for those regions 'left behind' very serious economic decay had set in.[27]

A brief review of the worsted and woollen industries provides a particularly good example of the regionality of proto-industrial development and reveals some of the implications of this regionality for our appreciation of the nature of the Industrial Revolution. In 1720, there were three major centres of worsted production. These were around Norfolk generally and Norwich in particular, around north Essex, and around Exeter and the Devon/Somerset border. There was also a nascent industry in West Yorkshire centred upon Halifax. However, between 1720 and 1820 the West Yorkshire industry accounted for the lion's share of the growth in worsted output at national level and while the industry still had a foothold in its older centres, in places such as Essex the hold was a tenuous one. When Frederick Morton Eden toured East Anglia to look at poverty and poor relief in the 1790s, he concluded that 'The Norwich trade has for some years been in a declining state', and also that there were more people working in textiles outside the city than within it.[28] By 1820 the textile workers outside the city limits were gone and the city trade was in terminal decline. The visible decay in the fabric of the town had become plain for all to see by the end of the 1820s.[29] In 1822 over three-quarters of all worsted output came from Yorkshire, whereas a century earlier it had accounted for very much less than one-fifth of output. In turn, the worsted industry was second only to the Lancashire cotton trade in terms of increased productivity and output from the later eighteenth century onwards, rapidly eclipsing the older woollen trade in these general indicators of 'modernisation'. Such growth was achieved largely without the transfer of capital, labour or entrepreneurial talent between expanding and declining regions, yielding, as we shall see below, structural problems in areas such as East Anglia which will be familiar from the modern decline of manufacturing.

The development of the woollen industry provides an even starker picture of regional proto-industrial concentration. In 1720, the woollen industry had centres in Westmorland, North Yorkshire, east Lancashire, West Yorkshire, Worcestershire, Coventry, Kent, Dorset, East Anglia and the West Country. The West Country trade in particular loomed large in national production figures, and was organised by a class of large clothiers who supplied the international market through Bristol and London. However, even counties such as Northamptonshire had parishes where 30 per cent or more of all males with a stated occupation were weavers between the 1720s and 1770s. By 1822, the whole situation had been turned on its head. As with the worsted industry, West Yorkshire had accounted for most of the phenomenal growth in national output during the eighteenth century. In 1770, Yorkshire accounted for one-third of all woollen output and one-half of woollen exports, rising from less than one-fifth in 1700. Thereafter, the attractiveness of Yorkshire woollens to the American market, and the fact that Yorkshire cornered the market for the cloth used in army uniforms, boosted demand further. By 1801 Yorkshire woollen producers accounted for over 80 per cent of all exports and well over two-thirds of total English wool cloth production.[30]

As a result of this process of regional concentration, peripheral regions such as Lancashire or Northamptonshire were stripped almost completely of woollen production, and the economic integrity of most of the other older regional centres outside the West Country was also fundamentally compromised. The West Country industry had been protected to some degree by its traditional concentration on fine woollens, but the main growth in demand during the eighteenth century had been for the medium and coarse woollens which were the traditional preserve of the West Riding industry.[31] By 1838, the West Country and West Yorkshire accounted for 71 per cent of *all* employment in woollen cloth production, rising to perhaps 86 or 87 per cent where we strip out small-scale local production. At this time, the West Country had 25,000 woollen workers, but the numbers were declining rapidly in the face of the final onslaught from Yorkshire. This was concentration on a scale only eclipsed by the experience of the English cotton industry and the de-industrialisation which accompanied it prompted re-ruralisation or, in places such as Northamptonshire, the development of alternative industries. In the latter case, the slow development of the shoe industry in the area between Northampton and Kettering was to eventually create a new industrial region, but only after thirty years of declining opportunities for textile workers.

In short, the proto-industrial textile development which drove the initial stages of the Industrial Revolution from the mid-1700s was a process which initiated, and depended upon, regional specialisation and concentration. When we talk of the woollen and worsted industries we thus mean the woollen and worsted industries in West Yorkshire. Even this is misleading, for as figure 2.1 shows the main core of the woollen *and* worsted industries in the early 1820s was concentrated into a limited area of the wider administrative county. Similar observations might be made about the spatial distribution of the silk, cotton and pottery industries, as we have already suggested. The ultimate result of this remarkable concentration was a sustained increase in the output of woollen cloth, and it is this feature which we see partly reflected in aggregate growth figures.

For those who lived within the confines of the proto-industrial woollen and worsted 'region', however, the consequences were much more revolutionary than simple output figures allow. Some of them are logically obvious. By the start of the nineteenth century, woollen and worsted production dominated the occupational structure and household economies of families and communities throughout the parishes around Leeds, Wakefield, Halifax, Bradford, and Saddleworth. In the parish of Calverley, for instance, independent artisan clothiers accounted for almost three-quarters of all of those who gave occupations when they baptised their children in the 1790s. In the worsted areas of Halifax parish from 1813 (when occupational data are more regularly given by parish registers) we can witness a similar concentration on industrial work. Proto-industrialisation also carried with it demographic consequences. It is now well established, for instance, that proto-industrial textile regions, as well as proto-industrial regions specialising in other trades such as metalwares or hats, looked very different in demographic terms from other rural areas or from towns. Marriage ages fell furthest in proto-industrial communities, and fertility rose most and fastest. Moreover when from the later eighteenth century the nation as a whole was experiencing lower infant and childhood death rates and stable adult mortality rates, proto-industrial areas in general saw significant increases in mortality rates over all age ranges.[32] More generally, at all stages of its development, proto-industrialisation can be linked to poorer public health and rising levels of occupational disease.[33]

Other consequences of proto-industrial development and concentration have been pinned down by detailed empirical work over the last ten years. Thus, the initial development of proto-industry allowed more people to stay in the locality of their birth, by providing alternative earning opportunities. Fewer people sought husbands and wives outside their own localities, and there is evidence that, except

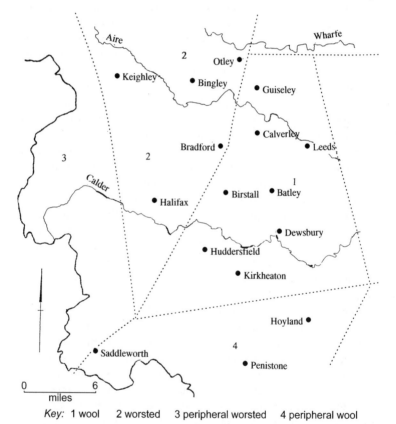

*Key:* 1 wool    2 worsted    3 peripheral worsted    4 peripheral wool

**Figure 2.1** Location of the wool and worsted industries in West Yorkshire, 1822

in the most developed of putting-out systems of the sort which we find in the Leicestershire hosiery industry, the existence of a substantial core of stable families allowed the creation of local dynasties and generated an important sense of local identity.[34] And proto-industrialisation also brought some brand-new experiences. While evidence is limited, there is some support for the idea that diets changed and that relationships between the generations became closer as early marriage left many young couples dependent upon the support of family and kin notwithstanding relatively high wages for the young adult worker in the proto-industrial system. Above all, commercial domestic production, whether by artisans or outworkers, generated a heavy reliance on the market and fickle international sales outlets, with all that this implied for periodic depression and enhanced life-cycle risks of poverty. We could go on, but the wider consequences of the proto-industrialisation process in the textile trades have been well covered elsewhere.[35]

The same basic observations about how regional industrial structures developed, how those structures related to national economic indicators, and what the socio-economic and cultural consequences of industrial production were for those living in the region of concentration, could be made about all of the regional centres which made up the proto-industrial textile industry by 1820. They could apply to other proto-industrial trades, too. We could have pointed to the eighteenth- and nineteenth-century regionality of the hosiery industry (around Nottingham and the east Midlands), the hatting trade (in Essex and southeast Lancashire), the fustian and then the domestic cotton industry (in central and east Lancashire), the carpet weaving industry (in the West Country and Derbyshire) and the metalware industry (in the west Midlands and South Yorkshire).[36] Each industry grew markedly from the later eighteenth century, and often at the expense of a wider spread of industrial penetration in other areas. Nowhere are these conclusions demonstrated more forcefully than in the domestic hosiery industry. Early centres of the industry in 'peripheral' areas such as Westmorland, Essex, Lincolnshire and East Anglia came to be superseded by that of the broadly defined 'east midlands', comprising Nottinghamshire, Leicestershire and south Derbyshire. Generally expanding demand for hosiery from mid-century was met almost entirely by producers in these three areas, and by 1762 the Nottinghamshire industry had managed to usurp the army contracts which had previously sustained an important hosiery industry in Westmorland. By 1812, 88 per cent of all stocking frames were to be found in these three counties, and this figure had risen to over 90 per cent by the early 1840s. In employment terms, 75 per cent of all people who stated an industrial occupation in Leicestershire in 1851 were engaged directly in the framework knitting trade. This was concentration indeed, and contemporary commentators lamented the change in morals, attitudes towards poverty and self-reliance, the landscape and culture which they believed flowed from rural industrial penetration.[37]

Figure 2.2 takes the analysis a little further, showing the broad geographical outlines of the English proto-industrial textile trades in 1810, after several decades of creeping concentration.[38] By this date, almost 90 per cent of all English textile workers were resident within these regional boundaries, which themselves understate the degree of textile concentration because the mapping scales involved here necessarily include parishes with relatively low occupational concentrations of textile workers. Bearing this caveat in mind, it should be clear just what the concept of 'regionality' means.

Of course, the striking thing about figure 2.2 is the amount of 'white space' on the map. Students must beware of reading this white space as a lack of industrial activity. Industries such as coal and metal mining, brewing, lacemaking, steelmaking, shipbuilding, the luxury sector and the making of sails, blankets and carpets also had distinctive regional development trajectories which complement figure 2.2 and which would fill some of the gaps if we mapped them. Indeed, in spatial terms relatively few areas of England were completely without some form of industrial (broadly defined) specialism. Much of this spatial pattern can be traced through the historical atlases that proved so popular in the 1980s and 1990s and which are listed in our bibliography. The purpose of this chapter, as we suggested earlier, is less to fill in all the details than trace the broad process and outcome of regional concentration.

In this sense, it is perhaps important to acknowledge that the consequences of regional concentration in the proto-industrial textile industries did not end at the broad regional boundaries that we can draw on the map. There were also 'unintended' consequences of proto-industrial concentration for other areas. The most immediate of these consequences, as we have already suggested, was relative or absolute de-industrialisation. In Essex, Norfolk and the West Country, the growth of Yorkshire as *the* production engine for woollen cloth

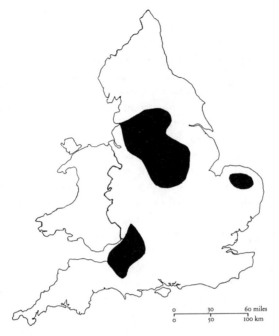

**Figure 2.2** The core of the English proto-industrial textile trades in 1810

stripped families of a traditional income-generation strand and opened up local populations even more fully to the vagaries of the season and overstocked regional labour markets. Indeed, it is precisely in the period of most rapid usurpation of economic power, in the 1760s and 1770s, that an enduring regional pattern of poverty and poor relief was created.[39]

Other 'unintended' consequences were less obvious or immediate, but no less important. Thus, the loss of industry in the process of inter-regional competition prompted higher out-migration rates (to London for those living in East Anglia and to the South Wales iron and coal industry for those living in the West Country) and a steady stream of emigration to the new world. In some places competition prompted industrial diversification such as the shoe industry in the former woollen parishes of Northamptonshire or glovemaking in various areas of the southeast, or it provided an impetus to the further development of exploitative and highly seasonal trades such as straw plaiting. The key point, however, is that there was a gap between the decline of one set of industries and compensation through the rise of another. The result was that, for women in particular, a definite form of structural unemployment can be observed rising out of full-blown proto-industrial development.

In turn, the unemployment, migration, exploitation, poverty and weakened household economies which we find in Essex, Westmorland or the West Country are as important for understanding the Industrial Revolution as proto-industrial concentration itself. These developments too changed lives, but did little to contribute to the national economic numbers that we reviewed in chapter one. Observing the decline of rural industries in the south in 1826, William Cobbett concluded that the loss of industry had 'made a vast change in the condition of the people, and in the state of property and of manners and of morals'.[40] Whatever agenda may have underlain such an observation, its broad substance finds support amongst other contemporary commentators, and suggests very strongly the importance of considering industrial concentration 'in the round' and of exploring regional interconnectedness.

It is also perhaps salutary to remember that areas which hosted proto-industrial concentration might themselves fall victim to de-industrialisation as industries either died out through changing patterns of demand and foreign competition or moved location as they moved into a new phase of industrial development. Even in areas which did use proto-industry as a springboard to factory development, dislocations could be fundamental. It is clear that by the 1820s hand textile producers in West Yorkshire were complaining loudly of decline in their trade and shifts in the organisation pattern away from cottage production to proto-factories and factories, from independence to dependence on a few large manufacturers and merchants. These complaints were overplayed, but it is nonetheless true that as cotton usurped wool in the international markets and as international competition in woollen cloth became more intense, the economy of West Yorkshire was compromised and the reaction was to promote larger-scale and mechanised production. What we measure in aggregate variables such as productivity or output is the rise of the factory and the proto-factory in the West Yorkshire industry. Yet what was really striking here was that the factory was superimposed on a co-existing domestic industry in which people had begun to suffer hardship by the 1820s as industrial involution augured structural unemployment, longer hours for less pay and disinvestment. These themes are revisited in our later discussion of household economics. What we measure as economic historians is increasing output not declining output, success not failure, investment not disinvestment, but it is the totality of the experience which makes revolution or not. Similar considerations apply to our interpretation of the significance of factory industry, as we shall see.

## Factory industry

For many contemporary commentators and foreign visitors the mechanised factory was the emblem of the Industrial Revolution in England by the 1840s. The manufactory – where larger-scale, hand or power aided production took place under one roof but without substantial mechanisation – was a recognised variant of the form. Both augured fundamental changes in the pace of work, the relationship between worker and employer, the nature of skill, and the regularity of work and leisure. No less than contemporary observers, many modern historians have also been caught up with factory fever.[41]

The basic narrative of the rise of the factory is well known, and we will consider it in more detail in later chapters. Apart from a few large production facilities in metal smelting and soap or salt boiling, and more common water-powered enterprises in textile preparation and finishing, centralised and mechanised production came first to the cotton spinning industry in Lancashire. Rural, water-powered spinning mills sprang up in the Pennine hills from the 1770s, to be followed rather later by similar mills in the worsted and then the woollen industries in the valleys of West Yorkshire. Thereafter, the development of steam power and continual refinement, and increase in scale, of cotton spinning technology combined to eradicate much of the domestic cotton spinning industry, and to push production facilities into urban areas concentrated heavily in central and southeast Lancashire. In the century after 1750, spinning technology alone was subject to 864 patents, and the cotton industry in general accounted for almost one-fifth of patented inventions up to the 1830s.[42] By 1820 what hand spinning remained was done on contract for millowners, and consisted of the coarsest grades of yarn or small runs, which machinery was unsuitable to produce. And by 1835, Britain, or by extension relatively small parts of Lancashire, accounted for 62 per cent of the entire world capacity of cotton spindles. This, then, was a remarkable case of sub-regional industrial concentration.

Weaving in cotton, worsted and wool was harnessed to power in a much slower process of evolution as innovation lagged behind invention for a considerable time. The theme of the spread of technology is taken up again in later chapters, but for now it is clear that the cotton handloom weavers survived, often barely subsisting, for much longer after their heyday in the late eighteenth century than has been generally acknowledged. As late as the 1850s, Lancashire handloom weavers numbered in their tens of thousands.[43] The powerloom did not make meaningful inroads into the cotton weaving trade before 1810, and even up to 1826 workers (and indeed many employers) were resisting the incursion of powered weaving. Depressed overseas markets, fear of the sorts of riots and violence which swept through the east Lancashire industry in the 1820s, and a precipitous fall in handloom weaving piece rates, all provided incentives for manufacturers to retain the status quo. Nonetheless, by the late 1820s urban powerloom factories had begun to take control of the cotton weaving industry, making stronger inroads by the 1840s under the influence of improving technology and trade-cycle fluctuations. In 1838 there were 110,000 powerlooms in operation, and by 1850 there were 250,000.

Paradoxically, in the initial decades of the nineteenth century worsted producers proved rather more willing to experiment with power-aided weaving than cotton producers. However, widespread industrial unrest and falling piece rates arrested such developments, and the worsted industry lagged perhaps a decade behind the cotton industry in achieving widespread mechanised weaving.[44] This said, by the mid-1840s, worsted production was substantially a factory-based enterprise. Developments in the woollen industry were slower. A witness to the 1806 inquiry into the state of the woollen industry observed that

> a young man of good character can always obtain credit for as much wool as will enable him to set up as a little master manufacturer, and the public mills which are now established in all parts of the clothing district, and which work for hire at an easy rate, enable him to command the use of very expensive and complicated machines, the construction and necessary repair of which would require a considerable capital. Thus, instances not infrequently occur wherein men rise from low beginnings, if not to excessive wealth, yet to a situation of comfort and independence.[45]

Three decades later, the development of factories, manufactories and powerlooms still had not blocked opportunities for independent production of this sort. As in the worsted industry, industrial unrest and falling rates for handworkers had undermined the economic viability of power-aided production, as did the 'company mill' (mills which were mutually owned and run by cloth producers) movement which grew strongly after 1800.[46] The number of powerlooms in the woollen sector increased from 5,000 in 1835 to 42,000 in 1850, while the number of factory employees rose from 15,000 to 154,000 over the same period. However, while in 1841 some 53 per cent of all English cotton workers were employed in the factory environment, the comparable figure for woollen workers was lower at 44 per cent.[47] Other proto-industries were similarly slow to embrace the factory. In the production of hosiery it was the 1830s which marked the advance of the machine and the factory, but even in 1850 the majority of all hosiery output was hand-produced. Similarly, in areas such as ribbon weaving hand production was very much the norm in the 1840s.[48]

Thus, in most branches of textile production factories emerged at the tail end of the most rapid and sustained period of economic growth in English history. At the aggregate level, it is probable that industrial machinery represented less than 5 per cent of the national capital stock in 1830.[49] A further 15 per cent was accounted for by industrial and commercial buildings and transport infrastructure, but factories represented only the smallest slice of this investment. In Manchester, the symbolic heart of the English cotton industry, more was invested during the second decade of the nineteenth century in public houses than in factories, and very much more was invested in warehousing than in either public houses or factories.[50] We should not be surprised to find, then, that the importance of factory work in the labour market was limited. In 1851, 30 per cent of the English adult male labour force was engaged in 'manufacturing', but, in so far as we can separate them from other industrial workers, factory workers probably made up no more than 5 per cent of the overall total. Even in Lancashire, factory workers made up only a minority of the adult labour force.[51]

In practice, proto-industrial production survived alongside factory development while in a whole range of industries the workshop or manufactory remained the representative organisation form well into the nineteenth century. Toolmaking is one interesting case in point, with hand tools and machine parts manufactured by skilled and semi-skilled workers in large sheds often with pedal-driven grinders and other hand equipment. In the metalware trades more widely, the workshop employing between perhaps four and eight people was the representative production unit in the early nineteenth century. Luxury goods were often produced in even smaller production units, though the biggest producers of furniture, pottery and other goods constructed considerable centralised workshops employing hundreds of people but little in the way of powered machinery. Nor perhaps should we forget the basic point that most of the trades that we might think of as broadly 'industrial' were incapable of transition to factory-type organisation. Some had always been organised on a large scale. Some, including bleachers, dyers and smelters, had always relied on capital-intensive, centralised production units. Other trades – carpenters, barrel makers, tailors, canal boat makers and food processors – satisfied local demand and had little to gain in economic terms from expanded, centralised or mechanised production.

Against this backdrop, it may seem strange to be focusing on the regionality of the factory system. Yet, we can draw many lessons about the process and consequences of regional concentration from a discussion of the development of textile factories, without making the factory the mainstay of the Industrial Revolution. What, then, were the exact regional dimensions of factory industry? Unsurprisingly, answering this question is far from easy. Poor source survival, the short life-span of firms and even industries, the product flexibility of many early factories, and the enormous local variations in industrial organisation highlighted by the factory inspectors, all impair our ability to do more than generalise at the most basic level. However, figure 2.3 attempts a broad survey of the prevalence of the factory system in the year 1821, based upon wide reading of industrial and firm histories, details given in the *Victoria County History*, and the data which can be gleaned from parliamentary returns. There are two initial caveats about this map. First, breweries and other enterprises with traditionally large capital requirements are excluded, as are *manufactories* of the sort which can be found in the pottery and metalware industries at this time. Second, the boundaries of our 'factory regions' are drawn very arbitrarily; the really important thing to look for is not the exact locations, but the size of these areas compared with those which are, by inference, 'non-factory'. The considerable sea of white space observed in figure 2.3 is telling in this respect, though as before students should not read it as a lack

**Figure 2.3** The location of significant concentrations of textile factory industry, 1821

of industrial or economic activity. When we talk about 'the factory', then, what we really mean is the factory *in relatively small parts of Lancashire, West Yorkshire, Nottinghamshire, parts of the northeast, Leicestershire, Derbyshire, the west Midlands, and in or around London.* In particular, we mean the cotton factory in Lancashire which, by 1830, had sounded the death knell (in terms of a 'national' importance) of production in other cotton centres in Scotland, Ireland, Nottinghamshire, Derbyshire and Cheshire. Not until the 1850s did factory production expand to any great extent geographically as the railways changed the location, marketing and production rules which had previously governed industrial production.

Despite such physical concentration, the importance of factories for the aggregate numbers which have been used to underpin one set of reinterpretations of the Industrial Revolution is obvious. It was factories in these areas – the so called 'modernised sector' – which, by 1831, were producing up to one-half of all English exports, and it was the early mechanised cotton industry which has long been credited with pumping up annual rates of English economic growth during the late eighteenth and early nineteenth centuries.[52] Yet, by concentrating on the aggregate consequences of factory development rather than the fact of its regional manifestation, we once again underplay the significance of the changes which the factory wrought. We have already noticed the structural unemployment which could accompany the transition from proto-industry to factory industry. The authors of the 1806 national inquiry into the state of the woollen industry thought that, 'the two systems [factory and domestic], instead of rivalling, are mutual aids to each other, each supplying the others defects and promoting the others prosperity'.[53] They may have been right for the best of economic times, but the tough times which often provided the incentive for entrepreneurs to consider factory development left little room for this sort of mutuality. Relatively few of those who worked in the domestic phase of any industry subsequently made the move to the factory. The cotton handloom weavers of Lancashire, for instance, did not move swiftly or easily to factory production and for them the concentration of factory development added structural unemployment to the seasonal and cyclical (trade cycle) unemployment forms which had always dogged the industry. One commentator suggested that handloom weavers 'live, or rather they just keep life together, in the most miserable manner, in the cellars and garrets'.[54] David Levine uncovered even more acute self-exploitation amongst the framework knitters of the east Midlands.[55]

For those who *did* engage in factory work, contemporaries differed sharply in their opinion of whether the consequences were negative or positive, and over how to characterise the broad factory movement. Themes like these are explored in chapter three. Modern historians have differed equally sharply. What all sides agree on is that factory workers experienced some fundamental changes in their lives compared with the experiences they would have had in the domestic system. With regard to earnings, for instance, skilled workers could earn substantial weekly wages in the factory. A mule spinner in a Lancashire cotton factory might earn 40 shillings or more per week, and overlookers or mechanics substantially more than that. The factory system was less generous to those lower down the skill scale, but (notwithstanding work stoppages and fines) for most employees the factory represented the highest-paying option within the locality. It was primarily for this reason that migrants to factory towns such as Preston used their relatives or people who had previously migrated from their own area to ease themselves into the factory labour force.[56]

Some commentators have suggested that employment was also more regular in the regionally concentrated factory system than it was in the domestic or other trades. Investment in fixed capital gave manufacturers an incentive to produce their way over short-term slumps related to market closure or war because they still had to meet the costs of machinery and premises even if they laid workers off. Moreover, since many firms continued to employ outworkers as a matter of routine, adjusting production volume or quality was often a matter of dispensing with handworkers rather than factory employees. Less tangibly, factory workers appear to have had a distinctive demographic experience compared with almost any other occupational group. Fertility in towns dominated by factory employment tended to be low, abortion relatively common, and infant and child death rates significantly higher than in rural areas or non-factory towns. There is also some evidence that factory families tended to contain more kin than was the norm in an English context. Meanwhile, factory workers rapidly caught up with the food-consumption habits of labouring people in the south, and public middle-class complaints about the factory worker (and more important the un-employed factory worker) demanding white bread, tea and sugar can be consistently found in the published ephemera relating to the 'factory regions'. More widely, it is clear that factory workers engaged in a very vibrant consumption culture, both in terms of clothing and the domestic environment. Bright clothing, pictures, plate and furniture were the regular investments of factory workers, a function of their desire to display earning power, of their need to invest in goods which could be liquidated in the inevitable bad times, and of the need to compensate for the drab and murky environment of urban England in the Midlands and north. Themes like these are revisited in Parts II and III.

We should not be too positive, of course. On the negative side, it is probably true that by and large, factory working conditions were poor. Occupational disease, accidents, long hours and harsh discipline were common features of factory work. They rank alongside concerns with moral degradation and female competition for male jobs as motivations for factory reform from the opening years of the nineteenth century. Both the earliest water-powered factories and the later urban factories used systems such as tokens (the employer's own money equivalent) or truck shops (factory shops where workers purchased goods out of wages yet to be given) to tie their employees into a debt relationship with the firm. Factory workers were as susceptible as their domestic counterparts to sharp practices by employers. These included the substitution of female for male labour and child for female labour where the machinery or processes allowed, irregular time keeping on the part of overlookers, irregular shift patterns, and the 'deductions' to wages which were incurred in setting up machinery or breaking workplace rules. Employees could leave (and did so in large numbers if we look at the workforce turnover in individual firms) but in the rapidly growing urban areas which characterised 'factory regions', recruiting more workers was rarely a problem. Only very late in our period did employers place a premium on keeping experienced or trusted workers.[57]

Moreover, employees of factory systems in most trades soon found out that what regularity of employment there was went with a commitment to wages going down as well as up, depending upon market conditions. And for some workers, stability of employment was an elusive goal. In the cotton and woollen industries, the lifespan of many textile firms was incredibly short. Of new firms founded in the Lancashire cotton industry between 1810 and 1820, the average life-span was just seven years. Giant firms like McConnel and Kennedy in Manchester were not representative of the industry as a whole, and the concern which rented just one floor in a factory building was susceptible to the loss of cargoes, fraud, non-payment of debts and other factors such as bank collapses. In the West Riding wool industry and the Nottinghamshire hosiery industry, the life-span of factory concerns was even shorter, as bankruptcy notices in local newspapers show.[58] Moreover, when firms did close due to trade downturn, there was a very considerable danger that they would not subsequently reopen when trade picked up. In 1842 William Cooke-Taylor suggested that:

> In any temporary crisis the factory labourer may generally calculate on escaping with comparative safety, but if the crisis be prolonged, if the losses on production begin to exceed the amount of losses which would result from deterioration of property, the consequence will be rendered more fatal, and the ruin more extensive, by the very circumstances which have delayed its arrival.[59]

Under such circumstances, the corollary of industrial and factory concentration on a spatial basis was that whole areas could be periodically reduced to beggary. Such was the experience of Lancashire, West Yorkshire and the Midland textile industries in 1842. Cooke-Taylor, again, noted during his tour of the depressed manufacturing areas in that year some of the consequences of wide regional factory failure. At Bolton:

> In all I visited eighty-three dwellings, selected at hazard. They were destitute of furniture save old boxes for tables, and stools, or even large stones, for chairs; the beds were composed of straw and shavings, sometimes with torn pieces of carpet or packing canvass for covering and sometimes without any kind of covering whatever. The food was oatmeal and water for breakfast, flour and water with a little skimmed milk for dinner; oatmeal and water again for a third supply, with those who went through the form of eating three meals a-day ... I was an eye-witness to children appeasing the cravings of the stomach by the refuse of decayed vegetables in the root-market.[60]

These and other consequences of a process of industrial development that created and was dependent upon regional industrial concentration are explored indirectly throughout this book. The key point at this stage in not whether factories had a net positive or negative impact, whether we should characterise them as 'good' or 'bad', but that even for a region with a very long history of industrial production, such as Lancashire, the factory movement wrought some really important changes on the lives of those directly or indirectly involved with it. A walking tour of any northern mill town would still provide ample testimony to their experience. The few remaining mills suggest how such buildings would have fundamentally transformed the skyline of industrial towns. The blackened fascias of so many public and private buildings in the 1860s and 1870s resulted from the systematic pollution of the urban airspace by factories after 1820. Above all, the mills demanded housing for their workers, and these still form a substantial component of the housing stock in many northern areas. We return to the important subject of the built environment in chapter ten.

In some respects the changing lives of factory workers are 'written into' the contribution of the cotton industry to national economic growth from the turn of the nineteenth century. However, the impact of the factory did not end in the factory districts, and the wider interlinkages between factories and regional economies are less easily encompassed in output figures. Thus, the demand of textile factories for labour was often seen as a threat to industries and agriculture in surrounding areas, forcing up the general level of wages. By the turn of the nineteenth century, carpenters and other tradesmen in Lancashire could expect to gain wages not too far behind their counterparts in London, and even agricultural labourers might attract a premium of up to 30 per cent compared with those elsewhere. There was less pressure in the Midlands and West Yorkshire, but here too there were complaints that factories siphoned off the labour force from the countryside.

Even firms and industries which did not compete with the factories for a labour force were tied into a complex economic arrangement with them. Carrying firms, bobbin makers, shipbuilders, machine makers, dressmakers, ribbon weavers, those engaged in food processing, brickmakers, iron smelters, and a whole plethora of other industries and occupational groups depended directly or indirectly on the health of the cotton factories of Lancashire. The same point might be made of the hosiery and woollen industries. Moreover, we must also remember that demand from the factory labour force intensified the inability of industrial districts such as Lancashire, the west Midlands or Yorkshire to feed themselves, such that, as in the case of Lancashire, agriculture in Westmorland, the North Riding, Cheshire and the East Riding received a significant boost to demand. The truism that when the cotton industry was recruiting, the whole northwest economy was vibrant, but when the cotton industry was shedding staff, the whole of the northwest battened down the hatches for a tide of depression, really does encapsulate the relationship between the narrow spatial concentration of factory industry and the wider regional economy within which the factories were located. These sorts of fundamental consequences of factory development and increasing concentration of industry are still not adequately considered in our determination of whether or not there was an Industrial Revolution and how we should measure it.

Nor should we forget that, as with the development of proto-industry, regional concentration of textile factories also carried a 'national' significance outside its impact on output or people in the regions specifically concerned. Some of the wider links are easy to see. If the factory system, with all that it implied for the intermittent nature of poverty in factory regions, had not existed, then the New Poor Law may well have met its central aims. The factory system was the first domestic rallying point (people had earlier rallied on slavery) for the economic and social reformers of late eighteenth-century and early nineteenth century England. Indeed, it could be argued that the factory forced itself on to the national psyche as a symbol of change, of progress, and even of dread, and that the existence of this symbol is as important for our understanding of the significance of the Industrial Revolution as measurements of the contribution of factories to industrial exports. In the cotton crisis of 1842, when most of Lancashire was out of work, publications such as *The Builder* were active in bringing the plight of factory workers to the southern urban heartlands, and food and clothing parcels were organised by a voluntary movement which operated, on and off, right up to the 1870s. Incidents such as this brought home the importance of the factory system to those without direct experience. Notwithstanding periodic depression, some saw the factory in its regional context as representing progress; the paintings which showed the smoky skyline of Preston in the 1840s and 1850s were sold throughout the urban south and might command considerable sums. Others lamented the factory; the Dickensian representations of Preston as 'Coketown' also sold well. Like them or loathe them, contemporaries did not ignore factories and we must attribute to them an importance which has, at least in the recent past, been stripped away.

## Conclusion

Clearly, this has been a very selective analysis. In terms of national occupational structure, it is well known that agriculture, food processing, domestic service and trades such as building remained the bulwarks of the labour market at the mid-point of the nineteenth century. Of the regionality of these trades, and of things like the luxury trades, woodworking, pottery, gun making or watchmaking, we have said almost nothing. This is not to say that the scale and organisation of production or the location of those industries did not change. Indeed, Berg and Hudson have, as we saw in the first chapter, mounted a stout defence of the importance of change in these sorts of areas in our understanding of the industrial, or perhaps 'industrious', revolution. These industries and trades, or more specifically the regionality of their development or decline, are not discussed here in part because of space constraints. We have also chosen, as was suggested at the start of the chapter, to try and draw general lessons about the regionality of industry and the usefulness of an understanding of that regionality in the process of making sense of the Industrial Revolution, rather than trying to provide a shallow overview.

The lessons to be drawn from our analysis are important and worth restating. First, in the woollen, worsted, cotton, iron, metalware and mining trades there was a regionality to industrial development which was in many instances clear to contemporaries themselves, particularly antiquarian historians and their readers. To return to one of the themes of the opening section, we can, albeit crudely, map and substantiate a 'regionality of the Industrial Revolution'. Second, the process of regional concentration and inter-regional competition created losers and gainers in regional terms. In this sense, understanding the Industrial Revolution is about more than measuring net output and productivity growth. Falling output matters as much as rising output, de-industrialisation as much as industrialisation, disinvestment as much as investment. Places which lost out on the regional specialisation bandwagon suffered economically, socially and culturally and for some structurally, and for some of these places there was a very direct stimulus to adopt the most innovative agrarian techniques in response. Others reinvented themselves as industrial regions exploiting their own comparative advantages after a period of structural decay. The major point, however, is that despite their obvious importance, these negative effects have an uncertain value when set in a framework of national economic statistics. Third, regional specialisation carried with it fundamental consequences for those directly or indirectly caught up in the process. Most importantly, it created a fragile form of capitalism, one which to a marked degree transformed the nature of work, the nature of the family economy and access to the means of production, but which was itself subject to trade depressions, business failures, banking failures, wars and a chronic tendency to overproduction and underemployment. Contemporaries saw these problems along with a whole range of new departures, including canals, the railways, enclosed fields, social commentary in literature, public buildings, industrial and commercial premises, urbanisation and then suburbanisation, and changing consumption standards. They could also see the development of distinctive regional and social cultures which marched hand in hand with the concentration of industry. The industrial middle class seeking to move into polite society came from the industrial regions. The impetus for self-help, co-operation and unionisation came from the industrialising regions, and the industrial regions were the fount of new popular challenges to the market and the established order of town and community governance. In sum, contemporaries could feel that 'something was going on'.

Regional industrial structures were rarely static and can at best only be pinned down in outline. However, this discussion has been a vital precursor to the discussion of more substantive issues in Parts II and III. It has demonstrated that the Industrial Revolution is a process and that it must be understood on a variety of different levels. For this reason, in the chapters which follow our aim is to suggest to students ways of approaching the Industrial Revolution, rather than providing all of the answers. We relate aggregate figures and general debates firmly and systematically to individual and regional experiences and detailed original sources, suggesting questions which remain to be asked and answered and prompting students to question prevailing assumptions.

## Notes

1  P. Hudson, 'The regional perspective', in P. Hudson (ed.), *Regions and industries: a perspective on the Industrial Revolution in Britain* (Cambridge, Cambridge University Press, 1989), p. 22.

2  J. Langton, 'The Industrial Revolution and the regional geography of England', *Transactions of the Institute of British Geographers*, 9 (1988) 145–67.

3  D. Gregory, 'The production of regions in England's Industrial Revolution', *Journal of Historical Geography*, 14 (1988) 50–8, and N. F. R. Crafts and C. K. Harley, 'Output growth and the British Industrial Revolution: a restatement of the Crafts–Harley view', *Economic History Review*, 45 (1992) 703–30.

4  D. Defoe, *A tour thro the whole island of Great Britain* (London, Penguin, 1987 reprint).

5  For some commentary from the end of our period, see W. Cooke-Taylor, *Notes on a tour of the manufacturing districts of Lancashire* (London, Cass, 1968 reprint), and E. Baines, *The social, educational and religious state of the manufacturing districts with statistical returns* (London, Augustus Kelley, 1969 reprint). Also G. Head, *A home tour through the manufacturing districts of England in the summer of 1835* (London, Augustus Kelley, 1968 reprint).

6  J. Fiske (ed.), *The Oakes diaries: business, politics and the family in Bury St Edmunds 1778–1800* (Woodbridge, Boydell Press, 1990).

7  J. Crowther and P. Crowther (eds), *The diary of Robert Sharp of South*

*Cave: life in a Yorkshire village 1812–1829* (Oxford, Oxford University Press, 1997), p. 90.

8  Lancashire Record Office (hereafter LRO), Uncatalogued James Collection, 'Certificate'. On wider migratory movements for work, see J. S. Taylor, *Poverty, migration and settlement in the Industrial Revolution: sojourners' narratives* (Palo Alto, SPSS, 1989).

9  See J. Walton, 'Proto-industrialisation and the first Industrial Revolution: the case of Lancashire', in Hudson (ed.), *Regions*, pp. 41–68. Also G. Timmins, *Made in Lancashire* (Manchester, Manchester University Press, 1998). On the historic roots of this regional structure, see J. Stobart, 'Geography and industrialisation: the space economy of north-west England 1701–1760', *Transactions of the Institute of British Geographers*, 21 (1996) 681–96.

10  It is important to beware of ascribing even these 'regions' economic, social or cultural unity. In the Staffordshire potteries the core towns remained economically, demographically and culturally distinct, while in South Yorkshire towns and villages actually competed against each other for markets, labour and capital.

11  On this issue, see E. Richards, 'The margins of the Industrial Revolution', in P. K. O'Brien and R. Quinalt (eds), *The Industrial Revolution and British society* (Cambridge, Cambridge University Press, 1993), pp. 140–69.

12  See, for instance, A. Everitt, *Landscape and community in England* (London, Hambledon, 1985), or J. Thirsk (ed.), *The agrarian history of England and Wales, vol. V: regional farming systems* (Cambridge, Cambridge University Press, 1984).

13  The amount of writing on this issue is considerable. See J. Thirsk, *England's agricultural regions and agricultural history* (London, Macmillan, 1987), and most recently M. Overton, *The agricultural revolution in England: the transformation of the rural economy* (Cambridge, Cambridge University Press, 1996). These themes are revisited in chapter six.

14  On the danger of identifying areas which were characterised by long-term occupational and economic stability in preference to areas characterised by frequent or short-term economic turmoil, and in the absence of comprehensive data on occupations before 1851, see P. Glennie, *Distinguishing men's trades: occupational sources and debates for pre-census England* (Historical Geography Research Series Number 25, 1990).

15  P. Laxton, 'Textiles', in J. Langton and R. J. Morris (eds), *Atlas of industrialising Britain, 1780–1914* (London, Methuen, 1986), pp. 106–13.

16  Historical atlases have tried to trace the broad outlines of industrial regions. See Langton and Morris (eds), *Atlas*, and R. Pope, *Atlas of British social and economic history since 1700* (London, Routledge, 1989). Sidney Pollard identified ten early industrial regions. See S. Pollard,

*Peaceful conquest: the industrialisation of Europe 1760–1970* (Oxford, Oxford University Press, 1981).

17  On this issue, see J. G. Williamson, *Coping with city growth during the English Industrial Revolution* (Cambridge, Cambridge University Press, 1990). Also E. A. Wrigley, *People, cities and wealth: the transformation of traditional society* (Oxford, Oxford University Press, 1987).

18  B. Deacon, 'Proto-regionalisation: the case of Cornwall', *Journal of Regional and Local Studies*, 18 (1998) 32.

19  L. Ashcroft, *Vital statistics: the Westmorland census of 1787* (Berwick, Curwen Archives Trust, 1992).

20  For a wider discussion of these issues, see S. A. King, 'Rethinking the English regions', in S. Brakensiek and A. Flugel (eds), *Regional history in Europe* (Stuttgart, Verlag Für Regionalegeschichte, 2000), pp. 46–69, and E. Royle (ed.), *Issues of regional identity* (Manchester, Manchester University Press, 1998).

21  But see Richards, 'Margins', and J. D. Marshall, 'Proving ground or the creation of regional identity? The origins and problems of regional history in Britain', in P. Swan and D. Foster (eds), *Essays in regional and local history* (Beverley, Hutton Press, 1992), pp. 11–26.

22  We could, of course, have focused on a wide variety of other industries which could be variously classified as 'modernised', 'modernising' or 'unmodernised' – craftsmen, bankers, brewing, the metalware industries of the west Midlands or South Yorkshire, or brickmaking, for instance – and their absence in this discussion reflects the need to clarify an approach at the expense of the sort of detail which can be gained from other books. Thus, on brewing, see P. Mathias, *The brewing industry in England 1700–1830* (Cambridge, Cambridge University Press, 1959), while for an overview of the metalware trades, see M. Berg, *The age of manufactures: industry, innovation and work in Britain 1700–1820* (London, Fontana, 1985), and D. G. Hey, *The rural metalworkers of the Sheffield region: a study of rural industry before the Industrial Revolution* (Leicester, Leicester University Press, 1972).

23  See B. Lemire, *Fashion's favourite: the cotton trade and the consumer in Britain 1660–1800* (Oxford, Oxford University Press, 1991).

24  For more on the history and meaning of this label, see R. Leboutte, 'Introduction', in R. Leboutte (ed.), *Proto-industrialisation: recent research and new perspectives* (Geneva, Droz Press, 1996), pp. 1–8.

25  For more on the detail of this spectrum, see E. Lipson, *History of the woollen and worsted industries* (London, Cass, 1921).

26  See P. Hudson and S. A. King, 'A sense of place: industrialising townships in eighteenth century Yorkshire', in Leboutte (ed.), *Proto-industrialisation*, pp. 181–210.

27  See Richards, 'Margins'.

28  F. M. Eden, *The state of the poor* (London, Cass, 1966 reprint), p. 479.

29  C. Chalklin, *English counties and public building 1650–1830* (London, Hambledon Press, 1998).

30  See D. J. Smith, 'Army clothing contractors and the textile industries in the eighteenth century', *Textile History*, 14 (1983) 153–64.

31  On the development of the West Yorkshire wool textile industries, see P. Hudson, *The genesis of industrial capital: a study of the West Riding wool textile industry 1750–1850* (Cambridge, Cambridge University Press, 1986) and W. B. Crump, *The Leeds woollen industry 1780–1820* (Leeds, Harper, 1931). Also, H. Heaton, *The Yorkshire woollen and worsted industries from earliest times up to the Industrial Revolution* (Oxford, Oxford University Press, 1920), and D. Gregory, *Regional transformation and Industrial Revolution: a geography of the Yorkshire woollen industry* (London, Macmillan, 1982).

32  See E. A. Wrigley, R. S. Davies, J. E. Oeppen and R. S. Schofield, *English Population History from Family Reconstitution 1580–1837* (Cambridge, Cambridge University Press, 1997); but see also S. A. King, 'English historical demography and the nuptiality conundrum: new perspectives', *Historical Social Research*, 23 (1998) 130–56.

33  J. C. Riley, *Sick not dead: the health of British workingmen during the mortality decline* (Baltimore, Johns Hopkins University Press, 1997).

34  See Hudson and King, 'A sense'. Also, D. Levine, *Family formation in an age of nascent capitalism* (New York, Academic Press, 1977). However, contrast these views with D. Rollison, 'Exploding England: the dialectics of mobility and settlement in early modern England', *Social History*, 24 (1999) 1–16.

35  See the contributions to S. C. Ogilvie and M. Cerman (eds), *European proto-industrialisation* (Cambridge, Cambridge University Press, 1996).

36  Moreover, we could even extend these conclusions to industries which were not strictly proto-industrial. A. Everitt, 'Country, county and town: patterns of regional evolution in England', *Transactions of the Royal Historical Society*, 29 (1978) 79–107, suggests that 'distinct occupational regions ... can clearly be observed in such industries as glove-making, shoemaking, lacemaking and plush making'.

37  See J. V. Beckett and J. Heath, 'When was the Industrial Revolution in the east midlands?', *Midland History*, 13 (1981) 77–94.

38  This figure excludes lace production and thus understates the importance of Leicestershire and a number of rural southeastern counties such as Berkshire. It also excludes silk, which, by the 1820s and 1830s was the mainstay of what textile employment there was left in Essex and Norfolk. Readers should also bear in mind our earlier distinction between domestic and workshop production for localities and regions and that under proto-industrial structures for national and international markets.

39  See S. A. King, *Poverty and welfare in England 1700–1850: a regional perspective* (Manchester, Manchester University Press, 2000).

40  W. Cobbett, *Rural rides* (Dent, Dalglish, 1932), p. 78.

41  For a brief chronology, see M. Berg, 'Factories, workshops and industrial organisation', in R. Floud and D. McCloskey (eds), *The economic history of Britain since 1700, volume 1: 1700–1860* (Cambridge, Cambridge University Press, 1994), pp. 123–50.

42  See R. J. Sullivan, 'England's "age of invention": the acceleration of patent and patentable inventions during the Industrial Revolution', *Explorations in Economic History*, 26 (1989) 424–52.

43  G. Timmins, *The last shift* (Manchester, Manchester University Press, 1993).

44  Timmins, *Made*.

45  For an extensive analysis of this commentary, see S. A. King, 'The nature and causes of demographic change in an industrialising township' (unpublished Ph.D. thesis, University of Liverpool, 1993).

46  Hudson, *Genesis*.

47  *Ibid.*

48  V. E. Chancellor (ed.), *Master and artisan in Victorian England: the diary of William Andrews and the autobiography of Joseph Gutteridge* (London, Evelyn Adams and Mackay, 1969).

49  See A. J. Field, 'On the unimportance of machinery', *Explorations in Economic History*, 22 (1985) 378–401, and C. Feinstein and S. Pollard (eds), *Studies in Capital Formation in the UK, 1750–1920* (Oxford, Clarendon, 1988).

50  See R. Lloyd-Jones and M. Lewis, *Manchester and the age of the factory: the business structure of cottonopolis in the Industrial Revolution* (London, Croom Helm, 1987).

51  At its peak in 1821, 35 per cent of the Lancashire labour force (sexes combined) was directly employed in cotton factories, falling to 19 per cent in 1851 as the labour force expanded and the regional economy diversified. These figures are almost certainly underestimates, but do suggest that factory employment was not the majority employer. Even in large parts of east Lancashire it is by no means certain that factories account for the majority of the labour force. See C. H. Lee, *British regional employment statistics, 1841–1971* (Cambridge, Cambridge University Press, 1979).

52  W. W. Rostow, *The stages of economic growth* (Cambridge, Cambridge University Press, 1991 reprint), and N. F. R. Crafts, *British economic growth during the Industrial Revolution* (Oxford, Clarendon, 1985).

53  King, 'Nature'.

54  Quoted in J. T. Ward (ed.), *The factory system, volume 1: birth and growth* (Newton Abbot, David and Charles, 1970), p. 141. The degree to which these observations are accurate will be contested by the present authors in other work.

55 Levine, *Family*. See also S. D. Chapman's instructive, 'Memoirs of two eighteenth century framework knitters', *Textile History*, 1 (1968) 103–18.

56 M. Anderson, *Family structure in nineteenth century Lancashire* (Cambridge, Cambridge University Press, 1972).

57 See M. Huberman, *Escape from the market: negotiating work in Lancashire* (Cambridge, Cambridge University Press, 1996).

58 See J. Hoppit, *Risk and failure in English business 1700–1800* (Cambridge, Cambridge University Press, 1987).

59 Cooke-Taylor, *Notes*, p. 119.

60 *Ibid.*, pp. 79–80.

PART II

# DEVELOPMENT OF THE ECONOMIC INFRASTRUCTURE

# CHAPTER THREE

# TECHNOLOGICAL CHANGE AND WORK ORGANISATION

### Conceptual framework

Part II of our book is essentially concerned with the development of economic infrastructure. In beginning our discussion, we turn to one of the best-known, but potentially most misleading, characteristics of the Industrial Revolution, namely the unprecedented rate at which industrialists adopted powered machines in place of hand technology. In doing so, we briefly tell the story of Joseph Habergam of Huddersfield, who in 1822 began work at the worsted spinning mill owned by George Addison. He told his story to a select committee of parliament established in 1832 to inquire into child labour in factories.

Joseph was just seven years of age when he started at Addison's mill. His job was to attend to the throstles, a type of spinning machine driven by steam power. He worked from five in the morning until eight in the evening with a thirty-minute break at midday for food and refreshment. Other breaks had to be taken as opportunity arose, 'standing or otherwise'. Indeed, having to stand so long during the day caused him particular discomfort. He also complained that he and his companions became increasingly drowsy from mid-afternoon and that, to maintain their work rate, one of the mill overseers hit them with a strap. 'The children could not be kept so long at their labour', he remarked, 'if they were not so treated.'[1]

Joseph Habergam went on to work at two other local mills, one owned by a Mr Brooks and the other by William Firth. Again, he worked long hours and endured physical abuse. Not surprisingly, his health deteriorated and eventually he had to give up work altogether.

> Mill labour has had a great deal of effect on my own health, I have had to drop it several times in the year. When I had worked about half a year, a weakness fell into my knees and ankles; it continued, and has got worse and worse. It was attended by very great pain, and

the sense of extreme fatigue. Under these circumstances I had to work as often as I could, otherwise not any allowance would have been made to me by the occupier of the mill. I live a good mile from the mill; it was very painful for me to move; in the morning I could not walk, and my brother and sister used out of kindness to take me under each arm, and run with me to the mill, and my legs dragged on the ground in consequence of the pain.[2]

To help with his condition, Joseph received treatment from Dr Walker at Huddersfield infirmary and then became an in-patient at Leeds infirmary. Here he was under the care of Mr Hay.

He examined me, and said that my deformity was caused by the factory system. He said he thought he could have done me good if he had me a few years ago; there would have been means of keeping me straight. He said it was all from the factory system; working so long and standing so many hours. Mr Hay said, there were but poor hopes of me. Dr. Walker says I never shall be right any more. The cause of my illness has been going on all along, but I have got rather worse since I was fourteen years of age. I cannot walk above thirty yards before my legs begin aching very bad, and then I cannot walk at all.[3]

Joseph Habergam's story is one of many we could have used to give insights into why contemporaries were so concerned about the growing use of powered machinery in factories and workshops. There may well be as much myth as reality associated with these concerns, but they are a stark demonstration of the awareness amongst contemporaries that theirs was a society in which profound change was taking place in the work environment. The potential impact of this change, of course, was strongest in those regions we noted in chapter two as becoming especially associated with 'modernised' industry. But as we also saw there were implications for other regions too.[4]

The experiences of people like Joseph Habergam have come to dominate popular understanding of the nature of technological change during the Industrial Revolution period. Yet the phrase 'technological change' has multiple meanings which we must understand and explore in the process of making sense of the Industrial Revolution. Thus it might mean the adoption of powered machinery. It might also mean improvements in hand techniques and tools; as we shall see, such improvements were common in industries that were not at the forefront in adopting powered equipment but they were by no means absent even in industries that were. Moreover, technological change might also be extended to encompass the application of advances in science to industrial processes. Adopting this broader perspective on technological change is important in helping us to identify industrial regions and sub-regions – some of which did not become strongly associated with the use of powered machinery, at least until the 1830s and 1840s – and in assessing the extent to which technological change was taking place and locating its significance for an understanding of the Industrial Revolution. But we can broaden our perspective still further by extending our definition to include the closely associated issue of the way in which manufacturing activity was organised. After all, even without technical changes to machinery, modifications to the nature or location of work processes could be described as 'revolutionary'. The rise of the factory using powered machinery is one key part of this issue. The development of centralised workplaces that did not use powered machinery and of the proto-industrial system are also important pieces of the organisational jigsaw. In what follows, therefore, we will be adopting a wide rather than a narrow conception of what technological change means.

We begin by discussing improvements in hand technology and why the use of hand technology persisted. Our attention then shifts to a consideration of advances in powered machinery as we examine the nature and causes of technological change more generally. As part of our discussion, we examine how closely the growing use of powered machinery was linked with the rise of centralised production and discuss the impact that technological change had in the industrialising regions. Finally, we consider the benefits and drawbacks contemporaries perceived to have resulted from the technological change that confronted them.

## The development and persistence of hand technology

The phrase 'hand technology' is as ambiguous as the term 'technological change'. It encompasses three distinct categories of technology. One comprises hand-held tools, such as builders' saws and planes, in the design of which there were important innovations during the period 1700–1850. A second category of hand technology is hand-powered machines. Developments in this category might take two forms. Thus we can identify new inventions in the period 1700–1850 which were subsequently modified to improve their efficiency. The spinning jenny, patented in 1765, is a case in point. The original patent specification for the machine shows that it was at first limited to spinning about sixteen threads simultaneously, a figure that eventually rose to 130.[5] Alternatively, changes to hand-powered technology might take the form of improvements to hand machines that had long been in use. The cotton handloom provides an example. Amongst the numerous improvements made to it, those associated with William Radcliffe of Stockport are often singled out. In 1802, he patented a device which enabled the woven cloth to be wound automatically onto a beam at the back of the loom. Radcliffe also invented a machine for dressing cotton warps with size, a paste made from flour and water. The size strengthened the warps, and because it was applied by the machine prior to weaving, the weaver was freed from having to stop periodically to apply it by hand.[6]

The general label 'hand technology' might also be applied to a wide range of industrial processes, some of which involved a substantial input of skilled labour. Again, there were significant developments in this area after 1700, amongst them the puddling process for making wrought iron. Patented by Henry Cort in 1784, the process required molten pig iron to be manually stirred with long iron rods in order to burn away the carbon it contained.[7] In the case of the pottery industry, we may note the major advances that occurred in the materials from which pots were made and in the means by which they were decorated. Thus, around 1800, Josiah Spode began to manufacture china using bone ash and feldspar, thereby producing a more transparent type of pottery known as bone china. Moreover, from 1780 coloured patterns were printed on pottery before glazing and second firing, so that the colours were given a rich, soft tone.[8] Also worthy of mention is the elliptical spring, patented by Obadiah Elliot in 1805. This device enabled road vehicles to be hung on springs, giving a more comfortable ride for passengers. As figure 3.1 shows, such springs were formed from plates of steel held together with a band of iron, which was hammered into position at the thickest part. The ends of the springs were left free, so that the impact of any pressure to which they were subjected could be efficiently distributed between the plates.[9]

The manufacture of sheet glass from cylinders also constituted a significant advance in hand technology. The process was introduced into England by Chance Brothers at their Birmingham works in 1832, and involved blowing a ball of hot glass – up to 40 pounds in weight – into a globe and then swinging it by hand in a deep trench so that it formed into a cylinder. The two ends were then cut off, the cylinder

**Figure 3.1** Making coach springs

was cut lengthways and, after being reheated, was smoothed out to form a flat sheet. The process enabled bigger pieces of sheet glass to be made than was possible with the alternative crown glass process, which involved spinning a globe of hot glass on a hand-held iron rod (or pontil) until centrifugal force caused it suddenly to flare out into a disc.[10]

In adopting this wide definition of hand technology we deal too with the application of scientific knowledge and procedures to industrial processes. The development of bleaching powder provides a notable example. In 1799, Charles Tennant of Glasgow devised a means of obtaining chlorine in concentrated form, which cloth bleachers merely had to dissolve in water to produce a bleaching solution of the strength they required. As a result, the time taken to bleach cloth was dramatically reduced.[11] Another example is the production of alkali (soda) which was used in manufacturing soap and glass. Until the early nineteenth century, English glass and soap makers had to rely largely on imported alkali derived from the ashes of burnt plants, especially wood and seaweed. However, in 1791, Nicolas Leblanc, physician to the Duke of Orleans, took out a patent for making soda by mixing salt with sulphuric acid. During the early nineteenth century, the process was being used on a small scale in Tyneside, but its development in England resulted more from the initiative of James Muspratt of Dublin. He established a works at Liverpool in the early 1820s, taking advantage of locally available salt and coal and of the repeal of the excise duty on salt in 1823.[12]

As this brief review suggests, hand technology broadly defined was subject to notable improvement during the period 1700–1850. On the face of it, this observation may seem strange, especially given that improvements in hand technology were taking place even in industries where powered machinery could have replaced it. After all, the productivity increases (output per person) that contemporaries suggested would occur by switching from hand to powered technology were striking, as we can see in the case of Edward Baines's figures for cotton weaving. According to his estimates:

> A very good *hand weaver*, 25 or 30 years of age, will weave *two* pieces of 9–8ths shirtings per week, each 24 yards long, containing 100 shoots of weft to the inch …
>
> In 1823, a *steam-loom weaver*, about 15 years of age, attending two looms, could weave *seven* similar pieces in a week …
>
> In 1833, a steam-loom weaver, from 15 to 20 years of age, assisted by a girl about 12 years of age, attending to four looms, can weave *eighteen* similar pieces a week; some can weave twenty pieces.[13]

Contemporaries also argued that qualitative advantages arose from using powered machinery. For instance, the self-actor (or semi-automatic) mule, a machine used in textile spinning, was said to wind yarn more evenly and firmly onto the cop (the package of yarn on the spindle), thereby reducing yarn breakages during weaving.[14] And woollen cloth manufacturers claimed that machinery upheld standards when rushed orders were required, though scribblers and cloth dressers argued that machines used in their work impaired quality.[15] Powered machines also offered cost reductions when compared with hand technology. For example, in cotton textile production, Knick-Harley has shown that yarn prices declined dramatically during the Industrial Revolution period, though to a greater degree in the case of fine yarns and for warps (the threads in the looms) than for weft (the threads interlaced into the warp by means of a shuttle).[16]

Why, then, did people bother to invent and improve hand technology in its various guises? In part they did so because there were many types of industrial work for which powered technology had not become available even by the mid-nineteenth century or for which it would never be available. Amongst them were such diverse activities as garment making and file cutting. The former offered widespread employment opportunities for females, though very often with low wages. In 1843, some years before sewing machines became available, the techniques used by London's garment makers were tellingly described by George Dodd:

> Here, from the Stepney seamstresses who wear out life by making shirts at a penny a-piece, to the court milliner who is surrounded by the luxuries of life, all produce their results by the slender needle and the supple thread, by dexterity of finger, by patience and endurance, and by such lengthened hours of labour as men would rebel against.[17]

As to file making, which involved using a hammer and chisel to make numerous cuts into both sides of a steel bar (see figure 3.2), attempts to use machinery had not proved successful. In 1862, one writer explained:

> Simple as the operation appears, there are certain qualities of manipulation which it seems almost impossible to impart by means of machinery. For instance, the clever workman not only adapts the strength of his blow to the kind of steel he is operating on, but, even in the same file, if he feels one part softer than another, he regulates the fall of his chisel so that the size of the teeth shall be the same in every part.[18]

Yet, even in industries where there was a very direct confrontation between hand technology, particularly hand-powered machines, and machinery powered by steam or water, hand technology frequently held its own or even won the confrontation. Part of the reason for this was that powered machinery did not always meet manufacturers' needs. In weaving finer grades of cotton cloth, for instance, the action of the powerloom often proved too harsh, causing frequent thread breakages and hence production stoppages. Accordingly, weavers could normally operate only one or two powerlooms, a situation that did not change until the improvements made by Kenworthy and Bullough.[19] There are other examples. In printing finer cotton fabrics,

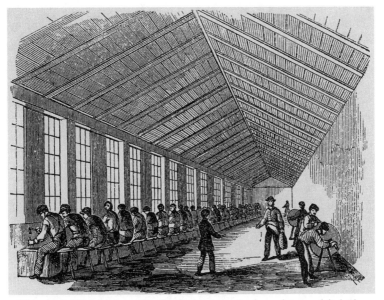

**Figure 3.2** File making. The file makers required good natural light by
which to work

for instance (a process illustrated in figure 3.3), it proved difficult to
rely solely on copper rollers, since the pattern could not be laid as
exactly as it could with hand blocks. Besides, the rollers could not
apply as many colours as the hand block, nor, it was said, could
they achieve the same richness and purity of colour. Similar problems
could arise outside the textile industry, as in the case of sawing planks
for ships' hulls. In describing work at a London dockyard in 1843,
George Dodd reported that tree trunks were cut into planks by two
men working with a long saw 'as in a common sawpit'. He continued,

> In a place where so much timber is used as in a ship-building yard, it
> might at first thought be imagined that machine-worked saws would
> be used; but the curvatures and angles of the timbers are so extremely
> varied, not only in different timbers, but also in different parts of the
> same timber, that the precision and regularity of machinery would be
> here thrown away, and indeed unavailable.[20]

A further reason for the persistence of hand technology was that
the improvements made in hand technology meant that, for a time
at least, the gap between the efficiency of steam or water-powered

**Figure 3.3** Printing calico by machine. The hand-block printer could add
further colour and pattern to the machine-printed cloth

and traditional technology may have widened more slowly than some
contemporaries would have us believe. This was so, for example, in
cotton weaving, with William Radcliffe's dandy loom raising the
productivity of hand weavers by perhaps as much as 50 per cent.[21]
Improvements made to the spinning jenny also increased spinners'
efficiency considerably, as is evident from rioting that occurred in
Lancashire during a time of severe trade depression in 1779. The
rioters directed their anger against textile machines, including jennies
with more than twenty-four spindles. These were considered to create
unfair competition and were either destroyed or cut down to an
acceptable size.[22]

Mention of jenny riots raises the question of how far advances in
steam or water-powered technology were held back by industrial
action. Adrian Randall's study of woollen workers in the West
Country and the West Riding during the late eighteenth and early
nineteenth centuries reveals that such action could have a significant
impact in delaying the introduction of new technology, though it
could not prevent it. In the former district, resistance to machines
was intensified by conservative cultural values based on the notion
of a 'moral economy', which were shared by domestic woollen
workers and others in the communities to which they belonged.

Accordingly, when serious rioting broke out in 1802 against the introduction of gig mills and shearing frames – both of which were powered machines used in finishing woollen cloth – memory of the intensity of its impact helped to maintain the use of hand technology for more than a decade. In West Yorkshire, however, where independent clothiers predominated, resistance to new technology proved less effective, though the machines destroyed during the Luddite riots of 1812 were not replaced for several years thereafter.[23] And, as Stephen Caunce has demonstrated, the traditional moral economy of the West Yorkshire woollen districts was modified rather than replaced. The prevailing social and economic conditions limited change with regard to the organisation of production and the introduction of new technology, but they still proved flexible enough for the industry to achieve a high degree of success.[24]

Aside from these considerations, industrialists also had to take into account the extra costs they would incur by installing powered machinery, along with a steam engine or water wheel to drive it and building or converting premises to house it. The sums involved might be appreciable, though they could be reduced by renting premises and machinery or by purchasing second-hand machinery, as we will see in the next chapter. Additionally, in industries converting from domestic outwork to centralised powered factories, the extra costs of equipment and buildings might be partly offset by savings from reduced raw material theft and from no longer having to transport materials between home and warehouse. Even so, the business risks involved in expanding production were not to be taken lightly, especially when borrowing money was involved.

A further possible drawback of investing in powered machinery arose because of periodic downturns in the trade cycle. These occurred with some frequency during the Industrial Revolution, and as a result industrial buildings and equipment could become underutilised, with the length of the working day or week being reduced and, in the worst instances, production ceasing altogether. At the same time, building and equipment costs still had to be met. For instance, interest would have to be paid on any loan that had been taken out to finance the purchase of capital equipment. Where hand technology was used, however, the fixed costs were, as a rule, comparatively low and the costs of idle equipment did not usually bring severe financial penalties. Indeed, where businesses organised their production on a domestic basis, the domestic workers might provide their own equipment and premises, and thereby meet a high proportion of the costs arising.

That industrialists retained the option of using hand technology when they might have turned to mechanised production was also made possible by the availability of an abundant labour supply. This was partly the result of the rapid population growth that occurred in the industrial districts. But it was also because industrial occupations could attract labour from the agricultural sector and because growing mechanisation in a range of industries achieved economies in labour usage. Furthermore, numerous people continued to make themselves available for handicraft work, women and children included, even if they experienced a marked decline in their long-term piece rates. In some cases, of course they had little option, because alternative work could be difficult to obtain. Older domestic workers, for example, were seldom considered suitable for factory work.[25] But advantage could also be found in domestic work compared with factory employment, reflecting the value attached to established cultural norms. One consideration was that a greater degree of choice in work regime could be achieved, with family members being able to keep the traditional 'St Monday' holiday.[26] Another consideration, bearing in mind the type of contemporary remarks we noted at the outset of this chapter, was the alienation that people felt with regard to working with powered machines in factories. And we must not forget that families wishing to remain in domestic work could devise strategies to do so, at least to a degree. For instance, as chapter two began to suggest, families could maintain an interest in handloom weaving by sending some or all of their children into factory work.[27]

Finally, we should note that demand considerations also played a part in the persistence and improvement of hand technology. This is partly because handworkers could be used to meet abnormal or specialist demand for products. The former arose periodically with trade-cycle upturns, the Lancashire handloom weavers benefiting during the mid-1830s, for example.[28] It could arise, too, in response to outbreaks of war, the handworkers in Birmingham's gun trades experiencing exceptionally high demand for their products during the hostilities with France in the early nineteenth century. The gun contractors who controlled the Birmingham gun industry were reluctant to intensify mechanisation at this time, or indeed later, since the traditional pattern of demand for their products was irregular.[29] As to specialist demand, changes in preference amongst fashion-conscious consumers required short production runs of higher-quality goods which could not be produced economically using powered machinery. Moreover some consumers retained an active preference for hand-made goods, which they perceived to have the edge in quality compared with machine-made goods.

We have tried to demonstrate in this section that 'hand technology' is a multi-layered phrase and that an important part of the technological change taking place during the Industrial Revolution period did not rely on the application of powered machinery. For various reasons, industrial processes depending on the use of hand techniques continued to be developed and applied in a wide range of industries. In some instances, such processes were gradually superseded by those requiring powered techniques, but in others they remained as the only or best means of production available. In this sense, it should be clear to students of the Industrial Revolution that the period 1700–1850 stands out because of the creation of a broadly based culture of technical development across a wide range of industries. This said, powered technology *was* becoming more intensively used in industrial processes by the later eighteenth century, and it is to a consideration of the nature of this technical development that we must now turn.

## The nature and causes of technological change

As we have suggested, growth in the use of powered machinery is undoubtedly the best-known characteristic of the technological changes that occurred in English industry during the Industrial Revolution period. Details of such famous inventions as Samuel Crompton's mule (which spun fine and strong cotton threads) and James Watt's separate condenser (which markedly improved the fuel consumption of steam engines) need not be given a detailed rehearsal here.[30] Indeed, to do so would be to simplify a process of invention and innovation which is in practice as complex and multi-layered as the development of hand technology. Instead, we begin our discussion by noting the crucial distinction historians have made between inventions arising from a radical new idea (macro-inventions) and inventions bringing improvements to existing techniques (micro-inventions).[31] Examples of the former in our period include the steamship and of the latter the spinning mule, which borrowed key features from earlier spinning machines. In manufacturing industry at least, von Tunzelmann

79

suggests that most innovations occurring during the early decades of the nineteenth century were the result of micro-inventions. However, they took place in a wider range of industries than previously, exerting a considerable impact on industrial productivity (output per head).[32] Mokyr too suggests the importance of micro-inventions, arguing that most macro-inventions during the Industrial Revolution era – apart from those concerning the steam engine and cotton manufacturing – originated in France and were *adapted and improved* in England. Indeed, he suggests that the secret of English technological success at this time lay in the country's comparative advantage over competitors in exploiting micro-inventions.[33]

One way to assess the nature and extent of micro-inventions and hence their importance is via the patent system. By no means all such improvements were patented, of course, so that data on numbers of patents – which show a marked rise during the Industrial Revolution period – are at best a minimal indicator of the changing level of technological advances being made. Even so, Dutton has argued that a very high proportion of inventors did patent their ideas during this period and that few major innovations by-passed the patent system.[34] Analysis of this material indicates that micro-inventions might take two forms. Improvement might take place as a series of relatively minor advances, perhaps resulting in notably more efficient machinery over the long term. The powerloom is a classic example, the refinements made to it gradually extending its capabilities, not least with regard to weaving finer threads. Yet, in some instances part of the advance achieved might be of a more fundamental nature, though it might require further adaptation before its general use was assured, as was the case with the self-acting (virtually automatic) mule. This machine was developed during the 1820s, with patents being taken out in 1825 and 1830, but could not be used economically to spin finer threads for some time. Whether the impact of these sorts of new micro developments can be regarded as more significant in promoting industrial growth than macro-inventions is debatable, but it is notable that Crompton's mule, the focus of a whole series of micro-inventions, became the dominant machine in cotton spinning by the early 1800s and thus one of the most important pieces of machinery in the world at that date. Much more could be said on these issues; the key lesson for students of the Industrial Revolution, however, is that there probably was a major discontinuity in the scale of inventive activity during the Industrial Revolution period.

Yet, rather than the level of inventive activity, the more important issue for contemporaries, and for our analysis of the Industrial Revolution, is the nature and extent of innovation – the process by which improvements in technology were employed by firms and industries to generate changes in the location, pace and experience of work. The nature of innovation is a complex issue. Landes, for instance, has suggested that innovation became a mushrooming process of 'challenge and response'. That is, 'the speed-up of one stage of the manufacturing process placed a heavy strain on the factors of production of one or more other stages and called forth innovations to correct the imbalance'.[35] The classic case of challenge and response is seen to have occurred in the cotton industry. Thus the improvement in weaving brought by the introduction of Kay's fly shuttle in 1733 is held to have created a technological imbalance which led to the introduction of new spinning machines – the jenny and the waterframe – in the 1760s. In turn, the new spinning machines, especially those that were power-driven, more than corrected the imbalance, leading to surplus yarn production. However, Griffiths, Hunt and O'Brien have challenged this view, arguing that the major technological breakthroughs in cotton manufacturing stimulated improved techniques in the same rather than related processes.[36] Yet, their argument fails to address Landes's further contention that the challenge and response principle applied *within* the spinning branch of the cotton industry, which in fact comprised several distinct processes. As he remarks, 'the mechanisation of spinning would have been unthinkable without a corresponding speed-up of the preliminary processes of cleaning, carding, and preparation of the roving'.[37]

There are, though, alternative models to underpin an analysis of the nature of innovation. For instance Maxine Berg suggests that innovation in machinery and industrial processes was driven by expanding markets and the introduction of a wide range of new products. Particularly important, she suggests, were new consumer goods – including household items, fashionable clothing and fabrics, and ornamental and semi-luxury commodities – which appealed to the middling classes. Her argument relies on a re-examination of patent records 'in the light of consumer culture rather than from the traditional perspectives of the historian of technology'. She also explores the type of connections that emerged between product innovation and broader technological innovation. For instance, she suggests that the skills developed in producing semi-luxury consumer goods contributed to the development of later technologies; these skills were widely valued and interchangeable from one industry to another.[38]

Of course, the idea that demand factors generated a tide of innovation is contentious. If rising demand was driving innovation it is difficult (though not impossible) to explain long time lags between major inventions being made and their widespread adoption, as in the case of Abraham Darby's process of smelting iron with coke. Unsurprisingly, historians have suggested alternative, 'supply-side', perspectives on the innovation process. The challenge and response idea is one such perspective, but others link innovation to the availability of skilled workers who could bring about technical advance; to adequate funds to invest in improved technology; and to a pool of scientific knowledge that might feed into advances in powered technology. Such views are themselves contentious. On the issue of scientific knowledge, James Watt acquired a scientific education by attending lectures, reading books and studying the construction of mathematical instruments. He also had a mathematics tutor. But more generally the question remains unanswered as to how far cultures of learning amongst labour forces aided technological advance.

Whichever model we choose as a vehicle for describing and understanding the process of innovation, it is important to acknowledge that there were a range of potential stimuli to the extensive adoption of improvements in technology where they were appropriate to the industrial process. Christine MacLeod has analysed 4,480 patents granted between 1660 and 1800, 2,618 of which (43 per cent) give details of the patentees' motives. She found that most patentees sought to improve the quality of products (29.3 per cent of cases) or to cut industrial costs, by saving on fuel, raw materials and power or by making equipment run more reliably (30.8 per cent of cases). Included in the former group is John Wilkinson's 1774 boring machine, which enabled James Watt to bore his steam-engine cylinders accurately, and in the latter group is Edmund Lee's 'fan-tail' of 1745, which turned windmills automatically so that they faced the wind. Relatively few patentees sought to save on capital costs associated with machinery, equipment and buildings. And this was also evident with inventions aimed at saving labour. They comprised only 4.2 per cent of the patent total, a figure that still rises to only 9.4 per cent if patents aimed at saving time (a coded way of referring to labour economies) are also taken into account. Yet, as MacLeod points out, we must be careful not to place too much credence on patentees'

declared motives. A patentee might consider it unwise to draw attention to the labour-saving potential of inventions given the threat
of job losses. In fact, MacLeod concludes that 21.6 per cent of the
patents probably *were* labour saving and that labour-saving innovation became of greater concern as the eighteenth century progressed.
Importantly, too, she points out innovation was sometimes more
concerned with overcoming difficulties arising with the industrial
workforce – such as absenteeism or careless work practices – than
with reducing the cost of labour.[39] The key point though is that while
it is difficult to trace the extent and pace of innovation with any
exactitude, there clearly were reasons why the desire and need to
innovate were building an unparalleled head of steam during our
period.

This said, we should not forget that there were also vigorous
constraints which could prevent the realisation of innovation. Some
of these – worker resistance, costs and improvement in hand technology – were outlined in the first part of this chapter. To this list
we might add institutional constraints. A good example is the patent
system. Kahn and Sokoloff have examined the differences between
the English and American patent systems between 1790 and 1850,
arguing that the British system tended to award patents to capital-
intensive technologies and to better-off people; patent fees were far
higher in England than in the United States. In contrast, the American
patent system awarded patent rights to a broader range both of people
and of new technologies. As a result, a more rapid diffusion of
technological information was encouraged in the United States than
in England.[40]

The relationship between industrialisation, invention and practical
innovation is thus a complex one. It might be fair to contend that
during the period 1700–1850 a number of influences worked in tandem
to ratchet up the pressure to innovate in the field of powered technology for some industries, and increased the returns for doing so.
Yet the extent to which this pressure was converted to practical
developments such as orders for new steam engines is buried in a
vast number of individual firm histories and, more importantly, in a
number of regional histories. Understanding the practicalities of technological change and locating its significance for our view of the
Industrial Revolution thus involves us in taking a regional perspective.

## The regional dimensions of innovation in powered and centralised technology

Many of the complexities of regional analysis have been dealt with in chapter two where we saw that industrial sectors varied in importance from region to region, giving rise to such shorthand (and somewhat misleading) descriptions as the 'Staffordshire Potteries' and the 'Lancashire cotton districts'. Economic activity could also vary in importance from place to place within an industrial district. For example, as we have already suggested, the woollen industry in West Yorkshire became centred in the Leeds, Wakefield and Huddersfield areas, whilst the worsted industry was mainly located further west in the Bradford, Halifax and Keighley areas. Such complexities mean that when we consider technological innovation in its various guises at regional level, we must deal with developments that had a general applicability, though they might be far more important in some regions than in others, alongside those which were largely applied in one or a small number of regions.

Most obvious amongst the former group are those relating to power sources. The importance of James Watt's separate condenser in improving the steam engine is well known, but this was only one amongst a number of major developments with which Watt and other engineers were associated. From 1781, for example, Watt steam engines were fitted with a 'sun and planet' device, which provided the rotary motion needed for driving machinery. And from 1845, William McNaught introduced an improved means of equipping steam engines with a high-pressure cylinder, enabling them to run more smoothly and economically. Such developments increased the range of uses to which steam power could be applied and, by the early nineteenth century, contemporaries were providing some impressive figures on the numbers of steam engines that were operating in the industrial districts. For instance, Edward Baines estimated that there were 1,541 in Lancashire (along with Stockport) during the mid-1820s, collectively delivering 30,835 horse power. For Manchester alone, the figures were 212 engines and 4,875 horse power.[41]

Important though the improvements made to steam engines were, they were by no means adopted universally. In fact, rather than buying Watt engines, many businessmen continued to prefer the pistonless steam engine developed by Thomas Savery in 1695 or the atmospheric steam engine introduced by Thomas Newcomen in 1712.

Colliery owners especially were often unwilling to buy Watt engines for pumping, at least before Watt's patent approached its expiry in 1800. The savings they made on fuel costs probably would not have outweighed the costs of re-equipping with a Watt engine and paying the annual premiums that Watt also demanded. In the case of pumping engines, these premiums were usually set at a third of the fuel savings achieved. Such reasoning may also explain the slow diffusion of high-pressure steam engines, though other considerations may also have operated, including fears about safety. Boiler explosions were a very real threat, with no fewer than 1,600 people being killed by them in the three years to November 1850.[42] Irrespective of the type preferred, the adoption of steam engines within the industrial districts was also limited by the continuing use of other power sources, especially waterwheels. This tendency was encouraged by improvements in waterwheel design and construction, including the growing use of components made of iron rather than of wood. Amongst those industrialists who persisted with water power were the Ashworth Brothers of Bank Top, near Bolton. In 1829, they bought a new mill at nearby Egerton and decided to complete the construction of a huge waterwheel, the diameter of which was no less that 62 feet and which was capable of generating an impressive 140 horse power.[43]

Not surprisingly, then, the degree to which steam power was adopted during the Industrial Revolution varied considerably from one region to another. By 1850, steam power had become very closely linked with the cotton textile industry, which was by then strongly localised in Lancashire and adjoining parts of Cheshire, Derbyshire and Yorkshire. Indeed, Taylor's figures show that in 1850 waterwheels generated a small fraction of the water power used in the county's cotton industry – about 7 per cent.[44] Furthermore, Lancashire's importance as a steam-power user was enhanced because other leading industries making use of steam power, especially coalmining and engineering, were also well represented in the county.[45] Reliable comparative data for other entire regions are lacking, but approximate figures for towns in the mid-1820s show that the horse power supplied by steam engines had reached 5,460 in London, 4,800 in Manchester, 4,500 in Glasgow, 2,300 in Leeds and 1,200 in Birmingham.[46] By 1870, admittedly outside our period, far more steam power was being used in Lancashire than in any other county, with Yorkshire second and Shropshire third.[47] The adoption of steam power, then, was a limited and regionally concentrated innovation.

Power systems were not the only type of technology with a potentially wide regional market. Engineering machinery and iron production techniques provide other examples, since they were used in industries that were widespread. Besides John Wilkinson's boring machine of 1784, which we have already noted, advances in engineering included James Nasmyth's steam hammer, invented in 1839. Compared with the traditional trip-hammers, the Nasmyth hammer enabled much bigger pieces of metal to be forged and gave the forgemen greater control over the metal they worked. In iron making, note has already been made of the puddling process, but its patentee, Henry Cort, is also credited with inventing (powered) grooved rollers, for which he took out a patent in 1783. The sets of rollers, which greatly quickened the production of iron bars, contained grooves of decreasing size, through which the bars were passed in turn, so that their thickness was reduced and their length increased. In the case of these and other major inventions, the extent and speed of application generally proceeded hand in hand with innovation in power sources, intensifying considerably the degree to which technological change occurred at regional level.

To the technological innovations that became widely diffused throughout the industrial districts must be added those that were much more strongly concentrated in just one or a few of these districts. The process of crucible steel making (illustrated in figure 3.4) provides a particularly striking example. Developed by Benjamin Huntsman around 1740, the process involved melting bars of carburised wrought iron (blister steel) in clay crucibles to give a hard steel of uniform quality. Kenneth Barraclough's extensive research into the industry has revealed that in England little crucible steel melting took place outside South Yorkshire; indeed, one contemporary estimate suggests that 2,113 crucible melting holes could be found at Sheffield in 1856, compared with 245 elsewhere in the country.[48] Similarly, though to a less marked extent, machinery used in textile production became regionally concentrated, as in the case of the powerloom. In 1850, factory inspectors' returns show that nearly 250,000 had been installed in Britain's cotton industry, of which about 70 per cent were in Lancashire factories. And this concentration in Lancashire becomes even more evident when powerlooms weaving other types of fabric are taken into account. In total, they amounted to around 50,000. About two-thirds were used in the worsted trade, of which about 42 per cent were also found in Lancashire.

**Figure 3.4** Crucible steelmaking. The 'puller-out' used long-handled tongs to remove the crucible, which might contain 50 pounds of molten steel at a temperature of about 1,600°C, from the furnace. The 'teemer' poured the crucible contents into an ingot mould

In touring England's industrial districts during the mid-nineteenth century, the interested observer would probably have been struck by the considerable degree of commonality that occurred in terms of the types of technology that were employed, in respect of both hand and powered equipment. At the same time, it would have been apparent that certain types of technology were better represented in some industrial districts than in others, as specialised technologies emerged to deal with particular industrial processes. Our observer would certainly have been struck by the sheer concentration of steam-powered machinery that was to be found in the Lancashire textile districts; not only had the county's dominant cotton industry become highly mechanised, but other industries that made considerable use of steam power, especially coalmining and engineering, were also well represented there. Yet, perhaps above all our observer would have been aware of a thriving culture of technology in the industrial regions. What was new about our period was that latent pressure to innovate was being turned into active innovation on a variety of fronts, a development that impinged strongly on the consciousness of contemporaries. But something else also struck them. This was the fact that technical innovation was often accompanied by, and was partly dependent upon, changes in the way that work was organised. It is to this theme that we now turn.

### Changes in the nature of work organisation

In the last chapter, we dealt with the eighteenth-century transition from domestic production and the proto-industrial system in its various guises. We suggested that the impact of this development on the working lives of those most closely engaged with the process at a regional level was profound. We drew similar conclusions about the impact of the factory. However, it remains to consider why factories and other types of centralised production arose. As a starting point, it is important to realise that centralised production in factories, workshops or other types of industrial premises did not always depend upon the introduction of powered machinery.

To illustrate the point we can cite examples from the textile and steel industries. Using evidence derived mainly from sale notices in local newspapers, Duncan Bythell has demonstrated that handloom-weaving sheds were constructed in various parts of the country during the eighteenth and nineteenth centuries. These could be of considerable size, some housing as few as 20 looms but others as many as 150 or 200.[49] As to steelmaking, rate-book evidence from Sheffield, the main centre of production, reveals numerous works which made steel alone, or steel and tools, without the need for powered equipment. Most of these works would have operated on a small scale, though they included Sanderson Brothers, one of the biggest of the specialist steelmakers. In the late 1830s, their West Street works comprised four cementation furnaces for making blister steel and eighty-three furnace holes for making crucible steel, along with warehousing and stabling.[50]

Other industries in which centralised production occurred without powered machinery necessarily being used are not difficult to identify, some of them developing new forms of workshop production during the eighteenth century based on an extensive division of labour and multi-site production.[51] However, the examples cited are sufficient to help us make the point that businessmen erected such premises for varying reasons. Quite plainly, neither those who ran the handloom-weaving sheds nor the steelmakers chose centralised production because they were concerned about powered equipment. Whilst the former might have wished to move away from domestic production, say, to improve quality control or impose greater discipline amongst their workers, the latter had no option other than to work from centralised premises at the outset.[52] Even a small steelworks may have required a four-figure outlay by the mid-1830s, as is indicated by extensions made to Marshes and Shepherd's works in Pond Street, Sheffield. These comprised an eight-hole crucible steel furnace, a three-stall stable, a storage cellar and a counting house at a cost of £616.[53] Additionally, to operate a steel furnace required the employment of several workers who were skilful as well as strong, whilst land had to be made available on which to erect the furnace and accompanying buildings. Such demands could not easily be met in the domestic environment.

To reinforce this point, the relatively high cost of non-powered equipment employed in some other industries characterised by centralised production may be briefly mentioned. The Dutch looms, which were used to weave smallwares (tapes, ribbons and the like) at Manchester and elsewhere, provide one example. Wadsworth and Mann note that these were complicated devices with multiple shuttles and were hence relatively expensive.[54] A further example is the dandy loom. This was made from iron rather than wood and its cost was augmented because a dandy-loom shop would require at least one dressing frame through which the warps were passed for sizing before weaving took place. Again such equipment would as a rule be too expensive for domestic producers to purchase, even if the necessary space was available, whilst those who owned it would be reluctant to hire it out to domestic workers because of uncertainty as to how fully and carefully it would be used.

Other reasons still for the rise of centralised production can be advanced, including reduced transport costs for goods and raw materials, lower levels of raw-material theft and the need to keep smaller stocks of raw materials. It is not surprising, therefore, that factories and other types of workplace that did not involve the use of powered machinery were constructed. For those who worked in such places, the consequences of centralisation for work routines were in some respects very different from, though potentially no less profound than, the consequences which sprang from centralised and mechanised production. While the 'factoryisation' of the labour force in Lancashire and elsewhere sharply engaged the attention of contemporaries and has done the same for some historians, the key change for many people in our period would have been the centralisation and other organisational changes that accompanied innovation in non-powered technology.

The diffusion of powered machinery and improved hand technology in conjunction with the changing organisation of work necessitated by proto-industrialisation brought ever rising numbers of people into factories and other types of industrial works. The fact of this shift provides support for the notion of an Industrial Revolution. Some contemporaries condemned these changes because they felt they had a profoundly adverse effect on the health and morals of industrial workers, especially women and children. Others, however, took an entirely different view, not only seeking to refute the arguments of the critics, but also to extol the benefits that centralised or mechanised production could bring. Historians have been no less divided, and so to complete the analysis of the impact of industrial development on the lives of ordinary people that we began in chapter two we must end with some contemporary views on what technological advance broadly defined meant in their society.

### Health and morals: the impact of centralised and mechanised production

In undertaking such an analysis, it must be borne in mind that the evidence provided by contemporaries cannot be regarded as entirely reliable, the more so because passions were often strongly aroused. It is possible, for example, that Joseph Habergam, with whose life story we opened this chapter, did not accurately report every detail of his experiences as a child factory worker. Moreover, his evidence contains inconsistencies on quite crucial matters. We have noted his doctor's diagnosis that he would never be 'right any more', but he also stated that 'the doctors have nearly cured me'. He also expressed differing opinions as to how hard his work was, at one point maintaining it 'was not very hard' and at another that 'it was rather hard of itself'. At least, though, he was recounting first-hand experiences in the three mills at which he worked over a ten-year period, whereas other contemporaries, Edward Baines amongst them, based their views on much scantier acquaintance with textile mill work. Owen Ashmore has suggested that Baines was 'a moderate reformer and supporter of "improvements" of all kinds', so he was always likely to have taken a positive stance with regard to the rise of power-driven factories, irrespective of how frequently he had visited them.[55]

To draw attention to the limitations of the evidence left by contemporaries is not to argue that it was without substance, however. The sheer volume of material they produced concerning appalling working conditions particularly in centralised facilities (mechanised and not) is far too great to be dismissed out of hand. We have already quoted some of this evidence in relation to the textile industry and it can easily be supplemented from investigations made into other industries. In the early 1840s, for example, children employed by Staffordshire potters were reported to be working from half past five in the morning to six at night and often until later, whilst the temperature in which they worked reached 100 degrees or more. During the same period, the Sheffield fork grinders were reported to be at exceptionally high risk of death from lung disease; they used dry rather than wet grindstones, with the result that stone and metal particles pervaded the atmosphere in their workshops. In fact, according to one contemporary calculation, those aged between 20 and 29 years experienced a death rate that was some 2.5 times the level of that for their age group in Sheffield as a whole.[56] And if further evidence of poor working conditions is required, it can be found in abundance with regard to coalmining, an industry in which accidents were all too frequent. Many of them occurred as people were ascending and descending the mine shafts, the 1842 Children's Employment Commission (Mines) pointing out that there were 'two practices peculiar to a few districts which deserve the highest reprobation'. They were,

> first, the practice not unknown in some of the smaller mines in Yorkshire, and common in Lancashire, of employing ropes that are unsafe for letting down and drawing up the workpeople; and second the practice, occasionally met with in Yorkshire, and common in Lancashire and Derbyshire, of employing boys at the steam-engines for letting down and drawing up the workpeople.[57]

Figure 3.5 provides a flavour of the nature of children's work in the mining industry.

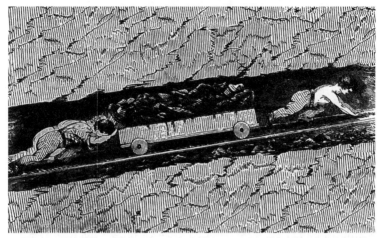

**Figure 3.5** Child coalmine workers. The question of health also related to the arduous nature of child labour, especially in coalmines, where both boys and girls were commonly employed in drawing – moving the coal from where it was cut to the bottom of the mine winding shaft

Contemporaries were also concerned about threats to the moral well-being of industrial workers in centralised facilities. Part of this concern was about the 'low moral condition' of child workers, which, according to the 1843 Children's Employment Commission (Trades and Manufactures), was characterised by:

> an absence of moral and religious restraint, shown amongst some classes chiefly by coarseness of manners, and the use of profane and indecent language; but in other classes by the practice of gross immorality, which is prevalent to a great extent, in both sexes, at very early ages.[58]

There was also a great deal of concern about the moral well-being of female workers. One mill owner is reported to have held the 'sincere conviction' that there was 'hardly such a thing as a chaste factory girl, at least in the large towns'.[59] That centralised production led to large numbers of young males and females congregating together was not seen to promote high moral standards, particularly where night working was concerned. Indeed, Michael Sadler, the famous factory reformer, remarked, 'I never did hear it denied that many of the mills, at least those in which night working is pursued, are ... little better than brothels.'[60] Such attitudes are neatly summed up by Deborah Valenze. The critics of the female factory worker, she comments:

unfurled a long list of indelicacies to which she was prone: unseemly behaviour created by the amassing of coarse workers, immodesty brought about by wearing scanty clothing because of the heat, precocious sexual development, fondness of drink and stimulants required by fatigue, solitary night travel necessitated by hours of work that lasted into the night, and cravings for excitement created by long hours of monotonous work.[61]

Part of the problem for women with regard to the morality issue was that, for a great many of them, their pattern of working changed fundamentally during the Industrial Revolution. A key dimension of this change was that they increasingly worked outside the home environment at an early and impressionable age, thereby coming into contact with influences that were regarded as being far from wholesome. But the line of argument also extended to older factory women, particularly those who were mothers. They clashed with the belief of middle-class observers and working-class men that the role of the mother was that of homemaker rather than breadwinner.

Yet, whilst many contemporaries were eager to voice their fears about the dangers to health and morals arising from centralised working, others took a quite different view. In the case of cotton mills, for instance, we have already noted Edward Baines's remarks about the extent of productivity advances arising from the use of powerlooms. With regard to cotton factories, he also argued that the use of powered machinery made work far easier:

> Factory labour is far less injurious than many of the most common and necessary employments of civilised life. It is much less irksome than that of the [hand] weaver, less arduous than that of the smith, less prejudicial to the lungs, the spine, and the limbs, than those of the shoemaker and the tailor. Colliers, miners, forgemen, cutlers, machine-makers, masons, bakers, corn-millers, painters, plumbers, letter-press printers, potters, and many other classes of artisans and labourers, have employments which in one way or another are more inimical to health and longevity than the labour of cotton mills. Some classes of professional men ... are subject to as great, and in many cases much greater, confinement and exhaustion, than the mill operatives.[62]

Cooke Taylor, who toured the manufacturing districts of Lancashire in 1842, took a similar view, suggesting that the tasks children were required to undertake in factories were not laborious, even though, for the most part, they were monotonous and fatiguing. He also sought to refute the idea of infants being employed in factories, and he argued for legal protection of children, not against employers, but 'against the extremes to which griping poverty in most instances, and grasping avarice in some, may drive their parents'.[63] Working conditions in industries other than cotton manufacturing could also evoke favourable contemporary comment. For instance, following his investigation into the Staffordshire pottery industry in the early 1840s, Samuel Scriven remarked that the employers were never known to inflict punishment on children or to allow others to do so. And though he came across appalling working conditions in the industry, he found that the more recently constructed works contained 'large, well-ventilated, light, airy, commodious rooms, in all respects adapted to the processes carried on in them'. In the potteries of the west of England, he did discover that corporal punishment was occasionally inflicted, but here, too, he considered that children were generally well treated.[64]

Allegations about the immorality of factory work could also be refuted by contemporaries. For instance, J. C. Holland expounded a counter-argument to the idea that immorality was encouraged when large numbers of people worked together. He maintained:

> The advantages of a large establishment, that is where the artisan is employed on the premises of the master, are great, in a moral point of view, from the beneficial influence of example. The industrious and well regulated habits of the many, restrain the irregular and intemperate conduct of the few, or at least control the tendency to dissipation.[65]

Holland drew a sharp contrast between factory workers and those working at home (or in small workshops) who were freed from 'all restraint and superintendence'. Such people, he suggested, could work when they wished, with the result that they were too often playing and drinking when they ought to have been otherwise employed.[66] As regards the charges contemporaries made about female factory workers being immoral, Angus Reach was sceptical. 'There exists amongst the mill girls', he remarked, 'a considerable degree of correct feeling – sometimes, indeed, carried to the extent of a species of saucy prudery – upon these subjects.'[67]

Clearly, contemporaries were divided with respect to the nature of the impact of technology and the changing organisation of work on the social, cultural and working lives of employees. On some of these issues, empirical investigation has subsequently offered more detailed perspectives. Thus, using a sample of census data from 1851,

Michael Anderson was able to suggest that only 23 per cent of women with children worked and that probably only about 15 per cent worked away from home for most of the day. Child neglect in this context was unlikely. Indeed, he argues, necessity often compelled these mothers to work, their husbands being unable to earn enough to provide the necessities of life, such that female work may actually have led to better domestic conditions for children.[68] Analysis of census material can also help in pinning down the question of the age at which children began work. Thus, taking England and Wales as a whole, figures extracted by Hugh Cunningham show that only 2 per cent of boys and 1.4 per cent of girls were recorded by census enumerators as having occupations. For boys, the main occupation available was agricultural labour (employing 5,463), followed by taking messages (employing 2,158) and cotton manufacturing (employing 2,072). For girls, straw plaiting led the way (2,746 jobs), followed by lacemaking (2,590 jobs) and cotton (1,477 jobs).[69] The exploitation of young children in centralised production units was thus, at least by the end of the period considered here, very small-scale. We could carry on with this sort of clarification. Yet, what is important for our analysis is that there was a debate at all amongst contemporaries. The fact of the debate conveys a powerful message that radical changes were overtaking the nature of work and its technological underpinnings. It was this above all, at least in the eyes of some contemporaries, that made the period 1700–1850 so different to what had gone before.

## Conclusion

Though in the mid-eighteenth century it was not unusual to find powered machinery used in English industry, a century later it was commonplace, its application being extended to a widening range of activities, as well as being intensified with regard to established uses. At the same time, steam power attained a dominant position over power derived from animals, wind and water, the uses to which it could be put being greatly extended by the development of rotary motion in the 1780s. Not only did the improved steam engine enable industrialists to develop much bigger industrial works, but it also freed them from having to locate mainly in river valleys. In fact, they increasingly concentrated their activities on coalfield sites in order to minimise the costs of transporting fuel. They also chose locations near to urban centres where their requirements for labour, transport and raw material supplies could most easily be met.

The impact of the growing use of powered machinery was potentially profound. Whereas in the mid-eighteenth century those employed in manufacturing industry as a rule worked within domestic premises, by the mid-nineteenth century it had become usual for the ever-rising number of industrial workers to find employment outside the home, especially, but by no means solely, in textile factories. The transition affected adults and children alike, enmeshing them in a much more regular working regime designed to ensure that expensive powered equipment was utilised to the fullest extent. It was a change which, as we have seen, brought impassioned debate amongst contemporaries with regard to its advantages and drawbacks, especially over the employment of women and children. The health and safety issue was paramount here – though moral considerations were important, too – with a plethora of evidence being deployed to show that the use of powered machines was associated with suffering. And its impact level was enhanced because it all too frequently drew attention to types of suffering which had rarely been experienced by previous generations.

Yet, the really important thing about the period 1700–1850 is that the rise of the mechanised factory must be understood as part of a generalised trend to technological development which involved vital advances in hand technology, the development of wider industrial 'processes', radical changes in the location and nature of work even outside the mechanised factory, the creation of a culture of innovation and the regional concentration of technological change at exactly the same time as technology became a 'national issue'. The 'process of technological change' is thus a complex and beguiling matter. Nowhere is this clearer than in deciding the importance to attach to improving hand technology. On the one hand such improvement potentially allowed people to lead lives that had much in common with those of their grandparents' generation, while on the other it was compatible with mass production, as was clearly the case with hand-woven textiles. Whichever angle we take, the key point is that locally, regionally and nationally, technological change was under the microscope of workers, industrialists, politicians and social commentators. This above all means that we must regard technological invention and innovation – widely defined to include hand technology and industrial organisation – as revolutionary in the period 1700–1850.

In turn, both the process of technical change and one of its partial consequences – more industrialists producing more goods on a wider scale and for the world stage – generated important knock-on effects for other yardsticks by which we might want to judge the Industrial Revolution. One of the potentially most important effects was on the scale and type of capital that entrepreneurs had to raise in order to establish or expand their businesses. This is the focus of the next chapter.

## Notes

1  S. Kidd, *The history of the factory movement* (New York, Augustus Kelley, 1966 reprint), pp. 285–6.

2  *Ibid.*, pp. 286–7.

3  *Ibid.*, p. 292.

4  D. Landes, 'The fable of the dead horse: or the Industrial Revolution revisited', in J. Mokyr (ed.), *The British Industrial Revolution: an economic perspective* (Boulder, Col., Westview Press, 1993), p. 161.

5  See J. Ayres, *Building the Georgian city* (New Haven, Yale University Press, 1998), pp. 162–8 and C. Aspin and S. Chapman, *James Hargreaves and the spinning jenny* (Helmshore, Helmshore Local History Society, 1964).

6  G. Timmins, 'Technological change', in M. B. Rose (ed.), *The Lancashire cotton industry* (Preston, Lancashire County Books, 1996).

7  L. Day and I. McNeil, *Biographical dictionary of the history of technology* (London, Routledge, 1996).

8  See J. Hammond and B. Hammond, *The rise of modern industry* (London, Methuen, 1925), p. 171.

9  P. S. Bagwell, *The transport revolution from 1770* (London, Batsford, 1974), and G. Dodd, *Days at the factories* (New York, Augustus Kelley, 1967 reprint).

10  T. Derry and T. Williams, *A short history of technology* (Oxford, Clarendon, 1960).

11  Day and McNeil, *Dictionary*, p. 696.

12  J. Mokyr, *The lever of riches* (Oxford, Oxford University Press, 1990).

13  E. Baines, *A history of the cotton manufacture in Great Britain* (London, Cass, 1966 reprint), p. 240.

14  Timmins, 'Technological change', p. 43.

15  A. Randall, *Before the Luddites* (Cambridge, Cambridge University Press, 1991), pp. 230–1.

16  C. K. Harley, 'Cotton textile prices and the Industrial Revolution', *Economic History Review*, 51 (1998) 49–83.

17  Dodd, *Factories*, p. 5.

18  *Pawson and Brailsford's illustrated guide to Sheffield* (Sheffield, S. R. Publishers, 1971 reprint), p. 150.

19  D. A. Farnie, *The English cotton industry and the world market, 1815–1896* (Oxford, Clarendon, 1979).

20  Dodd, *Factorie*, p. 553.

21  Aspin and Chapman, *Spinning jenny*, ch. 6

22  C. Aspin (ed.), *Manchester and the textile districts in 1849* (Helmshore, Helmshore Local History Society, 1972), p. 118.

23  Randall, *Luddites*, p. 289.

24  S. A. Caunce, 'Complexity, community structure and competitive advantage within the Yorkshire woollen industry, *c.* 1700–1850', *Business History*, 40 (1998) 26–43.

25  See M. Anderson, *Family structure in nineteenth century Lancashire* (Cambridge, Cambridge University Press, 1972).

26  See D. Reid, 'Weddings, weekdays, work and leisure in urban England 1791–1911: the decline of St. Monday revisited', *Past and Present*, 153 (1996) 135–63.

27  G. Timmins, *The last shift* (Manchester, Manchester University Press, 1993), ch. 6. See also J. S. Lyons, 'Family response to economic decline: handloom weavers in early nineteenth century Lancashire', *Research in Economic History*, 12 (1989) 45–91.

28  Timmins, *Last shift*, pp. 92–7.

29  C. Behagg, 'Mass production without the factory: craft producers, guns and small firm innovation, 1790–1815', *Business History*, 40 (1998) 1–15.

30  But the significance of such developments should not be exaggerated, as von Tunzelmann has demonstrated in the case of the early impact of Watt's steam engines. According to his calculations, the savings arising from using Watt engines compared with other types of steam engine amounted to only 0.11 per cent of national income in 1800, the year that Watt's patent expired. See N. von Tunzelmann, *Steam power and British industrialisation to 1860* (Oxford, Clarendon, 1978), ch. 6.

31  J. Mokyr, 'Technological change, 1700–1830', in R. Floud and D. McCloskey (eds), *The economic history of Britain since 1700, volume I: 1700–1860* (Cambridge, Cambridge University Press, 2nd edn, 1994), pp. 15–16.

32  N. von Tunzelmann, 'Technology in the early nineteenth century', in Floud and McCloskey (eds), *Economic history*, ch. 11.

33  Mokyr, 'Technological change', pp. 30–3.

34  H. I. Dutton, *The patent system and inventive activity during the Industrial Revolution, 1750–1852* (Manchester, Manchester University Press, 1984).

35  D. Landes, *The unbound prometheus: technological change and industrial development in Western Europe from 1750 to the present* (Cambridge, Cambridge University Press, 1968), p. 84.

36   M. Berg and K. Bruland, *Technological revolutions in Europe* (Chelten-ham, Edward Elgar Publishing, 1998), ch. 7.

37   Landes, *Prometheus*, p. 87.

38   M. Berg, 'Product innovation in core consumer industries in eighteenth-century Britain', in Berg and Bruland, *Revolutions*, ch. 8.

39   C. MacLeod, *Inventing the Industrial Revolution* (Cambridge, Cambridge University Press, 1988), ch. 9. See also N. von Tunzelmann, 'Techno-logical and organisational change in industry during the early Industrial Revolution', in P. O'Brien and R. Quinault (eds), *The Industrial Revol-ution and British society* (Cambridge, Cambridge University Press, 1993), pp. 256–8, and N. von Tunzelmann, 'Time-saving technical change: the cotton industry in the Industrial Revolution', *Explorations in Economic History*, 32 (1995) 1–27.

40   Berg and Bruland, *Revolutions*, ch. 15.

41   E. Baines, *History, directory, and gazetteer, of the county palatine of Lancaster, volume II* (Newton Abbot, David and Charles, 1968 reprint), p. 740.

42   Von Tunzelmann, *Steam power*, pp. 31–6.

43   R. Boyson, *The Ashworth cotton enterprise* (Oxford, Clarendon, 1970).

44   A. J. Taylor, 'Concentration and specialization in the Lancashire cotton industry, 1825–1850', *Economic History Review* 1 (1949) 114–22.

45   G. Timmins, *Made in Lancashire* (Manchester, Manchester University Press, 1998), pp. 98–107.

46   Von Tunzelmann, *Steam power*, pp. 31–6.

47   N. von Tunzelmann, 'Coal and steam power', in J. Langton and R. J. Morris (eds), *Atlas of industrializing Britain, 1780–1914* (London, Methuen, 1986), pp. 76–9.

48   K. C. Barraclough, *Steelmaking before Bessemer: volume 2 crucible steel* (London, The Metals Society, 1984), ch. 5.

49   D. Bythell, *The handloom weavers* (Cambridge, Cambridge University Press, 1969), pp. 33–4.

50   G. Timmins, 'Concentration and integration in the Sheffield crucible steel industry', *Business History*, 24 (1982) 65.

51   They include the Birmingham hardware trades and textile engineering in Yorkshire. For details, see M. Berg, 'Small producer capitalism in eighteenth century England', *Business History*, 35 (1993) 18–39; M. Berg, *The age of manufactures: industry, innovation and work in Britain, 1700–1820* (London, Fantana, 1985), pp. 203–4 and 264–9; and G. Cook-son, 'Family firms and business networks: textile engineering in Yorkshire, 1780–1830', *Business History*, 39 (1997), 9–12. Cookson sees the desire to improve standards as being central to the textile engineers moving into factories and suggests that they may also have been in-fluenced by established practice in other local industries.

52   On the labour control issue, see M. Berg, 'Factories, workshops and

industrial organisation', in Floud and McCloskey (eds), *Economic history*, pp. 146–7. More generally on the reasons for factory growth, see S. R. H. Jones, 'The origins of the factory system in Great Britain', in M. W. Kirby and M. B. Rose (eds), *Business enterprise in modern Britain* (London, Routledge, 1994), pp. 31–60.

53  S. Pollard, *Three centuries of Sheffield steel* (Sheffield, Butt, 1954).

54  A. P. Wadsworth and J. de Lacy Mann, *The cotton trade and industrial Lancashire, 1600–1780* (Manchester, Manchester University Press, 1935).

55  Baines, *History*, volume 1, 'Introduction'.

56  G. C. Holland, *The vital statistics of Sheffield* (London, Robert Tyas, 1843).

57  Parliamentary Papers, *1842, XV Children's Employment Commission (Mines) Appendix*.

58  Parliamentary Papers, *1843, XIII Second Report of the Children's Employment Commission (Trades and Manufactures) Appendix*.

59  Aspin (ed.), *Textile districts*, p. 19.

60  Kidd, *Factory*, p. 185.

61  D. Valenze, *The first industrial woman* (Oxford, Oxford University Press, 1995), pp. 98–9.

62  Baines, *History*, p. 121.

63  W. Cooke Taylor, *Notes on a tour of the manufacturing districts of Lancashire* (London, Cass, 1968 reprint), p. 241.

64  Parliamentary Papers, *1843 XV Children's Employment Commission, Appendix, part 1*.

65  Holland, *Vital statistics*, ch. 16.

66  *Ibid.*

67  Aspin, *Textile districts*, p. 19.

68  Anderson, *Family structure*, pp. 71–4. In his more recent work, which is based on an 1851 census sample for Lancashire and Cheshire, Anderson modifies this picture a little. He suggests that 40 per cent of the wives of textile factory workers with at least one child (but none in employment) had factory jobs. In fact, this figure only fell substantially when children in the family began to work, thereby replacing, at least in part, the income the mother had earned. See M. Anderson, 'What can the mid-Victorian censuses tell us about variations in married women's employment?', *Local Population Studies*, 62 (1999), p. 20.

69  H. Cunningham, 'The employment and unemployment of children in England *c.* 1680–1851', *Past and Present*, 126 (1990) 115–50.

# CHAPTER FOUR

# FINANCING THE
# INDUSTRIAL REVOLUTION

## Conceptual framework

How the finance required to promote regional industrialisation, and the technological innovation with which it was so closely associated, was raised and used are matters of vital concern in our understanding of the Industrial Revolution. The process has important implications with regard to such fundamental issues as the provision of industrial premises and the installation of machinery and equipment; the regularity of wage payments and the form they took; the purchase of raw materials; the provision of transport facilities; and the growth and appearance of the built environment. The need to provide much greater financing for these purposes enhanced the role of financial institutions, including banks. And the ability to secure and use such funds offered a means of attaining wealth and position. In other words, how finance was obtained and deployed within the industrial regions had a marked and widespread influence on the well-being and aspirations of people from all walks of life. These considerations lie at the heart of our present chapter, but before we launch into them, it is as well to note three crucial conceptual issues.

First, there is the question of terminology, and at the outset we must define two terms that historians commonly use in discussing industrial finance. One is fixed capital, which refers to the industrial premises (domestic or otherwise) and to machinery and other equipment (whether hand-driven or powered) used to produce goods and services. Adding to the stock of fixed capital is often referred to as fixed capital formation and to expenditure on it as fixed capital costs. The essential point about these costs is that they varied little, if at all, with output (at least in the short term). Not only were they of concern to those wishing to start a business, therefore, but also to established businessmen who experienced falling output – by no means an unusual situation given periodic downturns in the economy – or who wished to expand output to take advantage of an upturn in trade. The second term to note is that of variable (or working) costs – mainly the costs of labour, raw materials, power and transport – which fluctuated as output levels changed. Such costs could be lowered in various ways, including laying off part of the labour force or switching to short-time working. On the other hand, they could rise appreciably as a firm expanded, though the introduction of powered technology might reduce labour costs per unit of output by a considerable degree.

Second, we have to grapple with the sheer diversity of uses for which capital was required. There was a wide spectrum of experience. To take just one example, in the late eighteenth and early nineteenth centuries the poor-law authorities of North and East Yorkshire were deluged with appeals from paupers who sought small amounts of finance – between £1 and £4 – to enable them to purchase stock so that they could become hawkers (itinerant traders). The sums involved were working capital as surely as the thousands of pounds borrowed by the great textile concerns such as McConnel and Kennedy. Thus, while we will focus in this chapter on capital demand and supply in particular industries and regions, it is important to realise that the need for capital permeated all levels of society and all sectors of the economy after 1700 to an extent that would have been inconceivable half a century earlier.

The third conceptual problem is one of 'significance'. With regard to the demand for capital and its supply, what types of change took place and how, if at all, does an appreciation of these changes contribute to the idea that there was an Industrial Revolution? What marked out the period 1700–1850 compared with previous or later periods? To anticipate some of our conclusions, we can note that technological innovation, even where non-powered technology was involved, could appreciably increase the demand that individual business concerns had for both fixed and working capital. Meeting this demand involved a marked rise in national capital expenditure, if not to the extent that some historians have maintained. We can note, too, that to cope with the long-term capital needs of businessmen the partnership form of organisation – often arising through kinship or religious connections – came to assume high significance, whilst to meet businessmen's working capital needs a massive expansion of credit networks took place, in which the emerging banking system came to play a key role. There were, then, major developments in business finance which add considerable weight to the notion of an Industrial Revolution between 1700 and 1850.

With these conceptual points in mind, we begin our discussion by assessing the demand for capital. At the level of the individual business concern, we draw on extracts from the business records of Roberts, Cadman and Company, a Sheffield firm that manufactured tableware and other goods from Old Sheffield Plate. Established in January 1786, the firm was based at the Eyre Street premises of Samuel Roberts, the senior partner. The firm's earliest balance sheet, which gives valuations of its assets (what it owned) and of its liabilities (what it owed) has survived.[1] By considering its assets, we can determine the firm's relative expenditure on (and hence its demand for) fixed and variable capital. This is a matter of considerable interest to historians, since firms investing in the improved technology made available during the Industrial Revolution would sometimes have seen their fixed capital costs rising appreciably as a proportion of their total costs. In addition to discussing the demand for capital from the point of view of the individual firm, we also examine the demand for capital in particular industries and in the economy as a whole. This is because the sums spent on fixed capital by business and other organisations comprised an important part of investment expenditure, a major component of economic growth. We will return to this matter shortly, explaining the concept of investment expenditure in greater detail.

Having considered the growth in demand for capital, we turn to consider developments in the means by which it was supplied. At the level of the firm, we can again obtain useful insights from the Roberts and Cadman balance sheet, this time by considering the firm's liabilities. These give us some idea of the importance of the contributions made by the partners, as well as by others – such as raw-material suppliers – who granted credit to the partners. But we also move to more general discussion of major developments in the way that both long- and short-term business capital was supplied, particularly within some of the industrialising regions identified in chapter two.

### Capital demand and the business concern

In June 1787, eighteen months after they established their partnership, Roberts and Cadman held their first stocktaking. They made a detailed valuation of their business assets and by comparing the value of these assets with that of their liabilities, they were able to determine the extent of the profit or loss they had made. They set out the results in the form of a balance sheet and this is reproduced as table 4.1. In this section, we focus attention on the assets side of the balance sheet in order to consider the relative importance of the demand the partners had for fixed and working capital.

Table **4.1** *The Roberts and Cadman balance sheet, 1787*

| Assets | Valuation | Liabilities | Valuation |
|---|---|---|---|
| To materials in the workshops | 641 | By S. Roberts | 1,614 |
| To materials in the warehouse | 120 | By B. Naylor | 1,337 |
| To goods finished in the warehouse | 567 | By G. Cadman | 96 |
| To buildings, tools, fixtures, etc. | 1,246 | By debts owed | 1,164 |
| To cash in hand | 12 | By partners' stock gained | 852 |
| To debts owing | 2,477 | | |
| TOTAL | 5,063 | | 5,063 |

*Source*: Sheffield City Archives, Stock Book, Sis. 146.

As can be seen, the firm's fixed capital assets – comprising buildings, tools and fixtures – were valued at £1,246. The remaining items in the assets column comprise valuations of the firm's working capital. By far the biggest item, amounting to £2,477, was debts owing – in other words the sums that customers had yet to pay for goods supplied to them by Roberts and Cadman on short-term credit. Over sixty such customers are listed in the stocktaking book and they owed amounts ranging from a few shillings to several hundred pounds. In total, the sum of their indebtedness amounted to virtually half of Roberts and Cadman's total assets. That the firm was extending credit to its customers was normal business practice, though the risk of some customers defaulting was always present and would have been more intense during trade depressions.[2] The next biggest item of working capital – materials, etc. in the warehouse and workshops – formed about 15 per cent of the firm's asset value and mainly comprised silver plate, the quality of which varied appreciably. The remaining working-capital item of any note amongst the assets is the stock of finished goods, which comprised about 10 per cent of the asset valuation. The stock's value was discounted by 50 per cent, perhaps reflecting the lowest prices the firm might expect to receive for it.[3]

The main point to develop here with regard to the changes taking place in the financing of firms is the ratio of the partners' fixed capital requirements to their working capital requirements. As can be seen, the value of fixed capital stood at £1,246 compared with a working capital value of £3,817; the fixed to working capital ratio was thus about 1:3. The difference in the figures partly reflects both the partners' concern to extend considerable credit to customers as a means of generating sales and their lack of investment in powered technology. The one stage in their production process which did require the use of water or steam power, namely rolling out the plate so that the copper and silver were fused together, was probably carried out locally for them by Joseph Hancock, a specialist metal roller.[4] Plainly, the type of technology employed by a firm, and the extent to which its proprietors extended short-term credit to customers, could have a considerable influence on the ratio of its fixed to working capital. We might anticipate from the discussion in chapter three that the growing number of firms employing powered technology and/or more advanced hand technology would have been characterised by considerably higher ratios of fixed to working capital than was the Roberts and Cadman enterprise. But was this indeed the case?

Some insights into the matter have been provided by Sidney Pollard, who has concluded that only in the cotton industry did the value of firms' fixed capital exceed that of working capital during the Industrial Revolution period and even then by a very slim margin. And he warns that this would only have been the case where the most up-to-date cotton mills were concerned. Even in the iron industry, which might appear to be associated with particularly heavy expenditure on fixed capital, Pollard suggests that the ratio of fixed to working capital was low. For instance, at the Soho Foundry (near Birmingham) in 1822, fixed capital was valued at £3,200 and working capital at £33,300, a ratio of 1:10.4. The explanation for such low ratios is probably that the fixed capital equipment was usually made on site rather than being bought in, its value being calculated on the basis of the raw materials needed to build it and, perhaps, the labour costs involved.[5] In other words, firms were not having to pay for the value added in manufacturing fixed capital and for the profits that purchasing from other firms would have incurred.

With regard to changes in the fixed to working capital ratio over time, Pollard argues that a substantial rise occurred at an early stage of the Industrial Revolution in those industries that moved towards factory production or other capital-intensive methods. Thereafter, the pattern was one of a greater number of firms in each industry increasing their proportions of fixed capital, rather than the advanced firms extending theirs any further.[6] It might be added that, given the persistence of hand technology, many industrial concerns would not have extended their expenditure on fixed capital all that far beyond customary limits. Moreover, those that did would sometimes have bought second-hand equipment – which became available as firms' proprietors retired, died or became bankrupt – so that the impact of any rise in their fixed to working capital ratio was limited.[7]

The views expressed by Pollard have not gone unchallenged, however. Edwards is critical of Pollard's estimate that fixed capital represented just over half the capital invested by leading cotton firms. According to Edwards, the estimate is too generous, at least for the period 1780 to 1815.[8] He cites examples of the asset values calculated from the records of cotton firms for this period which, when used to compute ratios of fixed capital to total assets, give figures of 0.7 per cent, 14 per cent, 17.5 per cent, 21 per cent and 40 per cent.[9] Philip Richardson, on the other hand, believes that Pollard's estimate is too low. He uses data drawn from the account books of two leading cotton firms – Oldknow, Cowpe and Company of Pleasley and McConnel and Kennedy of Manchester – to calculate fixed capital ratios over fairly lengthy time periods. In the case of the former concern, he finds that the ratio averaged 65 per cent between 1786 and 1807 and in the case of the latter concern it averaged 71 per cent between 1797 and 1827.[10]

How can such differences be explained? In part, the answer is to be found in the method of calculation that is preferred. Using the data in the Roberts and Cadman 1787 balance sheet the ratio of fixed to working capital can be computed by expressing the value of fixed capital (£1,246) as a proportion of total assets (£5,063), giving a figure of 24.6 per cent. However, Pollard worked on the basis that such ratios can be calculated by defining working capital more narrowly, taking into account only stocks of raw materials, semi-finished goods and finished goods awaiting sale; he omitted trade credit from the calculation. In terms of the Roberts and Cadman balance sheet, using Pollard's approach would mean that the first three items in the asset column (valued at £1,328) are included as working capital, but the debts owing to the firm are not, so that the proportion of fixed capital rises to 48.4 per cent.

The Richardson and Pollard figures so far quoted were calculated leaving trade credit out of consideration. Accordingly, they are likely to be high, though the difference between them is nonetheless striking. Richardson, however, extends his analysis by making further computations taking trade credit into account. Adding in the credit extended by firms enables the value of fixed capital to be expressed as a percentage of the value of total capital employed. On this basis, fixed capital averaged 43 per cent of total assets during the years selected in the case of the Oldknow concern and 49 per cent in the case of McConnel and Kennedy.[11] The use of total asset values is also the basis on which the Edwards figures are calculated, which helps to explain why they are relatively low.

Plainly, therefore, the method by which fixed capital ratios are determined can have a marked impact on their magnitude, a reflection of the importance that trade credit could have. Yet, even when the same method of calculation is used, marked variations in fixed capital ratios from one firm to another are apparent. Some firms did of course have higher than usual expenditure on fixed capital perhaps because they purchased a new steam engine or built a new works. Equally, as Richardson's analysis shows, comparisons must be made between firms at a similar stage in their history. This is because fixed capital ratios were likely to have been high for firms at the outset, since some assets – stocks of raw materials, work in progress and finished products – would take time to accumulate.[12] Nor must it be overlooked that the stock-taking methods on which ratios of fixed and working capital are determined were by no means standardised from firm to firm as, for instance, with regard to allowances made for the depreciation of fixed capital. Both McConnel and Kennedy and Oldknow, Coupe and Company failed to make any depreciation allowances for a number of years after they began production and whereas those of the former company were then set at 10 per cent on their machinery and some of their buildings, the rate preferred by the latter never exceeded 5 per cent.[13] Finally, as Martin Daunton observes, fixed capital requirements could be much more important in extractive industry than in manufacturing industry, not only because considerable expense might be incurred by providing deep shafts, pumping equipment and wagonways, but also because working capital needs were low, since there were no raw materials to purchase and mine owners did not usually offer much credit to their customers.[14]

There are, then, considerable difficulties involved in calculating fixed capital ratios and assessing the change that occurred in their magnitude over time. However, the indications are that for firms in a range of industries, the ratio rose substantially during the Industrial Revolution period. This change reflected not only the growing use of powered machinery, but also the diffusion of relatively expensive capital equipment that was not power-driven and the construction of new industrial premises.

## Fixed capital demand at industry and national level: extent and impact

So far, our discussion on fixed capital has been undertaken with regard to the individual firm. However, historians have also been keen to calculate expenditure on fixed capital in the economy as a whole. In so doing, they have been concerned with the concept of capital formation, which may be defined as 'the additions made during a particular period of time to the stock of goods which are for use in future production'.[15] Expenditure on these items, which is usually measured annually, can be conveniently referred to as investment expenditure, the purchase of goods not used in future production being termed consumption expenditure. Historians are interested in the changing proportion that investment expenditure formed of national income – often termed the investment ratio – because of the impact it could have on the rate of economic growth. Since, according to some historians, marked changes occurred in the investment ratio during the Industrial Revolution period, it is clearly a matter we must consider.

Investment expenditure has two main components. One is the amount spent on fixed capital, which, for the economy as a whole, includes the buildings, machinery and equipment needed by agriculture, industry and commerce, along with public works and buildings, transport facilities and houses. The other is the expenditure on stocks of raw materials and work in progress. Calculations can be made of gross capital formation in order to take account of expenditure on both new capital as well as on replacing existing capital. However, figures of net capital formation are obtained by allowing for depreciation to the existing stock of fixed assets. Capital formation figures can either be given in current prices – the average prices that prevailed during the year for which the calculation was made – or in constant prices – the prices expressed in relation to those of a particular year, so as to allow for the effect of any price changes over time.[16]

Given the complexities involved and the limited amount of evidence available, measuring capital formation during the Industrial Revolution period is no easy task and has required a great deal of ingenuity on the part of historians. To provide some idea of the sources and techniques they have employed in measuring components of it, consideration can be given to two different means of calculating fixed capital formation in the factory sector of the cotton textile industry. The approach used by Chapman involved extracting details on the valuation of cotton mills and machinery from fire insurance records. These records have survived in some quantity from the Industrial Revolution period and though they do not cover every firm and they may not always provide accurate valuations of property, they nonetheless enable order of magnitude calculations to be made. Assuming that the ratio of small to large cotton firms in Lancashire was similar to that at Stockport, the Chapman calculations reveal that the fixed capital expenditure required for the northwest cotton factory industry amounted to about £1.25 million in 1795 out of a national total of around £2 million, rather more than 60 per cent. He regards this as a modest enough figure, reflecting the ease of converting water-powered sites to use Arkwright's roller-spinning machines and the improved efficiency of waterwheels. Thereafter, however, as the technological emphasis shifted towards mule spinning, fixed capital expenditure increased. Quoting revised figures made by contemporary observers, Chapman suggests that the nationwide figure had reached £5–6 million by 1812 and £34 million by 1834.[17]

The method of calculation used by Feinstein draws on the contemporary practice of estimating the cost of fixed capital in the cotton industry in terms of the amount per spindle in the case of spinning and the amount per loom in the case of weaving. During the middle decades of the nineteenth century, the former was given fairly consistently as 24 shillings and the latter as £24. Taking the numbers of spindles and looms in Great Britain reported in the 1861 factory inspectors' returns – respectively 30,267,000 and 398,000 – Feinstein was able to estimate a fixed capital value of £36.3 million in spinning and £9.6 million in weaving.[18] Those involved in calculating fixed capital expenditure have taken care to stress that only approximations can be achieved. In fact, Feinstein concedes that, textile production apart, the means he used to derive fixed capital values for manufacturing industry in general were 'highly conjectural'; at best, his figures may indicate broad orders of magnitude.[19]

Against the backdrop of this methodological uncertainty, a vigorous debate over the extent of aggregate demand for fixed capital at national level – and by inference debate over the nature of the industrialisation process – has developed. A key phase in the debate occurred with the publication in 1965 of Rostow's book *The stages of economic growth*. Some of Rostow's main ideas have already been noted, but of importance here is his contention that, during the 'take-off' phase, the proportion of national income devoted to investment rose 'from, say, 5% to over 10%'. As far as England is concerned, Rostow argued that the take-off occurred during the last two decades of the eighteenth century, when raw cotton imports increased dramatically.[20] Phyllis Deane, however, has suggested that the annual average rate of capital formation changed much more slowly than Rostow believed; it may only have reached around 6 per cent of national income by 1800 – very little more than the figure of about 5 per cent at the start of the eighteenth century – and did not attain a level of about 10 per cent until the late 1850s, when the heavy investment demands arising from railway building occurred.[21] Yet, Deane's estimates have in turn been challenged, both Pollard and Feinstein maintaining they are too low. Pollard's figures suggest that gross capital formation had already reached 6.5 per cent of national income by c.1770 and 9 per cent by the early 1790s. However, he sees a fall to 8 per cent occurring around 1815, before a rise to a historically high level of 11 per cent by the early 1830s. Feinstein's figures, which are the product of some remarkably detailed and painstaking research, suggest even higher rates. He estimates that, at constant prices, gross capital formation reached an annual average of 8 per cent of national income during the 1760s, reaching as much as 14 per cent in the 1790s – the sort of level envisaged by Rostow. During the first half of the nineteenth century, however, it ceased to grow at a faster rate, remaining at between 10 and 14 per cent. In direct contradiction to Deane's views, Feinstein concludes that the investment ratio rose by quite a substantial margin in the eighteenth century and was not significantly lifted by railway construction during the early Victorian years.[22]

Not surprisingly Feinstein's figures have met with criticism. Gourvish has argued that, given concerns about the quality of

Feinstein's data, we must be cautious in accepting his capital formation figures. He prefers a return to the proposition arising from Phyllis
Deane's work that it was railway investment in the early Victorian
era that took the capital formation rate into double figures.[23] Moreover, while Crafts concedes that Feinstein's capital formation figures
'represent an important advance in knowledge',[24] he nonetheless argues that the national income figures used by Feinstein in his
calculations are too low. By revising them upwards he derived a new
set of investment ratios which, before the 1820s, give much lower
figures than those provided by Feinstein. In fact, as Crafts point out,
his figures confirm the gradual advance suggested by Deane and
Cole's estimates; they fail to meet the Rostovian expectation of a 10
per cent or more level during the late eighteenth century and do not
reveal 'Feinstein's surprising result' that the investment ratio peaked
at the start of the wars with France.[25]

Given the marked disagreement that has arisen over the extent to
which the investment ratio grew at national level, what can be said
about the impact that investment expenditure had on the rate at which
the British economy grew? In briefly addressing the issue, we must
engage with the debate over the magnitude of growth in national
economic numbers, and over their meaning. As we saw in chapter
one, such numbers suggest that, for much of the Industrial Revolution
period, the English economy was characterised by slow growth. To
explain these findings it is suggested that capital formation was quite
modest when compared with that of other countries going through a
similar stage of industrialisation. In fact, throughout much of the
Industrial Revolution period, Britain was at war, with the result that
government revenue needs rose dramatically and whilst part of these
needs were met by extra taxation, the level of government borrowing in
real terms (allowing for price changes) rose from £134.7 million in
1761 to £387.3 million in 1811. A possible outcome was that expenditure which might have been directed towards investment in industry
and commerce was instead spent on fighting – productive investment
was 'crowded out'. Accordingly, both capital formation and economic
growth were lower than they might otherwise have been.[26]

The crowding-out notion has inevitably provoked debate, with two
key themes being addressed. One is the question of whether increased
government borrowing raised interest rates, thereby encouraging
greater purchases of government stock. The other is whether, as a
result, savings actually were diverted away from industrial investment.

We must briefly address both matters. With regard to the first, it is important to acknowledge that interest rates on consols – government stock without a maturity date – rose significantly during the war years.[27] In 1797 and 1798, the rate rose marginally above 6 per cent and was generally above 4.5 per cent. However, when these rates are linked to changes in the level of consumer prices to give real (as opposed to nominal) interest rates, a different picture emerges. Thus, according to calculations made by Heim and Mirowski, whereas the real interest rates on consols averaged 2.31 per cent during the war years of 1793–1815, they averaged 6.27 per cent during the peacetime years from 1784 to 1792 and 1816 to 1823. A similar pattern arises when the real interest rates on India bonds – which were six-month bonds issued by the East India Company – are also considered. When these interest rate figures are related to those showing the net sums that governments borrowed each year (again allowing for price changes) the strong direct relationship that might be expected is not apparent. Accordingly, doubt is cast on a key element in the crowding-out hypothesis.[28] A re-examination of the evidence concerning the effect of government borrowing on interest rates has led Black and Gilmore to a different conclusion, however. They maintain that wartime borrowing in Britain did raise long-term nominal interest rates, but with a time lag of two years.[29]

As to the idea that high interest rates diverted savings towards the purchase of government stock and away from industrial investment, several objections have been raised. One is that the priority amongst industrialists was to invest in their own businesses rather than helping to finance government needs; even high interest rates may not have tempted them to buy government bonds. Nor was England a closed economy, so that the government could meet some of its additional requirements from borrowing abroad, whilst investment that might have gone abroad could have been used to purchase government stock. And even within England it is by no means certain that a national capital market existed, with the result that government borrowing may not have extended into all the industrial areas. This is so despite the work of Buchinsky and Polak, which suggests that the relationship between London interest rates and West Yorkshire property transactions had become strong by the late eighteenth century, thereby giving a tentative indication that a national capital market had emerged.[30] This debate over how closely regional capital markets were integrated is one that we return to later in the chapter.

Whether any marked reduction in overall investment rates actually did take place during the war years is also in doubt. Crafts' investment ratio figures, which are calculated using Feinstein's capital formation data with his own estimates of national income, reveal a steady decennial rise during the late eighteenth and early nineteenth centuries.[31] Those of Feinstein show that the ratio was higher in the 1790s (11 per cent) than in the 1780s (10 per cent) though he suggests a fall to 10 per cent in the first decade of the nineteenth century. Yet, in absolute terms, Feinstein's figures indicate that total domestic investment did not actually fall, rising from an annual average of £13 million in the 1780s to £17.5 million in the 1790s, the same level as in the first decade of the nineteenth century.[32] Of course, these figures cannot be taken too literally, but they suggest that, if anything, the impact of the French wars on investment was delayed until the early nineteenth century. It may also be the case that any crowding-out effect was far more apparent in some economic sectors than others. Thus, Heim and Mirowski note Williamson's suggestion that building and construction were the main victims of crowding out and point out that, since buildings did not form a significant proportion of business investment at the time, the case for crowding out is weakened.[33]

It is apparent from our discussion that the extent to which the national investment ratio changed during the Industrial Revolution period cannot be assessed with any exactitude and that attempts to calculate it are always likely to provoke disagreement amongst historians. However, the indications are that it rose significantly. Moreover we must bear in mind that the national figures underplay the extent to which investment ratios would have risen within particular industries and industrial regions. There are numerous examples of rising demand for capital at the level of individual firms and entrepreneurs (because of technological or organisational change or greater production levels using traditional techniques), and it is clear that the period 1700–1850 witnessed the emergence of capital demands that were different in both order and degree from those that had gone before. Such observations themselves stimulate the need for further discussion. Could rising demand for capital be met? Did sources of capital change? And what were the regional dynamics of capital supply and demand? These are the foci of the rest of this chapter.

## Fixed capital supply and the type of business organisation

In switching our discussion from the demand for capital to its supply, we can usefully return to the Roberts and Cadman balance sheet, this time to consider the firm's liabilities. As can be seen, most of the capital was supplied by the firm's three partners, Samuel Roberts, George Cadman and Benjamin Naylor. The firm's partnership deed reveals that Naylor was 'desirous of being excused and totally exempted from acting in the said Joint Co-partnership Trade'.[34] In other words, he wished to be a sleeping partner. The deed also tells us that Roberts pledged to bring into the enterprise 'money, stock debts and implements' valued at £1,600, which would represent four-sevenths of the firm's capital. Of the remaining capital, Naylor was to supply two-sevenths (£800) and Cadman one-seventh (£400). Additionally, Naylor agreed to lend the partnership £1,200 at an interest rate of 5 per cent per annum. All these sums were to be subscribed within twelve months of the agreement being signed. Profits were to be shared out in proportion to each partner's capital holdings. The management of the firm was vested in Roberts and Cadman, who were both to receive a salary of £60 per annum.

The firm's other liabilities relate to its short-term capital supply, which we consider in the following section. Here we focus on the firm's long-term capital needs – for meeting fixed capital expenditure – which the subscriptions of the partners more than met. In fact, Roberts and Cadman was merely one amongst a great number of business concerns that adopted the partnership form of organisation during the Industrial Revolution era, a strong motivation to do so being the need to meet the relatively high levels of fixed capital expenditure associated with centralised production. The sums required, which had to be available on a long-term basis, were often beyond the level that an individual was able to raise, especially when powered machinery was involved.

To illustrate this point, and to set it into context, evidence contained in town and county trade directories is available. Compiled for businessmen, these directories normally give classified lists of local firms, the style used to record the firms' names revealing whether they were run by partnerships or by single proprietors. There is always concern, of course, that the compilers did not make a complete record, or an entirely accurate one, either of the number of firms or of the trading names that firms adopted. However, the data for

Newcastle-upon-Tyne (presented in table 4.2) are derived from a directory published in the late 1840s by F. White & Company, who appear to have been amongst the more careful compilers.[35] The table relates only to those industries, trades and professions in the town which were most strongly associated with partnerships, though the very range of the list tells us something about the pervasiveness of partnerships.

**Table 4.2** *Partnerships in Newcastle, 1847*

| Activity | No. of partnerships | No. of firms | Percentage partnerships |
|---|---|---|---|
| Academies | 19 | 99 | 19 |
| Attorney | 15 | 74 | 20 |
| Banks | 5 | 8 | 63 |
| Brick and tile makers | 10 | 16 | 63 |
| Coal fitters and owners | 32 | 93 | 34 |
| Corn merchants and factors | 9 | 22 | 41 |
| Earthenware manufacturers | 6 | 10 | 60 |
| Engine builders | 6 | 8 | 75 |
| General merchants | 36 | 71 | 51 |
| Glass makers | 8 | 11 | 73 |
| Iron founders | 9 | 15 | 60 |
| Iron merchants | 9 | 12 | 75 |
| Iron manufacturers | 5 | 8 | 63 |
| Sawmills | 5 | 7 | 71 |
| Shipbuilders | 4 | 9 | 44 |
| Ship and insurance brokers | 38 | 100 | 38 |
| Timber merchants | 12 | 30 | 40 |
| Wine and spirit merchants | 14 | 42 | 33 |
| Woollen drapers | 11 | 18 | 61 |

*Source*: White & Co., *General directory*, pp. 153–208.

Of course, care is needed in interpreting the data, since by no means every partner brought additional capital into an enterprise. Thus sons and nephews of businessmen were frequently given partnership status in order to ensure that family control, or influence, was passed on from one generation to the next. The eventual inclusion of Samuel Roberts junior in his father's partnership provides one illustration. Partners might be brought in to contribute particular types of skill or knowledge as well as to inject capital. This might happen, for instance, in such professions as teaching and the law. And finance contributed by partners was not necessarily needed to meet substantial expenditure on buildings and equipment. In banking, for instance, an adequate level of reserves had to be made available for discounting bills of exchange (see below, pp. 121–3) and for making loans, whilst high levels of stock had frequently to be maintained by merchants.

Notwithstanding such considerations the data reproduced in table 4.2 are telling. For the most part, the highest percentages of partnerships occurred in manufacturing industries which sometimes required specially designed buildings and equipment, including powered machines. This was the case, for instance, in iron foundries, glass works and saw mills, all industries in which partnerships exceeded 70 per cent of the total. Furthermore, it is probable that the firms not listed as partnerships would normally have been the smaller-scale operators in each of the industries listed in the table, as well as more generally.

Further evidence taken from trade directories can be used to suggest the growth in the importance of partnerships over time in the industrialising districts. For instance a directory of Manchester and Salford published in 1788 lists fifty firms of bleachers from the surrounding areas, representatives of which regularly attended Manchester for business purposes. Of these firms, only two were partnerships. A similar list for the mid-1820s records forty-one bleaching concerns, twenty-two of which (54 per cent) were partnerships. In the case of calico printing concerns, the same sources show that partnerships rose from one out of seven (14 per cent) to nine out of thirteen (69 per cent).[36] Additionally, partnerships were well represented in the capital-intensive machinery-making industry, which became of importance in several industrial areas as steam engines and powered machines became more widely used. Thus, at Manchester, thirty-seven firms of machine makers could be found in the mid-1820s, of which nearly half were partnerships.[37] Finally, we may note Peter Mathias's research on brewing firms. During the late eighteenth and early nineteenth centuries, these firms required major injections of long-term capital to purchase leases on public houses and the only way they could meet their needs was to attract additional partners. The number of partners in the Truman concern, for instance, rose from two in 1780 to six in 1830.[38]

Whilst partnerships are important in showing how some businesses raised the much increased amounts of long-term capital they required to finance fixed capital expenditure, their significance must not be overstated. In terms of absolute numbers of firms partnerships were less common than single-proprietor concerns as a form of business organisation in most industries throughout the Industrial Revolution period. This reflected the limited scale on which many business concerns operated and the rural industrial roots of many industries which had propelled the individual proprietor to the fore of business organisation from an early date. Their proprietors did not need to raise large sums of money to cover the initial costs of fixed capital, often being able to rent premises from which to operate (if they were needed) and requiring very little in the way of equipment (which they might anyway purchase second-hand). Nor would existing proprietors necessarily have wished to expand to a point where they would have to spend heavily on premises and equipment; earning a reasonable return may have been a stronger motivation than that of seeking to maximise profits. Retaining sole control of a business rather than maximising its size might also have been regarded as especially important given a prevailing business culture that stressed self-reliance and mistrust of outsiders.[39] And in any case, we must not forget that all too many firms starting out as single proprietorships failed before they were able to expand, with or without the aid of partners. As the work of Hoppit and others has vividly demonstrated, the number of bankruptcies showed a marked upturn during the Industrial Revolution period.[40]

The argument that those establishing businesses in many industries did not generally need to raise particularly large sums of money to begin operations should not be taken to mean that most people could easily raise the capital sums required. Studies of several industries point to entrepreneurs having generally been drawn from families that had already generated at least modest levels of wealth. For instance, Katrina Honeyman's study of cotton-mill owners recorded in Patrick Colquhoun's survey of 1787 reveals that over 90 per cent of the 230 that can be traced (there were 282 in total) were from upper social groups. Most had already established businesses in textile production or merchanting. Those who had not were drawn from quite a wide range of backgrounds, including landowning, brewing and banking.[41] There are clear indications from such evidence that those from the lower ranks of society who might have wished to establish themselves in business would not as a rule have been able to obtain the necessary finance, however limited this may have been.

Whilst the marked rise in the number of business concerns during the Industrial Revolution was mostly associated with single proprietorships and partnerships, the finance required to establish or expand a business could sometimes greatly exceed the sums that even several well-to-do partners could raise. The formation of canal companies, which had to spend heavily on constructing transport routes before they started to earn revenue, are cases in point. Harold Perkin notes that the average canal company had a capital of £165,000 in 1825, though much larger sums might be involved in canal construction, as in the case of the Rochdale Canal, the completion of which required an expenditure of £600,000. But even such an extraordinary sum was dwarfed by the investment levels associated with railways; the average cost of constructing the twenty-seven railways opened between 1830 and 1853 was nearly two million pounds.[42]

To raise such vast sums, large numbers of investors had to be found, an objective which could be achieved by selling shares in the company. Under the provisions of the 1720 Bubble Act, companies of this type, which were known as joint-stock companies, had each to be established by an act of parliament.[43] Shares in the company were sold to the general public, the shareholders becoming part-owners of the company and hence entitled to a share in any profits arising. Those running joint-stock companies owned the majority of the shares that were issued, though they were accountable to their shareholders.[44] Shareholders were given limited liability, so that, in the event of the company failing, they would not lose a sum greater than the value of the shares they held. Sole proprietors and business partners, in contrast, did not enjoy such immunity, as the experience of the unfortunate John Spear, a Sheffield toolmaker, illustrates. He was declared bankrupt in 1821 and, at a meeting of his creditors, he was forced to surrender all his belongings save 'the wearing apparel of himself and his family'.[45]

Apart from the investments made by partners and shareholders, how else was long-term capital obtained? In particular, what were the routes open to the sole proprietor? One possibility was that having become successful, businessmen could hope to derive at least part of their needs from the profits they earned. In fact, studies of individual firms reveal that this course was commonly taken and Crouzet has remarked on 'the overwhelming predominance of self-finance'.[46] William Greaves and Sons, steel and toolmakers of Sheffield, provide a striking case in point. The enterprise existed in 1774 and by the mid-1820s, as a result of 'prudential habits through many years of profitable business', the partners had accumulated the £50,000 they needed to erect their celebrated Sheaf Works, the first in Sheffield to bring together on one site the various stages of steel and metalware manufacture.[47] The policy of self-financing further reflects the individualistic nature of the business culture in which firms operated, as well as the fact that, in the early years, businesses may not have acquired a sound enough reputation to enable them to borrow from external sources. But even when they were established, firms would sometimes have been unable to rely solely on profits to finance expansion, one problem being that new investment often entailed a heavier expenditure than could be met from gradually accumulated profits. Accordingly, they would have had to seek external finance. The wool textile industry during the 1830s and 1840s provides a case in point, reinvestment (or 'ploughing back') of profits probably being less important than bank loans as a means of expanding capacity.

A second possibility is that, as in wool textiles, businessmen could increasingly take advantage of the facilities made available by the growing number of provincial banks, a development of considerable importance in the industrialising regions, but more generally as well.[48] The role of these banks in providing business finance is considered more fully below (pp. 123–4), but note may be made here of Michael Collins's suggestion that, during the Industrial Revolution era, the 'generality of banks would have provided some long-term finance'.[49] Instances of this practice have certainly been noted in several industries, especially textiles, even though individual firms do not seem to have relied heavily on banks for this purpose. In some cases, banks might provide long-term finance by periodically renewing short-term loans, retaining the option of calling them in at each renewal date. If payment of a short-term loan could not be met, the bank might grant an extension in the hope that the borrower might eventually pay. In the case of Quaker brewers borrowing from Quaker bankers, loans sometimes ran for ten years or more. Moreover, by providing short-term credit, banks could enable businessmen to use the profits they earned for long-term investment purposes.[50]

Other possible sources for long-term loans included family and friends, some of whom might become business partners, whilst merchants and landowners might also lend to businesses on a long-term basis, as long as those in charge of the businesses owned land or other suitable property which could be offered as loan security. In seeking such loans, the help of financial intermediaries could be sought, amongst whom provincial attorneys were predominant. During the eighteenth century, they became highly active in arranging loans for those who could offer land as a security, sometimes becoming wealthy enough to make loans from their own resources. They placed both small and large amounts, with varying repayment times, and though the loans were used for a number of purposes, at least some helped to finance business expansion.[51] It is perhaps pertinent to bear in mind that the very appearance of intermediaries such as this is testimony to substantial change in the nature of capital demand and supply in the period 1700–1850.

Overall, then, it is evident from our discussion that the greater demands businessmen made for fixed capital in the Industrial Revolution was met from a variety of sources. However, partnerships of the type formed by Roberts and Cadman increased considerably in importance, especially in the industrialising districts. Prior to the mid-eighteenth century, partnerships would have been relatively infrequent, but a century later, as trade directory evidence makes clear, they had grown to prominence in many industries, especially those adopting the more advanced forms of technology that were becoming available. This said, our analysis so far has focused on just one part (and in some industries the least important part) of the capital needs of eighteenth- and nineteenth-century entrepreneurs. We must also consider how they met their short-term, working capital needs.

## Working capital

To begin our discussion, we can usefully refer back again to the liabilities side of the Roberts and Cadman balance sheet. We have already noted the sums advanced by the three partners, but we have yet to consider the other major item, namely the debts that the partners owed to their suppliers. The sum involved amounted to £1,164, about 23 per cent of the total liability value. Such indebtedness arose because businesses had to raise capital for relatively short periods of time to cover their day-to-day expenses, including the purchase of raw materials, the payment of wages and the costs of transport. Since they were not always able to finance such expenditure from payments made to them by customers – in modern parlance they could have cash flow problems – they often needed to borrow sums of money, perhaps for just a few weeks or months, until they had sufficient revenue to settle their debts. In fact, because it was normal business practice to allow customers time to make payments for goods supplied to them, in effect to give them credit, business concerns were both short-term borrowers and short-term lenders.

By comparing the amounts of debt recorded on each side of the balance sheet, it becomes apparent that Roberts and Cadman were granting their customers more than twice as much credit as they were receiving from those who supplied them. Perhaps, in order to generate custom, the firm at such an early stage in its history needed to offer credit more readily, and on terms that were more generous, than it would ideally have wished. Yet the partners were not in a particularly vulnerable position. This is partly because the valuation of their stock of finished goods was cautiously made so that the value of their assets was unlikely to have been exaggerated. It is also because they were not receiving more credit from their suppliers than they were offering to their customers. Had they been in such a position, the risk would have arisen of the creditors insisting on payment being made which could not be met by the firm even if all its debtors could have been persuaded to meet their obligations on time and in full. Should need have arisen, firms in the position of Roberts and Cadman at least had the option of trying to call in sufficient sums from those to whom they had given credit in order to meet their obligations. Even so, as Pat Hudson has shown in the case of several West Yorkshire textile firms, allowing too large a gap between credit granted and credit received could lead to firms seeking large bank overdrafts in order to meet their requirements for cash.[52]

Probably the most usual way in which businessmen came to make short-term credit (working capital) available to each other during the Industrial Revolution period was through issuing bills of exchange. The firm supplying goods to another firm (maybe a merchant forwarding raw materials to a manufacturer or a manufacturer dispatching finished goods to a wholesaler) would draw up the bill. The bill would specify that a certain sum should be paid to the supplier at a future date, perhaps in two or three months. This sum would be somewhat greater than the value of the goods supplied, the difference (in effect a rate of interest) providing compensation for the delay in payment. The bill would be sent to the debtor, who would sign (endorse) it and return it to the creditor, thereby acknowledging that the debtor would settle in full by the date due. The supplier could keep the bill until it matured, thereby earning a rate of interest, but he was more likely to have passed it on to settle one of his own debts, either fully or in part; the bill thus became a substitute for money. In this case, the person receiving the bill would accept it at less than the value of the bill at maturity, again to compensate for the delay in receiving payment. In fact, a bill might be passed on several times in this way to settle debts before it was returned to the endorsee for final payment. The value of the bill would gradually rise (and the rate of interest it earned would fall) until it reached its maturity value.[53] A further way a supplier could dispose of an endorsed bill of exchange was to sell it to someone else. The buyer would offer a lower price than the maturity value (he would buy at a discount), again to provide a rate of interest which would compensate for the delayed payment.

Not unexpectedly, the bill of exchange system did not always operate precisely in the intended manner. There was concern, of course, that borrowers might be unable to make good their indebtedness, though less so with regard to the more reputable firms and when trade was good. And for those holding bills at or near maturity, there was the possibility that payment might be delayed because debtors were unable (or unwilling) to meet their obligations. For instance, in 1806, the Sheffield steelmaker George Hague received the following communication from one of his London customers, Thomas Lewis:

> In consequence of being disappointed in remittances, which I expected to receive several weeks back, it will be impossible for me to pay my acceptance to you for £90 6s. 5d. due the 18th Inst – therefore shall be obligd in your having goodness to secure it for three Months longer, when you may rest satisfied that it will (with the other two) be regularly paid when due.[54]

Lewis was in effect asking for a credit-free period of three months, perhaps because he was being forced to grant credit to those customers whose remittances he had hoped to receive in time to settle his debt with Hague. Hague may well have taken the view that his best way forward was to agree to the request, since it at least gave him the possibility of securing his money in due course. Yet delays in payment could lead to substantial amounts of debt arising, no doubt bringing anxiety to borrower and lender alike. For instance, in September, 1789, the Huntsman steelmaking concern at Sheffield was owed over £42 by a local customer, Barber and Genn. By August, 1792, the level of Barber and Genn's indebtedness had risen more than fourfold to nearly £174. Perhaps at this stage Huntsman's patience ran out, for during the next few months he received a fairly regular flow of commercial bills from Barber and Genn, leading to their debt being settled in February 1793.[55] In both these examples, the debtors plainly had a vested interest in settling their debts as quickly as possible if they were to avoid gaining an unenviable reputation in the business world.

The role of merchants in providing short-term credit was crucial. We have noted that they commonly gave credit to manufacturers they supplied by drawing up bills of exchange, but we should also note that, in some cases, the credit period might be of considerable length. For instance, up to the late 1820s, Hull merchants were said to be supplying bar iron to Sheffield steelmakers with a credit period of twelve months or more, whilst during much the same period, Manchester traders were allowing local spinners from four to eight months credit on raw cotton.[56] Plainly, the manufacturers were being given a generous period of time to convert these raw materials into finished products and to sell them on, though they, too, may have needed to give their customers lengthy credit periods. Merchants might also assist manufacturers by advancing short-term loans. McConnel and Kennedy, for instance, asked their main Dublin suppliers for a sum of £2,000 'for a few months' in August 1805.[57] Furthermore, in selling manufactured goods, merchants might advance cash or short-dated bills of exchange (bills due for payment in a relatively short time period) ahead of the goods being sold. And the amount of the advance might be considerable. For instance, the London agent of Samuel Crompton, the inventor of the mule and a cotton manufacturer, advanced up to two-thirds of the value of the goods supplied.[58]

The function of discounting bills of exchange was increasingly undertaken by provincial banks, which had numbered only twelve in 1750 but which had reached a total of around 700 by 1825. Commonly, provincial banks arose as local merchants and industrialists accumulated funds which could be profitably lent to others, especially by discounting bills. Lloyds of Birmingham, for example, were originally involved in the iron trade, as were many others in the west Midlands.[59] The next stage was for bankers (or concerns undertaking banking functions) to accept deposits, thereby making additional funds available for loan. In many instances, provincial bankers also issued their own notes, thereby extending the currency supplies needed to facilitate a wide range of local transactions, including the payment of wages. As long as the provincial bankers could maintain the confidence of their customers, they provided invaluable help to the business communities they served. To help them to do so, they forged direct links with banks in London, giving them a much higher degree of stability than would have arisen by depending on local resources alone. Yet the possibility that banks could default on payment was real, no fewer than ninety-three of them in England and Wales (about 15 per cent of the total) being unable to meet their commitments during the depression of 1825–26.[60]

This brief discussion by no means exhausts the range of options available to businessmen in meeting their short-term capital needs, particularly when we consider the financing of proto-industrial expansion, which required large amounts of working capital. In this context, entrepreneurs might tap the sources they used to obtain long-term finance, including family members, retained profits and the sums they initially brought into their enterprises from other industries, practices which remind us that we can draw too sharp a distinction between the sources of long- and short-term capital. However, the key point to make is that the financial system through which short-term credit was channelled from lender to borrower became far more extensive after 1750. The growing use of bills of exchange and the emergence of a widespread provincial banking service to discount them was particularly significant. This developing financial system gave form to the complex pattern of borrowing and lending within the business community, with firms expecting both to give credit and to receive it. It also carried potentially fundamental consequences for the financial infrastructure of individual regions, and it is to this matter that we finally turn.

## Local and regional capital supplies

So far, we have only indirectly addressed the question as to how frequently businessmen would have been able to meet their financial needs from within the localities or regions in which they were based. In the preceding section we have drawn attention to instances of manufacturers receiving help with working capital from merchants who resided outside the industrial regions concerned, including London. And we have noted the tentative suggestion of Buchinsky and Polak that a national capital market may have emerged by the late eighteenth century. Yet we have also mentioned that successful businesses would have generated a great deal of the finance they required from the profits they earned, so that, at least as far as fixed capital expenditure was concerned, they did not have to resort to external finance. Moreover, we have seen that family businesses (partnerships as well as single proprietorships) predominated in English industry, thereby suggesting that immediate kin would have been heavily relied upon for financial help, perhaps to meet fixed capital expenses in particular. But where did the balance lie between regional and more distant sources of financing and were changes taking place during our period? Was there, in fact, an emerging national capital market?

In addressing these matters, we can usefully begin by noting Chapman's research into the textile industry during the first half of the eighteenth century. Focusing on the west of England, East Anglia and the Midlands, he concludes that the limited amounts of long-term capital that were required in the industry at this time were drawn from the localities. Indeed, entrepreneurs found that it was relatively easy to switch capital from one industry to another within the region in which they operated.[61] Local financing also prevailed within the Derbyshire lead mining industry as Katrina Honeyman has demonstrated. She finds that before 1700, only small amounts of capital were normally required by the county's lead mining ventures and that most was supplied by local landowners. From the early eighteenth century, there was some diversification of sources, but most of the industry's capital continued to be obtained from within the locality.[62] Indeed, the reliance on local financing remained important in all the industrial regions outlined in chapter two. With regard to the West Riding, for instance, Pat Hudson's research has revealed that the capital market remained 'overwhelmingly a local phenomenon' with little evidence of long-term finance being obtained from elsewhere.[63] Crucially, capital within industrial regions continued to be transferred from one industry to another. This happened in the Midlands textile districts, for instance, as a small group of entrepreneurs moved capital from declining industries – including silk, lead mining and iron smelting – into cotton manufacturing.[64]

To illustrate the ways in which businesses obtained local finance, we can begin by considering the long-term capital provision made by families. Thus, Samuel Roberts was advanced money by his father to start the Eyre Street silver plate works in 1784. At the firm's first stocktaking, as we have seen, the value of these works (including tools and fixtures) was given as £1,246. Additionally, the business records of the brothers William and Daniel Doncaster of Sheffield, who became partners as steelmakers in 1830, show that their mother Jane lent them £250 at an interest rate of 3 per cent.[65] But such sums pale into insignificance compared with those derived from family sources by the brothers Henry and Edmund Ashworth, cotton spinners and manufacturers of Egerton and Bank Top, near Bolton. In 1831, they were indebted to their father for £21,207 and to their uncle for £6,519. As in the case of Jane Doncaster, family members could hope to make a return on their investment, though they were also motivated, no doubt, by a desire to assist their kin.[66]

Examples of firms that have been shown to have used the profits they earned as a means of financing expansion of their productive capacity include McConnel and Kennedy, the leading Manchester cotton spinners, and Marshes and Shepherd, one of Sheffield's more important producers of steel, tools and cutlery. The former concern built new factories in 1797 and 1818, but there is little evidence to show that money was borrowed to finance their development. In the early years the partners had little to offer in the way of security had they wished to seek a loan, whilst they quickly prospered and so had no need for outside finance thereafter. Marshes and Shepherd were similarly placed. As the firm prospered during the 1820s and 1830s, considerable extensions were made to its capacity and they were almost entirely financed from profits earned; the occasional bank overdraft was required, but was quickly repaid.[67] And to provide a further example, the experience of the Doncaster brothers' steelmaking concern can be cited. During the 1820s, the firm was in considerable difficulty, but its fortunes were transformed after Daniel Doncaster relinquished the partnership with his brother in 1833. During the next two decades, profitability showed a marked upward trend and the firm erected three new furnaces and associated buildings.[68]

Beyond family loans and retained profits, businesses could also draw on other local sources for long-term capital. Landowners provide a case in point, being of considerable significance in coalmining. However, as the costs and risks rose in this industry, they increasingly preferred to draw royalties on the coal obtained from their land, leaving others to undertake the actual mining.[69] Local merchants, too, might go beyond merely lending to manufacturing businesses and actually transfer capital into them, as in the case of textile production. One example was Peter Drinkwater, a Manchester fustian wholesaler and manufacturer, who opened a steam-powered spinning mill in the town during 1789.[70] More generally, industrialists were able to tap into the finance made available by people from a wide range of backgrounds, as can be illustrated in the case of Cardwell, Birley and Hornby, cotton spinners, manufacturers and merchants of Blackburn. Between the 1780s and 1812, ninety-seven people living within about a thirty-mile radius of Blackburn invested in the firm, including widows, spinsters, clergymen and friendly societies.[71]

Whilst most of the long-term finance that businessmen required during the Industrial Revolution period may have continued to be raised at regional level, the indications are that it was sometimes being obtained from further afield as well. Chapman's work on the Midlands textile industry has demonstrated that, whilst most hosiers entering into spinning found local partners, a number were able to draw on finance provided by London contacts.[72] Flows of long-term capital could also take place from one provincial locality to another. In coalmining, for example, financiers from Workington bought coal-bearing lands in northeast England following the opening of the Stockton Darlington railway in 1825.[73] Again Derbyshire lead merchants diversified their interests into the coal and iron industries of South Yorkshire, whilst Yorkshire iron and coal producers invested in Derbyshire lead mining. Mention may also be made of capital flows arising as those investing in business, perhaps as partners, actually moved from region to region. One example is the Revd Benjamin Naylor, the sleeping partner in the Roberts and Cadman's enterprise. He withdrew from the partnership in 1798, and in 1805 he left Sheffield to become a partner in a Manchester cotton firm.

Working capital, meanwhile, continued to be supplied in quantity from sources outside some industrial regions. The Lancashire cotton industry, for instance, had long relied on credit supplied by London merchants and during the late eighteenth and early nineteenth centuries the proprietors of cotton concerns often made use of London bankers, particularly if they had large numbers of customers there. London customers might also be approached to provide credit for cotton manufacturers. For instance, John Watson and Sons, leading cotton spinners at Preston, had obtained credit of more than £10,000 from their London customers at the time of their bankruptcy in 1807.[74] And external credit available in the industrial regions also had an important international dimension as foreign merchants increasingly came to settle in England. In some cases they brought capital with them, but the smaller concerns had to rely on the credit of others, including that provided by merchant houses in the cities from which they had come. Writing in the mid-1820s, Edward Baines noted this occurrence at Manchester, remarking that the town's commerce had flourished to such an extent that 'foreigners had established agents, and sometimes had resident principals in this town, to conduct their commercial transactions'.[75]

In seeking long-term as well as short-term capital, therefore, businessmen were able to draw on sources both within and beyond the region in which they were based. Yet, as Pat Hudson has shown in relation to the West Riding textile industry, they could find themselves operating under quite different circumstances with regard to capital provision from one locality to another. In the wool zone, the indications are that links between clothier families were strong, thereby facilitating the flow of funds from one family to another. In contrast, the worsted zone was characterised by less close social relationships, and by the late eighteenth century impersonal lending associated with attorneys and banks had become more fully developed. Indeed, the worsted producers appear to have been readier to look beyond their region for the finance they required. Hudson also points to changes that occurred in the provision of capital within regions over time. Again using the West Riding as her example, she finds that, prior to the late 1820s, both local and regional sources were available to reputable businesses, but, thereafter, the regional orientation became stronger. This tendency benefited the larger and better-established firms, which were more influential and which could offer more in the way of security than the small concerns.[76]

### Conclusion

Technological change (hand and powered), changes in industrial organisation and the sheer increase in the number of business enterprises greatly increased demands for both fixed and working capital in the period 1700–1850. In textiles especially businesses had to spend much greater amounts on fixed capital than had been customary. And this tendency was also evident in other industries, including iron making, transport and mining. Firms involved in capital-intensive production methods might spend more on fixed capital than on working capital, particularly when they started out in business. Such developments should not of course be exaggerated. Many business concerns would have required much greater amounts of working capital than fixed capital, a reflection of the limited demand for the use of mechanised techniques and specialised buildings and equipment. To meet working capital needs, firms both granted and received credit, aiming to ensure that their level of indebtedness did not exceed the level of credit they allowed their customers. For the most part, though, firms did not need to resort to external financing, partnerships normally being able to raise the sums they required for capital expenditure from their own resources.

Taking the economy as a whole, a great deal of attention has been directed towards calculating the extent of capital formation, a key determinant of economic growth. Only rough estimates can be made, however, despite the ingenuity and effort involved in their compilation. Moreover, attempts to compute ratios of investment to national income have yielded varying results. With the move towards centralised production and the greater use of powered machinery, the ratio undoubtedly rose to markedly higher levels than had hitherto been the case, but the precise rate at which it did so remains unclear.

Taken together, the aggregate, regional and individual firm experiences suggests a widespread reworking of the financial system in the 150 years after 1700. Such changes were symptomatic of a tremendous increase in the number of business concerns during the Industrial Revolution, the growing scale on which the more successful businesses were able to operate and regional industrial concentration. In turn, these developments augured wider changes to the English economic infrastructure than are simply encompassed by a revamping of regional capital markets. In particular, more and bigger concerns producing a wider variety of goods had to find new ways to market their products and to stimulate consumer demand. It is this theme that we take up in the next chapter.

### Notes

1 Sheffield City Archives (hereafter SCA), Stock Book, Sis. 146.
2 Besides as David Kent has shown in relation to small business, disaster could all too often strike because firms could not regulate customer credit effectively, irrespective of whether they granted credit to a few

or to many of their customers. See D. Kent, 'Small businessmen and their credit transactions in early nineteenth century Britain', *Business History*, 36 (1994) 47–64. Publicans were amongst those who gave small amounts of credit to relatively large numbers of customers.

3 SCA, Stock Book, Sis. 146, p. 14.

4 SCA, Stock Book, Sis. 146, p. 21. At this time, Joseph Hancock was rolling silver plate for another Sheffield firm, T. Bradbury and Sons.

5 S. Pollard, 'Fixed capital in the Industrial Revolution in Britain', *Journal of Economic History*, 24 (1964) 120–41.

6 *Ibid.*

7 For examples in the cotton industry, see M. M. Edwards, *The growth of the British cotton trade, 1780–1815* (Manchester, Manchester University Press, 1967), pp. 203–4.

8 *Ibid.*, p. 213.

9 Edwards, *Cotton trade*, pp. 258–9; F. Crouzet, *Capital formation in the Industrial Revolution* (London, Methuen, 1972), p. 37.

10 P. Richardson, 'The structure of capital during the Industrial Revolution revisited: two case studies from the cotton textile industry', *Economic History Review*, 41 (1989) 497–8.

11 *Ibid.*, 493–500.

12 *Ibid.*

13 *Ibid.*, pp. 496–7.

14 M. J. Daunton, *Progress and poverty* (Oxford, Oxford University Press, 1995), p. 242.

15 J. Hibbert, 'Modern practice and conventions in measuring capital formation in the national accounts', in J. P. P. Higgins and S. Pollard (eds), *Aspects of capital investment in Great Britain, 1750–1850* (London, Methuen, 1971), p. 11.

16 C. H. Feinstein, 'Capital formation in Great Britain', in P. Mathias and M. M. Postan (eds), *The Cambridge economic history of Europe, VII* (Cambridge, Cambridge University Press, 1978), p. 35; F. Crouzet, *The Victorian economy* (London, Methuen, 1982), p. 129.

17 S. D. Chapman, 'Fixed capital formation in the British cotton industry, 1770–1815', *Economic History Review*, 23 (1970) 235–66.

18 Feinstein, 'Capital formation', pp. 52–6.

19 *Ibid.*, p. 55.

20 W. W. Rostow, *The stages of economic growth* (Cambridge, Cambridge University Press, 1991 reprint).

21 P. Deane, *The first Industrial Revolution* (Cambridge, Cambridge University Press, 1965), pp. 153–6.

22 Feinstein, 'Capital formation', pp. 31 and 90–2. See also C. H. Feinstein and S. Pollard (eds), *Studies in capital formation in the United Kingdom, 1750–1920* (Oxford, Clarendon, 1988).

23 T. R. Gourvish, 'Railways 1830–70: the formative years', in M. J. Freeman

and D. H. Aldcroft (eds), *Transport in Victorian Britain* (Manchester, Manchester University Press, 1988), pp. 60–2.

24 N. F. R. Crafts, *British economic growth during the Industrial Revolution* (Oxford, Clarendon, 1985), p. 72; and Crouzet, *Victorian economy*, p. 132.

25 Crafts, *Economic growth*, pp. 72–3.

26 J. G. Williamson, 'Why was British growth so slow during the industrial revolution?', *Journal of Economic History*, 44 (1984) 687–9.

27 R. A. Black and C. G. Gilmore, 'Crowding out during Britain's Industrial Revolution', *Journal of Economic History*, 50 (1990) 128–9.

28 C. E. Heim and P. Mirowski, 'Interest rates and crowding out during Britain's industrial revolution', *Journal of Economic History*, 47 (1987) 117–27.

29 Black and Gilmore, 'Crowding out', pp. 109–23.

30 M. Buchinsky and B. Polak, 'The emergence of a national capital market in England, 1710–1880', *Journal of Economic History*, 53 (1993) 1–22. For further discussion, see P. Hudson, 'Financing firms, 1700–1850', in M. W. Kirby and M. B. Rose (eds), *Business enterprise in modern Britain* (London, Routledge, 1994), pp. 107–8, and Daunton, *Progress*, pp. 252–8.

31 Crafts, *Economic growth*.

32 Feinstein, 'Capital formation', p. 71.

33 Heim and Mirowski, 'Interest rates', pp. 131–2.

34 SCA, Partnership deed, 1786, Sis. 1.

35 F. White & Co., *General directory of the town and county of New-castle-upon-Tyne and Gateshead* (Sheffield, 1847), pp. 153–208. For more general discussion on trade directories, see S. Porter, *Exploring urban history* (London, Batsford, 1990), pp. 69–70.

36 *Lewis's Manchester directory for 1788* (Radcliffe, Richardson, n.d. [1788]), p. 31.

37 E. Baines, *History, directory, and gazetteer of the county palatine of Lancaster, volume 2* (Newton Abbot, David and Charles, 1968 reprint), p. 380.

38 P. Mathias, *The brewing industry in England 1700–1830* (Cambridge, Cambridge University Press, 1959), pp. 300–4.

39 J. F. Wilson, *British business history, 1720–1994* (Manchester, Manchester University Press, 1995), pp. 46–7.

40 J. Hoppit, *Risk and failure in English business 1700–1800* (Cambridge, Cambridge University Press, 1987). Also L. Neal, 'The finance of business during the Industrial Revolution', in R. Floud and D. McCloskey (eds), *The economic history of Britain since 1700* (Cambridge, Cambridge University Press, 1994), pp. 173–81.

41 K. Honeyman, *Origins of enterprise* (Manchester, Manchester University Press, 1982), pp. 59–61. For details of landowner involvement in wool and worsted production, see P. Hudson, *The genesis of industrial capital:*

a study of the West Riding wool textile industry 1750–1850 (Cambridge, Cambridge University Press, 1986).

42  H. Perkin, *The age of the railway* (Newton Abbot, David and Charles, 1970), and P. S. Bagwell, *The transport revolution from 1770* (London, Batsford, 1974), p. 18.

43  P. Payne, *British entrepreneurship in the nineteenth century* (London, Macmillan, 1988), p. 14.

44  M. B. Rose, 'The family firm in British business, 1780–1914', in Kirby and Rose (eds), *Business enterprise*, pp. 65–7; D. A. Farnie, *The English cotton industry and the world market, 1815–1896* (Oxford, Clarendon, 1979), p. 212.

45  See G. Timmins, 'The commercial development of the Sheffield crucible steel industry' (unpublished M.A. thesis, University of Sheffield, 1976), pp. 83–4.

46  Crouzet, *Capital formation*, p. 188.

47  G. Timmins, 'Concentration and integration in the Sheffield crucible steel industry', *Business History*, 24 (1982) 68–9.

48  For a map of bank offices in England and Wales in 1842, see J. Langton and R. J. Morris (eds), *Atlas of industrialising Britain, 1780–1914* (London, Methuen, 1986), p. 151.

49  M. Collins, *Banks and industrial finance in Britain, 1800–1939* (London, Macmillan, 1991), p. 25.

50  P. Mathias, *The first industrial nation* (London, Methuen, 1969).

51  See B. L. Anderson, 'The attorney and the early capital market in Lancashire', in J. R. Harris (ed.), *Liverpool and Merseyside* (London, Cass, 1969), pp. 50–71, and M. Miles, 'The money market in the early Industrial Revolution: the evidence from West Yorkshire attorneys, *c*. 1750–1800', *Business History*, 23 (1981) 28–54.

52  Hudson, *Genesis*, pp. 198–203.

53  For examples of the use of bills of exchange, see T. S. Ashton, 'The bill of exchange and private banks in Lancashire, 1790–1830', *Economic History Review*, 15 (1945) 25–35, and Hudson, *Genesis*, pp. 111–30.

54  Timmins, 'Commercial', p. 50.

55  *Ibid.*, pp. 48–9.

56  Edwards, *Cotton trade*, p. 226.

57  *Ibid.*, pp. 225–6.

58  *Ibid.*, p. 228.

59  M. B. Rowlands, 'Continuity and change in an industrialising society', in P. Hudson (ed.), *Regions and industries* (Cambridge, Cambridge University Press, 1989), pp. 127–8. Also S. D. Chapman, *The early factory masters* (Newton Abbot, David and Charles, 1967), pp. 142–3.

60  Collins, *Banks*, p. 24.

61  S. D. Chapman, 'Industrial capital before the Industrial Revolution: an analysis of the assets of a thousand textile entrepreneurs 1730–50', in

N. B. Harte and K. C. Ponting (eds), *Textile history and economic history* (Manchester, Manchester University Press, 1973), pp. 113–37.

62 Honeyman, *Origins*, pp. 26–9.

63 Hudson, *Genesis*, pp. 265–6.

64 Chapman, *Factory masters*, p. 100.

65 Timmins, 'Commercial'.

66 R. Boyson, *The Ashworth cotton enterprise* (Oxford, Clarendon, 1970), p. 33.

67 S. Pollard, *Three centuries of Sheffield steel* (Sheffield, Butt, 1954), pp. 17–18.

68 Timmins, 'Commercial'.

69 R. Church, *The history of the British coal industry, volume 3* (Oxford, Clarendon, 1986), pp. 122–5.

70 A. Kidd, *Manchester* (Keele, Keele University Press, 1993).

71 Edwards, *Cotton trade*, pp. 255–7.

72 Chapman, *Factory masters*.

73 Church, *Coal industry*.

74 S. D. Chapman, *The cotton industry in the Industrial Revolution* (London, Macmillan, 1987), p. 34.

75 Baines, *History*, vol. II, p. 135.

76 P. Hudson, 'Capital and credit in the West Riding wool textile industry *c.* 1750–1850', in Hudson (ed.), *Regions*.

# CHAPTER FIVE

# SELLERS AND BUYERS: DEMAND AND THE INDUSTRIAL REVOLUTION

## Conceptual framework

So far, our discussion of the social and economic changes that occurred in England during the Industrial Revolution period have concentrated on matters concerning the production of goods and services rather than their consumption. To use more technical terminology, we have been concerned with 'supply-side' matters rather than with 'demand-side' matters; with producers rather than with consumers. Yet, there is a view amongst historians that in seeking to explain the economic changes associated with the Industrial Revolution far too much attention has been given to production and not enough to consumption, even though, in recent times, efforts have been made to redress the imbalance.

In this chapter, we consider aspects of demand, focusing on two major issues that have been seen to be associated with 'revolutionary' change. One is concerned with how the proprietors of business concerns sought to take advantage of the growing market opportunities, both within their own localities and further afield, yielded by higher levels of economic growth. Some of them, most notably Josiah Wedgwood, the famous Staffordshire potter, responded by devising their own highly innovative sales strategies designed to capture regional, national and international markets. But we also consider major developments in the type of sales strategies that were more generally employed, which might rely on marketing services that evolved to meet the needs of particular industries and which were often provided by external agencies. In fact, as in the case of the silver-plating concern founded by Roberts and Cadman (to which we drew attention in chapter four), firms might develop their own methods of selling as well as taking advantage of the services provided by agents to sell on their behalf.

The second issue we consider relates to demand in the economy as a whole, since there has been a good deal of discussion amongst historians about the overall impact of rising demand in stimulating economic growth. Indeed, the argument has been made for nothing less than a consumer revolution accompanying the Industrial Revolution – a revolution on the supply side being balanced by a revolution on the demand side. To an extent, our discussion will still be concerned with the micro-dimension, because a key element in the research historians have undertaken into this matter relates to changing patterns of household consumption, both during and before the Industrial Revolution. The issue is complicated because disagreement exists over precisely which groups of domestic consumers were buying the expanding range and quality of goods that were becoming available. Class, gender, life-cycle and regional considerations are all seen to apply, creating a formidable agenda for discussion which, given limits of space here and the need for additional research findings, we can only deal with briefly.

Other conceptual matters that impinge on our discussion require mention. One relates to the nature of demand changes. These could arise for a number of reasons. Thus, the demand for cotton products is likely to have risen because their price fell sharply during the Industrial Revolution period. But other influences would also have operated, especially changes in individual and household income and changes in consumer taste. It might even be the case that the demand for a product might vary because the price or popularity of a complementary product changed. For instance, a fall in the price of tea might increase the demand for sugar, even if the price of sugar remained unaltered or even rose. Plainly, in trying to understand why demand for particular products increased we must go beyond considerations of price, even if the available evidence is limited and difficult to interpret.

We must also draw a distinction between long- and short-term changes in demand. For the most part, we are concerned with the former than with the latter – with considering how producers and consumers were initiating changes that were not only profound but that also endured. Without doubt, demand for a wide range of goods and services rose strongly during the Industrial Revolution period, both in home and overseas markets. Yet periodic upturns and downturns in the trade cycle, which had long been present in the English economy, continued to bring fluctuations in demand. Such fluctuations had been traditionally linked with variations in harvests and overseas trade, but as industrial activity became more important than agriculture in the English economy, demand fluctuations associated with overseas trade assumed greater significance. So, too, did those relating to levels of investment expenditure, especially in the capital goods industries – industries such as engineering, iron and steelmaking, coalmining and shipbuilding. They were dependent on orders arising in the consumer goods industries – textiles, food and drink manufacturing, furniture making and so on – and in the building and transport industries. Such orders occurred mainly as the trade cycle moved upwards, when business was brisk, profits were rising and confidence in future sales was high. Quite possibly, therefore, a trade upturn could lead to an investment upturn. As the trade cycle peaked and demand began to drop, however, orders for investment goods would tail off. In the worst instances, the economy would be plunged into deep recession, with high levels of unemployment and acute social distress. Upturns in the business cycle were a different matter, of course, though they could still create problems for entrepreneurs. For instance, labour shortages might arise, whilst existing capacity might be insufficient to meet demand. Thus, in 1813, John Spear, a Sheffield steelmaker, wrote to a would-be customer:

> In reply to your favour of 2nd inst. I am sorry it is not in my power to execute any orders at present having more than one half on hand that have been in my book several months. If at any other time when I am more disengaged you should think proper to favour me with your orders I shall attend to them with pleasure.[1]

Finally, we must distinguish between home and overseas markets. As far as the former is concerned, we shall need to bear in mind the greatly increased opportunities that were opening up to entrepreneurs as the number of urban consumers expanded massively, especially in London and the industrial regions. We should also be aware that, for firms selling abroad, more distant markets assumed increasing importance. From 1784 to 1786, 42 per cent of Britain's manufactured exports by value were sent to Europe and a further 39 per cent to North America and the West Indies. By 1854–56, the proportion dispatched to the former area had fallen to 32 per cent and to the latter to 28 per cent – a reflection of intensifying industrialisation in both these areas – though, in absolute terms, sales expanded around sixfold in each case. At the same time, the proportion sent to Asia and Australia increased from 14 to 22 per cent and to Latin America from some 0.05 per cent to 9 per cent.[2] The more distant markets, of course, presented formidable problems with regard to the speed of communication in the days before telegraphic communications were available, but we need to recognise, too, that firms might view the expanding sales to these areas as opening up important new opportunities for them.

Essentially, our discussion is divided into two main parts. The first considers developments in marketing strategies, beginning with Neil McKendrick's account of the novel methods devised by Josiah Wedgwood. We adduce new evidence to suggest that other firms were commonly adopting elements of the sales techniques used by Wedgwood and we draw on existing findings to demonstrate other developments that occurred with regard to the direct selling methods that firms employed. Additionally, we consider developments in indirect selling through agencies, a trend reflecting a move towards greater specialisation in marketing. The second part of our discussion turns to consider demand from the consumers' perspective. We are particularly concerned to identify new sources of domestic demand and to make an assessment of how far they can be seen to add to the notion of revolutionary change.

## Developments in direct selling

Josiah Wedgwood made high-quality, fashionable goods, which he sold at relatively high prices. At the same time, he sought to make large sales to a widespread market. To achieve these aims, he could not rely on new inventions or new ideas alone, since both would be quickly imitated by his competitors. Accordingly, he turned to an ambitious sales strategy based on capturing the world of fashion. In particular, he sought to produce wares that exploited the growing preference for neo-classical designs, which, in contrast to the extravagance and exuberance of the late Baroque and Rococo styles prevailing during the middle decades of the eighteenth century, emphasised 'purity, simplicity and antiquity'. His ambition extended to seeing his pottery as future works of art and, with publicity in mind, he even invited famous artists to include his products as background items on their canvases.[3]

As far as winning the home market was concerned, Wedgwood set out to secure the patronage of the King, Queen and other members of the royal family, realising the value this would have in advertising his wares to the general public. His approach embraced a willingness to undertake challenging commissions, including a specially designed teaset for Queen Charlotte, which other potters refused. Though uneconomical to produce, these 'uniques' had immense commercial value, enabling Wedgwood to advertise himself under such styles as 'Potter to her Majesty and their Royal Highnesses the Duke of York & Albany & the Duke of Clarence'. He strove, too, to gain the patronage of the nobility and gentry, again by producing uniques for them, but also by such measures as seeking their advice on artistic matters and ensuring they saw his new wares first. To promote sales lower down the social scale, he could rely partly on the imitation of upper-class fashions. Yet, realising that more was required, he took such measures as lowering prices and naming his pottery wares after their patrons, giving rise to such lines as Queensware and Royal pattern. To widen the geographical spread of his sales he opened warehouses and showrooms in London (on which he lavished particular attention), Bath, Liverpool and Dublin, as well as a special display room at his Etruria works near Stoke-on-Trent. And besides advertising his products in newspapers, he benefited from flattering articles that appeared in the press.[4] In 1777, he also introduced travelling salesmen, having for some time been hostile to them on the grounds that they gave the impression of hawking, a practice too readily associated with selling other than high-quality goods. However, given the need to exploit markets more fully, Wedgwood changed his mind and after some initial difficulties the policy proved successful. From 1790 the procedures to be adopted by his salesmen were set out in a book of rules.

In developing more distant markets, Wedgwood's determination to sell quality wares at high prices remained undiminished and again he sought to ensure that kings and aristocrats gave the lead in purchasing his goods. To gain their custom, he first won the allegiance of British ambassadors, offering presents and flattery to pave the way. He realised that diplomats were keen to promote English prestige and would speak favourably of his products to those in the high social circles in which they moved. And he was also prepared to manufacture uniques for overseas dignitaries, most notably a 1,282-piece table service for Catherine the Great, the completion of which in 1774 required over a thousand original paintings. Nor were the wider commercial possibilities of such an astonishing achievement lost on Wedgwood, for he displayed the service at an exclusive exhibition in London, attracting no lesser personages than Queen Charlotte and the King and Queen of Sweden. To generate more general overseas demand he designed wares to appeal to more popular tastes in individual countries, including cameo medallions of monarchs, though he also dispatched his outdated goods to Russia and his cheaper wares and seconds to America. Importantly, too, he produced sales catalogues in translation, offered generous discounts, employed clerks who spoke European languages and opened overseas warehouses.[5]

Josiah Wedgwood was probably unusual in devising such a remarkably comprehensive approach to marketing and in being prepared to finance it. Yet McKendrick has pointed out that Matthew Boulton, the Birmingham hardware manufacturer, adopted similar strategies to those of the Staffordshire potter, despite favouring a pricing policy which aimed at bulk sales from low prices.[6] Moreover, it is not difficult to unearth evidence to show that, in part at least, numerous businessmen were making use of the strategies he employed. We can usefully explore this matter in relation to the advertising and display of goods. Such approaches had long been used in the business world, but it seems probable they came to feature far more prominently in the selling process during the Industrial Revolution, strengthening the argument that a fundamental change was occurring in the business world.

With regard to advertising, the first point to make is that businesses were extremely keen to announce royal and aristocratic links. Amongst them were Fourness and Ashworth of Sheffield who, in 1792, grandly proclaimed themselves as 'Engineers to their Royal Highnesses the Prince of Wales and Duke of Clarence'.[7] Far more impressive, though, was the list of eminent personages with which another Sheffield firm, the cutlers Joseph Rodgers and Sons, could claim to be connected. By the mid-1840s, they were advertising themselves as:

### CUTLERS TO THEIR MAJESTIES
AND TO THEIR
ROYAL HIGHNESSES THE DUKE & DUCHESS OF CAMBRIDGE,
*THE DUCHESS OF KENT, THE DUKE OF SUSSEX,*
AND PRINCE LEOPOLD OF SAXE COBURG;
ALSO, TO THEIR GRACES THE DUKES OF NORFOLK, DEVONSHIRE,
AND WELLINGTON,
*And to His Majesty the King of Sweden and Norway*

This distinguished list was no doubt built up over many years of trading and care was evidently taken with regard to the order of precedence.[8] By the early 1860s, Rodgers and Sons were describing themselves as cutlers 'by special appointment' to the Queen, a form of words that may have been chosen in an attempt to give themselves special status over other suppliers of cutlery to royalty.

The practice of advertising the patronage of royalty and the nobility evidently became commonplace and related to a wide range of goods and services that we can do no more than indicate. Thus, during the late 1820s, John Bennett's self-cleansing filtering machine for purifying water was advertised as being used in the residences of the King and many of the nobility, as well as being sanctioned, amongst others, by 'the Lord High Admiral, the Lords Commissioners of the Admiralty, and the Honourable Commissioners of the Victualling Department'.[9] At the same time, Rowland's macassar oil, a hair-care product, was advertised as being used by 'his Majesty and the Royal Family',[10] whilst, in the early 1850s, Gorst and Co. of Liverpool, coach builders and harness manufacturers, were advertising their products as being 'by appointment to the queen'.[11] Lastly, we can note the case of a Mrs Thomas Holding and her daughters. In 1833, they were advertising themselves as the inventors of wax flowers, and offered tuition in making them, again claiming royal patronage for their business.[12]

At least some of the firms we have cited, including Wedgwood and Rodgers, established close business connections with members of the royal family and continued to supply them with goods over lengthy periods of time. Many businesses, however, exploited connections with royalty that were tenuous and misleading. For instance, John Watts, a Manchester draper, advertised himself in 1821 as an agent for Urlings lace, a product 'under patronage of the Royal Family'.[13] In the mid-1820s, William Entwistle, also of Manchester, who was a cupper, bleeder and dealer in leeches (wholesale and retail), advertised his gruesome services 'without fire in the glass, being the new and improved plan which is adopted by MR. MAPLESON, Cupper to his present Majesty'.[14] To take another example, Mons. J. M. Mallan, a Liverpool dental surgeon, advertised his services in 1833 using the heading 'Liverpool Grand Musical Festival' which, according to his advertisement, was patronised by French as well as English royalty.[15] And the famous artist Madame Tussaud was able to profit from royalty in a very novel way. Following the accession of George

IV to the throne in 1820, she created a travelling exhibition representing the coronation scene 'upon which no expense had been spared to render it worthy of so great an occasion'.[16]

Turning to advertising more generally, it is plain that business proprietors were keen to take advantage of the increasing opportunities that came to them. As our discussion so far indicates, the growing number of provincial newspapers – the distribution of which was facilitated by improved means of transport – became a far more significant advertising medium, which could bring benefit to local and out-of-town businesses alike. The respectful tone of newspaper advertisements, the fashionable luxury products to which they often referred and the relatively high price of newspapers all point to the type of customer being sought, a consideration to which we will shortly return. Newspapers tended to provide more advertising space towards the end of our period than earlier, a reflection of the growing awareness amongst businessmen of the value that advertising their products could have. No doubt, too, newspaper proprietors were alive to the value of advertising revenue.[17]

A similar line of argument can be made with regard to advertising in trade directories. Those available prior to the early Victorian years tend to contain little in the way of advertisement, beyond giving classified and/or alphabetical lists of local or regional business concerns including those providing transport services. Thereafter, however, they incorporate advertisements that often give considerable detail on the product ranges of individual firms, sometimes listing technical description and noting products for which patents had been obtained. Since trade directories were intended primarily to disseminate commercial information to businessmen, they offered particular opportunities for advertising producer as well as consumer goods. Furthermore, the incorporation of visual images into trade directory advertisements became increasingly fashionable, especially for the larger concerns, depicting both the products they sold and the premises from which they operated. Such illustrations supplemented the more detailed ones that appeared in the growing number of trade catalogues that were published from the last third of the eighteenth century and which were used especially to promote overseas sales.[18]

Of course, describing and illustrating goods were likely to have had much less impact than showing them and it is plain that displaying goods to prospective customers came to be regarded as a highly important part of the marketing process during the Industrial

Revolution. It is equally clear that a range of display strategies were adopted. Not infrequently, as with the Wedgwood concern, permanent showrooms were provided. In 1821, for instance Rodgers and Sons created a sensation by opening the world's first cutlery showroom at their Sheffield works. An insight into the care and expenditure that could be lavished on these showrooms is evident from a description of that belonging to the London Marble and Stone Works in Esher Street, near Vauxhall Bridge. A visitor in 1843 remarked on the 'very beautiful appearance' of the showroom and continued:

> It is a kind of gallery, well adapted for the reception and exhibition of finished works in marble. The room is of great length, and is lighted by ranges of windows situated near the ceiling on both sides of the room, leaving ample space for monumental tablets, &c. beneath them. A clear passage is left through the middle of the room from end to end; on either side of which are ranged very numerous specimens of finished works in marble, such as chimney-pieces, pillars, pilasters, vases, urns, tables and table-tops, statues, busts, monumental tablets, mouldings, &c. Some of these are very elaborately worked; and, from the diversified colours of the specimens of marble employed, and the taste with which they are arranged, the whole presents a very elegant appearance. Others are nearly plain, and exhibit the accuracy with which the machinery employed can produce flat surfaces of marble, for such purposes as paving for halls, conservatories, dairies, shop-fronts, &c.[19]

Displaying goods in opulent premises of this type was a far cry from the long-established practice of using inns as places to store goods for prospective purchasers to view. Chapman has described such practices in relation to the eighteenth-century textile industry, reporting instances of country clothiers, hosiers and others retaining a room in a local town inn, which gave them a base to conduct their regular business and a place to stay overnight.[20] We should not forget that inns might be the only suitable places available in towns to store goods and they also provided convivial places to meet, allowing prospective buyers to benefit from the hospitality of those wishing to sell to them. Moreover, some town inns became highly popular venues for country textile manufacturers: the New Boar's Head in Manchester, for example, provided storage and accommodation facilities for over fifty of them during the 1790s.[21] The number of country manufacturers visiting Manchester's inns continued to grow during the early decades of the nineteenth century, well over a thousand of them attending on one or more of the town's three market days by the mid-1820s.[22] Even so, Manchester's country manufacturers were increasingly utilising storage and display facilities in town-centre warehouses, giving rise to a highly distinctive feature of the town's economy and appearance.[23] And Manchester also attracted sales of cotton cloth from other towns, especially Bolton. Writing in 1824, Edward Baines noted that, in the early days of cotton manufacture, extensive warehouses and sale rooms of 'singular and ornamental' construction were erected in Bolton's main streets. However, Bolton's manufacturers increasingly began to meet the London merchants in Manchester, with the result that Bolton declined as a trading centre for cotton goods. By the time Baines wrote, all the Bolton warehouses had been demolished.[24]

Apart from providing storage and display facilities for those businessmen who were regular visitors to a particular town, it seems likely that inns were also increasingly used to show samples of goods, perhaps for several days at a time, carried from town to town by commercial travellers. The type of facilities that became available at commercial inns and the means by which travellers might obtain the best from them is evident from the letters written by Evan Smith (a partner in the former Roberts and Cadman enterprise) to William Sissons (his successor) in the early 1850s. In the highly competitive business environment that emerged in the silver-plate industry, both careful planning and the close co-operation of hotel staff were required if an effective display was to be achieved.[25] Thus Smith advised:

> I always find a table set out in center of room, which you may walk round, the best. Those which they often want to put you off with, narrow and placed against the walls, altho' well enough for some goods, don't show off well.
>
> The mode of arranging must depend on your taste. I always place the Epergnes, Candelabra, Urns, Ice Pails and big things in the centre, sloping them down to sides and ends of table or tables, with the covers, kettles and next big things, until at the edges come the Mustard pots, bottle stands and small things. A white cloth is the best to cover table with. This and a Screw-driver to open boxes which you may get from the Boots [general hotel servant] ...
>
> Even to those who know what plated things are, to shew them tarnished or on dirty cloth will ruin your sales. Therefore don't keep them open longer than you can avoid and when open make friends with the Chambermaid or Boots to lend you some blankets.

To mount a display at an inn was one thing, but to persuade prospective customers to view it was quite another, especially when they were being visited by a constant stream of sellers. Evan Smith seems to have relied on the personal contacts he could make, and in approaching prospective customers he stressed the need to be polite, considerate and prompt.

> It will be necessary to make your calls early; after one at latest you must not call because their own customers are then likely to come in so that it is necessary to make the most of your morning, especially as few care to do their business before 10-o'clock ... Even before one o'clock it is not so easy to gain an entrance; there are the Agents of all the other Sheffield Platers and a host of Jewellers always about and, so you can only take your turn, it requires to be all alive and quick to get a chance of even shewing what you have to exhibit; there are more sellers than buyers and the shopkeepers are so pestered that they are not over civil, but the tact necessary not only to get the ear but the confidence of your customer constitutes the difference between a good and a bad salesman.

Even with established customers, success was by no means assured and Smith's reference to customer confidence is a sobering reminder that orders could as easily be lost as won. For those who could not be persuaded to visit the hotel to see the display of goods, he outlined an alternative strategy.

> I used to take a blue bag with me and if all my endeavours to get customers up to the Inn to look were in vain, I put a new thing or two into a bag and watched for an opportunity to take it in to show.

Other means of attracting people to view displays were increasingly tried, including advertisements in newspapers. For example, in July 1833, George Morduant, a Sheffield cutler and dealer in silver and plated goods, placed an advertisement in The *Blackburn Alfred* announcing that he was staying for a few days at 14 Clayton Street in the town. He planned to offer an assortment of his wares 'for the inspection of those parties who may favour him with a call'.[26] More personal and pressured approaches were also adopted, as in the case of 'hookers-in' – men who were employed by the Manchester textile manufacturers to meet the arrival of stage coaches in order 'to solicit the attendance of possible customers at the warehouses'.[27]

In focusing our discussion on advertising and display, we must not overlook other developments that occurred in the way businesses undertook their own marketing. Amongst such developments was a tendency to move towards greater specialisation, one manifestation of which was to employ a salesman or, as in the case of the Roberts and Cadman enterprise, to devolve responsibility for sales to a partner. In April 1813, a Manchester fustian manufacturer employed a former cotton trader as a salesman on a seven-year contract. The salesman's salary was to be £50 a year and he would receive commission of up to a third on sales value. Such a person would no doubt have been particularly useful as a salesman because of the business contacts he would already have made in the cotton trade.[28] Furthermore, sales trips were increasingly made overseas, as in the case of Sheffield manufacturers visiting the United States. The cutler George Wosten-holme, for instance, made no fewer than thirty visits there, starting in 1836. Such trips gave the opportunity for Sheffield businessmen to sell goods they produced particularly for the American market, including plantation hoes and Bowie knives.[29]

We know from the records of Roberts and Cadman that Evan Smith visited customers in various parts of the north of England; whether he moved further afield is unclear from the surviving records. However, in the cotton industry at least, Edwards has suggested that a further change to occur in the marketing of goods was the decline – though by no means the demise – in the use of 'riders-out', who travelled over considerable distances to secure orders. Such men began to be replaced by manufacturers' representatives who operated from Manchester warehouses. The change was fuelled by the growing awareness that sales representatives would meet far more prospective customers by operating in Manchester than by travelling long distances. Premises would need to be secured in Manchester, but these would be at least partly offset by savings in travelling expenses.

Other changes in direct selling took place with regard to particular industries, a prime example being the Yorkshire woollen cloth industry. The clothiers in the county worked with their families as domestic producers and had long sold their products to merchants at street markets. However, later in the century special cloth halls were built to better accommodate the rising volume of cloth sales in the region. That at Halifax, for instance, was opened in 1775; it was built around a large open square and contained over 300 rooms where trading could take place.[30] Much of the woollen cloth bought at cloth halls was sold abroad, though the clothier would know little or nothing about its final destination. In the context of effective marketing, it is important to note the crucial role that the merchants played in providing the clothiers with information about the types of cloths that prospective customers required. Indeed, providing market information was a role that merchants in general were well placed to fulfil.[31]

Much more research could be done – not least on local newspapers and directories – to assess the development of the marketing strategies adopted by business concerns during the Industrial Revolution period. Even so, the examples discussed here suggest that such leading innovators as Wedgwood may have been less exceptional in developing new approaches to marketing than is often realised. It may be that a great many concerns were keen and willing to imitate the type of methods he used, at least in part. It is certainly clear that, as far as advertising was concerned, firms were commonly prepared to take advantage of the new opportunities that became available to them. Equally, as the case of the cloth halls reminds us, long-established selling techniques could be adapted to meet changing circumstances and still prove highly effective. In other cases, though, traditional means of selling became less important, such as from cotton cloth sales at fairs and local markets, from warehouses in the smaller towns and by travelling salesmen. Plainly we are looking at a complex picture here. Firms throughout the country would often have developed their sales strategies in similar ways. Yet they also had to take account of the varying circumstances in which they found themselves, so that the type of innovations that proved successful in some industries and regions were quite inappropriate for others.

### Developments in indirect selling

Not all businesses made direct contact with those consuming the goods they produced. In many cases, business concerns depended entirely or in part on wholesalers who, using the type of marketing strategies outlined in the previous section, sold on their behalf. These wholesalers might purchase consignments of goods directly from producers, taking the risk of not being able to sell them all at a profit but being free to take whatever actions they thought best without reference to the producer. Alternatively, they might sell goods supplied to them and earn a commission on sales (often then being called commission agents) and returning any unsold stock, their freedom of action being to a degree prescribed by the wishes of those who owned the goods. Attempts have been made to distinguish between the different types of wholesaler – merchants, factors and brokers being the terms commonly used according to the particular functions they had – but in practice these functions often overlapped.[32] We may note, too, that agents might be used to sell services, as in the case of fire insurance to business in the industrial districts.[33]

The use of wholesalers had the major advantage of helping to keep marketing costs to an acceptable level, but, as Peter Payne has noted, it could have drawbacks. First, since agents normally acted for several firms, the products of any one concern they represented would not necessarily have been pushed very strongly or persistently; understandably, the agents would have sought to maximise their own returns by concentrating on the lines that they found most marketable. Second, to achieve a high degree of success with one firm's products might prove disadvantageous to the agent in that the firm might be encouraged to employ its own salesman. Third, the difficulties a firm encountered in using agents were likely to be more pronounced in overseas than in home markets, partly because overseas agents tended to act for a greater number of firms, but also because distance, language and lack of familiarity with a market gave the firm less control over the agent's actions.[34] It may be noted, too, that the agents would not necessarily know a great deal about the technicalities of the products with which they were dealing, so that customers' enquiries about quality, for instance, would not always be satisfactorily answered. Nonetheless, the use of wholesalers was an important feature of the marketing of goods during the Industrial Revolution and we need to look at the ways in which the services they offered were developed.

The first point to make is that a massive expansion occurred in the wholesaling services that were available to businesses in the industrial regions, giving greater opportunities to exploit wider markets, especially for small-scale producers who lacked marketing expertise. The extent of this expansion is difficult to judge with any exactitude. Much-increased numbers of merchants, factors and other wholesalers can certainly be counted in trade directories relating to the industrial regions, but these are likely to understate the extent of growth. This is partly because they give no real indication of the scale on which businesses conducted their wholesaling activities. But it is also because we cannot be certain that firms undertaking merchanting activities always declared as much in their directory entries.

Even so, some striking changes can be noted. In Sheffield, for example, little merchanting activity at all took place before the late eighteenth century, but the growth of the American market for Sheffield goods brought much-increased activity thereafter. By the start of the nineteenth century, eighteen Sheffield concerns were exporting to the United States and nine to other overseas markets.[35] In other industrial regions, local merchants were much better represented at an earlier date, the first generation of them at Wolverhampton and Birmingham, for example, numbering thirty-four by 1767.[36]

In part, as we noted in chapter four, the increased level of merchanting services that emerged in the industrial regions, especially in Manchester, was provided by foreigners, and after the Napoleonic Wars a new generation of these merchants made their presence felt. They came from the United States, Germany and elsewhere, buying the goods they required on commission. In response, British commission agents began to supply more distant and well-developed markets. Wartime trading difficulties were instrumental in reducing the power of the older English merchant houses and there was an unwillingness amongst their proprietors to adapt to changing trading circumstances after the war which required high-volume trade with low profit margins. Both English and foreign commission agents were also greatly helped by the rise of accepting houses, which included such famous names as Rothschild and Baring. With large capital sums at their disposal and special knowledge of overseas markets, these concerns were prepared to make substantial credit available to their clients. The London-based commission agents, however, took advantage of overproduction and falling prices to seize back the initiative, establishing new types of high-throughput warehouse.[37]

Apart from the greatly increased numbers of merchants in the industrial regions, an important development also occurred in the nature of merchant enterprise as manufacturing firms became increasingly involved in trading.[38] This development brought substantial benefits to local businesses. During trade upturns, for example, the merchant manufacturers might secure large orders for their products, only part of which they might be able to execute, prompting them to turn to local firms in their own line of business to help out. They might also secure orders for a range of the goods manufactured in the region in which they were based. The point can be illustrated in the case of the Huntsman family, steelmakers of Sheffield. During the late eighteenth century, as the firm's proprietors moved into merchanting, they built up extensive European sales dealing directly with such continental buyers as J. C. Grill of Augsburg and Carl Wurs of Vienna and through London agents, including Dubois and Sons. The firm's order books for the period 1797–1814 have survived and they reveal that it was heavily involved in placing orders with local firms on behalf of its leading customers, amongst them J. H. Reinhard of Winterthur.[39]

In the Lancashire cotton industry, trade-directory evidence reveals that some sixty leading firms were combining manufacturing with merchanting by the mid-1790s, the great majority having started out as manufacturers.[40] Indeed, as Lloyd-Jones and Lewis have demonstrated, Manchester firms selling cotton yarn on commission were commonly weaving cotton also. For example, as rate-book evidence shows, the firm of Joseph Massey and Sons occupied two warehouses in Marsden Square in 1815 and was described in the trade directory of that year as manufacturers and dealers, agents and commission dealers.[41] The same sort of trend is also evident amongst Sheffield's steelmakers. Using trade directories to trace the way they expanded their activities, it is striking how often they came to describe themselves as 'merchants' or as 'factors and merchants'. For instance, Charles Hodgson had commenced business as a hinge, shovel and trowel maker at Workhouse croft in 1787, had become a 'factor' by 1815 and, in partnership with his sons and others, was regularly describing himself as a 'factor and merchant' from 1821.[42]

The increased amount of commerce that characterised the Industrial Revolution period encouraged greater specialisation amongst merchants, though the degree to which this took place is hard to measure. Such specialisation might occur with regard to geographical area, as trade-directory entries sometimes reveal. Thus, in the mid-1820s, a number of Liverpool merchants were describing themselves as either American or West India merchants, whilst several in Manchester concentrated either on the American or the continental trade. But growing specialisation is also evident with regard to mercantile functions.[43] In the case of Liverpool merchants, for example, Williams has concluded that, compared with the range of functions performed by the eighteenth-century merchants – including banking and insurance and selling on the produce they imported – Liverpool merchants during the first half of the nineteenth century were far more specialised. As far as importing raw cotton was concerned, the leading thirty firms showed a strong tendency to specialise in importing that commodity and to confine their activities to importing and exporting.[44] Other instances of mercantile specialisation have also been noticed, as in the case of those London-based commission agents who tended to specialise in selling cotton cloth. They also advised the cotton manufacturers about changing market conditions, offered them financial assistance and collected debts on their behalf. As in the case of William Gray of Bolton, a cotton manufacturer might deal with several London agents, thereby spreading business risks and widening sources of credit and of market intelligence.[45]

In indirect as well as in direct forms of marketing, therefore, major developments were taking place as businessmen sought to find more effective means of selling the rapidly growing volume of goods that they produced. Not only were wholesaling services greatly expanded in the industrial regions, but they were adapted to meet particular needs, giving rise to more specialist provision. Their contribution should be seen as part of the marked expansion of the services that became available to businesses in the industrial regions, their successful development being closely linked with the provision of much-improved transport facilities on which the commercial sector so strongly depended. We do not have the space to deal with the transport infrastructure in this book.

### Sources of demand

In the final part of this chapter, discussion turns to the question of the level of demand from the consumer point of view. We are particularly concerned with trying to identify new sources of demand for industrial products that were generated amongst English consumers, bearing in mind considerations of gender, social class and life-cycle stage. In doing so, we are not attempting to enter the broader debate on how far changes in home and overseas demand influenced England's industrial growth. This is a matter that is well covered in the literature, with recent work undertaken by Cuenca Esteban re-opening the possibility that exports could in fact have played a highly significant part in promoting economic growth during the Industrial Revolution period.[46] Instead, in line with our general approach, we engage with discussions on the role that different consumer groups played in generating new demand for industrial products, an issue that has recently become much discussed amongst historians and which offers a great deal of scope for further research.

We can usefully begin with a line of discussion centring on Neil McKendrick's contention that a consumer boom occurred in England during the eighteenth century. He suggests that the boom reached revolutionary proportions in the third quarter of the century and that, by the closing decades, a greater proportion of the population than 'in any previous society in human history' was able to purchase consumer goods. He sees the Industrial Revolution as one of the great discontinuities in history and maintains that it was matched by the consumption revolution, which provided 'the necessary convulsion on the demand side of the equation to match the convulsion on the supply side'. The rich led the way in the consumer revolution, he argues, as they engaged in 'an orgy of spending' on a wide range of fashionable goods, including stylish houses. Building on the comments made by Elizabeth Gilboy,[47] he maintains that the middle ranks of society imitated the rich in their desire to spend and, in turn, so did the rest of society as far as it was able. As a result, demand in the economy was stimulated to an unprecedented degree.[48]

In articulating the influences on the consumer revolution, McKendrick identifies an intellectual underpinning arising from a growing approval of the idea that it was acceptable for all ranks of society, and not merely the rich, to acquire new wants and the means to purchase them, hence expanding demand. He suggests that because the structure of English society was less strongly differentiated than elsewhere in Europe, thereby facilitating social mobility, it proved conducive to the spread of the consumer revolution. So, too, he considers, was fashionable London, which was the biggest European city and the one that housed the highest proportion of any national population. Also important in encouraging spending were domestic servants, a numerous group who were well aware of the spending habits of their social superiors and who transmitted these habits more generally. To complete his thesis, McKendrick argues for the emergence of a stronger desire to consume goods, which was generated through advertisement, sales promotion and the exploitation of fashion, and an increased ability to do so, the result of family incomes rising as women and children found greater work opportunities in an expanding economy.[49]

A different approach linking demand to the Industrial Revolution has been proposed by Jan de Vries. He suggests a 'companion concept' to the Industrial Revolution, which he terms an 'industrious revolution'. Essentially, his concept centres on the identification of two key changes in household behaviour which are seen to have had a significant impact on the demand for manufactured goods. One is a reduction in the amount of leisure time taken by household members, the implication being that they earned more and therefore could afford to buy more. The other is a reallocation of household labour away from the production of goods that household members themselves consumed, in favour of the production of goods that were sold to others. These changes, de Vries argues, 'involved a reduction of typically female supplied home-produced goods' and the emergence of women as autonomous wage earners. In terms of timing, de Vries believes that there is evidence that an industrious revolution took place from the mid-seventeenth century to the early nineteenth, so that it 'preceded and prepared the way for the Industrial Revolution'.[50]

A common element in the McKendrick and de Vries approaches to explaining demand increases concerns the additional spending that women were able to undertake as their earning opportunities increased. It is a conclusion that a number of historians have supported, at least with regard to certain types of goods. Beverly Lemire, for instance, suggests that as women became wage earners they became more active consumers, extending the range of their purchases beyond the clothing and furnishing textiles they had traditionally bought for their households. She cites evidence from the 1820s to show that at the factory village of Styal in Cheshire women were spending more than usual on shoes and hats (as opposed to clogs and shawls) during the relatively prosperous year of 1825.[51] However, Pat Hudson warns that the argument cannot be taken too far since there is little supportive evidence to show that women were at the forefront of consumer spending beyond the purchase of food and drink and the household and personal essentials that they had previously made.[52]

To take this point further, we need to consider the research undertaken by Sara Horrell, which suggests that the mass of the population may have been unable to afford the fashionable consumer goods that were increasingly becoming available during the Industrial Revolution period. Computing changes in real wages for working-class people during this period is notoriously difficult, but Horrell's analysis, based on a sample of 283 household budgets, indicates that the real expenditure – expenditure allowing for changes in prices – of working-class households increased by one-third between the late eighteenth and mid-nineteenth centuries, though with a decline during the 1840s. Yet this expenditure was channelled towards traditional rather than new industrial products. Thus, between 1787 and 1796, the sample households spent 87.7 per cent of their income on necessities (food and housing) and 73.5 per cent on food alone. For the years 1840–54, the corresponding figures were 83.5 per cent and 64 per cent. That the overall reduction in the proportion of income spent on necessities was so small was largely the result of increases in house rent. If this evidence is representative – and some variation is apparent according to occupation and hence earnings – it is plain that little of the additional real expenditure by working-class families went on anything other than necessities. The budgets are not detailed enough to give a clear picture of how expenditure by working-class families on non-essential goods was distributed, but they suggest that it was directed towards clothing, furniture, household goods and services.[53] Certainly we know from the comments made by those who visited working-class houses in the early Victorian era that possession of durable consumer goods was common, even if they were not always bought new. Indeed, even in houses in 'the older and less improved localities' of Manchester in 1849, the journalist Angus Reach found that:

> Sometimes there is a large cupboard, the open door of which reveals a shining assortment of plates and dishes; sometimes the humbler dinner service is ranged on shelves which stretch along the walls; while beneath them suspended on hooks a more or less elaborate series of skillets, stewpans, and miscellaneous cooking and household matters. A conspicuous object is very frequently a painted and highly-glazed tea tray ... which, by its superior lustre and artistic boldness of design, commonly throws into the shade the couple or so of tiny prints, in narrow black frames, which are suspended above it.[54]

And we also know that, as was the case with the Ashworth Brothers of Egerton and Bank Top, near Bolton, employers might make loans to their workers for the purchase of various types of household goods.[55]

Horrell's findings are also revealing in two other respects. First, they cast further doubt on the notion, revisited in Part III below, that women's work boosted family income and allowed for spending on non-essentials. In fact, such work was associated with higher shares of expenditure on cheaper foodstuffs and on soap and candles.[56] Second, she calculates that, taking all households in the country, the surplus remaining for expenditure on non-essential items (using constant prices) rose from £4.5 million in 1801 to £86.7 million in 1841. Plainly, these figures represent a massive increase in expenditure, which, since it did not emanate from working-class families, must have been generated by middle- and upper-class families. Such a conclusion is certainly consistent with the view taken by some historians that income inequality increased during the Industrial Revolution period. Horrell warns that we should not read too much into her analysis with regard to the impact that upper- and middle-class expenditure had on home-manufactured goods, since some of it would have been directed towards services and to imported goods. Nevertheless, she concludes that 'domestic demand for the products of new industries was undoubtedly important'.[57]

In addition to criticising the notion that women's expenditure played a key role in raising demand, historians have also been sceptical about the question of emulative demand. Amanda Vickery does find some evidence of emulative expenditure with regard to dress amongst her sample of women drawn from the higher social echelons, but she notes that this idea is misleading if we try to apply it generally and she draws a provisional conclusion that female consumption was 'repetitive and predominantly mundane'.[58] For the pre-1750 period, Pat Hudson notes that the evidence of probate inventories (lists of individuals' possessions made after death) casts doubt on the idea that either the gentry or London were the main driving forces behind rising demand. The purchases made by middle-class consumers and by consumers in provincial towns may have been more significant and these purchases did not necessarily arise through emulation. And evidence on emulation derived from other sources for the eighteenth century tends to be drawn from comments made by contemporaries about clothing fashions. Not only may such evidence be a poor guide to consumer expenditure in general, but it may also be misleading. Thus lower-income groups may often have worn fashionable clothes that they bought second-hand rather than new (and which they may have modified themselves) so that they were not necessarily making purchases that contributed to the demand for newly produced clothes.[59] Finally, we should note that evidence for a regional dimension to emulation also needs to be qualified. In discussing the probability that, in the later eighteenth century, ready-made clothing (as opposed to clothing made at home) was more widely available in London and the home counties than in the north of England, John Styles suggests that the influence of the metropolis was probably crucial, but that other considerations, such as the density of the retailing network, must also be taken into account.[60]

Our discussion so far seems to point to the crucial role of greatly increased demand from middle- and upper-class groups in accounting for a massive expansion of home demand for 'non-essential' goods during the Industrial Revolution period. And this is a theme that has recently been developed by Maxine Berg. She argues that, during the eighteenth century, a dynamic market developed amongst middling groups in society which 'pushed producers to create new products, finishes and tools'. By examining a set of patents for the period 1627–1825 that relate to metalware, glass, ceramics, furniture, and clocks and watches, she discerns the consumer orientation to which much of it was directed. This orientation embraced not only the development of new products, but also of existing goods by, for example, using new materials and types of ornamentation. She finds that patents dealing with product changes were by no means random, but were concentrated around specific problems or themes. One such theme was portability, which, from the 1760s, led to the introduction of a range of portable products including mangles and stoves. Berg also uses product information from the growing number of trade catalogues to add weight to her views, pointing out that catalogue entries demonstrate the complementarity of product development with, for example, improvements in metalware goods being associated with those in glass (see figure 5.1).[61] Here she echoes the theme rehearsed by Beverly Lemire regarding the cotton textiles and complementary goods. Writing of the 1750s and 1760s, Lemire notes:

> Just as cotton textiles appeared in greater numbers, so too did the many assorted accessories: buttons, buckles, caps, handkerchiefs, hose and mittens, that multiplied over the first half of the eighteenth century, reflected a strong and persistent consumer demand.

She further observes that all these articles fell within a broadly middling price range and that new articles continued to appear throughout the second half of the eighteenth century.[62] We may note, too, that the impression of remarkably extensive product ranges being generated can sometimes be gained from trade-directory evidence. For instance, the Sheffield cutlers Joseph Rodgers and Sons were advertising forty categories of goods in 1833, a number of which they sub-divided into several other categories and to which they sometimes added the description 'of all sizes' or 'of all kinds'. The type of

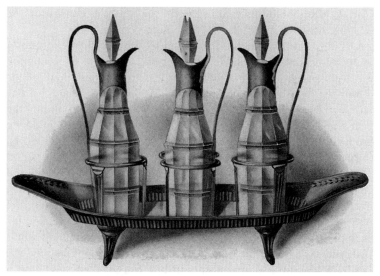

Figure 5.1 Jugs made from glass and Old Sheffield Plate. The jugs, which date from the period 1784–1820, provide a useful illustration of complementarity in product development

consumer they were aiming at is evident from a number of references to silver wares and to goods for ladies and gentlemen, but also to such undoubtedly luxury products as fish knives, asparagus tongs, gold thimbles and portable travelling knives and forks with a cork-screw (see figure 5.2).[63]

In suggesting the importance of expenditure by the better-off in promoting much higher levels of demand for fashionable consumer goods, we must not overlook other aspects of demand. Thus Styles's work on the move from self-provision to purchase of clothing brings a life-cycle dimension to the issue of household demand. He draws attention to several references made by Fredrick Morton Eden in 1797 to married couples making do with the clothes they acquired as single people given the heavy expenses associated with the early years of marriage. He notes, too, the evidence on this matter contained in the household accounts of Richard Latham, a yeoman of Scarisbrick in west Lancashire. Entries for the period 1724 to 1743 show that Latham and his wife bought very little woollen cloth until their children grew older, at which time a dramatic increase in their purchases occurred.[64] More generally, we might surmise that as rising

**Figure 5.2** Papier-mâché trays. Manufactured by Walton and
Co. of Wolverhampton during the mid-nineteenth century,
these trays illustrate the type of product differentiation that
could be achieved by varying design and ornamentation

population led to numerous new households being formed, demand
from newly married couples for a range of basic household goods
would have risen appreciably, even allowing for such goods being
passed from generation to generation, for second-hand goods being
purchased and for time being taken to acquire them. One example

157

that has been noted is that of clocks. According to Angus Reach, writing of the Manchester working class in 1849, 'a clock is very frequently the first article of household stuff which a young married couple procure'. He reasoned that a clock was indispensable because of the need to keep regular working hours in the mills.[65]

Lastly, we must turn to the issue of the producer goods mentioned in our introduction to this chapter. So far, we have concentrated our discussion on consumer goods, but we need to remember that businessmen would have bought producer goods for their workplaces as well as the consumer goods for their homes. Again, such goods might be bought second-hand, but since productive capacity in English industry extended enormously during the Industrial Revolution, the argument cannot be taken too far. Indeed, we are looking at a very considerable rise in demand for new producer goods during this period (as chapter three suggested), as well as for new premises in which they could be housed. Moreover, we must be aware that there was a strong regional element in the demand for such goods, with businesses often coming into existence as part of ancillary industries, the main function of which was to supply the major industry or industries in that region. The emergence of local engineering industries in the textile districts provides a case in point. Of course, not all the products of such firms would necessarily have been sold locally. Many firms branched out into wider markets, sometimes selling directly to overseas customers. And firms manufacturing producer goods were certainly alert to the sales possibilities arising in other industrial districts, as is quite evident from advertisements in trade directories. These were often directed towards the sale of producer goods, including machinery, hand tools and a range of industrial equipment such as steam engines and boilers, forge bellows, vices and safes. The Sheffield tool and steel makers, to take one example, were regularly advertising their products in local and regional trade directories, a reflection of the wide range of industries in which their products could be used.

It is clear, therefore, that both consumer and producer goods must be taken into account in seeking to identify new product demand emerging during the Industrial Revolution period. Both are likely to have been purchased mainly by the better-off, though as the prices of some consumer products, cottons amongst them, showed sharp long-term falls, more and more people would have been able to afford them. Moreover, industrialists made great efforts to introduce new products and to improve existing ones with both households and fellow industrialists in mind. Indeed, it seems likely that the increased demand for producer goods formed an important part of any consumer revolution that can be identified at this time.

## Conclusion

The degree to which firms developed their marketing strategies during the Industrial Revolution period varied considerably, much depending on the resources that could be made available for the purpose. In the case of Josiah Wedgwood, a remarkably sophisticated and comprehensive strategy was initiated, and though this may well have been exceptional, elements of his approach became widely employed. What is clear is that businesses were often keen to take advantage of new opportunities to bring their products to the attention of prospective and established customers alike. The advertising potential offered by the appearance of many more provincial newspapers and by the growing number of trade directories was highly significant in this respect. Additionally, businesses were able to take advantage of the expansion in wholesaling services, which tended to become more specialised. Drawing on both their own initiatives and those of external agencies, therefore, businesses in general were able to benefit from greatly improving marketing facilities, especially where, as in the case of the Sheffield area, they seem to have been ill-developed during the early eighteenth century. It is for this reason that we may identify the period 1700–1850 as revolutionary.

As to the groups of consumers at which marketing effort was particularly directed, the indications are that much attention was being paid to enhancing demand for a wide range of consumer and producer goods that the better-off needed for both domestic and business purposes. In both these dimensions a good deal of attention was being devoted to developing wide product ranges, so that consumer choice was greatly extended. Such an approach gave full scope to incorporating fashionable designs which would help to differentiate the products of one firm from those of another, even though, in so far as they were functional, these products were equally efficient. Studying the advertisements of the early Victorian era leaves a strong impression that great strides had been made in developing a consumer culture. And such a highly visible expression of change would not have been lost on the contemporary mind. Once again, they would have been aware of 'something happening'. We take up another aspect of this broad theme in the following chapter on agriculture.

## Notes

1  G. Timmins, 'The commercial development of the Sheffield crucible steel industry' (unpublished M.A. thesis, University of Sheffield, 1976), p. 28.
2  See R. Davis, *The Industrial Revolution and overseas trade* (Leicester, Leicester University Press, 1979), pp. 88–9.
3  N. McKendrick, 'Josiah Wedgewood: an eighteenth century entrepreneur in salesmanship and marketing techniques', *Economic History Review*, 12 (1959/60) 410–12 and 415–16.
4  *Ibid.*, 412–15 and 418–25.
5  *Ibid.* Also M. Berg, *The age of manufactures: industry, innovation and work in Britain, 1700–1820* (London, Fontana, 1985), pp. 425–33.
6  N. McKendrick, J. Brewer and J. Plumb (eds), *The birth of a consumer society* (London, Longman, 1982), pp. 69–77.
7  Timmins, 'Crucible steel', pp. 13–14.
8  W. White, *History and general directory of the borough of Sheffield* (Sheffield, White, 1833).
9  Pigot and Co., *National commercial directory for 1828–9* (Norwich, Winton, 1995 reprint).
10  *Ibid.*
11  *Slater's royal national classified commercial directory of Lancashire* (Manchester, Slater, 1851).
12  *Blackburn Alfred*, 1833.
13  *Manchester Guardian*, 12 May 1821.
14  *Pigot and Dean directory for Manchester, Salford, etc. for 1824–5* (Manchester, Pigot and Co., 1825).
15  *Blackburn Alfred*, 18 September 1833.
16  *Manchester Guardian*, 29 December 1821.
17  On the development of advertising, see B. Lemire, *Fashion's favourite: the cotton trade and the consumer in Britain, 1660–1800* (Oxford, Oxford University Press, 1991), and C. Y. Ferdinand, 'Selling in the provinces: news and commerce round eighteenth century Salisbury', in J. Brewer and R. Porter (eds), *Consumption and the world of goods* (London, Routledge, 1993), pp. 393–411.
18  M. Berg, 'Product innovation in core consumer industries in eighteenth-century Britain', in M. Berg and K. Bruland, *Technological revolutions in Europe* (Cheltenham, Edward Elgar Publishing, 1998), pp. 149–51.
19  G. Dodd, *Days at the factories* (New York, Augustus Kelley, 1967 reprint), pp. 236–7.
20  S. D. Chapman, 'Industrial capital before the Industrial Revolution: an

analysis of the assets of a thousand textile entrepreneurs 1730–50', in N. B. Harte and K. C. Ponting (eds), *Textile history and economic history* (Manchester, Manchester University Press, 1973), pp. 128–36.

21 S. D. Chapman, 'The commercial sector', in M. Rose (ed.), *The Lancashire cotton industry* (Preston, LCB, 1996), pp. 63–4.

22 E. Baines, *History, directory and gazetteer of the county palatine of Lancaster, volume 2* (Newton Abbot, David and Charles, 1968 reprint), pp. 379–90.

23 M. M. Edwards, *The growth of the British cotton trade, 1780–1815* (Manchester, Manchester University Press, 1967), pp. 172–5.

24 Baines, *History*, p. 543.

25 Sheffield City Archives, Scrapbook, Sis. 10.

26 *Blackburn Alfred*, 17 July 1833.

27 Edwards, *Cotton trade*, p. 173.

28 *Ibid*, p. 169.

29 G. Tweedale, 'English versus American hardware: British marketing techniques and business performance in the USA in the nineteenth and early twentieth centuries', in R. Davenport-Hines (ed.), *Markets and bagmen* (Aldershot, Gower, 1986), p. 62.

30 N. Pevsner, *The buildings of England: Yorkshire West Riding* (London, Penguin, 1967), p. 231.

31 S. Caunce, 'Complexity, community structure and competition advantage within the Yorkshire woollen industry 1700–1850', *Business History*, 32 (1998) 26–43.

32 S. D. Chapman, *Merchant enterprise in Britain* (Cambridge, Cambridge University Press, 1992), pp. 3–4.

33 O. M. Westall, 'Market strategy and the competitive structure of British general insurance, 1720–1980', *Business History*, 36 (1994) 22–6.

34 P. Payne, *British entrepreneurship in the nineteenth century* (Basingstoke, Macmillan, 1988), p. 41.

35 Tweedale, 'Marketing techniques', p. 58.

36 Chapman, *Merchant enterprise*.

37 *Ibid.*, Parts 1 and 2.

38 *Ibid.*

39 Timmins, 'Crucible steel', pp. 22–8.

40 Chapman, *Merchant enterprise*, p. 58.

41 R. Lloyd-Jones and M. Lewis, *Manchester and the age of the factory: the business structures of cottonopolis in the Industrial Revolution* (Beckenham, Croom Helm, 1987).

42 This information is taken from a database compiled by one of the authors.

43 Baines, *History*.

44 D. Williams, 'Liverpool merchants and the cotton trade 1820–1850', in J. R. Harris (ed.), *Liverpool and Merseyside* (London, Cass, 1969), pp. 192–201.

45  Edwards, *Cotton trade*, pp. 147–56.
46  J. C. Esteban, 'The rising share of British industrial exports in industrial output, 1700–1851', *Journal of Economic History*, 57 (1997) 879–901.
47  E. Gilboy, 'Demand as a factor in the Industrial Revolution', in R. M. Hartwell (ed.), *The causes of the Industrial Revolution* (London, Methuen, 1967), pp. 46–64.
48  McKendrick et al., 'Introduction', *Consumer society*, p. 6.
49  *Ibid.*
50  J. de Vries, 'The Industrial Revolution and the industrious revolution', *Journal of Economic History*, 54 (1994) 98–128.
51  Lemire, *Fashion's favourite*, p. 55.
52  P. Hudson, *The Industrial Revolution* (London, Edward Arnold, 1992), pp. 176–7.
53  S. Horrell, 'Home demand and British industrialisation', *Journal of Economic History*, 56 (1996) 564–82.
54  C. Aspin (ed.), *Manchester and the textile districts in 1849* (Helmshore, Helmshore Local History Society, 1972), pp. 5–7.
55  R. Boyson, *The Ashworth cotton enterprise* (Oxford, Clarendon, 1969).
56  Horrell, 'Home demand', 582–91.
57  *Ibid.*, 591–7.
58  A. Vickery, *The gentleman's daughter* (New Haven, Yale University Press, 1998), ch. 5.
59  Hudson, *Industrial Revolution*.
60  J. Styles, 'Clothing the north: the supply of non-elite clothing in the eighteenth century north of England', *Textile History*, 16 (1994), 160.
61  Berg, 'Product innovation', pp. 138–54.
62  Lemire, *Fashion's favourite*, pp. 87–9.
63  White, *History*.
64  Styles, 'Clothing'.
65  Aspin (ed.), *Manchester*, p. 46.

# CHAPTER SIX

# FEEDING THE
# INDUSTRIAL REVOLUTION

## Conceptual framework

In 1829, the agricultural writer Rudolph Schmidt landed at Dover to begin a three-month tour of rural Britain. He was principally interested in English experiences of the decline of co-operative (open field) farming in the light of intense debate on the value and long-term future of this form of farming in different Prussian regions.[1] His itinerary took him through Kent and the home counties, East Anglia, Lincolnshire, East Yorkshire, the Scottish lowlands and then back through Westmorland, Staffordshire, the Welsh Marches and to Dover again, via Dorset. The commentary he made points to the regionality of agricultural change, but also paints an approving picture of the 'progressive tendencies' in British agricultural practice and institutions. Of Berkshire and Buckinghamshire, he noted that:

> The farms in the numerous small villages are by and large of considerable extent, and while the landholding situation in some places has made enclosure a difficult end to achieve, it is true to say that the landscape is a marvellous patchwork of the most advanced agricultural techniques.[2]

Of Northamptonshire, he wrote that, 'The place is dominated by a mass of great estates, where well informed gentlemen are engaged in vigorous estate improvement and do much to encourage the best practice amongst their tenants.'[3] His highest praises, however, were reserved for the counties of Norfolk, Lincolnshire and the East Riding, which he felt to be models of advanced agriculture, combining extensive enclosure, new crop rotations, and the most 'modern' labour force practices, tenancy arrangements and estate management techniques. He suggested that:

> In these places there is little land left to be enclosed and the peasant farmer no longer has a place. Labourers are generally employed on

short contracts or by the piece, to work on crops which seem in endless variety. I am told by one farmer that 25 bushels an acre or more can be got from a single planting of wheat. Can there be any stronger confirmation of the advantage of individual farming?[4]

Penned by someone who was enthusiastic about agricultural change, these words undoubtedly contain a hidden agenda. Certainly contemporary English commentators such as William Marshall were less inclined to give such blanket praise to English agriculture, even as it was practised in the 'progressive' counties.[5] However, the key point is that to a foreign commentator the changes in English agriculture that had been developing cumulatively since the seventeenth century appeared radical and seemed to mark England out from other European countries. His final thoughts on the tour as a whole are particularly important. He noted the recent great increase in the British population (as revealed by the censuses, and to be reviewed below in chapter seven) and suggested that despite debate over the symbolic and practical role of the corn laws, 'it is remarkable that the country has managed to feed such a great population from its own resources'.[6]

The Schmidt narrative seems to implicitly confirm many of the characteristics of English agricultural history that have become accepted pillars of writing on the subject. English food needs were met without recourse to substantial imports except during the most severe harvest crises, and this despite a rapidly growing population.[7] What is more, while data on people's heights provide contradictory evidence of the level at which these needs were met, a recent review of the likely course of stillbirths has suggested persuasively that mothers became better and better nourished during the course of the eighteenth century. In other words, not only were food needs met, they were met at an increasing level.[8] They were also met by an ever shrinking percentage of the labour force as urbanisation and industrialisation competed with agriculture for rural residents and rural workers, suggesting that agricultural efficiency (however we measure it) must have increased substantially.[9] These sorts of contentions will be familiar from most textbooks, and their heroic nature dominated early characterisations of the process of agricultural development which was labelled 'revolutionary'.[10] It is this theme that we take up in the next section.

## Rural England: an economic perspective

If we accept for the moment these broad generalisations about the wider importance of English agriculture, the natural corollary is that the economic life of rural England must have witnessed substantial change in the two centuries before 1850. The aggregate evidence for this perspective is persuasive. A growing population required substantial increases in total agricultural output, but given the limited potential for extension of the cultivated acreage at times of normal prices,[11] this had to come from rising productivity – that is increased outputs per unit of input, with each worker and each acre producing more over time. The fact that we can look at output and productivity for a range of different crops and that the sources to accurately quantify agricultural output do not exist complicates our appreciation of the success or otherwise of English agriculture. Nonetheless, it has been suggested that over our 150-year period aggregate output more than trebled, a function primarily of a rise of approximately 200 per cent in land productivity and 150 per cent in labour productivity.[12] In terms of historic agricultural experiences and the experiences of other European countries, these were considerable advances. Indeed, by 1851 output per worker in English agriculture was over double that in any other contemporary European state.[13] More widely, Crafts has suggested that total factor productivity growth in agriculture outstripped that in industry (modernised and unmodernised combined) by a factor of three, placing agriculture at the forefront of a widely conceived Industrial Revolution.[14]

Many of the potential explanations of increasing total output and productivity may be familiar to students from some of the numerous textbooks on enclosure, the agricultural revolution and rural unrest. A breakdown in rigid distinctions between pastoral and arable land, new crop rotations, selective animal breeding, enclosure, improvements in hand technology, greater professionalism amongst a progressively smaller number of predominantly tenant farmers, changes in the size and structure of farms – which in aggregate grew by over a third between 1700 and 1850 – and the application of more fertiliser, have been seen to underpin rising agricultural outputs. We can bring these bland explanations to life, and begin to gain an appreciation of their individual and collective importance, by looking at the records of contemporary farmers and estate managers. Lord Lilford, for instance, had estates in Lancashire, Cheshire, Shropshire,

Warwickshire, Herefordshire and Somerset, and his archives remain one of the great unexplored sources in English agricultural history.[15] The farming books of his stewards reveal much about the small everyday developments which may have lain behind the notional figures reviewed above. In March 1808, Richard Hodgkinson from the Lancashire estate noted that:

> Sowed 18 and a half bushels of yellow oats which I bott off John Wright of Culcheth, ... and on the 24th I sowed upon the same plot 10 pounds of trefoil, 6 pounds of white clover and 4 pounds of red clover seed and 5 sacks of my own hay seed and had them rolled in with the large roller.[16]

The use of diversified grasses and clovers in rotations, planted so as to follow on directly after the taking in of a cereal crop, afforded food to animals, helped in the replenishment of land nutrients after harvest and meant that land which might previously have had to stand fallow could be brought into productive use nationwide. For the most progressive agricultural counties, these sorts of new rotations were increasingly being adopted as early as the second decade of the eighteenth century.[17] Meanwhile, a greater appreciation of the role of organic fertilisers, and greater ingenuity in getting and applying fertilisers, also contributed to output improvement. All of the Lilford estate stewards gave detailed attention to setting dunghills, cleaning out ditches and spreading the contents on land, and invested heavily in networks of dung buying and selling. In August 1808, Hodgkinson:

> set a dunghill which I bott off Geo Durnell butcher for 14 pounds ... I had the ditch from the Stock Platt cleared and the slutch of this covered more than half an acre ... what this compost was short of covering ... I made out with lime unmixed ... so that it has all been manured except about three quarters of an acre at the south end where a good hedge affording shelter to the cattle usually lie which makes it of equal if not superior to any part of the field.[18]

In the same month he 'Covered with lime and soil all the south side which had been covered with black dung in 1802. At the same time covered with good butchers dung ... all the north side which had been covered with lime and soil in 1802'.[19] He also used industrial waste as a fertiliser. In 1822, 'The Hall field was set over with soap waste and lime and soil, about three quarters of an acre on the west side with soap waste and the remainder with lime and soil.'[20] Soap waste was just one of many innovative fertilisers that farmers had increasingly come to value by the opening decades of the nineteenth century, from a list which included crushed bones, cotton rags, the dregs from the brewing process and sawdust. The range of manures is important, but more significant for long-term productivity was whether farmers invested in a cycle of manuring to maintain land fertility. In this case there was evidently an estate-wide manuring plan in force, but it is unlikely that a similar appreciation of the importance of soil fertility could have been found even fifty years earlier.

Lilford and his stewards were also active in seeking out the best seeds in a *national* seed market. Richard Hodgkinson purchased oat seeds from Bedford, Norfolk, Staffordshire, Essex and Hampshire, as well as places within Lancashire, while the wheat seeds that he did not generate himself were taken from dealers in the East Riding, Berkshire and Oxfordshire. Clover and other grass seeds were sometimes imported from abroad but more often were purchased in bulk from dedicated clover growers in the Midlands. When neighbours and friends informed him of a particularly good strain of plant, Lilford would dispatch local agents to seek out regular supplies and order his stewards to undertake substantial experimental planting. The Parker family of Lancashire were also eager to seek out the best plant strains using James Prown, the Bradford seedsman, to acquire items that came to their attention in conversations and through agricultural shows and writing.[21] These were very considerable advances, akin to genetic engineering in our own day but on a more ad hoc basis. The fact that the Parkers attended agricultural shows and read pamphlets also points to important but ultimately unquantifiable advances in background knowledge on farming issues during the eighteenth century. As Gregory Clark points out, the eighty years after 1770 saw a very considerable increase in the number of agricultural pamphlets published annually, and this observation might be allied with an increasing awareness amongst medical historians in particular, of an exponential increase in writing on plants and agricultural issues in books and magazines after 1780.[22] A reading of the published letters of major estate holders in different parts of England also suggests that, from the late eighteenth century, there was an increase in formal visiting by landowners and their stewards for the purposes of learning different estate management practices.

For those further down the landholding and farming scale, financing change was as much of a problem as obtaining knowledge on what needed changing in the first place. Landlords might help with both problems, as the great barn building and rebuilding programme evident in estate records for central and southeastern England during the later eighteenth century shows. But there is also evidence that networks of lending and borrowing to finance local farm improvement were more extensive and more active than had been the case earlier in the eighteenth century. The farming memoranda book of Rowland Parke from Kirkby Lonsdale provides a particularly good example of this trend. In the early part of his book, the central concerns for Parke were how much his servants would be paid for the year, where he sold his produce and upon what terms. By the 1790s, however, he was lending Mr Picard, a local gentleman farmer, £210, and Edward Beaushaw (another farmer and the first person to become a dedicated clover grower in the area) £24, and by 1833 he had at least £430 out at interest to local farmers. At the same time, he himself had borrowed from other people for farm improvements. His creditors included Margaret Jackson, the widow of Samuel Jackson who was the first entrepreneur to produce a printed catalogue of hand-tools.[23] Much more work needs to be done on structures of finance for tenant farmers, but the key point is that by the later eighteenth century tenant farmers like Parke were investing in their plots and that their farming generated the money to invest and to lend.

Importantly, tenant farmers like Parke were also much more numerous by the later eighteenth century than they had been before. Customary tenure (by will of the Lord of the Manor, or according to the length of a number of lives) may well have continued in more peripheral agricultural areas such as Cumberland and Westmorland even into the nineteenth century. However, for the vast majority of those who owned land a process of consolidation (which was not necessarily linked to enclosure), more professional estate management and the need to make rents more responsive to market conditions gave an impetus to change the representative tenure to a fixed period of years. We know surprisingly little about the regional timing of this change in tenure arrangements, about whether it generated conflict or about its nature. Certainly, we should beware of assuming that tenure reform meant more productive farming. In good times the landlord had the option to easily remove or not renew the leases of those tenants who did not come up to scratch. However, numerous estate records suggest that questions of morality and custom continued to pervade many tenancy arrangements, and even good and efficient tenants could be removed because of a moral lapse. In bad times, when the supply of farms exceeded the supply of tenants with the knowledge and capital to run them, the tenancy system could break down and result in farms lying empty or being rented to inappropriate people, retarding the growth of agricultural output in a locality. Nonetheless, as a crude generalisation, it might be appropriate to suggest that new tenancy arrangements coming into force between the late seventeenth and late nineteenth centuries gave landlords all of the personal knowledge about their tenants that customary tenure had offered, but more flexibility than the older system in terms of rent levels and of who they accepted as tenants. In short, it is possible that new tenurial arrangements gave both tenants and their landlords a greater incentive to take an interest in efficient land management. There are few detailed anatomies of the farm renting process – some landlords advertised, some depended on word of mouth – but archives such as those of the Parker family certainly suggest that the process was one to which landowners came to devote detailed attention. Thus in 1775, 'William Folds, John Hindle and John Smith came to talk over taking Lane Head Farm. My son sets it on a term of 11 years, a clear yearly rent of 45 guineas a year.'[24] The renting of the farm took the entire evening and evidently involved detailed discussion of terms and conditions, as well as, we learn later, capital incentives for improvements made by the tenants.

We could go on with examples like these, but the key point is that detailed archival evidence does much to support generalisations which point logically to substantial improvements in the agrarian economic infrastructure of England before 1850. Indeed, most commentators agree on what the important nominal changes in the rural economy were – enclosure, new tenancy arrangements, drainage, better manuring practices – and they acknowledge a considerable rise in productivity even if they cannot agree on its exact magnitude. Where they disagree is on the timing of the changes to the agrarian economy (and therefore the productivity rise), the spatial distribution of changes and their overall significance. We consider the issue of regionality in the agrarian economy in the next section, but the inter-related questions of the timing of change and whether we can in fact see an agricultural revolution in the eighteenth and nineteenth centuries demand our immediate attention.

Logically, as Clark points out, there should be little dispute over the significance and timing of agrarian reorganisation and development. Rising real incomes and faster rates of population growth and urbanisation from the 1770s (and particularly after 1800) should have prompted the most rapid agrarian innovation and production growth from the late eighteenth century. As we have suggested already, Crafts subscribes to this idea. So does Wrigley, who suggests that there was a substantial rise in eighteenth-century labour productivity, partly underpinned by the greater use of horses.[25] And our archival material certainly supports the idea that there must have been very substantial eighteenth- and nineteenth-century adjustments to farming practice. However, Clark argues that such commonsense views are problematic, and that at the level of individual crops the most spectacular increases in yield per acre were achieved before 1770, and largely before 1700. Allen likewise casts doubt on the likelihood of revolutionary productivity gains between 1750 and 1850.[26] The heroic advances which are often seen to lie at the heart of an eighteenth-century agricultural revolution, and which are brought to life so well by our archival material – enclosure, better drainage and a better appreciation of the role of manuring – can be seen to have had much deeper chronological roots. Turnips, clover, swedes, the watering of meadows, and initial attempts at animal and plant breeding were seventeenth-century innovations in the most progressive rural counties of the south and east. Parliamentary enclosure, the epitome of eighteenth-century advance, affected 21 per cent of the cultivatable acreage but a larger proportion of total acreage had been regularised through enclosure by agreement or piecemeal creation of closes well before the two peaks of parliamentary enclosure in the late eighteenth century. We could go on with examples like this. For now, the contention of Clark that, 'There was no agricultural revolution between the early eighteenth and mid nineteenth centuries, merely modest productivity gains',[27] is significant and picks up on a wider body of literature that talks of agricultural evolution, running anywhere from the Black Death to the great depression of the later nineteenth century, rather than agricultural revolution.

As Clark reminds us, it is possible that commentators have overstated the scale of agricultural advance needed to feed a growing late eighteenth-century population, given a transfer of labour to occupations requiring less calorific intake, and that they may also, whatever the recent thoughts of Wrigley on stillbirths, have overstated the degree to which real wage rises underpinned increasing demand for food.[28] Jackson has likewise suggested that the most significant changes in English agriculture predated 1750, and that the ability to feed a rapidly growing population had thus been latent for a considerable time by the early nineteenth century. Indeed, at the very time it would be logical to expect rapid growth of agricultural output and productivity rates during the later eighteenth century, the rate of growth was actually falling off.[29]

Kussmaul's study of marriage seasonality has provided substantial support for the idea of a seventeenth-century development spurt, arguing that the really fundamental changes to the landscape of farming were a seventeenth-century phenomenon associated with the rise of distinct agricultural regions where none had existed before. Put crudely, Kussmaul suggests that by 1740 the relatively homogeneous arable production that had characterised the early seventeenth century had been replaced with a broadly pastoral 'west', a broadly arable 'east' and 'south', and a mixed industrial, arable and pastoral 'Midlands'. In turn, specialising agricultural regions connected by increasingly elaborate trade routes bolstered total output. And they did so without increasing inputs or resorting to new productivity-raising techniques, offering support to those who see a latent ability in English agriculture to respond to higher demand as early as the first few decades of the eighteenth century. By contrast, in the 1780s and 1790s the relatively rigid regional specialisations in place for over a century had begun to break down due to the incentive that high grain prices gave to converting marginal land in all regions. Consequently, some of the benefits to productivity that regional specialisation could generate were undermined at the very time when notional demand for higher productivity should have been felt most keenly.[30] Both Jackson and Kussmaul suggest that the changes of the seventeenth century provided a solid launchpad for future innovation on a wide regional basis, and they implicitly accept the rosy view of English agricultural achievements with which we began this chapter. Hudson disagrees, suggesting that the pace of agricultural change after 1750 was insufficient to prevent rising prices for basic foodstuffs, crowding out higher demand for industrial products and thus acting as a brake on the whole Industrial Revolution process.[31]

Students of the Industrial Revolution thus face a straight choice between two historiographical viewpoints. One locates the seat of widespread change in the English agricultural economy in the eighteenth and nineteenth centuries and interprets these changes as broadly revolutionary. The other sees the changes of the eighteenth century underpinned by a raft of gradual developments from at least 1600 and interprets the later changes at most as one part of a process of evolution. Reconciling these very different perspectives is a difficult task. It is important, for instance, to judge developments in the agrarian economy against what was possible, not what was desirable. In the absence of chemical fertilisers, land fertility remained one of the major constraints on agricultural output and advances in agricultural productivity. Not until the very end of our period had this constraint even begun to give way. We must also beware of underplaying – as so many agricultural history textbooks seem to do – the weather. Eighteenth- and nineteenth-century farmers remained heavily dependent upon the vagaries of the weather, and poor harvests over a run of years could depress notional aggregate numbers of the sort we cited at the start of this section. The records of farmers are littered with references to weather problems. One nineteenth-century farmer commented that:

> The spring of 1802 being remarkably dry this field did not seem likely to grass well. I had it bush harrowed but the weather still continuing dry the grass made but little progress. I then put 10 pounds clover seeds and 10 pounds trefoil and having sowed it had the ground well rolled. The crop of hay was light not more than 2 tons upon an acre.[32]

These were disappointing returns on so much capital and labour input, and highlight the need for a realistic yardstick against which to judge both aggregate numbers and the economic outcomes of individual processes such as enclosure or animal breeding.

The recent work of Mark Overton provides one way forward. Questioning the tendency to underplay the achievements of English agriculture after 1700, he suggests that we need to give more weight to two fundamental developments in a process of re-establishing the notion of an eighteenth- and early nineteenth-century agricultural revolution.[33] The first is the considerable rise in total productivity (compared to what was possible at the time). The second is the change that occurred in the social and institutional structure of rural society to accommodate the rise of aggressive agrarian capitalism. Part of this 'process' involves Overton in taking an overtly regionalised view of the agricultural revolution. In the same way that chapter two shows relatively small areas to have provided the heartbeat of a narrowly defined *Industrial* Revolution, so Overton suggests that the agricultural revolution in strict economic terms must also be understood as a phenomenon played out most intensively on individual farms within a structure of leading and lagging regional agrarian economies. Thinking of the agricultural revolution against this backdrop means that we must attach considerable significance to even limited land and labour productivity rises in the eighteenth century. Meanwhile, another part of the process of re-establishing an agricultural revolution is to understand the notion of 'revolution' in the round – encompassing social, institutional and cultural as well as more traditional economic variables. Aggregate productivity numbers and stories of agricultural change of the sort which we have so far deployed in this chapter provide only a partial index of the degree to which rural society as a whole changed for those who lived in it during the eighteenth and nineteenth centuries. In other words, to understand the changes which did occur after 1700 and to locate them within the broad sweep of agricultural and economic history, we must understand the regionality of the process by which initial advances become generalised techniques. We must also include in our assessment some of the wider impact which nuts-and-bolts changes in farming practice and structure stimulated. These two tasks will lie at the heart of the rest of this chapter as we attempt briefly to understand whether there is a case for re-establishing the English agricultural revolution.

## The regionality of the agrarian economy

Were changes in agricultural output caused or accompanied by an increasing regional specialisation in the rural economy? What were the effects of this regional concentration if it existed? Does an understanding of regionality help in confirming or denying that an agricultural revolution was played out during the eighteenth century? Asking and answering questions like these is complicated in at least four senses. First, the term 'agriculture' masks a number of different production specialisms (wheat, barley, oats, sheep, cows, pigs and market gardening to mention just a few) which could be followed in combination or singly at any point in time by the individual farmer and which could change markedly over time in a given area. Some areas, for instance the northern uplands, were consigned by their basic topography to long-enduring forms of agricultural production, and little changed or could change between 1700 and 1850. Farmers and landowners in other areas, such as the Lincolnshire Wolds or the

Essex plains, could switch production between arable, pastoral and specialist production of items like vegetables with relative ease.[34] In this case, our patchy and relatively static historical sources can at best offer only a broad characterisation of 'regional' production systems.

Second, to decide whether there was a regionality to the rural economy we must understand what the term 'region' means and have some way of recognising how the boundaries of these 'regions' changed over time. As our basic unit of analysis, we might classify farming areas according to the type of production (mixed, arable, cereal, specialist), topography, markets, farm size, proximity to centres of urban demand or perhaps penetration of industry in the rural occupational structure. Yet, even if we had the primary data to undertake this sort of mapping exercise (which by and large we do not), different 'regions' would overlap and generate a problem of how to cull the essence of the regionality of the agrarian economy. Joan Thirsk suggested two ways of making sense of this complex problem. One is to distinguish three main types of 'region' (arable, intermediate and pastoral), distinguishing eight sub-types under these general headings.[35] The other, and more intuitively appealing, is to refer to the French term, *pays* – areas given some unity by their topography and soil typology. Thirsk identified (figure 6.1) a number of these 'regions', running from the fells and moorlands of the north-west and north to the marshlands of Essex, Kent and Hampshire.[36] These perspectives are useful, but 'regions' drawn in this way are still relatively static entities when in some senses the changing regional boundaries are part and parcel of unlocking the significance of changes in agriculture and the contribution of regional concentration to the overall increase in production.

The third problem is that however we choose to draw spatial boundaries there were also substantial intra-regional differences in farming practices between the most and least efficient farms and the most and least efficient sub-regions. Overton thus calls for 'more specific regions, appropriate to the particular question being addressed', and continues, 'Where it is possible, the individual elements of the rural economy should be mapped separately, unless there is a demonstrable, consistent link between them.'[37] What happens to our understanding of the rural economy and its achievements if we start to map some of the individual components of change as Overton suggests? Figures 6.2 to 6.5 undertake a small part of this task, mapping respectively the geography of parliamentary enclosure, the proportion

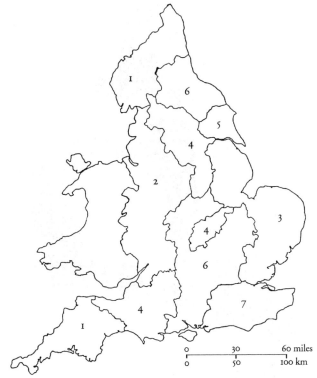

*Key:* 1 Moorland   2 Pastoral   3 Fenland and low-lying arable
4 Forest and wold   5 Down and moorland   6 Arable
7 Forest and arable

**Figure 6.1** English 'local countries', *c.*1720. This is a simplified version of the model offered by Thirsk. The broad regional divisions exclude much sub-regional detail, particularly in terms of the existence of forest lands, but at this stage such abstractions reveal more than they conceal

of the 1851 labour force employed in agriculture, the percentage of farm servants in the agricultural labour force and the percentage of the occupiers of land who employed labour (acting as a proxy for farm size). Of course these are relatively clumsy and absolutely static instruments but unfortunately we are still very far away from the year-by-year and place-by-place mapping that we ideally need.

Nonetheless, a 'virtual' synthesis of these maps would begin to suggest that there were distinctive agrarian regions to mirror the

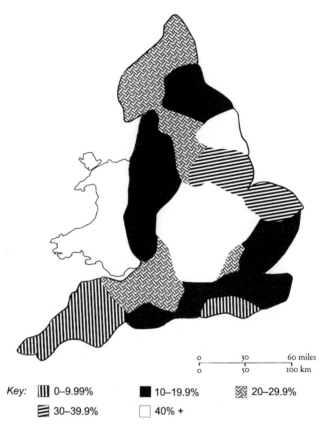

**Figure 6.2** Proportion of county acreages (fields and commons) affected
by parliamentary enclosure, 1750–1850

industrial regions outlined in chapter two. These may be familiar,
and can largely still be seen in England today. The Midland counties,
East Anglia and the southeast experienced the heaviest parliamentary
enclosure and these were also the areas where traditional relations
between employers and labourers appear to have changed most, where
new tenancy arrangements developed fastest, and where aggregate
farm sizes grew the most. Within this general framework, it was
places such as Norfolk or Berkshire that experienced the most fundamental changes in landscape, work practices and the organisation
of farming during the eighteenth century.

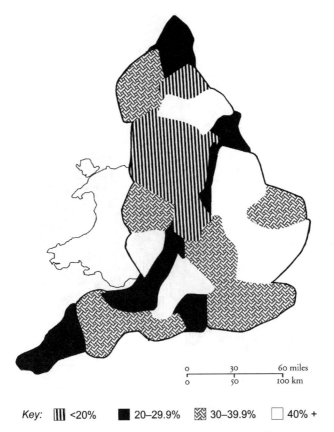

Key:  [|||] <20%   ■ 20–29.9%   ▧ 30–39.9%   ☐ 40% +

**Figure 6.3** Proportion of county labour forces employed in agriculture,
1851

We have already encountered Kussmaul's idea that the east and
the southeast had come to specialise in arable production during the
late seventeenth century, and during the eighteenth century this trend
was to continue, with a particular focus on the commercial production
of wheat. Such regional specialisation drove forward cereal productivity and total output in much the same way that textile production
in Lancashire provided the heartbeat of industrial development.

These maps are ill-suited to really pinning down the regionality of
the pastoral trade, but the wider historiographical literature once
again identifies key 'regions' such as Staffordshire and Cheshire where

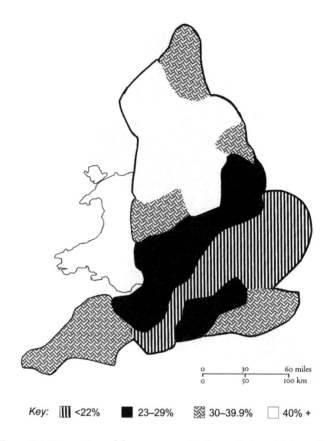

Key: ▌▌▌ <22%　■ 23–29%　▨ 30–39.9%　☐ 40% +

**Figure 6.4** Proportion of farm servants in the agricultural labour force,
*c.* 1831

specialisation according to regional comparative advantage contributed to powerful rises in both total output and land and labour
productivity. Kussmaul and Thirsk are clearly correct to emphasise the
ancient origins of these broad cow and corn regions, but it seems likely
that the impetus of better transport, sustained home demand (arising
out of population growth and urbanisation) and the lure of the foreign
marketplace during the eighteenth century served both to increase the
intensity of specialisation and to foster the inter-regional integration
that was required to optimise the output possibilities of such specialisation. We return to this issue in the final section of the chapter.

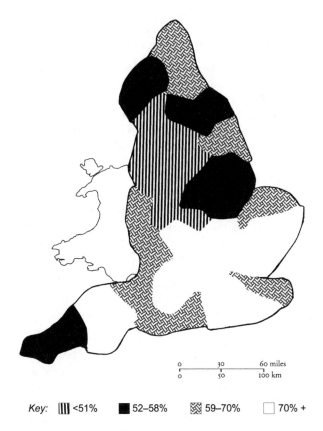

Key:  ||| <51%   ■ 52–58%   ▨ 59–70%   □ 70% +

**Figure 6.5** Proportion of owner-occupiers employing labour, *c*.1831

These broad conclusions on regionality are inherently appealing. Norfolk, Suffolk and the 'home counties' were at the forefront of agricultural innovation in the seventeenth century and such roots must necessarily have contributed to a strong productivity performance. Similarly, Cheshire farmers had been specialising in pastoral production for at least two centuries by 1800, and it is reasonable to suppose that they knew a thing or two about pastoral farming. On the ground, this regionality was played out in subtle ways – in knowledge of crops for instance. Richard Hodgkinson in 1801 noted:

> The wheat Croft I gave 5 plowings and 2 harrowings and on 1st June sowed it with Swedish turnip seed ... They came up very well, but

179

having no person who understood hoeing them, and being busy in the hay harvest, they became overrun with weed. After hay harvest I had all the weed drawn up by hand which cost me 30s.[38]

The costs of this ignorance were considerable, approaching sixpence per bushel of harvested crop, so that Lilford made a loss on this experiment. The same sorts of mistakes were unlikely to have been made in, say, Lincolnshire (which had 19 per cent of its cultivated land under turnips in 1801) where, even if Lilford had had no knowledge, neighbouring estates would have been able to share their own experiences. This sort of pooled knowledge is an example of what economists call externalities – benefits from concentration of production that reduce costs or increase output without requiring more capital and labour input at the level of the individual business – which remains one of the key benefits of specialisation. Meanwhile, in 1803 the Lilford estate steward was in Wiltshire, and he observed that:

The hay ... does not seem nutritious or well flavor'd. This I conceive may partly be owing to it being impossible to cover so large a tract of meadows with dung as frequently as might be wished, and of course the grass must become dry and tasteless. The farmers use no lime, or purchase any species of manure whatever. Their corn land is manured solely by folding of sheep, and without this they c'd get no corn. They fallow and fold for wheat; then take a crop of oats laid down with grass seeds, mow the clover etc. the third year and fallow and fold the fourth, and this is their scale of cropping. Upon this scale they say they only get a crop in 4 years, that is, they are unwilling to call anything a crop but wheat.[39]

By implication Hodgkinson was comparing the situation in Wiltshire unfavourably with his own farming on the Lancashire plain. If accurately observed, then the attitude of farmers in Wiltshire to cropping and manuring would also seem very backward compared with the imaginative and systematic approaches taken by many farmers in places like Norfolk or Northamptonshire. Such observations represent regionality in action, and they clearly suggest the existence of leading and lagging sectors in the agrarian economy.

Yet, the Hodgkinson material also suggests some of the weaknesses in the impression of regionality conveyed by figures 6.2 to 6.5 and the accompanying narrative. Lancashire is often portrayed as one of the more backward counties in agrarian terms in the eighteenth and nineteenth centuries, and yet here we have Hodgkinson lamenting the poor farming practices of an agrarian county. While it is true that many farmers in north Lancashire understood as little about rotations and manuring as did their counterparts in Wiltshire, tenant farmers on the Lancashire plain or in the Fylde – the so-called bread basket of Lancashire – were as well acquainted with the most advanced techniques as their counterparts on larger farms in Norfolk or Berkshire. Our broad-brush picture of regionality does not allow for this sort of experience. Nor can it, for figures 6.2 to 6.5 map only proxy variables for what we would really like to have, namely a county-by-county or region-by-region hierarchy of productivity growth or agricultural innovation. While the work of Overton has given us very detailed estimates of arable productivity using data from Norfolk probate inventories, this work has not been duplicated in other arable areas let alone pastoral regions.[40] And even if it had been, inventories give us reliable and substantial data only up to the early decades of the eighteenth century. By implication, our maps highlight the *fourth* problem with trying to map the regionality of agrarian England in the sense that they both simplify the complex process of farming and divorce farming from its institutional, social and cultural context.

As Overton has suggested, productivity, the timing of innovation within and between agricultural regions, and the interaction between agricultural regions are important questions. But to really understand whether there was an agricultural revolution, and to locate the changes in agriculture within the framework of the Industrial Revolution, we must understand the complexities of the farming process as a whole. From the point of view of the farmer, this involved growing cash and other crops, engaging and managing labour, serving local offices, going to church, buying stock, engaging with other farmers and landowners, paying taxes, finding and buying seeds, dealing with day-to-day disasters like the stock getting into the fields of other farmers, and managing the social side of rural life from weddings and funerals to fairs and dinners. The diary of James Newton of Nuneham Courtenay in Oxfordshire (1736–86) provides an excellent example of the process of farming.[41] On 14 March 1759 he 'Draw'd home faggots from forewood and begun plowing turnip land'.[42] In the same month he talked on several occasions with the major local landowner Lord Harcourt about farming matters, exchanged land with other owners to create more contiguous holdings, slaughtered some pigs, and collected and paid rent. A close reading of his diary suggests that in the course of an average agricultural year, he might have to undertake a couple of hundred different farming or farming-related tasks. The entries for the week between 11 and 18 August 1759 provide some idea of the variety of the tasks and concerns:

> William Field and another made an estimate of the damage done by my asses at Clifton. The cows got out of Long Mead ... Begun making a wheat rick at Tom Anderson's. Us'd one of my Lord's teams. The cart ladder could not be found. James Lawrence cut down a tree in the rong place. Nine load of wheat from Forewood and five from Nineveh ... Finish'd the first wheat rick and begun another. Lord Harcourt came here ... Finish'd the second wheat rick and begun a little one in my lower yard. Sent Winter and his wife to reap beans. William Clark finished my last land of wheat ... a carriage kill'd a small hog ... Pounded a sow and two pigs out of Windmill Field ... Ball began mowing barley ... Paid one year's Land and Window tax ... Brought a calves head.[43]

This was quite apart from the seven social occasions which living in a rural society obliged him to attend during the same week. Other actors within the rural economy had an equally complex set of experiences, and so the question is not just whether we get more corn or cows per acre over time, but how the whole process of being a farmer or labourer changed. Equally, in order to decide whether there was an agricultural revolution and what its regional manifestations were, we must also have an appreciation of how the whole tenor of rural life changed or remained the same during the eighteenth and nineteenth centuries.

Visualising rural life in this way given the current state of our knowledge is clearly impossible. However, figure 6.6 offers something a little different. It combines the broad regional thrust suggested by figures 6.2 to 6.5 with our appreciation of the degree of cultural, social and institutional change in rural society after 1750 gleaned from reading numerous diaries, letters, newspaper reports, the proceedings of commissions of inquiry and secondary studies of regions and localities.

What the map portrays is a broad 'index of change' for the period 1750–1850. A rating of 1 or 2 suggests very little change in economic and social life and a rating of 8 suggests the wholesale transformation of rural society. The map is purely speculative and we cannot rely on the observations to be drawn from it. However, let us speculate

**Figure 6.6** An index of change in the social, cultural and economic life of rural England, 1700–1850. An index score of 1 implies little change to rural economy and society in the region as a whole. A figure of 5 implies moderate and incremental change. A score of 7 or more implies both substantial and relatively rapid change

a little further for effect. If we were to accept this index approach, then it is clear that rural life was transformed first and furthest in East Anglia and the southeast in the vicinity of London. The broadly defined 'home counties' and Midlands experienced radical change in economic, social, cultural and institutional life. These 'regions' will be familiar from the earlier discussion. However, less obvious centres of change also stand out; rural Lancashire south of the river Ribble, Staffordshire, the northern part of the West Riding bordering on the North Riding and some of the West Country as it was forced to adapt to the loss of rural industry. The latter places may have contributed little to aggregate productivity figures, but they stand out more strongly in a widely defined search for an agricultural revolution because they seem to have experienced profound and relatively rapid change in economic, social or cultural structures. By contrast, a broadly defined west, and particularly northwest, merits relatively low scores on our index. Again, these will be familiar 'regions' from the foregoing discussion, but once more there are a few surprises. In the East Riding, for instance, productivity increases in cereal production may have made a significant contribution to aggregate numbers, but that productivity rise was achieved in the face of continuity of method and in the wider process of farming. Farm servants, for instance, survived longer here than elsewhere. The county thus merits only a low rating on our scale.

This map may be entirely spurious. Even if it is not, other commentators might draw different boundaries; some might give Dorset a higher rating than Lincolnshire, or Leicestershire might attract a higher score than Cambridgeshire instead of the rough parity that we have assigned them. The ultimate fact remains, however, that counties such as Durham, West Yorkshire, Cumberland, Westmorland, Devon, Shropshire, Dorset, Nottinghamshire did not, despite their largely rural status, contribute substantially to the productivity increases, social upheavals and institutional transformations that we must come to regard as synonymous with the notion of 'agricultural revolution'. To borrow the words of Hudson and Berg on the Industrial Revolution, the agricultural revolution was a region-specific process that added up to more than the sum of its parts. And while much more work needs to be done on identifying these 'parts' our map does at least have the advantage of making sense when set against other yardsticks. The poverty experiences of those places to which we attach a high rating lay behind the formation of the new poor law, and also behind earlier attempts to regulate poor relief through select vestries. Moreover, there is also evidence that the development of a class of wealthy landowners and tenants in the regions to which we ascribe a high rating lay at the heart of some of the regional dimensions of the consumption revolution in the eighteenth century, as considered in chapter five. We make no rash claims for the value of this discussion, but to return to the questions with which we started this section, it is clear that there was a regionality to the development of agrarian England, and it is possible, indeed probable, that the very fact of this regionality should encourage us to think in terms of what Overton labels an agrarian revolution. The rest of the chapter develops this theme.

## The social fabric of rural England

Rightly or wrongly, figure 6.6 suggests that by incorporating an appreciation of the course of non-economic variables into the search for an agricultural revolution our characterisation of developments post–1700 experiences subtle changes. This section looks at a few of those non-economic indicators – the social outcomes of enclosure, rural unrest and experiences of poverty – concentrating particularly on those areas to which we ascribed high ratings in figure 6.6. We could have looked at other areas and other themes. The consolidation of a tripartite landholding and working structure – landlord/tenant/landless labourer – within a framework of largely enclosed fields during the eighteenth and early nineteenth centuries changed fundamentally the life experiences of the vast majority of rural workers, and is ripe for a detailed and regionalised discussion, for instance. As elsewhere in this book, however, our aim is not to provide a shallow and easily digestible overview, but to encourage new ways of thinking about established problems.

Let us first turn to the question of the parliamentary enclosure process and its social outcomes.[44] The recent willingness of historians to return to traditions of historical writing current in the 1960s and to tell stories of enclosure and its effects, rather than simply trying to measure the quantifiable aspects of enclosure, can help us here. Indeed, the 'story' surrounding the enclosure of Otmoor near Oxford is particularly instructive for those wanting to gauge whether enclosure was 'revolutionary'. This was an area of perhaps 1,800 acres of common land bordered by seven villages. Some of the residents from these villages held the 'right of common' while others used the common by customary rather than legal right. The first move to formally enclose the common was made in 1777 by a prominent local landowner and a draft bill for the enclosure of the common was put before parliament in 1788. However, the Earl of Abingdon, another major local landowner, sided with 149 other protestors from the seven villages (not all of whom held common rights) to defeat the draft bill. A second attempt to enclose was made in 1801, but the passage of the final enclosure bill was not until 1815 and the enclosure process was not formally completed until 1829 as the principal beneficiaries of the enclosure argued over issues such as tithes. In all, the enclosure process from start to finish had taken fifty-two years. This is an extreme example (though not unusual in Oxfordshire), but it does highlight the point that enclosure did not just 'happen'. Where it was undertaken under the auspices of a parliamentary bill it required someone to organise the vote of the owners of three-quarters of the land, it involved sponsoring the bill through parliament, the appointment of commissioners, hearings to establish rights of common, redrawing the landscape of the village (often with new roads and bridges and always with new fences and hedges and different access to water supplies), and it involved the formal payment of fees and squabbling over minor issues such as tithes and rights of way. At each stage the enclosure process could be short-circuited, and perhaps one-fifth of all potential enclosures never made it to the final 'signing off' stage. More importantly, that the enclosure process under law was so drawn out and the taking of common rights with little or no compensation so transparent, left plenty of room for festering divisions in rural society.

This is precisely what happened in Otmoor, and while the protest outlined below is just one example and form of the covert and direct unrest and dispute that we can see all over rural England, it acts as a useful focus for the issues that we need to explore here. Thus, in 1830 the decision of a local judge to release prisoners apprehended for breaking the banks of a river diverted in the Otmoor enclosure process questioned the validity of the whole enclosure movement in the locality and was the starting point for a concerted outburst of fence and hedge breaking by those dispossessed of common rights. There was a mass demonstration on 6 September 1830, and hostilities resumed again on some scale in 1832 and 1833 when 150 men mounted a campaign of guerilla warfare against the physical symbols of the enclosure process. Even in counties such as Northamptonshire, where enclosure seems to have been more rapid than in Oxfordshire, enclosure meant considerable changes to the local landscape and social and economic life, and might generate very considerable unrest.[45]

Of course, interpretations of the significance of common rights and entitlement to them in the first place, and hence of the significance of the loss of those common rights, vary considerably. Snell and Neeson regard common rights as an important supplement to the household economies of labouring people and therefore their loss was catastrophic, especially in the sense that enclosure also changed labour patterns and compromised the employment of women in rural areas.[46] Generally the areas assigned high scores in figure 6.6 were also areas of substantial (parliamentary and non-parliamentary) enclosure and we have attached considerable weight to this fact. Other historians have been less keen on the idea that enclosure had purely negative consequences, suggesting that heavy exploitation of the commons, the impact of encroachment and limited rights to common in the first place meant that their loss was only a minor economic blip, whatever the psychological impact of full proletariani-sation. Even Chambers and Mingay suggested that enclosure created more economic opportunities than it destroyed, so that there may have been a net addition to welfare.[47] In any case, it has been suggested, we have often been beguiled into focusing on parliamentary enclosure when much the most significant elimination of common and common rights had been achieved before 1750. Historical opinion is even divided over how we should interpret the Otmoor incidents. After all, the protestors of the 1830s would have had almost twenty years to get used to the idea of enclosure, and it might be argued that the protests represented less opposition to enclosure than general and temporary discontent in the countryside of the south and east during the 1830s.[48]

We return to this theme shortly, but what seems certain is that in the Otmoor case the number of people with access to land, however we might value that access as objective historians, fell by over 70 per cent during the enclosure process. Those who had used the commons but had no 'rights' lost access except in the sense of allotments which were given to each township in the enclosure process for the benefit of the poor. Those who gained some land through the compensation for common rights or who already had small plots augmented by an additional allowance in lieu of common right had to find the cost of enclosing their own fields and also a contribution to the common pot for funding new bridges, roads and river diversion. So while the number of small 'owners' nominally increased after the enclosure was formally finished, their number fell precipitously within three years as they sold out to larger landowners and tenants. Average farm size in the seven villages increased by 25 per cent between 1826 and 1836 and the end of the enclosure process marks the start of a relative (to other rural Oxfordshire villages) and in some years absolute depopulation process which was not to be reversed until the twentieth century.

Ambiguous evidence and the different strains of ideological baggage that historians bring to their analysis of the enclosure movement means that debates over the social outcome of enclosure will continue. However, taking students out to Otmoor, showing them old and new bridges, old and new houses and tracing the changing course of the river demonstrates very forcibly the degree of change that local people must have seen in the fabric of their communities. Accordingly, it is unsurprising to learn of strained social relations between landlords or tenants and those who did not benefit from enclosure. In turn, it is for reasons such as this – rather than its advanced farming techniques – that Oxfordshire is assigned a relatively high value in figure 6.6. The tenor of life changed and, as in neighbouring counties such as Northamptonshire, parliamentary enclosure and its social outcomes held the key to this change.

Meanwhile, we should not forget that the Otmoor incident took place within the context of widespread rural unrest in the south, east and Midlands during the 1820s and 1830s. Students will be familiar with relatively isolated incidents of animal maiming, rick burning, fence breaking and ducking which collectively have come to be known as the Swing Riots. These are capable of being interpreted as a radical class statement or an expression of the stagnant economic situation in many rural parishes of the south and east of England.[49] However, there is a danger of focusing too narrowly on this issue. Townships and parishes throughout rural England were in practice faced by serious but less well-publicised forms of unrest and social tension that say much more about the changing dynamics of rural society by the 1830s. Such tensions were apparent at all levels of society. The select vestry system introduced formally in 1818 and 1819 provided a forum for major ratepayers to play out their political and social divisions, such that whereas the rural select vestries of the north of England came to police the poor with considerable efficiency, in the south select vestries were often paralysed by endemic in-fighting. The payment of rates swelled by the demands of the poor law also provided a focus of discontent, with distraint of goods for non-payment of rates much more common after 1800 than it had been before, and with rate strikes in 150 parishes or townships in the south and Midlands between 1790 and 1834. Non-resident vicars, the increasing intrusion of extra-local officials into the day-to-day running of anything from schools to markets, and conflicts between old and new money in urban hinterlands, all added to the pressures which can be seen to have built up in nineteenth-century rural society, particularly in the south and east.

For the poor and labouring people trying to keep together ever weaker family economies (a subject to which we return in Part III), the growing tensions of rural society were strongly felt. Leisure practices were undergoing considerable modification, and while it has been usual to focus on seaside holidays and urban leisure patterns, those of the increasingly poor rural labourer also deserve some attention in understanding the changing fabric of rural society. Nineteenth-century middle-class attempts to reform leisure practices so as to eliminate the ale house and the 'sports' involving animal cruelty or violence weighed heavily on traditional rural pastimes, particularly in the small parishes of the south and east. Bare-knuckle boxing, cock throwing, bull baiting and hare coursing all suffered under the drive to reform leisure, and while the number of ale houses rose significantly in urban areas during the Industrial Revolution, their number often fell in rural areas. In the seven villages surrounding Otmoor, for instance, the number of ale houses fell from eleven in 1821 to just six in 1834. Even without the moral imperative, movements like enclosure whittled away opportunities for leisure by enclosing the spaces where traditional pursuits had been followed. In Oxfordshire, for instance, the number of village fairs actively celebrated fell by more than half between 1770 and 1820, and by half again between 1820 and 1850 as common land and village greens were abolished totally or cut back and put to other uses. Beset by a changing landscape, changing work practices and clumsy attempts to shape leisure time, it is small wonder that sporadic outbursts of protest and minor vandalism became more common from the 1780s and 1790s. Such tensions and explosions of unrest were less common in those areas such as Cumberland, Westmorland, the North and West Riding and Somerset where relatively large areas of common and waste remained well into the nineteenth century. It is for this reason, as well as for their limited farming improvements, that these areas achieve only moderate rankings in figure 6.6.

Other strands in the fabric of rural life were also changing, though again more so in some places than others. By the later eighteenth century wealth and poverty, as we will see in later chapters, were becoming polarised in a much more obvious way than had been the case before. The consumer revolution reviewed in chapter five opened up to the families of landlords, tenant farmers, larger butchers and others amongst village ratepayers by the 1780s and 1790s a richer variety of domestic possessions and the ability to tap into fashions of dress and diet in a way that would not have been possible in 1730. Small towns like Bury St Edmunds had by the early nineteenth century become year-round (rather than seasonal) magnets for rural social elites from a wide range of surrounding villages, providing milliners, booksellers, clockmakers, cakemakers, teachers and quacks to relieve increasingly heavy rural purses, and providing also assembly rooms, baths and reading rooms. There was much money to be made here, as the records of the Oakes family show, but the opposite side of the coin is that if more and more money was being spent by rural elites in Bury St Edmunds, less and less was being spent in the localities from which these local elites were drawn.[50] Occupational information from the parish registers of eleven of the small villages around Bury St Edmunds between 1813 and 1830 suggests that these communities were progressively denuded of their traditional crafts, with blacksmiths, cabinet makers, bakers and shoemakers disappearing over time. Meanwhile, a tour of these eleven villages today demonstrates very clearly a rebuilding during the first half of the nineteenth century which on purpose or by accident had tended to cut off the increasingly wealthy elites from their poorer neighbours with fences, hedges and walls. No longer did the poor and the wealthy live side by side; the geography of social status had changed, in this town at least.

This is important, because there were ever more poor people and they were increasingly poor. The national statistics are reviewed in later chapters, but for now it is important to note that rural counties by 1802/3 accounted for eight of the ten poorest counties expressed in terms of the percentage of the population on poor relief or the amount of poor relief expenditure per head. What is more, as later chapters will argue, there was a progressively greater chance of poverty being a whole-life experience and of children inheriting the poverty of parents. These were significant changes from the situation in the early eighteenth century, and they were felt most keenly in all of the regions save one to which we have ascribed high index values in figure 6.6.[51] In the villages surrounding Bury St Edmunds, and in the town itself, the growing 'poverty problem' resulted in a trebling of the number on poor relief between 1790 and 1830, two workhouse riots, two collections amongst the major ratepayers to meet the dire circumstances of particular years and a problem of begging that had reached epidemic proportions by 1815.[52]

Part III takes up the poor-law theme. There were also important changes to rural demography, rural architecture, the rural household economy, the nature of the rural labour force, and the nature of rural migration patterns, and these are addressed in some depth in Part III as well. What we have tried to do in this brief chapter is to follow up our suggestion that understanding the agricultural revolution is about more than counting cows and corn. It is also about more than tracing the regionality of economic variables. We must understand changes in the process of farming, heroic movements like parliamentary enclosure and the aggregate productivity numbers. But we must also understand what was happening to the fabric of rural society if we are to make a case for an agrarian revolution. Instead of asking whether productivity growth rates accelerated or decelerated after 1700, we need to be asking how the experience of being a landowner, tenant farmer or labourer changed in the eighteenth century. In doing so, our contention is that a distinct hierarchy of leading and lagging regions emerges and that collectively these experiences of rapid and more serene change amount to an agrarian revolution of the sort that Overton suggests we look for. In the final section of this chapter, we will argue that changes in the way that agricultural produce was sold adds to our impression of a revolutionary period in English agriculture during the eighteenth and early nineteenth centuries.

## Changes in the marketing and distribution of agricultural produce

As with the industrial products mentioned in chapter five, there were substantial pressures to change the way in which agricultural produce was marketed after 1700. One was growing urbanisation. By 1750, London accounted for around 12 per cent of the national population and thereafter, while its contribution to national totals remained roughly stable, the absolute numbers of its inhabitants grew hugely. Other urban areas were also growing. By 1750, 17.5 per cent of the population lived in towns of more than 10,000 people, well above the European average, and the urban industrial growth that followed created an inexorably increasing demand for agricultural produce on the part of urban dwellers. While towns like Bristol and Liverpool retained urban dairies and other livestock keeping for much longer than is often realised (and while a vigorous glasshouse-based market gardening movement also developed within the confines of towns) most urban areas were substantially dependent upon their immediate hinterlands for perishable goods and on wider inter-regional and national markets for cereals and some livestock. Moreover, urban dwellers were relatively wealthy consumers. Williamson has done much to highlight the wage premiums which attached to urban work, and even when we make some allowance for the higher costs of rent and a notional monetary adjustment for poorer urban conditions, it is nonetheless true that the differences in effective wages and thus potential demand between urban and rural communities were significant.[53] London above all had a surplus of disposable income which filtered through to the regions, and it is no surprise to see some commentators contending that London stood at the hub of vigorous demands for agricultural produce at a national level in the eighteenth and nineteenth centuries. Indeed, Chartres suggests that in certain agricultural markets – those for meat and fresh produce for instance – London 'may have doubled its proportionate share'.[54] He also reminds us that England in the eighteenth century was an intermittent exporter of cereal products. While the exact magnitudes of the trade and the timing of its high and low points might be in dispute, what is not is that at certain times substantial amounts of wheat were exported. Richard Hodgkinson was in Worcester in 1795 and observed:

> I breakfasted at Worcester with a gentleman who was in the coach when I got in at Bromsgrove, who told me during breakfast that the day before he had been in company with an American captain who was just come from Brest, who informed him that he had seen 18 vessels laden with corn, 15 of which belonged to Liverpool, come into Brest-water and deliver their cargoes to the French.[55]

Trade on this scale necessarily involved wholesalers, middlemen and production to contract, as well as large-scale product-storage capacity, notions which would have been largely alien to the open-market retail culture still in force by 1750 when 'the market town and even market day remained the primary focus for trade'.[56] In chapter five, we pointed to the emergence of the same sort of middlemen in the selling and distribution of industrial goods.

Despite the intensifying forces making for changes in agricultural marketing in the eighteenth century, Chartres suggests that really significant steps were taken towards the creation of national and integrated regional food markets and 'a more mature marketing system' in the late seventeenth and early eighteenth centuries, as transport improvements began to make a national grain market a reality.[57] He concludes that, 'After 1700, at any rate, such were the flexibilities of the national market and transport system that the ultimate penalty for abandoning subsistence farming, the Malthusian famine, had effectively vanished from England and Wales'.[58] This is powerful language and imagery and its corollary must have been a decline in the business done by non-animal fairs (if not their number) and the emergence of challenges to the primacy of the open market as a forum for selling and buying agricultural produce. By implication, too, initial moves would have occurred to replace farmers' wives and hawkers as the main conduits between farmer and consumer with corn factors, merchants and more powerful drovers in the pastoral trade. Kussmaul likewise suggests the early emergence of a national market in key products such as wheat, tracing an intimate connection with the emerging regionality of the agricultural revolution in the seventeenth century, such that autonomous local markets in some products had gone by the turn of the eighteenth century.[59]

So, do we see an eighteenth-century revolution in agricultural marketing to mirror that in industry, or just the faster evolution of established trends? Certainly the changes of the seventeenth century were important, but attaching too much importance to them masks the complexity of agricultural production and lays too much importance on the early London experience. The wheat market may have been fully integrated at an early date, as might the market for rye. Certainly wheat prices in regional markets reacted in the same way and at roughly the same time to exogenous changes such as war. There was also a national market in seeds at an early date, as we have already implied. For other products (including oats and barley), however, regional markets and regional pricing systems were still the norm in the early eighteenth century. And while it is certainly true that the need to supply London stimulated places like Terling in Essex to adopt advanced farming practices at an early date, and provided an incentive for pastoral farmers everywhere to fatten and breed for Smithfield, the very fact of rapid agricultural development in the capital's immediate hinterlands reigned in some of the powerful tentacles which London directed towards English agricultural regions throughout the eighteenth century. More work needs to be done on the issue of the timing of advances in distribution and marketing. Meanwhile, O'Brien's contention that fundamental transport improvement was required to really create national markets and realise the latent potential of English agriculture seems inherently attractive.[60]

Even against this backdrop, we should avoid assumptions that transport 'improvements' were a sufficient stimulus to the development of wide spatial markets. While it is true, as Chartres reminds us, that most of the wheat needs of London were met by overland trade using packhorses and wagons right up to the 1830s, it is also true that the road system outside of the London nexus left plenty to be desired. One of Richard Hodgkinson's journeys took him to Tenbury in Herefordshire in 1794, and he noted:

> I passed three toll-gates, at 2 of which I paid before I got half way to Tenbury. In some places the road was so bad that I got over into the fields, and in other places the road leads thro the middle of corn fields for half a mile together without any fence on either side.[61]

On this road at least the damage to crops must have been considerable and the possibilities of transporting wagons of wheat or other agricultural produce largely non-existent. Transport improvement before the railways could do little to create national markets in products such as fruit and milk, and even in the early nineteenth century visits from traditional itinerant hawkers of food and other products were common. As well as functionally better (as opposed to nominally better) transport, the creation of national markets required tenant farmers with market knowledge and the flexibility to respond to changing market demands, the infrastructure to store products, a core of middlemen to create new conduits between farmer and producer, and new means of financing the inter-regional food trade.

Clearly we cannot cover all of these topics here, but it is important to note that traditional ways of doing business *were* waning by the mid-eighteenth century. Outside livestock selling, but even here, open markets and (to a lesser degree) fairs as a way of selling declined in favour of wholesale merchants, middlemen and fixed shops. This decline was not rapid nor regionally homogenous. Richard Hodgkinson visited Bristol in 1794 and noted that:

> The market is very well supplied with butchers meat of excellent quality ... Bristol is exceedingly well supplied with vegetables. Tis astonishing to see the quantities of all kinds of garden stuff produced in the market; there was also great abundance of fruit of all sorts.[62]

Bristol's port status helped of course, but we clearly see that Hodgkinson walked through an open market and that there must have been a considerable market gardening specialism around and inside Bristol. We must also be aware of the implication of the tone of Hodgkinson's observations that he did not see comparable markets in Lancashire. This perhaps shows how little he was in Preston and Manchester. Certainly Scola's authoritative work on the way in which the food needs of Manchester were met by road and canal testifies to a rich market culture in Manchester in particular, as we saw in chapter five.[63] Moreover, and paradoxically, Hodgkinson himself was engaged in the supply of urban open markets. In a letter to the renowned farmer John Curwen of Workington, he observed that:

> I hold a farm under his Lordship [Lilford] of abt one hundred and seventy statute acres, which lying in a populous neighbourhood, I employ a considerable part of it as a milk farm, raising a large quantity of meadow hay. I breed my own cows chiefly. One piece of land of abt 25 acres I stock with ewes bot at Chester Fair the last Thursday in Feby and sold at Michelmas, never wintering any sheep.[64]

Such testimony also suggests that animal fairs as the staple of the inter-regional animal trade were alive and well in the nineteenth century.

Yet, these caveats notwithstanding, the number and frequency of fairs and markets did decline. In those that remained, the work of Scola on Manchester and Thwaites on Oxfordshire demonstrates very powerfully that both the form and symbolism of marketing changed. The fixed stall replaced the itinerant stall, marketing times were formalised, women and other irregular sellers were driven out of the markets, and the customers changed from those buying small amounts to those buying larger amounts for local resale.[65] The same phenomenon can be observed in Leeds, where the Tuesday grain market was largely populated by 'customers' who bought by the bushel and then sold in their own localities by the peck. But, crucially, much produce by the later eighteenth century failed to make it to the retail market at all, being dealt with instead by wholesalers or contractors. The age-old role of wool factoring spawned many imitators as the eighteenth century wore on, and amongst the farming families whose records we used earlier the Parkers sold tallow, butter and cheese to local northeast Lancashire wholesalers, while Rowland Parke from Kirkby Lonsdale sold some of his produce to local people, but most of it went on contract before it was ever harvested to three Kendal wholesalers, Nicholas Huggan, Robert Cragg and John Parkinson. Even Richard Hodgkinson in his later years can be found walking around the Lilford estates talking to a factor who had come from Manchester to buy cereals on a sample basis. In the main grain-growing belt of the east and southeast (with high values in figure 6.6) these experiences were more common and more refined, and went hand in hand with new systems of credit to finance the delays in remuneration that middlemen and factors inevitably incurred. We can see similar experiences in the industrial sector, and whatever happened to productivity, the generation and regeneration of powerful national and inter-regional flows of agricultural produce, and the development of new methods of marketing that produce, add weight to interpretations which suggest the presence of an eighteenth- and nineteenth-century agricultural revolution.

We can perhaps demonstrate the importance of these observations by turning away from the ubiquitous focus on grain and cereal products to talk instead about the provision of herbs to a vigorously growing commercial medical marketplace from the later eighteenth century. While this may seem a strange way of ending a section on marketing, the growth of the trade in herbs probably far outstripped that in any other 'agricultural' produce, and the herb trade epitomises wider changes in the process of selling. Thus, the late seventeenth century had witnessed the initial publication of popular guides to herbs in book form for the first time. This coincided with the initial stirrings of a vibrant medical market which was, by the later eighteenth century, to lead to substantial demand for the services of all forms of formal practitioner, as well as a seemingly insatiable desire for the remedies of quacks and a deep interest amongst middling and other families in self-dosing. New medicines emerged even though understanding of disease and diagnosis changed relatively little in the key period of the formation of the medical marketplace. In particular, saffron became a recognised cure for fever amongst ordinary people. And while some of the ingredients for these medicines came from overseas (for instance opium), at base the eighteenth century medical marketplace was dominated by medicines, particularly for the middling and labouring people, that relied on herbs and herbal knowledge. Even many quack concoctions demanded the use of basic herbs.

Notwithstanding substantial urbanisation, herbs were a common feature of English hedgerows in the early nineteenth century and this was one potential source of supply. However, the recipes for medicine containing herbal ingredients become increasingly precise during the eighteenth century and measurements move from 'handfuls' or weights of herbal ingredients to monetary valuations of herbal ingredients. Pennyworths of herbs become a common feature of the recipes that we can see in written family records. By implication, there must have been a market in herbs, particularly in urban areas or for those families who might increasingly have had books which identified herbs but had less experience in identifying them on the ground and gathering them to best effect. It is for this reason that the herb trade evolved with the medical marketplace. By 1750 the north of England in particular had a network of itinerant herb sellers, some of whom have left records for our use, but by 1800 the herb trade had been transformed into a modern business. While families might still gather their own herbs, even in urban areas, they were more likely to get them from the increasing number of herb sellers who took the place of grain sellers in the markets of urban England. While these people seem to have been relatively rare in places like Oxfordshire (owing perhaps to its overwhelmingly rural character and the relative slowness of the enclosure process), Manchester had 16 herb sellers in 1801, Leeds had 11, Norwich had 6, Huntingdon had 3 and Northampton had 7. Smaller towns and communities without regular markets were served by itinerant herb sellers, but they came on carts rather than foot and carried with them a considerable variety of British and foreign herbs. The much-maligned quack would also usually carry herbs as well as his own patent remedies. Such people were supplied by groups like artisan botanists, but the scale of their operations demanded a rather steadier source of supply, and this was to be found in specialist herb growers. The Parker family in Lancashire grew herbs on a considerable scale for their own medicine (which they sold), but also for public sale. More widely, we have been able to identify twenty-three specialist herb growers in northwest England between 1790 and 1820, and it seems likely that this sort of grower/wholesaler lay at the heart of the herb trade by the early nineteenth century. Such experiences represent in microcosm the changes taking place in the marketing and distribution process for most agricultural produce between the late seventeenth and early nineteenth centuries, a movement which was to produce national integrated markets (and national prices and price movements) in most products by 1850.[66]

## Conclusion

Clearly there is much more to be said about the nature of the English rural economy and society than can be conveyed in a single chapter of a book like this. Indeed, even Mark Overton's excellent survey of the transformation of rural England only barely scratches the surface of the local diversity of experience that we really need to understand, and leaves a whole range of questions – for instance on the relationship between centre and periphery in the process of 'agricultural progress' – unasked or unanswered. Nonetheless, we can attempt some general conclusions. In terms of the narrowly defined agricultural economy – productivity levels and changes in aggregate output – there seems little reasonable doubt that what we see between 1700 and 1850 is a period of sustained but gradual development, a process of evolution which, along with latent productive capacity in English agriculture, was sufficient to feed a growing and urbanising population, even if only just. However, there are also other indicators from the rural economy that may have suggested rather more radical change to contemporaries. Some are familiar (the changing landscape associated with enclosure had a symbolism rather more important than simple numbers suggest, for instance) but others are less so – the gradual disappearance of some of the traditional rural crafts from rural villages, the decline of fairs and markets, regional product specialisation, or the appearance of crops such as turnips and swedes in a locality. There were also potentially radical social and cultural changes in some areas – the revision of the tenancy system, the intensification of seasonal unemployment amongst the labouring classes, inexorably increasing poverty and the creation of niggling class tensions.

How to balance the aggregate numbers with our observation of regionality in the agrarian economy and of a complex mix of continuity and change in rural society and rural culture is of course a difficult nut to crack. For us, however, Richard Hodgkinson typifies the new breed of farmer that was driving English agriculture forward by the later eighteenth century and was increasingly changing the culture of rural society. Well-educated, relatively well-to-do, tied into a network of other tenant farmers and buying and dispensing of labour as a commodity, this man's philosophy on farming looked radically different from that which might have been expressed in the early eighteenth century. On 10 May 1815 he wrote:

But theory alone will make but a sorry farmer. The man who turns his attention to agricultural pursuits with the least degree of seriousness will soon find it not to be learned by inspiration or intuition, there is no royal road to it, we must pursue the scriptural maxim of laying line upon line, precept upon precept, and I may add experiment upon experiment and after all too often reap only disappointment. It seems strange that a *science* upon the exercise of which has depended the existence of every human being since the creation of the world ... sh'd be so little understood, But be that as it may, its practice and its improvement will now be forced upon us.[67]

Hodgkinson was unusual in articulating these views so well, and in sending his own son to learn the trade of farming from John Curwen, but for farmers and estate managers in Norfolk, Northamptonshire and a range of other counties, experiment and science were increasingly the order of the day by the turn of the nineteenth century. Failure, the reaping of disappointments, adds nothing to aggregate output or productivity growth figures, but it tells us much about the way the agriculture economy, and its underlying social and ideological structure, were changing. The experiences of Hodgkinson, allied with our thoughts on the regionality of change in the agrarian economy and society and in agrarian culture, convinces us that Schmidt was right to see 'something big' happening in rural England. In Part III of this book, we will explore more of these social and cultural issues in our attempt to make sense of the Industrial Revolution.

## Notes

1 For the record of Schmidt's perceptions of British agriculture, see R. Schmidt, *An agricultural journey* (Hanover, Willhelm Back, 1835). The book is published in German, and the quotes which we use are our own translation. On the wider debate in the Prussian regions, see S. Brakensiek, 'Agrarian individualism in north-western Germany, 1770–1870', *German History*, 12 (1994) 137–79.

2 Schmidt, *An agricultural*, p. 43.

3 *Ibid.*, p. 64.

4 *Ibid.*, p. 89.

5 W. Marshall, *The review and abstract of the county reports to the Board of Agriculture, 1811* (New York, Augustus Kelley, 5 volumes, 1968 reprint).

6 Schmidt, *An agricultural*, p. 264.

7 Even after repeal of the corn laws in 1846, England imported less than one-fifth of its total food requirement. Over the eighteenth century as

a whole, it is likely that England was a net corn *exporter*. See J. Chartres, 'The marketing of agricultural produce, 1640–1750', in J. Chartres (ed.), *Agricultural markets and trade 1500–1750* (Cambridge, Cambridge University Press, 1990), pp. 157–274.

8 See E. A. Wrigley, 'Explaining the rise in marital fertility in England in the long eighteenth century', *Economic History Review*, 51 (1998) 435–64.

9 Evidence on occupations prior to 1851 is patchy and ambiguous, but it seems likely that the proportion of the male labour force engaged solely in agricultural occupations at least halved between 1700 (around 47 per cent of the labour force) and 1851 (22 per cent of the labour force).

10 For a review of this early writing, see J. D. Chambers and G. E. Mingay, *The agricultural revolution 1750–1880* (London, Batsford, 1966).

11 The cultivated acreage (all crops) increased by just 10 per cent between 1700 and 1837, with a slight blip in the 1790s as unusually high wartime prices made more completely marginal land viable.

12 N. F. R. Crafts, *British economic growth during the Industrial Revolution* (Oxford, Clarendon, 1985), and R. C. Allen, 'Agriculture during the Industrial Revolution', in R. Floud and D. N. McCloskey (eds), *The economic history of Britain since 1700* (Cambridge, Cambridge University Press, 2nd edn 1994), pp. 96–122. However, see also N. F. R Crafts and C. K. Harley, 'Output growth and the Industrial Revolution: a restatement of the Crafts–Harley view', *Economic History Review*, 45 (1992) 703–30.

13 For European comparisons, see G. Clark, 'Agriculture and the Industrial Revolution, 1700–1850', in J. Mokyr (ed.), *The British Industrial Revolution: an economic perspective* (Boulder, Col., Westview Press, 1993), pp. 227–66.

14 N. F. R. Crafts, 'British economic growth 1700–1850: some difficulties of interpretation', *Explorations in Economic History*, 24 (1987) 245–68.

15 The Lilford papers, and those of his estate stewards, can be found in several locations and they underpin the analysis which follows. See Lancashire Record Office (LRO), DDX 211, Hodgkinson papers, and LRO, DDLi Uncatalogued (192 boxes of assorted estate papers), and Manchester Central Library, L15/2, Estate papers. We are grateful to Alan Weaver, who is conducting an exhaustive study of the Lilford papers, for providing some of this material.

16 LRO, DDLi Box 92, Farming book.

17 Stories such as this also serve to show the complexity of farming and farming improvement; it is all too easy to get an impression from textbooks on agricultural history that fields of clover were interspersed with fields of arable crops in rather rigid field rotations, whereas the Lilford material clearly shows that this was not the case.

18 LRO, DDLi Box 74, Farming book.

19 *Ibid.*

20  LRO, DDLi Box 90, Farming memoranda.

21  LRO, DDB 81/71, Diary.

22  Clark, Agriculture.

23  LRO, DDX 115/91, Farming memoranda, 1785–1838. Though the catalogue entries refer to the author as unnamed, the writer clearly identifies
himself under the entry for Good Friday 1790.

24  LRO, DDB 81/71, Diary.

25  E. A. Wrigley, *Continuity, chance and change: the character of the Industrial Revolution in England* (Cambridge, Cambridge University Press,
1988).

26  R. C. Allen, 'The two English agricultural revolutions, 1459–1850', in
B. M. S. Campbell and M. Overton (eds), *Land, labour and livestock:
historical studies in European agricultural productivity* (Manchester,
Manchester University Press, 1991), pp. 236–54.

27  Clark, 'Agriculture', p. 246.

28  *Ibid.*

29  R. V. Jackson, 'Growth and deceleration in English agriculture 1660–
1790', *Economic History Review*, 38 (1985) 333–51.

30  A. Kussmaul, *A general view of the rural economy of England 1538–1840*
(Cambridge, Cambridge University Press, 1990).

31  P. Hudson, *The Industrial Revolution* (London, Arnold, 1992).

32  LRO, DDLi, Box 92, Farm account book.

33  See M. Overton, 'The critical century? The agrarian history of England
and Wales 1750–1850', *Agricultural History Review*, 38 (1990) 185–9,
and M. Overton, *The agricultural revolution in England: the transformation of the agrarian economy* (Cambridge, Cambridge University
Press, 1996).

34  For an example of early commercialisation and specialisation under the
influence of London, see K. Wrightson and D. Levine, *Poverty and piety
in an English village: Terling 1525–1700* (London, Academic Press, 1979).
For later discussion of the Essex example, see P. Sharpe, *Adapting to
capitalism: working women in the English economy 1700–1850* (Basingstoke, Macmillan, 1996).

35  J. Thirsk (ed.), *The agrarian history of England and Wales, vol. VI:
1640–1750* (Cambridge, Cambridge University Press, 1984), p. 20.

36  J. Thirsk, *England's agricultural regions and agrarian history 1500–1750*
(Basingstoke, Macmillan, 1987), p. 39.

37  Overton, *Agricultural revolution*, p. 56.

38  LRO, DDLi Box 92, Farming book.

39  F. Wood and K. Wood, *A Lancashire gentleman: the letters and journals
of Richard Hodgkinson 1763–1847* (Stroud, Sutton, 1992), p. 177.

40  M. Overton, 'Estimating crop yields from probate inventories: an example
from East Anglia 1585–1735', *Journal of Economic History*, 39 (1979)
363–78, and M. Overton, 'Re-estimating crop yields from probate

inventories', *Journal of Economic History*, 50 (1990) 931–5. An alternative might be to use an index of rental values per acre in different counties in order to see how contemporaries valued productive land. However, amongst many potential problems with this approach, we have to bear in mind that where competition for land was strong (for instance where it might be used for town expansion or industrial purposes, or where land was held at a premium because it was gathered in by those with urban and industrial fortunes) so rental values would be very high indeed. North of the river Trent, for instance, the highest individual rents per acre of which we are aware related to land which had a potentially dual agricultural and textile use as a place for siting tentering frames. See M. E. Turner, J. V. Beckett and B. Afton, *Agricultural rent in England 1690–1914* (Cambridge, Cambridge University Press, 1997), pp. 184–98.

41 G. Hannah (ed.), *The deserted village: the diary of an Oxfordshire rector, James Newton of Nuneham Courtenay 1736–86* (Stroud, Sutton, 1992).

42 *Ibid.*, p. 16. 'Faggots' here means firewood.

43 *Ibid.*, p. 48.

44 Other forms of enclosure are ignored here because of space constraints rather than because we attach no importance to them.

45 For the Otmoor material, see Oxfordshire Record Office (ORO), CPZ/15.

46 K. D. M. Snell, *Annals of the labouring poor* (Cambridge, Cambridge University Press, 1985), and J. M. Neeson, *Commoners: common right, enclosure and social change in England 1700–1820* (Cambridge, Cambridge University Press, 1993).

47 Chambers and Mingay, *Agricultural revolution*.

48 See B. Reaney, *The class struggle in nineteenth century Oxfordshire* (Oxford, Clarendon, 1970), A. V. Brown, 'Last phase of the enclosure of Otmoor', *Oxoniensia*, 32 (1967) 35–52, and D. Eastwood, 'Communities, protest and police in early nineteenth-century Oxfordshire: the enclosure of Otmoor reconsidered', *Agricultural History Review*, 44 (1996) 35–46. The article by A. V. Brown represents just a tiny part of a much wider research paper, and we are grateful to him for letting us have access to this work, from which the next section of our chapter draws.

49 J. E. Archer, *By a flash and a scare: incendiarism, animal maiming and poaching in East Anglia* (Oxford, Clarendon, 1990).

50 J. Fiske (ed.), *The Oakes diaries: business, politics and the family in Bury St Edmunds 1778–1800* (Woodbridge, Boydell Press, 1990).

51 The exception is south Lancashire and Cheshire, where harsh poor-relief systems appear to have covered up the scale of underlying rural poverty.

52 Fiske, *The Oakes*.

53 J. G. Williamson, *Coping with city growth during the British Industrial Revolution* (Cambridge, Cambridge University Press, 1990).

54  J. Chartres, 'Introduction', in Chartres (ed.), *Agricultural*, p. 7.
55  This despite poor harvests and the threats of war. See Wood and Wood, *A Lancashire gentleman*, p. 86.
56  Chartres, 'The marketing', p. 223.
57  *Ibid.*, pp. 252–3.
58  Chartres, 'Introduction', p. 9.
59  Kussmaul, *A general*.
60  P. K. O'Brien, 'Agriculture and the home market for English industry 1660–1820', *English Historical Review*, 50 (1985) 773–800.
61  Wood and Wood, *A Lancashire gentleman*, p. 69.
62  *Ibid.*, p. 73.
63  R. Scola, *Feeding the Victorian city: the food supply of Manchester 1770–1870* (Manchester, Manchester University Press, 1992).
64  Wood and Wood, *A Lancashire gentleman*, p. 281.
65  Scola, *Feeding*, and W. Thwaites, 'Women in the market place: Oxfordshire 1690–1800', *Midland History*, 9 (1984) 43–69.
66  For a larger discussion of the medical marketplace, self-dosing and herbal remedies, see S. A. King and A. Weaver, 'Lives in many hands: the medical landscape in Lancashire 1700–1830', *Medical History* (forthcoming, 2000).
67  Wood and Wood, *A Lancashire gentleman*, pp. 287–8.

# PART III

# THE INDUSTRIAL REVOLUTION AND ASPECTS OF EVERYDAY LIFE

# CHAPTER SEVEN

# THE DEMOGRAPHY OF THE
# INDUSTRIAL REVOLUTION

## The conceptual framework

In Part II, we dealt with the development of different aspects of economic structure. We argued that in order to understand the process of the Industrial Revolution, it is necessary to look at regional dimensions, to understand continuity as well as change, and to take a wide view of the sorts of experiences which can help us to decide what the Industrial Revolution meant. In particular, we used individual stories to try and suggest that part and parcel of making sense of the Industrial Revolution is an understanding of how the process might have looked on the ground to those living through it. What we want to do in Part III is to take forward the latter theme in particular, investigating how the Industrial Revolution process influenced key areas of everyday life after 1700 – basic demography, the form and function of the family, the character of the household economy and the built environment. This is not – and is not meant to be – a thoroughgoing 'social history of the Industrial Revolution'. As we said in our introduction, the aim of this book is to allow students to engage with some of the nuts and bolts of the complex and wide-ranging process that we have come to label the Industrial Revolution, rather than trying to provide a detailed synthesis of all of the dark nooks and crannies of the process itself. We start, then, with demography, and we start with a story.

In 1821, James Harker, an agricultural labourer from Dorset looked back on his life in an autobiographical account. He had been born in Poole in 1752, and by age ten was working on his father's rented farm. His father died when he was aged thirteen, the farm lease was revoked and the family split up. James went to work for a farmer in Puddletown, while his mother and siblings moved to Bournemouth to live with an uncle. The job at Puddletown did not last long, and

Harker moved through a series of temporary labouring positions until he was aged nineteen. Then, he started to court Betty Hargreaves, a servant aged seventeen, and eight months later they married. With Dorset wages low, Betty heavily pregnant by the time she married and work highly seasonal, life was a struggle and hunger not unfamiliar. This notwithstanding, they had children regularly. Eleven were born in the twenty years 1772–92. Of these, 3 died in infancy, 2 died between five and ten years old and 2 more before they were fifteen. In 1793, Betty died and James married again less than a year later. His new marriage yielded two children, but both died in infancy. His second wife died of a fever in 1811, and only two of James's children were still alive when he wrote his autobiography. During his life, he had conducted nine migratory movements between towns as well as moves within the same neighbourhood.[1]

The story of James Harker is interesting in itself, and typical of many other stories that we could have told. However, it also highlights the main themes addressed in this chapter – marriage, fertility, death, migration, and sex outside marriage. Harker was living through a period of sustained national population growth, and while contemporaries were unsure of the exact magnitude of growth they were keenly aware that it was rapid compared with anything in living memory. Indeed, as we have seen already in this book, Thomas Malthus believed that population had the capacity to outgrow the means available to support it in terms of food, clothing and shelter. He maintained that population growth must reach a ceiling at which it would be blocked either by disease, famine or war raising the death rate (the so called positive check) or by 'moral restraint' in terms of later marriage, lower fertility or more non-marriage (the so-called preventative check). These doom-laden prophecies were overtaken by considerable increases in agrarian and industrial productivity of the sort which we highlighted in Part II of this book, and by the gradual globalisation of trade in primary resources, but the fact remains that population growth *was* rapid.[2] For students seeking an understanding of the Industrial Revolution process the first question must be 'how rapid?', but the more important issues are how and why the population grew nationally and regionally, and what this population growth meant for ordinary people at the level of the locality and family. James Harker's tale will provide invaluable signposts to these key issues.

## Population growth: how rapid?

Prior to 1981, estimates of English population size and growth rates were imprecise. Figures for the nineteenth century could be obtained on a decennial basis from census returns, but the first four (1801–31) were unreliable.[3] For the period before 1801, no national figures are available except the very rough estimates of Gregory King on population size in the late seventeenth century.[4] Even at the level of individual communities, population listings and counts appear to have been rare prior to 1801, and historians wishing to discover population size have had to use estimates based upon multiplying the number of people appearing in military surveys, religious returns or tax data according to a notional average family size of 4.5 people.

In 1981, however, E. A. Wrigley and R. S. Schofield took a new approach to calculating English population totals, pioneering a technique called back projection. Crudely put, they started with the 1871 census and counted backwards, subtracting deaths and adding births for five-year periods, in effect providing a census-type population figure for each five-year period back to 1541. Between 1837 and 1871 national birth and death totals were obtained by taking and adjusting the figures published by the Registrar General. Prior to 1837 records of baptisms and burials recorded at parish level are the closest approximation to birth and death totals. However, data in this form present two major problems. First, how to count the number of baptisms, burials and marriages in the registers of over 15,000 English parishes. Second, how to discern the extent to which baptisms and burials (not all of which were recorded) reflected births and deaths. To overcome the first problem, Wrigley and Schofield calculated baptism, burial and marriage totals for a sample of 404 parish registers. These were corrected for likely under-registration and weighted to allow for the fact that there were too many large parish populations in the sample. The 1811 census population figures for each of the 404 parishes in the sample were then added together, re-weighted and divided by the national population figures for 1811 (excluding London) to produce a multiplication figure of 22.82.

The second problem – how closely baptisms and burials relate to births and deaths – is potentially more thorny because nonconformity, a retreat from religion generally, and infant deaths before baptism could all reduce the 'fit' between recorded events and the actual number. In line with commentators before them, Wrigley and

Schofield found that this sort of under-registration of births and deaths was worst between the early 1790s and the early 1820s, with up to one-third of births and deaths not registered as baptisms and burials in some years. A series of 'correction figures' were thus applied to the weighted totals of baptisms and burials to produce a 'best guess' of births and deaths which were then used in back projection.[5]

These techniques have not been without their critics. It has been claimed, for instance, that slight changes in assumptions about the scale of nonconformity or the effect of a birth–baptism interval on registration could result in different population estimates. Even if the assumptions are correct, critics have been quick to point out Wrigley and Schofield's inadequate treatment of the issue of urban demography, which hardly figures in their analysis. At a time when, as we shall see, larger and larger proportions of the population were living in larger and larger urban areas, such neglect is a potentially serious issue.[6] Some of this critical commentary is misleading. *The population history of England* was as much an exercise in pushing back the methodological barriers of historical demography as it was an attempt to create fully accurate figures of the rate of population change and the mechanisms of growth.[7] In any case, if some of the assumptions which underpin back projection are inaccurate, this probably does not compromise the broad validity of the magnitudes and rates of change which Wrigley and Schofield identified. Indeed, in their follow-up volume Wrigley et al. use a new technique called inverse projection and a new set of assumptions on the necessary correction figures to show that while they may have understated population figures for the early eighteenth century the differences compared with their 1981 estimates were very small indeed.[8] Figure 7.1 charts both sets of figures for English population growth in the period covered by this book. Broadly, the population grew from just over 5 million in 1701 to 8.6 million by 1800 and 16.7 million by 1851. This was a spectacular and sustained rise when compared either with historic growth in England or with the rest of Europe, and it was achieved without substantial immigration from other countries except Ireland. In terms of growth rates, the generation of James Harker was responsible for much of the most rapid advance. Between 1701 and 1771 the population grew by only just over 1.3 million, with an average compound growth rate of under 0.5 per cent per year. The next seventy-year period saw an increase of just over 7.5 million, with an annual compound growth rate of over 1.3 per cent.[9]

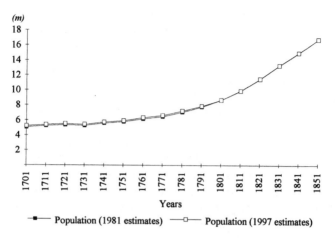

**Figure 7.1** Population totals as calculated by Wrigley and Schofield (1981) and Wrigley et al. (1997), 1701–1851

Little wonder that travellers from the continent portrayed England as an increasingly teeming and industrious country.[10] What was also abundantly apparent to contemporaries was that people were increasingly becoming urban dwellers. Historians have been unable to reach a consensus over what size of population constituted an 'urban' environment, but if we think in terms of a range of 2,500 to 5,000 as a lower boundary, then it is clear that by 1801 more than one-third of the population were urban dwellers, rising to over one-half by around 1848. This 'urban' development gave some of the regional character to population change, much of it taking place outside the hierarchy of southern and Midlands towns which had dominated the urban scene in 1700. Indeed, traditional urban centres such as Norwich barely kept pace with national population growth rates during the eighteenth century. Towns like this were replaced in the rank order of urban population size by the rapidly growing northern and Midlands towns with economies based upon manufacturing industry, services or mining. They carried county population totals with them. Of the thirteen counties which experienced population growth of over 67 per cent between 1700 and 1801, eight were in the north and Midlands. Lancashire in particular was transformed from a relatively sparsely populated county in 1700 to the most populous and urbanised in England by the 1830s. Between 1790 and the depression of 1842, Lancashire could boast seven of the top ten fastest growing towns and cities in the country, and contemporary commentators as diverse as Arthur Young, James Caird and the artist Fuseli marvelled at the density and size of population in the county.[11] The rest of the fastest growing eighteenth-century county populations were arranged along the south coast (Kent, Sussex, Hampshire) where commercial agriculture to serve the demands of London rapidly became established alongside the holiday industry, and around Bristol. These broad regional divisions persisted in the nineteenth century, though with renewed emphasis on the growth of mining communities in the northeast and Midlands.[12] Certainly by the 1830s the focus of population growth had moved from the south to the Midlands and north.

These broad regional patterns might be familiar to students of the Industrial Revolution, but perhaps less familiar are population growth profiles at sub-regional level.[13] In Lancashire, for instance, rapid rates of population growth at *county level* masked substantial differences of experience. Textile and/or merchanting centres such as Preston, Blackburn, Bolton and Manchester had very rapid growth rates, as did the coalfield areas of southwest and central Lancashire and the rural industrial area of Rossendale. Lancashire north of Preston, however, remained distinctly rural, and townships here experienced relatively slower growth in population during the eighteenth and nineteenth centuries, and indeed some even experienced absolute decline.[14] A similar picture of regional complexity emerges when we switch our attention to the agrarian south. In the early eighteenth century, low-lying areas prone to fever-related deaths could be experiencing absolute population decline while other townships not far away were experiencing substantial growth.[15] Later, the growth of market towns, the regional impact of parliamentary enclosure, the demand for migrants from London, and the extension of 'open' and 'closed' parishes could all stimulate very different population growth trajectories at sub-regional level.[16] If we look at James Harker's Dorset, for instance, it is clear that Poole and surrounding parishes maintained healthy growth rates between 1770 and 1850. More widely, villages and parishes in the east of the county experienced relative or absolute population decline during the wave of parliamentary enclosure in the 1770s, but then gained population as the west of the county experienced the same changes late in the century. Within this framework, so called 'open' villages like Bere Regis grew relatively quickly at all times while 'closed' villages dominated by one landowner, such as Cerne Abbas, grew relatively slowly or even declined.

And above all of these individual community experiences stood the magnet of London, drawing off surplus rural population from a range of southern counties to meet its own yearly population deficit caused by a total (infant, child and adult) mortality rate which, while not as high as some urban areas, was still high enough to ensure that natural increase alone could not power continuing growth rates.[17]

A detailed local mapping of experiences of population growth remains beyond the grasp of historical demographers, but we can make three basic points to use as a springboard for further analysis. First, at a national level population grew steadily to 1770 and relatively fast thereafter. Second, population growth, particularly after 1750, was intricately tied up with the development of a range of new towns and the growth of existing urban areas, and with a fundamental shift in the demographic significance of the English regions. Finally, whatever was happening to population at a national or regional level, ordinary people might have had very different experiences depending on where they lived. Indeed, given the ubiquity of migration, explored below, it was quite possible for a single person to have experienced the whole gamut of population regimes during a life-course, living in both towns and rural communities, and living in communities faced with declining, stagnating or rapidly growing populations. This 'life-cycle vision' is one of the keys to unlocking the lived experience of the Industrial Revolution.

### Influences on English population growth

Accepting that complex local and regional patterns underpin national trends in absolute population numbers, the question becomes *how* population changed. Once again Wrigley and Schofield offer new interpretations. Before 1981, the relative merits of explanations which saw population growth driven by falling mortality versus those which saw growth fuelled by a rising birth rate could not be adequately balanced. While the English birth rate was never anywhere near its biological maximum, many contributors to the debate favoured mortality-based explanations. It is not hard to see why. After 1730 national mortality crises (though not local ones) disappeared from the English demographic scene, providing the scope for falling death rates, particularly amongst infants. At the same time, a determined crusade against smallpox was often thought to have paid dividends in the form of reduced incidence and fatality of the disease. And *The population history of England* used family reconstitution studies from twelve communities to confirm that 'national' death rates among infants in particular did indeed fall from the mid-eighteenth century.[18] However, the same reconstitutions seemed to show that the really significant changes in demographic experience were centred not on mortality but on the rate and age at marriage (nuptiality) and, to a lesser degree, on fertility. According to Wrigley and Schofield in 1981, during the period from the 1700s to 1820s the 'national average' female age at first marriage fell by almost three years, from 26.2 to 23.4. While this might seem a moderate fall, it freed up part of the most fertile years of the female reproductive life-cycle to childbearing and might have meant an extra one or two children per marriage.

Trends in non-marriage are also important. The generation born around 1700 could expect to see roughly 11 per cent of their number unmarried by the time they reached forty-five and this figure had fallen to only 5 per cent for the generation born at mid-century. Non-marriage then rose more or less consistently, reaching 11 per cent again for the generation born in the early nineteenth century.[19] In other words, during the key decades of population explosion in the late eighteenth and early nineteenth centuries, marriage ages were tumbling and the number of women taken out of the marital fertility equation by 'celibacy' was at its lowest point. The 1981 estimates pointed to less spectacular change in marital fertility.[20] This appears to have been remarkably stable, varying by only 8 per cent over time and a little more between regions. Illegitimacy, on the other hand, almost doubled during the 1700–1820 period, from under 3 to almost 6 per cent of all births, fuelling growth in the total fertility rate. Overall the 'big picture' is one in which at least two-thirds of population growth in the period considered here reflected changes in nuptiality and fertility, leaving a relatively small role for mortality.[21]

These conclusions are not unproblematic. Quite apart from the small number of family reconstitutions on which they are based, some commentators have suggested that they underplay the significance of mortality decline. Peter Razzell, for instance, has argued that because of uncorrected flaws in the burial recording process Wrigley and Schofield understated the scale of mortality in the early eighteenth century and thereby understated the role of mortality decline in the 'population revolution' of the later eighteenth century.[22] Whether he is right or wrong, it is clear that mortality was the most spatially variable of demographic indicators and it is by no means certain that the small number of reconstitutions used in 1981 really encompass the full potential range of English mortality regimes. This said, it is significant that the 1997 analysis of twenty-six family reconstitution datasets by Wrigley et al. not only confirms the broad mechanisms of change identified in 1981, but also gives fertility overall more weight.[23] Thus, the average age at first marriage for women fell from 26 in 1700–9 to 23.1 in 1830–7, while that for men fell from 27.4 to 24.9.

As Goldstone noted of Wrigley and Schofield's 1981 analysis, much of this fall in the aggregate female age at marriage is to be explained by a sharp fall in the number and proportion of brides marrying over the age of thirty, and a more than commensurate rise in the number marrying at or around the age of twenty. The majority of women did not change their marriage behaviour. These observations have important implications for how we interpret the wider demographic regime, but the overall fall in female marriage ages in this period was sufficient to yield a minimum increase of 15 per cent in the number of children born to a women who married at the average age and remained married until the end of her childbearing period. In turn, the extension of the childbearing period through earlier marriage was reinforced by changes in marital fertility which increased by roughly 10 per cent between the mid-seventeenth and early nineteenth centuries. These figures represent more extensive change than Wrigley and Schofield allowed in 1981, and would have been sufficient to add between one and two children to the tally of a complete reproductive life-cycle. Interestingly, the effect seems particularly notable among youthful brides, who not only married earlier but had children at a faster rate too.[24]

The broad pattern of mortality outlined in 1981 is also confirmed in Wrigley and Scholfield's most recent analysis. Infant mortality at the start of the eighteenth century stood at 174 deaths per thousand babies born, rising further to around 190 between 1710 and 1749. Thereafter, rates fell markedly, reaching a low point of 133 deaths per thousand in the decade 1810–19, before rebounding to reach 144 between 1825 and 1837. Childhood mortality also declined. Mortality between age one and age four peaked at around 113 per thousand children entering the age group during the period 1700–49, and then fell (though not in a linear fashion) to under 100 by the opening decades of the nineteenth century. Mortality in the age ranges 5–9 and 10–14 peaked in the period 1725–49 (at 50 and 28 per thousand

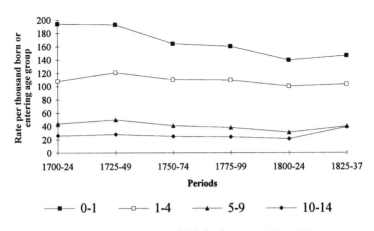

Figure 7.2 Infant and child death rates, 1700–1837

entering the age group respectively) and then fell until the second quarter of the nineteenth century.[25]

Figure 7.2 reproduces the infant and childhood mortality figures for the period covered by this book, and clearly indicates these trends. Adult mortality rates are generally harder to calculate from family reconstitution data, but in so far as estimates are reliable they show that in the early eighteenth century adult life expectancy was rising sharply while by the later eighteenth century average gains had reached a plateau, only for the upward trend to resume from the mid-1790s. If we add all of these figures together, then expectation of life at birth fell from 37 in the decade 1700 to 1709 to 35 in the decade 1720 to 1729. Thereafter, improvement was substantial, with life expectancy at birth in the decade 1800 to 1809 reaching almost 45. Later in our period the impact of urbanisation in particular was to compromise life expectancy once more, as figure 7.2 suggests. The key point remains, however, that in contrast to many European neighbours, England started the eighteenth century with comparatively low mortality rates and it retained those comparatively low rates well into the nineteenth century.[26]

We should not, of course, take the newly confirmed 'big picture' – that England had a fertility- rather than a mortality-dominated demographic system – at face value. In practice broad 'national' statistics on the reasons for demographic change could be the outcome of communities going in very different demographic directions, and there are certainly important regional, sub-regional and socio-economic differences of which students of the Industrial Revolution need to be aware. Consider the mortality issue first. Most rural communities appear to have had relatively moderate mortality levels. Around 1750, infant death rates in the 'agricultural' parishes assembled by Wrigley et al. stood at 124 per thousand, with figures below 100 per thousand a regular feature of the demographic history of places like Hartland in rural Devon. In the late 1830s, the infant death rate was 113 in these parishes. Such a pattern contrasts with rural industrial communities. While infant and childhood mortality rates almost everywhere were improving by the later eighteenth century, in rural industrial communities they rose, from 126 per thousand between 1675 and 1749 to 169 between 1838 and 1844. This experience was shared by rural industrial communities not analysed by Wrigley et al., suggesting that the rapid population growth often achieved in rural industrial areas happened despite high mortality rates.[27] Meanwhile, the most substantial improvements in mortality appear to have occurred in market towns, which saw infant mortality improve from the very high level of 240 per thousand in 1750 to a moderate 136 per thousand by the late 1830s. The demographic experience of larger urban areas was equally distinctive. In 1700 these places were growing by in-migration, had a younger age structure than many rural areas and appear to have combined high fertility and (at least among urban natives) early marriage ages with substantial death rates amongst infants and children. By the early nineteenth century, however, it becomes increasingly clear that most urban areas outside the rapidly growing Lancashire towns shared in the death rate decline observable in other communities, with London in particular developing a relatively moderate mortality regime.[28]

These socio-economic characteristics shape the regional geography of mortality. While Michael Flinn, writing in 1981, could find no significant regional and local patterns in infant mortality rates during the Industrial Revolution there were certainly very real regional divisions at the end of our period when we look at the level of registration districts.[29] Many of these post-1837 regional divisions will come as no surprise. Industrial and mining districts, and large urban concentrations in the north and Midlands, were associated with relatively high infant death rates, while the rural south and east had a much more moderate experience. Places like Preston and Liverpool had particularly poor experiences, an idea which gains much support from contemporary sources like the autobiographical writings of the Preston mechanic Benjamin Shaw.[30] However, for the pre-1837 period the regional outlines of mortality can be identified with less certainty. Key eighteenth- and early nineteenth-century growth areas such as Lancashire, most coal communities and the industrial west Midlands have little or no family reconstitution coverage on which to base mortality calculations, and even in the rural south reconstitution coverage can hardly be described as dense. Logically, we would perhaps expect the urban industrial concentrations of the north and Midlands to have had a substantial impact in raising relative mortality levels after 1750. Yasumoto thought so when he traced a series of overlapping, urban-centred, mortality regimes in the West Riding.[31] The work of Steven King on mortality in the industrial communities of the West Riding and Paul Huck on industrial communities in Lancashire also suggests this to have been the case.[32]

Indeed, contemporary commentators highlighted this regionality too; one claimed, for instance, that the fertility rates of the West Riding far outstripped those of the more rural East and North Ridings, but that fewer people reached the age of forty in the West Riding than East or North.[33] Rural counties, by contrast, experienced relatively moderate death rates, despite the fact that low wages and endemic poverty characterised the lives of agricultural labourers such as James Harker. The picture is not of course simple. Rural areas of the north – the Fylde of Lancashire, Westmorland and the East Riding – experienced infant death rates roughly one-third higher than similar rural communities in the southwest or southeast, so that the north in general might be styled 'high mortality'. Moreover, mortality rates could vary widely between communities even in the same physical and socio-economic settings, reflecting diverse influences such as cultural practices on hygiene and childcare, attitudes towards physical expansion of the village, and the gender organisation of work. In the West Yorkshire parish of Calverley, two communities separated by less than five miles and sharing the same broad economic and social structures could nevertheless demonstrate infant death rates which diverged by almost 100 children per thousand born.[34] Nonetheless, if we accept these general conclusions, then it is clear that sustained population growth from the 1750s generated or coincided with enduring regional as well as intercommunity inequalities in death rates.

Regional and socio-economic variation in the experience of

(particularly female) marriage ages also provides scope for generalisation. In terms of level, the reconstitutions used by Wrigley et al. suggest very considerable variation between communities, but this was determined less by geography than by socio-economic type. Communities which were to later become rural industrial appear to have started the eighteenth century with relatively high marriage ages, for instance, while agrarian communities serving large urban areas appear to have had relatively low marriage ages from the same date.[35] In terms of trend, the fall in female marriage ages was faster and further in rural industrial communities and other areas which saw a shake up in the local economy during the course of the eighteenth century, than in rural communities generally.[36] Areas where mining came to dominate the occupational structure also appear to have experienced rapid decline in female marriage ages.[37] Ultimately, however, while the range of variation between mean marriage ages was still notable by the 1830s (even as between communities of the same basic socio-economic type) the enduring feature of the later eighteenth century and after was a convergence in experiences of female marriage ages in communities of different socio-economic types.

Compared with mortality and nuptiality, the socio-economic and regional profile of fertility is much more difficult to plot. In 1984, Wilson contended that while it might be possible to argue that marital fertility rates were higher in urban or rural industrial areas, the overall variation between the highest and lowest reliable figures for total marital fertility in the eighteenth century was small.[38] Wrigley et al. likewise found little variation in the level of fertility between communities of different socio-economic type, with total marital fertility in the period 1750–1837 varying between 7.24 children per completed family in communities where handicrafts dominated the male occupational structure, and 8.15 children where manufacturing was the main occupation.[39] Indeed, it is clear that some rural communities in Kent matched or exceeded the marital fertility levels recorded in West Yorkshire rural industrial communities by the early nineteenth century.[40] Not surprisingly, no consistent regional patterns emerge either. Communities in Lancashire and West Yorkshire appear to have experienced consistently high marital fertility, and mining areas such as the northeast were also (in)famous for their high fertility levels. Yet, once we allow for the fact that these were the areas of highest infant mortality (at a time when infant death could artificially speed up the pace of childbearing by curtailing breastfeeding and increasing the risks of earlier conception), marital fertility might have exceeded the average national figure by only 5–6 per cent.[41]

There was rather more variation in non-marital fertility, as the work of Peter Laslett, Richard Adair and others shows.[42] The eighteenth century appears to have opened with a broad east–west divide; an overall illegitimacy rate amounting to around 2 per cent of all first births in 1700 masked the fact that illegitimacy rates were much higher in Lancashire, Staffordshire or Cheshire than they were in Norfolk or Essex. By the mid-eighteenth century there had been a convergence between rates in different regions, but by 1800 the overall rate had grown to 6 per cent and the broad divide between east and west had re-emerged. Within this regional framework simple socio-economic differences are difficult to pinpoint. In 1800, illegitimacy in rural Westmorland was roughly one-third higher than that in rural Essex, while illegitimacy in some North Riding pastoral communities was roughly double that in similar pastoral communities in north Lincolnshire. Clearly, simple socio-economic classifications offer little predictive value on bastardy levels and trends. These indicators fare little better at sub-regional level. Figure 7.3 uses new data from Lancashire on the percentage of all births that were illegitimate in various parishes during the period 1811–21 to throw light on sub-regional illegitimacy patterns. The map shows clearly that a generally high illegitimacy rate could understate very considerable differences in experience at the level of individual communities. Illegitimacy for the county fluctuated between 1 per cent of all births in Barton and 19 per cent in Culcheth, but there was no socio-economic logic to this; the industrial town of Haslingden had an illegitimacy rate of 7.5 per cent, while the exactly similar town of Cowpe just up the road had an illegitimacy rate of less than 2 per cent. More work needs to be done in this area before we can make wider generalisations.

In broad summary, then, the state of the evidence suggests that English communities were locked into a nuptiality-driven demographic regime with a falling female age at first marriage opening up the possibility of cramming more children into a life-cycle. Falling adult mortality meant that more marriages lasted longer, increasing the overall number of children born, while illegitimacy increased substantially at the same time as national population figures were taking off. The exact combination of mortality decline and fertility increase varied between regions, and between communities within

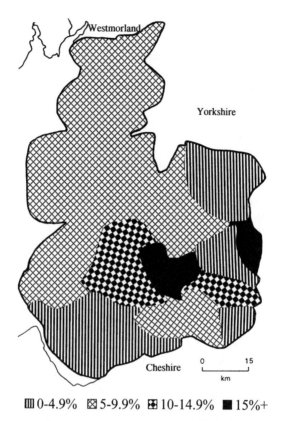

▥ 0-4.9%   ▨ 5-9.9%   ⊞ 10-14.9%   ■ 15%+

**Figure 7.3** Illegitimacy as a percentage of all births in Lancashire
townships and parishes, 1811–21

regions, but ultimately the effect was sustained natural increase. For
students of the Industrial Revolution, these may be comfortable conclusions, but it would be more in keeping with the central theme of
this book to ask what changes in demographic life would really have
been visible to contemporaries within and between the generations.
They would certainly have seen more illegitimate children being born,
and nineteenth-century census studies indicate that grandparents
played a key role in caring for such children, generating a powerful
intergenerational awareness of the issue of illegitimacy.[43] By the later
eighteenth century, parents would almost certainly have noticed that
their adult children were experiencing fewer stillbirths and that their
daughters and daughters-in-law were spending more of their time

pregnant. By the early nineteenth century, the marriage ceremonies stood a more than even chance of involving a bride in the advanced stages of pregnancy, something which would have been a rarity for the generation married in the 1750s.

Paradoxically, what contemporaries might have noticed much less was changing infant and childhood mortality. The autobiographical testimony of James Harker suggests why. From two marriages Harker lost nine children before they reached the age of fifteen, but the overall mortality levels in Dorset were probably relatively light by the late eighteenth century when Harker was baptising his children. The corollary of this is that many other people living around and about Harker would have had little direct experience of infant death. This same tendency for just a few families to account for much of the infant and childhood mortality in a community can be observed even in high mortality proto-industrial areas.[44] The picture is less clear for urban areas, but logically the families of in-migrants would have been more prone to endemic town-based diseases than would the families of urban natives who may have attained and passed on some immunity.[45] As an extension of these observations, it is clear that falling mortality at national and community levels could have reflected a fall in already low risks of infant death amongst the majority, or improvement in the experiences of that small core of families prone to heavy infant and child death. In Dorset and other rural communities, the latter explanation would seem more relevant, and in this sense changing mortality patterns may have been largely invisible to the contemporaries who had in any case never experienced substantial risks of infant or child death. For national population history the significant point is that infant and childhood mortality fell, but for those experiencing the Industrial Revolution the questions of who died and how widely known their experience was may perhaps have been more important than how many.

Changes in mean marriage ages might also have been invisible to contemporary observers. The calculation of an average has little purchase on everyday life. If we take James Harker's wife and the wives of his friends as a representative sample, then the average of eight marriage ages (17, 19, 21, 23, 27, 29, 30, 31) was 24.6 years, but this figure would be nowhere near the real experiences of the people concerned. More importantly, we have already seen that the main feature of nuptiality in the later eighteenth century was the disappearance of a core of late marryers and the creation of a core of early marryers. These two groups account for between one-fifth and one-third of all female marriage partners depending on the nature of the community under the microscope. In other words, the majority of women may have seen relatively little change in their marriage ages, though there may have been rather more visible changes in their marriage chances. Students of the Industrial Revolution must thus take careful note of the gulf between the understandings of contemporaries and those of historians. But there is also another lesson to be learnt from contemporary appreciation of the demographic situation; for many contemporary commentators the most significant component of local demography was not birth, death or marriage, but migration. It is to this, until recently relatively neglected, corner of national, regional and local demography that we now turn, before offering some preliminary attempts at understanding *why* key demographic variables changed.

## Migration and mobility

Strictly speaking, migration is not a 'demographic event' at all. While changes in age at marriage, marital fertility or death rates increase or decrease the population, migration simply redistributes what is already there. However, Pooley and Turnbull suggest that 'migration was central to the process of social, economic and cultural change in the past', and certainly no discussion of historical demography is complete without considering this topic.[46] In fact, migration might take many forms, for instance within regions, between rural and urban areas, between regions and overseas. Not all of these themes can be explored here, but James Harker and his family would seem to reflect the 'normal' migratory experience of people in eighteenth- and early nineteenth-century England. In his own lifetime Harker moved frequently, but usually within a radius of five to fifteen miles of where he was born. Peter Clark suggests that nationally during the eighteenth century between two-thirds and three-quarters of all people (depending on sex and place of residence) could expect to move at least once during their lifetime.[47] Pooley and Turnbull, using the life-histories of over 16,000 people assembled by British genealogists and family historians, can be more precise, suggesting that in the period 1750–1819 individuals averaged 3.3 moves during a lifetime. Between 1820 and 1849 this figure had risen to 4.5 lifetime moves, but at least some of the discrepancy between the two periods reflects the fact that movement is more difficult to trace in the eighteenth century than in the nineteenth century.[48]

Harker was not, then, unusual in the number of times he moved, and this conclusion is reinforced by studies of individual communities. In the Hampshire village of Odiham, for instance, Stapleton found that for some cohorts almost two-thirds of those who migrated into the village subsequently left again, and that many of them stayed for less than five years. The Odiham data also suggest that Harker's tendency to circulate around his place of birth during a number of short-distance moves was common. Some 70 per cent of the people who appear to have moved into Odiham came from distances of less than fifteen miles.[49] Pooley and Turnbull provide more systematic data, suggesting that between 1750 and 1839, 53.3 per cent of all life-cycle moves were to places less than six miles away and that 65 per cent of all moves were to places less than thirteen miles away.[50] Similar experiences can be observed in industrial Lancashire and West Yorkshire, and as Souden points out there appears to be no consistent pattern to mobility experiences either in terms of regions or socio-economic community types from the mid-eighteenth century onwards.[51]

The experiences of James Harker's two surviving adult children show that the character of migratory patterns was not static. They had both moved to London, one on a temporary and one on a permanent basis, whereas Harker had remained all his life in a small corner of Dorset. This is testimony to the enormous pulling power of the capital (a fact confirmed by Pooley and Turnbull), but also reflects a growing eighteenth- and early nineteenth-century tendency for circulatory migratory patterns to be supplemented by rural–urban migration either on a permanent basis or as part of a life-cycle of movement. This is unsurprising. From the 1770s the corollary of excess death rates in towns was heavy migration from rural areas, and Williamson traces rural losses of between 0.87 and 2.1 per cent per annum for the period 1816–71.[52] In Lancashire, these bland figures might mean that at least three-quarters of the population of the county would have spent some of their lives in urban areas by the early 1830s. Thereafter, we might observe a second modification to long-term migration patterns. As urban areas became relatively self-sustaining towards the end of our period, so movements (and often longer-distance movements) between urban areas became much more common.[53] This said, there is no denying that localised migration provided the quantitative heart of mobility throughout the period covered by this book.

James Harker's life-cycle is also instructive in other ways. Almost all of his migration was conducted while he was young. His children apparently had the same experience. This tendency for migration to be disproportionately concentrated amongst the young and the single can be observed in a range of other areas too. In Lancashire, for instance, 65 per cent of all moves in some rural industrial areas represented the mobility of single people under the age of twenty-four.[54] Pooley and Turnbull confirm the importance of the young in the migration stream, and also suggest that there was a linear tendency for the distance moved to fall with advancing age. Those under twenty, for instance, moved an average distance of twenty-five miles. The extension of this observation is that single people moved almost double the distance of married people before 1850.[55] Within this broad framework, there were important urban–rural divisions; migration to towns was concentrated in the early part of the age range 11–30 while migration in rural areas concentrated in the latter part of the same age range.[56] Nor were gender experiences amongst young and single people uniform. James Harker moved frequently, but the wider literature suggests that even where we exclude migration which was likely to have been for marriage purposes, women were more mobile than men. Women were also more likely than men to migrate between or to towns and to stay there longer once they arrived.[57]

These characteristics of the migration framework prior to 1850 reflect a rationale for mobility which is simultaneously complex and simple. Once more, the experience of James Harker provides important clues. Most of his migratory movements were for work purposes, and Pooley and Turnbull confirm that work was the single most important cause of male mobility. Domestic servants, as well as those with skills and professional qualifications, tended to move the longest distances and to move most frequently, while agricultural labourers such as Harker tended to move shorter distances and less frequently.[58] Meanwhile, Harker's wife had moved to his home after their marriage had taken place in her home parish, and more generally marriage seems to have been a significant spur to female migration. Stapleton, for instance, claims that the female domination of migration into and out of Odiham was directly linked to movement for marriage purposes.[59] In Yorkshire, at least 45 per cent of all female in- and out-migration reflected movement for marriage purposes in the communities for which reconstitution evidence is available.[60] Indeed, Pooley and Turnbull suggest that together work and marriage explain almost 75 per cent of all life-cycle moves before 1839. This, then, is the simple part of explaining migration motivations.

Grappling with the other 25 per cent of moves is rather more complex. Movement might have reflected apprenticeship or migration to be near kin, or it might have been involuntary, with the settlement and removal system operating strongly in some areas.[61] Unemployment, the formation of 'migration societies' in the south, or life-cycle crises such as widowhood and old age might also stimulate migration. Clearly, more work remains to be done before we will really understand the detailed nooks and crannies of localised migratory systems. And we might inject a further note of caution to students of the Industrial Revolution; a quantitative discussion of the migration framework tells us only part of the story of migration. By the early nineteenth century, a life-cycle with 3, 4 or 6 moves might encompass several types of migration and several different migratory rationales. This, rather than the fact that quantitatively most migration was local and explained by work and marriage, is the key to understanding how migration would have looked to contemporaries on the ground.

None of this analysis denies, of course, the existence of longer-distance and inter-regional movement. Evidence on apprenticeship in Lancashire mills suggests that there was a considerable traffic in young children from urban and rural workhouses in the south to northern industrial areas.[62] By the early nineteenth century many southern rural communities had begun to institute funds for the export of poor children and families either overseas or to the northern and Midlands industrial areas. Vagrants, and particularly seasonal Irish workers, also made the north–south migration on a regular basis. Overall however, this sort of long-distance north–south movement constituted only perhaps 10 per cent of inter-regional movement. Much more took place over shorter distances on the borders between counties and regions. In Lancashire, for example, the key interchange point between cotton-producing Lancashire and woollen-producing West Yorkshire was the border between Halifax parish and Rossendale. More industrial workers passed along this route than anywhere outside the west Midlands, and yet by moving just a few miles residents of Halifax parish had entered into a very different economic and social region in the Rossendale valley. Inter-regional migration was dominated not by movement from the rural south to the industrial north and Midlands, then, but by movement between urban and industrial areas within the north and Midlands, and from rural counties such as the East Riding and Westmorland to industrial counties such as Lancashire and West Yorkshire.

Yet, the distances involved could still be considerable; the tramping artisans identified by Humphrey Southall thought little of moving fifty or a hundred miles in search of work.[63] Coalminers were also willing to move long distances. New mines usually took the core of their workforce from other mining areas, with movement between South Wales and Lancashire or Lancashire and Nottinghamshire being relatively frequent. Men moved first, with their families following, and a simple analysis of surname turnover and range in Wigan reveals names commonly associated with Wales, Scotland and the northeast alongside probable population turnover approaching 80 per cent over fifteen years.[64] These examples notwithstanding, however, there is now persuasive evidence that to understand the world view of those living during the Industrial Revolution, we must understand localised migration structures which circulated people around the locality of their birth and, in many cases, placed them squarely within extensive kinship networks centred on the 'local country'.

This has been a necessarily brief review of a much wider topic. Much has been missed out or glossed over. An enduring feature of English agriculture, for instance, was the flows of seasonal migratory workers; as late as the 1830s urban industrial workers left their factories for the harvest in areas where industry and agriculture co-existed. Some industrial tasks also tended to attract migrant labour because of a distinct seasonality in the possibilities of industrial production. The experience of miners is salutary, with the regular workforce in some Lancashire and Nottinghamshire mines shrinking by over two-thirds in January and February as migrant miners went back to other occupations. Nor has it been possible here to consider the impact of permanent Irish migration on English demography and migratory patterns. Such questions have been extensively covered elsewhere and thus merit only a mention here. Emigration and immigration more generally are also topics which fall victim to space constraints.

Finally, one other important form of internal migration has been largely excluded here, and that is chain migration. In some guises this is indistinguishable from localised or rural–urban migration patterns, but a basic model would suggest that people were informed in their decision on when and where to migrate by the previous migration of relatives and/or the presence of kin elsewhere which might have reduced some of the costs and uncertainty of the migratory process. Analysis of census data in various early nineteenth-century contexts has suggested that kin could be much more important than has previously been thought in offering shelter, contacts and employment to migrants, with many of those labelled as employees of a household in the census data actually related to the head of household by blood or marriage. Further work will be done in this area in the next few years, and neglect of chain migration in this discussion is perhaps not a reflection of its limited importance.[65]

## Explaining demographic experiences

The lessons of the chapter so far can be succinctly put. England experienced a low-pressure fertility-driven demographic system in which the basic demographic actors were highly mobile. There were important regional and socio-economic characteristics within this broad framework, but basically, England stood out compared with most of the rest of Europe at this time. Why was this so? Clearly, explaining the individual components of demographic behaviour and tracing the interaction of different demographic variables is a vast topic, and also one that has been relatively neglected compared with the attention devoted to establishing what the demographic framework actually was in the first place. We will be unable to offer a comprehensive analysis, but there are a number of key points that we can make about demographic motivations, particularly with respect of changing marriage behaviour.

Conventionally, explanation of falling female marriage ages has centred on three interrelated bodies of theory. First, the idea that the poor law from the mid-eighteenth century onwards underwrote many of the demographic consequences of less restrained marriage behaviour. Put crudely, because England had a poor-law system which had a legal duty to relieve the deserving poor, couples deciding whether to marry did not have to think about the short-term viability of a household or the immediate consequences of childbearing because they knew that the poor law would bail them out if they could not cope.[66] The poor law in the southeast in particular appears to have systematically supported the wages of those in work by the later eighteenth century, negating any real need to save and plan for a wedding. While this idea was dismissed in the work of Blaug in the 1960s, it has been revived by George Boyer for the southeast, and more recently has been generalised by Solar in his attempts to locate some of the impetus to early English industrial development.[67]

The second body of theory links rural industrialisation and marriage ages.[68] Formulated in 1971, the theory of proto-industrialisation saw the development of large-scale, systematically organised rural industries working to supply national and international markets, as essentially disruptive of social structures and conventions, and of demography. It gave young people an alternative source of income to the land and freed them from the constraints on early marriage imposed by the need to inherit land. Given this and more opportunity to mix with the opposite sex in the work context, it appears that young proto-industrial workers approached courtship in a more purposeful way than had previous generations. If they needed further incentive to early marriage, then it was provided by the fact that rural industry placed a premium on physical efficiency, with the highest wages earned in the late teens and early twenties, and so it made sense to marry young and get the main burden of childbearing out of the way before physical efficiency and earnings declined later. Continental scholars have questioned this link between industry and marriage strategies, emphasising that a host of factors – the gender distribution of work, the place of rural industry in the overall household economy, the resilience of traditional patterns of behaviour and belief, the type and quality of the product and the exact organisation of the rural industrialisation process – might influence whether marriage ages fell, and if so how far.[69] In the English context, however, proto-industrialisation as an explanation for changing marriage behaviour has proved resilient. Proto-industrial communities experienced the most dramatic falls in female marriage ages, and since they were generally much bigger than the rural communities used in the Wrigley et al. reconstitution sample, they carry a disproportionate weight in creating a picture of 'national' decline in female ages at first marriage.

The third theoretical pillar in the analysis of marriage motivations centres on the resource-acquisition strategies of young people when conceived more widely than as just their involvement in proto-industry. In 1965, and again in 1981, Hajnal suggested that the relatively high age at marriage amongst west European youth reflected the fact that new households were supposed to form residential units which were spatially and economically separate from that of their parents or other relatives.[70] It took time to accumulate the resources needed to do so, and hence marriage was delayed. Where either the accepted level of resources necessary to form a household eased or the means of getting those resources became easier, there was scope for a reduction in marriage ages. Some commentators have suggested that both developments occurred after 1750. Proletarianisation and urbanisation upset accepted norms which linked household formation to access to land and sole occupation of houses, and the 'necessary level of resources' for household formation may have come more and more to be represented by the ability to find six months' rent and some basic furniture. Changes in inheritance practice might also have diluted norms for household formation. There was a distinct eighteenth-century tendency for bequests in English wills to be confined only to the very closest family. People could thus be more certain of inheriting or not inheriting in 1800 than had been the case in 1700 and might not have postponed marriage whilst the drama of inheritance was acted out.[71] Whatever the accepted level of resources, there is some evidence that they became easier to obtain. The high wages offered in the eighteenth-century rural industrial sector had a role here. So too did changes in the institution of farm service, as the practice of servants on farms living with their employers declined and was substituted by a wage relationship, giving more ready money for resource accumulation and removing a practical constraint on marriage.[72] More generally, in 1981, Wrigley and Schofield observed a relationship between real wages and changes in marriage ages where the two variables were lagged by a generation. While we might doubt that this observation was underpinned by any meaningful relationship, it is potentially true that changes in real wages and/or work opportunities linked to agrarian, commercial or industrial change could have stimulated a later eighteenth-century change in the ways in which young people internalised risk and formed the expectations of the short- and medium-term future which we might expect to have influenced the decision on when and if to marry.

On their own, none of these theoretical perspectives can explain the experience of English female marriage ages. However, it should be easy for students of the Industrial Revolution to conceive some combination of the themes which might provide an adequate explanation for falling marriage ages. It could be argued, for instance, that greater certainty of inheriting or not inheriting by the later eighteenth century, allied with enhanced earning opportunities in rural industry and an awareness that the poor law would act to relieve life-cycle crises, and would look after parents in old age, interacted to encourage more people to marry and to marry at an earlier age. Alternatively, we might suggest that those in proto-industrial and urban areas married more and earlier because waged labour offered substantial resources earlier in the life-cycle, while young people in rural areas married earlier simply because they knew that wages were likely to remain stagnant in the long term, and hence there was little to gain by waiting.

As students should be keenly aware, however, such conclusions are based upon a raft of largely unproven assumptions about the nature of courtship and marriage. They assume that young people really did want to get married, and that couples making the decision to marry were rational actors, responding to an expansion of economic opportunities by marrying sooner than had previously been the case. They also assume that the households formed as a result of the marriage decision had to be economically and spatially independent from the households of their parents and other kin in anything other than the very short term. And there are more subtle assumptions which underpin these theoretical explanations. There is the idea that men and women thought in the same way about courtship and marriage, and that they reacted to common influences in the same way. These theories also implicitly assume that there were few real barriers in the marriage market, and that imperfections such as parental interference dwindled over time. But how realistic are these assumptions?

Bridget Hill and Alison Mackinnon question the invisibility of women in historical demography, formalising the obvious but often missed point that men and women entered the marriage arena with different expectations, experiences and opportunities. For some women, marriage was the only way in which they could expect to survive in the medium term, given the structure of work, pay and social power, and hence the marriage decision was not a decision at all.[73] Even if women had more choice than this view allows, it would be misleading to think that balancing the need for long-term material security, the demands of parents for a say in the marriage process or for long-term nursing care, the need for love and affection, the desire for independence, and the demands of fashion, friendship and work routines was done in the same way or had the same outcomes as was the case for men. Meanwhile, England would be very unusual indeed amongst contemporary European states if local communities did not have highly segmented marriage markets.[74] The children of landowners and tenants might have been socialised to shun the children of proletarians in the marriage market, or the children of shopkeepers, craftsmen and tradesmen might have avoided, say, the children of artisans in the courtship process. While 10 per cent of any local population, depending on age structure, would have been in the marriage market at any one time, where considerations of status, occupation, age or reputation closed off some potential marriage partners there may have been a very restricted 'choice' in the courtship and marriage process. Moodie's perceptive comment that women in particular 'married when they could not when they should' reflects exactly this segmentation.[75]

Other implicit assumptions fare no better when we look at them closely. To assume that men and women were engaged in any active or rational balancing of economic possibilities is problematic, as is the related assumption that couples were constrained by the need to achieve a spatially and economically separate residential unit. Indeed, much anecdotal autobiographical evidence can be assembled to suggest that exactly the opposite was true. James Harker married in his teens, apparently without prospects and certainly with no savings. Despite the fact that his new wife had been engaged in farm service, she too had failed to make any provision against the formation of a new household. They had barely forty shillings between them at marriage, considerably less than the hundred shillings which renting a property and furnishing it at the barest of levels might have cost in the later eighteenth century. The early nineteenth-century autobiography of the Coventry ribbon weaver, Joseph Gutteridge, is even more explicit.[76] He married for the first time while still an apprentice, and against the wishes of his kin, a young woman he had barely courted. He married again (with the help of friends in the courtship process[77]) after the death of his first wife and after an equally short courtship. On both occasions he married without planning, without resources, without future prospects and without having the means to be economically or spatially independent. Kin were vital in both fostering and thwarting his marriage plans, and there seems to have been no conception of what the 'necessary' level of resources was to be able to start thinking about marriage. Gutteridge married for love and companionship, not economic rationality. More widely, David

Levine has explored the relationship between marriage ages and a range of material factors (inheritance, parental survival, birth order and wealth), concluding that people timed marriage decisions 'for their own reasons'.[78]

Clearly, the theoretical explanations might sit uneasily with historical reality because they are based upon erroneous assumptions about courtship and marriage before 1850. They are also inadequate in another way, since they are framed to deal with the marriage behaviour of all men and women. Yet, at the centre of English nuptial experience from 1750 was the disappearance of a core of late marryers and the appearance of a core of early marryers, while for most women behaviour changed hardly at all. There are two things to explain here; first, why marriage behaviour changed so radically for a minority of women, and second why it hardly changed at all for most women. Any explanation of marriage ages must consider both problems side by side. We have neither the space nor the data to offer a refined alternative explanation of falling female marriage ages. However, some commentators have begun to think about this issue, and in doing so they have moved away from explanations which link economics with demographic behaviour. They have suggested that the poor law may have released more women from the job of nursing elderly parents in the later eighteenth century, thus wiping out in a single sweep a core of women who would have married late for this reason prior to 1750. They have suggested that most people had a number of failed courtships prior to the one that resulted in marriage, and that changes in the role of parents, friends and reputation in the courtship process may have resulted in fewer failed courtships and hence earlier marriage in the later eighteenth century. And they have suggested that chance factors may have a big part to play in the emergence of a core of earlier marryers.[79] Whether such commentary is right or wrong, students of the Industrial Revolution need to think very carefully about how we explain changes in marriage ages.

A similar point might be made about explanations of changing mortality. On the face of it, the falling mortality that we can observe in the later eighteenth century could have occurred for three reasons – because exposure to disease was reduced, because resistance to disease was increased or, in the case of infant mortality, because the level of stillbirth and genetic defect was reduced over time. The last influence on mortality figures is very difficult indeed to pin down, but recently Wrigley has argued that stillbirths, and by extension genetic defect, probably did dwindle in the course of the eighteenth century as improving maternal nutrition appears to have filtered through to improved foetal and newborn health.[80] Balancing changing exposure and resistance to disease is also a complicated matter. Analysing proto-industrial communities gives good reason to think that exposure was the key variable. Rapidly growing proto-industrial populations, the in-filling of open space, larger family sizes, greater contact with urban areas and the requirements of industrial production (which often polluted the local water supplies) created declining standards of public and private health. The shabby state of many proto-industrial villages and their populations was clear to contemporaries, and it is tempting to draw a direct association between these experiences and rising infant, childhood and adult mortality.[81]

By extension, we might be tempted to link improving mortality almost everywhere else with better public and private health conditions. Such a view would be misleading. Many of the places where mortality fell also experienced very poor public health conditions, and indeed some of the most rural communities for which we have evidence appear to have had poorly built, overcrowded and damp housing which had an uncertain access to water and other basic necessities.[82] The evidence on public and private health is thus contradictory, while on other elements of exposure to disease the evidence is almost non-existent. We know almost nothing, for instance, about the way in which towns acted as a pool of disease which came to be transferred out to rural hinterlands by returning town migrants, and we know even less about autonomous changes in the virulence of common eighteenth-century killing diseases such as smallpox or measles. Nor are we much better off in considering resistance to disease as a factor in mortality decline. Data on heights in eighteenth- and nineteenth-century populations provide us with contradictory indications of nutritional status, and in any case we are often unsure how nutrition and resistance to disease were related. Doctors and medicine provided little in the way of drugs to enhance resistance, but the tendency for larger numbers of communities to reach a notional population threshold above which diseases such as smallpox became endemic rather than epidemic may have helped to fuel resistance. Yet, alongside the endemicisation of disease we must place increasing pressure on the family economy which meant longer working hours and more intense life-cycle crises, hardly experiences likely to foster disease resistance.

The picture, then, is a complicated one. However, we can complicate it more by noting that in most communities death rates rose or fell not because the experiences of all families changed, but, as we have already seen, because those families which had been particularly prone to experience large numbers of infant deaths increased or decreased in number while the number of deaths accruing to them rose or fell. Crudely put, somewhat less than one-fifth of local families experienced well over one-half of all infant and child deaths, so that the vast majority of local families had very low risks indeed. As with marriage ages, then, there are two things to explain – the concentration and trends in concentration, and the fact that most families really had moderate risks of seeing infant and child death even in high-mortality proto-industrial communities. Differential access to water supplies might have a role to play here, as might the tendency for some families to experience disproportionate chances of genetic defect amongst their children.[83] Alternatively, those with the highest risks of infant death may have been among the poorest strata of local society or migrants without access to local kinship and credit networks.[84] Or those with the greatest levels of infant and childhood mortality may have been those families where women abandoned breastfeeding earliest and devolved care of younger children to older children soonest. There are a range of potential explanations for the trends, but the key point is that historical demography has a long way to go before it really effectively provides explanations of the demographic patterns that it has observed so well.[85]

## Conclusion

Important areas have been left unconsidered in this analysis. The fact that eighteenth- and nineteenth-century improvements in expectation of life at birth were accompanied by a rising tide of sickness amongst those living longer is significant. If we want to know how contemporaries thought about their lives, then sick rather than dead may not have been the preferred option.[86] We do not have the space to open this line of inquiry. Nor can we say more about the potentially very important issue of widowhood and remarriage, despite the fact that the breaking of marriage had important demographic consequences in the area of fertility and of sex ratios in the marriage market, and may have coloured contemporary perceptions of the demographic life-cycle.[87] We can, however, make a number of key points in summary. First, England appears different from the rest of Europe, notwithstanding some of the caveats deployed in this chapter. It had a demographic system which was driven by nuptiality and fertility rather than by mortality as was the case on the continent. And by comparison with Germany or France, English regional demography was incredibly uniform in both trend and level for most measures from fertility to mortality. Second, the English population grew most strongly from the 1750s, and within this framework urban growth was particularly rapid. By 1851, a majority of people lived and worked in towns and most of the large urban areas had become, or were becoming, self-sustaining in their growth patterns, as mortality fell but fertility remained high. Third, it is possible to trace broad regional or socio-economic patterns in variables such as infant mortality or marriage ages, but explanations of these experiences have lagged considerably behind their observation. Finally, and linked to this, the analysis of how demography worked at the level of ordinary people still waits to be systematically explored, particularly for the industrial, rural industrial and urban areas which provided the bedrock of economic growth during the Industrial Revolution period.

The consequences of demographic change were manifold. While economic historians continue to argue over the relative importance of home and overseas demand in fuelling industrial expansion and creating the supply bottlenecks which partly forced invention and innovation, there can be little doubt that a bigger population meant a bigger home market. More important, the demand created may not have been illusory; before 1790 and after 1820, and in some areas possibly throughout the period covered by this book, aggregate living standards seem to have improved and left more room for the purchase of industrial goods. This theme was explored in chapter five and is taken up again in chapter nine. For now, students of the Industrial Revolution must realise that population growth also had more perceptible effects on manners, on the size of the middle classes, on the function and scope of the press and on the possibilities of leisure for labouring people. Potentially too population growth carried with it important consequences for the size and internal coherence of the family and household, for the nature of the relationships between the generations and for the ways in which families made ends meet. These and other consequences are explored in more depth in the chapters which follow.

## Notes

1 V. E. James (ed.), *The autobiography of James Harker, a Dorset labourer* (London, Greenwood Press, 1954). For background on Dorset, see J. H. Bettey, *Dorset* (London, Cass, 1974).

2 For much more on Malthus, see D. Winch, *Malthus* (Oxford, Oxford University Press, 1992), and P. Laslett, 'Malthus and the development of demographic analysis', *Population Studies*, 41 (1987) 269–81.

3 For a discussion of the practical impact of these problems, see C. Jarvis, 'The reconstitution of nineteenth-century rural communities', *Local Population Studies*, 51 (1993) 45–63.

4 P. Laslett, 'Gregory King, Robert Malthus and the origins of English social reason', *Population Studies*, 39 (1985) 351–62.

5 E. A. Wrigley and R. S. Schofield, *The population history of England, 1541–1871* (London, Arnold, 1981), pp. 1–154.

6 See G. Kearns, 'The urban penalty and the population history of England', in A. Brandstrom and L. G. Tedebrand (eds), *Society, health and population during the demographic transition* (Umea, Umea University Press, 1986), pp. 213–36. Over time the importance of a failure to deal systematically with urban mortality conditions dwindles as the scale of the 'urban death penalty' is watered down. For attempts to model the role of urban demography, see N. Goose, 'Urban demography in pre-industrial England: what is to be done?', *Urban History*, 21 (1994) 273–84, and C. Galley, 'A model of early modern urban demography', *Economic History Review*, 58 (1995) 448–69. Also E. A. Wrigley, 'Brake or accelerator? Urban growth and population growth before the Industrial Revolution', in A. Van Der Woude, A. Hayami and J. de Vries (eds), *Urbanisation in history: a process of dynamic interactions* (Oxford, Oxford University Press, 1991), pp. 101–12.

7 R. S. Schofield, 'Through a glass darkly: the population history of England as an experiment in history', *Journal of Interdisciplinary History*, 15 (1985) 571–94.

8 E. A. Wrigley, R. S. Davies, J. E. Oeppen and R. S. Schofield, *English population history from family reconstitution 1580–1837* (Cambridge, Cambridge University Press, 1997).

9 But see Peter Lindert's sophisticated critique of Wrigley and Schofield which suggests that they substantially understate the birth rate in the eighteenth century and overstate it post-1810. In effect, national population probably rose faster in the post-1750 period than has thus far been allowed, emphasising the importance of the seven decades 1750–1820 for English demographic history. See P. Lindert, 'English living standards, population growth and Wrigley and Schofield', *Explorations in Economic History*, 20 (1983) 131–55. Also J. Goldstone, 'The demo-

graphic revolution in England: a reexamination', *Population Studies*, 40 (1986) 5–34.

10  R. Nettel (ed.), *Journeys of a German in England in 1782* (London, Cape, 1965).

11  For more on broad regional trends, see R. Lawton, 'Regional population trends in England and Wales, 1750–1971', in J. Hobcraft and P. Rees (eds), *Regional demographic development* (London, Croom Helm, 1978), pp. 29–70.

12  See P. Deane and W. A. Coale, *British economic growth, 1688–1959* (Cambridge, Cambridge University Press, 1967), and contributions to Hobcraft and Rees (eds), *Regional.*

13  For benchmark population indicators, see P. Clark and J. Hosking, *Population estimates of English small towns 1550–1851* (Leicester, Leicester University Press, 1989).

14  See C. B. Phillips and J. H. Smith, *Lancashire and Cheshire from 1540 AD* (London, Longman, 1994).

15  See M. J. Dobson, 'The last hiccup of the old demographic regime: population stagnation and decline in late seventeenth and early eighteenth-century south-east England', *Continuity and Change*, 4 (1989) 395–428.

16  For general reviews of some of these issues, see M. Overton, *The agricultural revolution in England: the transformation of the rural economy* (Cambridge, Cambridge University Press, 1996).

17  See J. Landers, *Death and the metropolis: studies in the demographic history of London 1670–1830* (Cambridge, Cambridge University Press, 1993), and A. Hardy, 'Diagnosis, death and diet: the case of London 1750–1909', *Journal of Interdisciplinary History*, 28 (1988) 387–401. Also N. Williams and G. Mooney, 'Infant mortality in an age of great cities: London and the English provincial cities compared 1840–1910', *Continuity and Change*, 9 (1994) 185–212.

18  Family reconstitution was pioneered in the English context by E. A. Wrigley in the mid-1960s. While the process itself is extremely complex, we might crudely style it as the production of a family tree for all people who registered demographic events in a place over a given period. Because the process yields life-cycle records which record demographic events *and* the length of time someone spent at risk of experiencing those events, it is possible to use reconstitution data to calculate very precise demographic measures such as average age at first marriage or the infant death rate. See E. A. Wrigley (ed.), *Identifying people in the past* (Cambridge, Cambridge University Press, 1972). The technique is not without problems, and these are of three types. First, the question of whether the relatively few communities with sufficiently good records to allow reconstitution to take place are really representative of other communities which will never come under the reconstitution microscope.

P. G. Spagnoli, 'Population history from parish monographs: the problem of local demographic variations', *Journal of Interdisciplinary History*, 7 (1977) 427–52, in an under-used article is highly sceptical of how far the experience of one parish can be used to represent that of another even when they share the same basic socio-economic and institutional characteristics. Second, the fact that reconstitution can tell us little about the demographic history of in- and out-migrants, so that we have to assume that migrants had the same basic demography as the small group of stable families whose demography is usually more completely traced. On this issue, see S. Ruggles, 'Migration, marriage and mortality: correcting sources of bias in English family reconstitutions', *Population Studies*, 46 (1992) 507–22, and E. A. Wrigley, 'The effects of migration on the estimation of marriage age in family reconstitution studies', *Population Studies*, 48 (1994) 81–97. Finally, reconstructing family trees involves relying on the raw material of parish registers which might or might not contain substantial inaccuracies, and thus lead to flawed demographic measures. See S. A. King, 'Historical demography, life-cycle reconstruction and family reconstitution: new perspectives', *History and Computing*, 8 (1996) 62–77.

19  These are 'national' estimates calculated as an adjunct to back projection. They provide support for David Weir's argument that it was changes in the rate of non-marriage rather than changes in the ages of those who did marry, which drove population increase between 1700 and 1750. See D. Weir, 'Rather never than late: celibacy and age at marriage in English cohort fertility, 1541–1871', *Journal of Family History*, 9 (1984) 340–54. At the level of individual reconstitutions, female non-marriage can only be detected very roughly by looking at the numbers of single women buried, while that for men cannot be gauged at all.

20  Such terminology is confusing. A falling age at marriage increases fertility simply by adding to the number of children that can be conceived and born in a reproductive life-cycle. Marital fertility refers to the rate of childbearing in marriage. So, if marital fertility increases it means that women, irrespective of the age at which they marry and therefore the total number of births that are possible, are having children faster. If marital fertility falls, then it means that women are having children more slowly.

21  For a concise review of the 1981 findings, see E. A. Wrigley and R. S. Schofield, 'English population history from family reconstitution: summary results 1600–1799', *Population Studies*, 37 (1983) 157–84, and E. A. Wrigley, 'The growth of population in eighteenth century England: a conundrum resolved', *Past and Present*, 98 (1983) 121–50.

22  See P. Razzell (ed.), *Essays in English population history* (Chichester, Caliban, 1994).

23  See Wrigley et al., *English*. For a more condensed version, see R. S.

Schofield, 'British population change 1700–1871', in R. Floud and D. McCloskey (eds), *The economic history of Britain since 1700, volume I* (Cambridge, Cambridge University Press, 1994), pp. 60–95.

24  P. Lindert, 'English', called for this sort of re-evaluation of the role of fertility in 1983. For the best recent attempt to synthesise the evidence of rising fertility and an interesting attempt to explain this rise, see E. A. Wrigley, 'Explaining the rise in marital fertility in England in the long eighteenth century', *Economic History Review*, 51 (1998) 435–64.

25  It is important not to lose sight of absolute numbers. Risks of death were highest in historical populations in the first two years of life, with the link between infant mortality and early childhood mortality provided by weaning, which had a negative effect on child survival chances given the lack of sterilised quality alternatives to breast milk. After year two, the real number of deaths falls off markedly, so that death figures for the age group 10–14 are based on so few cases that much of any 'trend' could be explained simply by extreme values in just a few years.

26  For comparative material, see J. Knodel, *Demographic behaviour in the past: a study of 14 German village populations in the eighteenth and nineteenth century* (Cambridge, Cambridge University Press, 1988).

27  See Wrigley et al., *English*. This feature was observed originally by David Levine in his reconstitution study of the Leicestershire village of Shepshed. See D. Levine, *Family formation in an age of nascent capitalism* (New York, Academic Press, 1977). See also S. A. King, 'Profitable pursuits: rural industry and mortality in the proto-industrial West Riding 1650–1830', *Local Population Studies*, 59 (1997) 26–40. Not all rural industrial areas grew rapidly but all appear to have had death rates. See R. Houston and K. Snell, 'Proto-industrialisation? Cottage industry, social change and the Industrial Revolution', *Historical Journal*, 27 (1984) 473–92.

28  Urban demography has become a popular subject in the last two decades. For three important pieces, see J. G. Williamson, *Coping with city growth during the English Industrial Revolution* (Cambridge, Cambridge University Press, 1990), J. Landers, *Death*, and A. Sharlin, 'Natural decrease in early modern cities: a reconsideration', *Past and Present*, 79 (1978) 126–38.

29  M. W. Flinn, *The European demographic system 1500–1820* (Brighton, Harvester, 1981), and R. I. Woods and N. Shelton, *An atlas of Victorian mortality* (Liverpool, Liverpool University Press, 1997).

30  A. Crosby (ed.), *The family records of Benjamin Shaw, mechanic of Dolphinholme and Preston* (Manchester, Manchester University Press, 1991).

31  M. Yasumoto, *Industrialisation, urbanisation and demographic change in England* (Nagoya, Nagoya University Press, 1994).

32  King, 'Profitable pursuits', and P. Huck, 'Infant mortality and living

standards of English workers during the Industrial Revolution', *Journal of Economic History*, 55 (1995) 528–50.

33 E. Parsons, *The civil, ecclesiastical, literary, commercial and miscellaneous history of Leeds, Bradford, Wakefield, Dewsbury, Otley and the district within ten miles of Leeds* (Leeds, Hobson, 1834).

34 King, 'Profitable pursuits'.

35 Wrigley et al., *English*.

36 For suggestions that there may actually have been substantial differences in demographic indicators between rural industrial communities in England as on the continent, see P. Hudson and S. A. King, 'A sense of place: industrialising townships in eighteenth-century Yorkshire', in R. Leboutte (ed.), *Proto-industrialisation: recent research and new perspectives* (Geneva, Droz Press, 1996), pp. 181–210.

37 See W. Seccombe, *Weathering the storm: working class families from the industrial revolution to the fertility decline* (London, Verso, 1993).

38 C. Wilson, 'Natural fertility in pre-industrial England 1600–1799', *Population Studies*, 38 (1984) 225–40. Total marital fertility in this case means the total number of children born within marriage to the average woman marrying at age 20 and remaining in the same marriage until she was 49.

39 Wrigley et al., *English*.

40 B. Reay, 'Before the transition: fertility in English villages 1800–1850', *Continuity and Change*, 9 (1993) 91–120. Communities in other southern counties from Essex to Devon experienced relatively uniform marital fertility rates at or just below the national average. R. Woods and C. Wilson, 'Fertility in England: a long term perspective', *Population Studies*, 45 (1991) 399–415. See also G. R. Boyer, 'Malthus was right after all: poor relief and birth rates in southeastern England', *Journal of Political Economy*, 97 (1989) 93–114.

41 But see also D. Loschky and D. Krier, 'Income and family size in three eighteenth century Lancashire parishes: a reconstitution study', *Journal of Economic History*, 29 (1969) 429–48, who argue that craftsmen and the gentry in the Lancashire rural communities of Over Kellett, Gressingham and Claughton practised family limitation between 1650 and 1812.

42 P. Laslett, K. Oosterveen and R. M. Smith (eds), *Bastardy and its comparative history* (Cambridge, Cambridge University Press, 1981), and R. Adair, *Courtship, illegitimacy and marriage in early modern England* (Manchester, Manchester University Press, 1996). For interesting local work, see B. Reay, 'Sexuality in nineteenth century England: the social context of illegitimacy in rural Kent', *Rural History*, 1 (1990) 219–47.

43 M. Anderson, *Family structure in nineteenth century Lancashire* (Cambridge, Cambridge University Press, 1972).

44 S. A. King, 'Dying with style: infant death and its context in a rural industrial community', *Social History of Medicine*, 10 (1997) 3–24.

45  Williamson, *Coping*.
46  C. Pooley and J. Turnbull, *Migration and mobility in Britain since the 18th century* (London, UCL Press, 1998).
47  See P. Clark, 'Migration in England during the late seventeenth and early eighteenth centuries', *Past and Present*, 85 (1979) 57–90.
48  Pooley and Turnbull, *Migration*.
49  B. Stapleton, 'Migration in pre-industrial southern England: the example of Odiham', *Southern History*, 10 (1988) 47–93.
50  Pooley and Turnbull, *Migration*.
51  S. A. King, 'Migration networks in Lancashire', in D. Ebeling and S. A. King (eds), *Community, locality and life-cycle: migration and mobility in eighteenth and nineteenth century Europe* (Hanwood Press, forthcoming, 2000), and D. Souden, 'Movers and stayers in family reconstitution populations', *Local Population Studies*, 33 (1984) 11–28.
52  Williamson, *Coping*. Southern cities and towns, and smaller towns more widely, appear to have been more dependent on the migration of young single people than northern or Midlands towns and cities.
53  C. Pooley and S. Da Cruz, 'Migration and urbanization in north west England *c.* 1760–1830', *Social History*, 19 (1994) 339–54.
54  King, 'Migration'.
55  Pooley and Turnbull, *Migration*.
56  P. White and R. I. Woods (eds), *The geographical impact of migration* (London, Longman, 1980).
57  B. Hill, 'Rural–urban migration of women and their employment in towns', *Rural History*, 5 (1994) 185–94.
58  Pooley and Turnbull, *Migration*.
59  Stapleton, 'Migration'.
60  Hudson and King, 'A sense'.
61  For a review of this, see K. D. M. Snell, 'Parish registration and the study of labour mobility', *Local Population Studies*, 33 (1984) 29–43.
62  M. B. Rose, 'Social policy and business: parish apprenticeship and the early factory system, 1750–1834', *Business History*, 31 (1989) 5–32.
63  H. Southall, 'The tramping artisan revisits: labour mobility and economic distress in early Victorian England', *Economic History Review*, 44 (1991) 272–91.
64  See J. Langton, 'People from the pits: the origins of colliers in eighteenth century southwest Lancashire', in D. R. Siddle (ed.), *Migration, mobility and modernization in Europe* (Liverpool, Liverpool University Press, 2000).
65  See K. Schurer, 'The role of the family in the process of migration', in C. Pooley and I. White (eds), *Migrants, emigrants and immigrants* (London, Routledge, 1991), pp. 106–42.
66  For a much more sophisticated discussion of the potential influence of the poor law, see Schofield, 'British'.

67  M. Blaug, 'The myth of the old poor law and the making of the new', *Journal of Economic History*, 33 (1963) 151–84, and G. Boyer, *The economic history of the English poor law 1750–1850* (Cambridge, Cambridge University Press, 1990). Also P. Solar, 'Poor relief and English economic development before the Industrial Revolution', *Economic History Review*, 58 (1995) 1–22. However, Williamson, *Coping*, argues that because rural–urban migration was so heavy in the south of England, the focus of generous poor relief was actually on an ageing population in rural areas, rather than principally on young couples.

68  For a particularly perceptive analysis of this issue, see R. M. Smith, 'Fertility, economy and household formation in England over three centuries', *Population and Development Review*, 7 (1981) 595–622.

69  For the most recent review of the state of proto-industrial research on the wider European stage, see S. Ogilvie and M. Cerman (eds), *European proto-industrialisation* (Cambridge, Cambridge University Press, 1996). J. R. Lehning, 'Nuptiality and rural industry: families and labor in the French countryside', *Journal of Family History*, 8 (1983) 333–45, provides a particularly concise review of many of these issues.

70  H. J. Hajnal, 'European marriage patterns in perspective', in D. V. Glass and D. E. C. Eversley (eds), *Population in history* (Cambridge, Cambridge University Press, 1965), pp. 101–46, and H. J. Hajnal, 'Two kinds of pre-industrial household formation systems', *Population and Development Review*, 8 (1981) 449–94. Even an average female marriage age of twenty-two years in England in the early nineteenth century was high compared to Mediterranean or Indian society.

71  J. A. Johnston, 'Family, kin and community in eight Lincolnshire parishes 1567–1800', *Rural History*, 6 (1995) 179–92

72  See A. Kussmaul, *Servants in husbandry* (Oxford, Oxford University Press, 1981). Farm servants were generally paid by the year, while other labour was paid more regularly, enabling workers in the latter context to be much more in touch with their economic position from week to week.

73  B. Hill, 'The marriage age of women and the demographers', *History Workshop Journal*, 29 (1989) 129–47, and A. Mackinnon, 'Were women present at the demographic transition? Questions from a feminist historian to historical demographers', *Gender and History*, 7 (1995) 222–40.

74  D. Gaunt, D. Levine and E. Moodie, '*The population history of England 1541–1871*: a review symposium', *Social History*, 8 (1983) 139–68.

75  *Ibid.*

76  See V. E. Chancellor (ed.), *Master and artisan in Victorian England: the diary of William Andrews and the autobiography of Joseph Gutteridge* (London, Evelyn Adams and Mackay, 1969).

77  For a review based on sixteenth-century evidence of the importance of friends in the decision of when and who to marry, see D. O'Hara, 'Ruled

by my friends: aspects of marriage in the diocese of Canterbury *c.*1540–1570', *Continuity and Change*, 6 (1991) 9–42.

78  D. Levine, 'For their own reasons: individual marriage decisions and family life', *Journal of Family History*, 7 (1982), 255–64.

79  See S. A. King, 'Chance encounters? Paths to household formation in early modern England', *International Review of Social History*, 44 (1999) 23–46, and J. R. Gillis, *A world of their own making* (Oxford, Oxford University Press, 1997).

80  Wrigley, 'Explaining'.

81  W. Cudworth, *Round about Bradford* (Queensbury, Mountain Press, 1968 reprint).

82  M. J. Dobson, 'The last hiccup'.

83  King, 'Dying'.

84  *Ibid.*

85  For the first real attempts to explain rather than observe fertility experiences, see Wrigley, 'Explaining'.

86  H. Southall and E. Garrett, 'Morbidity and mortality among early nineteenth-century engineering workers', *Social History of Medicine*, 4 (1991) 231–52. Also J. C. Riley, 'Working health time: a comparison of pre-industrial, industrial and post-industrial experiences in life and health', *Explorations in Economic History*, 28 (1991) 169–91.

87  For the latest writing on this issue, see S. Cavallo and L. Warner (eds), *Widowhood in medieval and early modern Europe* (London, Longman, 1999).

# CHAPTER EIGHT

# FAMILIES, HOUSEHOLDS AND INDIVIDUALS

## Conceptual framework

The last chapter identified fundamental changes in demographic patterns stretching from the 1740s or earlier. Our period was associated with rapid population growth, greater longevity, a more youthful age structure (because of higher birth rates and greater infant and child survival) and the emergence, towards the middle of the nineteenth century, of a demographic life-cycle which we might begin to characterise as 'modern'.[1] However, demographic historians have often seen much less change in the way people were organised into their social units – families and households – claiming that a rapidly increasing population had always been, and continued to be after 1700, concentrated into small and simple residential units. The nuclear family, in other words, was the foundation stone of social organisation in the period covered by this book. To discern whether such conclusions are valid, and to draw out the implications of domestic organisation for the wider Industrial Revolution process, students first need to confront some complex problems of terminology and evidence.

Conventionally, the term 'family' is used to characterise all of those living in the same place who are related by blood or marriage, and the term 'household' is usually taken to represent all of those living in the same finite residential unit. The family might be synonymous with the household, but the latter might also include a range of unrelated persons, such as servants, lodgers or apprentices, bound to the family by implicit or explicit contract. However, such seemingly commonsense definitions encounter three basic problems when we attempt to use them to identify and understand social and domestic units in historical populations. First, general definitions such as these do not do justice to the full spectrum of domestic structural experiences. While adult life expectancy rose and risks of maternal mortality fell during the Industrial Revolution period, it is nonetheless true that families frequently broke up because of death or desertion, and then re-formed through remarriage or informal cohabitation. It was not uncommon for men in particular to go through three or more marriages, and these sorts of experiences were reflected in the appearance of a range of half-children, adopted children and step-children in sources which deal with the structure and working of families and households. Illegitimate children and the very tangled in-law relationships which were often created through marriage add to this complexity. So does the possibility that mothers, fathers, brothers, sisters, nephews and nieces might join related households temporarily in order to cope with common life-cycle experiences such as illness or old age.

For these reasons, historians have tried to create typologies of experience. The 'standard' classification scheme based upon the work of Laslett and Wall in 1972 makes a distinction between five household/family types. The *solitary* household consisted of just a single person; the *simple* family household consisted of individual couples, a nuclear family or widow(er) and unmarried children; the *extended* family consisted of a couple (with or without children) and a range of other people related by blood or marriage; the *multiple family household* represented situations where two or more distinct families were present in the same household; finally, the *no family household* consisted of collections of individuals who might or might not have been related but who did not form a family in a conventional sense. Co-residing brothers and sisters and widows sharing houses with other widows would fall into this category.[2] Of course, there are many other ways to start classifying family and household types, but for the purposes of our analysis the basic Laslett criteria will be sufficient.

While these more sophisticated classifications might clear up some of the terminological problems and better reflect family experiences on the ground, imposing them on a poorly or ambiguously documented past raises a second basic problem. Historical demographers have only the crudest evidence available to address the structure of social units. The decennial censuses which were instigated in 1801 provide no useful information on family and household structure before 1851. Even if they did, and even if information was accurately stated and recorded, census lists do no more than represent snapshots of family and household structure on one day every ten years. Some communities in the years before the instigation of effective national census procedures can boast their own local listings, taken for religious, legal or political reasons. On the face of it such listings promise much, but some give insufficient information for the historian to discern family and household structure with confidence, while in other instances it is unclear who was included and excluded and thus whether the listing really was an accurate representation of population numbers and domestic organisation. Servants, apprentices, visitors and lodgers may have been particularly prone to exclusion from these sorts of listings, as might kin who were temporarily resident. Moreover, even the best listings have to face the question of provenance – in almost all cases there is little definitive guidance as to why a local listing was made or who made it, so that we can never be sure that listings made for different communities or in different years are strictly comparable. In any case, the available returns (fewer than 500) are small beer when set against the tens of thousands of communities which could have been subject to census listing in the seventeenth and eighteenth centuries.

Nor are other sources necessarily more reliable. Family reconstitution can allow the reconstruction of kinship networks, but it can tell us little that is concrete about the people who lived together at any point in time because the focus of analysis is the demographic life-cycle rather than the residential unit. Autobiographies and other contemporary narratives can provide much richer information about the form and function of families, but potentially suffer from problems of representativeness and partiality. Of course, historical demographers are well aware of these problems, and there is a sense in which those studying in this area have to make the best use of the tools available. The alternative to using local censuses to look at family structure is to abandon family history altogether. However, students of the Industrial Revolution must be as aware of the problems with the figures which they use as they are of the figures themselves.

Meanwhile, a third basic problem is that we must always beware of imposing labels and understandings of labels which would have seemed alien to contemporaries. This may be true of general terms such as 'family', and even more true of the detailed classification labels (extended, simple, solitary, etc.) which English family historians currently adopt. A number of commentators, for instance, have suggested that when contemporaries used terms such as 'brother', 'sister', 'cousin', 'kin' and 'family', they actually included many people under these headings who were not really related. Apprentices, servants, friends, neighbours, occupational colleagues, those with the same religious affiliation, and even strangers who happened to originate from the same town or region, might all be considered 'family' as much as those who had real blood or marriage relationships.[3] In turn, being labelled as 'kin' or 'family' in this way opened up a range of obligations and expectations between unrelated people which might match or compete with the strength of duty felt to blood relatives. These issues are taken up later in the chapter, but the need to appreciate contemporary understandings of terms which we accept as uncomplicated is an important issue.

Clearly, any attempt to analyse English families and households should be conducted with some caution. Yet, get to grips with the size, structure and functionality of families/households at different points in time and over the life-cycle we must. The family and the household were the basic building blocks of the communities which experienced the Industrial Revolution. In the words of one commentator households were 'miniature societies'.[4] They were also probably the institutional structures which did most to shape how individuals made sense of the Industrial Revolution. And as we said in our introduction, the historian's characterisation of this period matters much less than contemporary understanding of the risks and failures, opportunities and successes, which the Industrial Revolution yielded. Let us turn first to the form of historical families before looking at their functionality.

## Size and structure of domestic units[5]

A number of basic generalisations, most of them stemming from the work of Peter Laslett in the 1960s and 1970s, dominate our appreciation of English family and household history.[6] These can be simply stated. When measured at any point in time, English social units were both 'small'[7] and relatively simple.[8] As late as 1998, Richard Wall concluded that in England, 'simple family households predominated' in contrast to the situation in Corsica and Hungary where complex (extended and multiple) households were more numerous.[9] Moreover, while there was some variation around this norm in different communities there was remarkably little *systematic* spatial or socio-economic variation, or indeed variation over time.[10] In turn, these small and simple social units were located in a relatively barren kinship landscape, with mortality and migration rapidly stripping away pools of relations in most localities. Finally, within individual communities there were few systematic connections between household size and form and occupation, but rather more in the way of variation according to social status. Crudely put, it has become a commonplace that the households of peers, the gentry and, later, the urban middle class were larger and more complex than those of working people, while those of the poor were on balance smaller.[11] Servants rather than kin appear to have been key actors in variations of household size.

There is much evidence to support these crude generalisations. Consider first the idea that domestic units were both small and consistently small. Most census-based studies indicate that average household sizes varied within the range of 4–5.2 people, with a 'natural' level at around 4.7.[12] And while late eighteenth-century households may have been bigger than those of the early eighteenth or nineteenth centuries, and late nineteenth-century households were certainly smaller than those of 1800, really marked changes in mean household size are noticeable by their absence.[13] It is rare to find two population listings covering the same place at different points in time, but where they do occur the similarity in mean household size is usually striking.[14] Consider next the idea that domestic units were simple as well as small. In his analysis of 1790 data from Corfe Castle, Richard Wall suggested that 14 per cent of all households consisted of just solitary people, 72 per cent were households in which one or both parents lived with unmarried children, 9 per cent had co-resident kin outside the nuclear family, and just 4 per cent had two or more related families living together to form multiple-family households.[15] Corfe would seem to exemplify a much more widely applicable picture. Barry Reay's analysis of three nineteenth-century Kent parishes, for instance, has suggested that in 1851 between 74 and 83 per cent of all households were 'simple'. Families extended by the presence of kin accounted for only 16.5 per cent of households in the village of Broughton, and less in the others.[16] In urban Preston at the same date, 73 per cent of families were 'simple' and just 10 per cent extended.[17] For Braintree (Essex) in 1821, 83.4 per cent of non-pauper households and 77.8 per cent of pauper households were 'simple'; 4.2 per cent and 8.6 per cent of households respectively were 'extended'. The Essex village of Ardleigh in 1796 was equally polarised between these two household types – 80.7 per cent of non-pauper households were 'simple' as against 84.1 per cent of pauper households, while 10.9 per cent and 14.6 per cent of households respectively were 'extended'.[18] Other examples abound. In the Bedfordshire parish of Cardington in 1782, for instance, a local census indicates that just 8.1 per cent of households were extended.[19]

The other major generalisations can also find empirical support. Consider the role of servants in households. While the Industrial Revolution created an implicit tension between old and new money, what unified both camps was that claiming and keeping social status was usually tied up with funding a substantial household. Servants figured heavily in the size difference of these households compared with that of other lower-status households.[20] The 1787 census of parts of Westmorland highlights this feature of English domestic life very well. In the constablewick of Kings Meaburn, for instance, servants averaged one per household, highlighting the potentially elastic supply of servants even in this relatively isolated part of the world. Elsewhere, the connection between social status and the presence of servants is also starkly illustrated. In the constablewick of Hackthorpe and Whale in Lowther parish, for instance, the wealthy farmer William Hobson had four servants (domestic and farm), while the less wealthy William Tompson had two servants and the majority of smaller farmers and ordinary labourers did not generally retain any servants. There was also, of course, a link between life-cycle position and the presence of servants. In most of the constablewicks, widows and the old showed a greater tendency to employ servants than did young families with plenty of child labour.[21]

Census data of this sort are less useful for substantiating the idea that small and simple domestic units were situated within shallow and loose kinship networks at the level of the locality. In this task, however, family reconstitutions and evidence from sources such as wills prove very powerful. Lord, for instance, has used testamentary evidence from a sample of ten parishes from southeast Surrey to suggest that between 1750 and 1850, under 30 per cent of households were related to each other.[22] These figures have resonance in the Essex village of Terling where in the late seventeenth and early eighteenth centuries less than one-third of all households were related to at least one other.[23] Households in parishes in and around York during the eighteenth century were locked into a similarly shallow local kinship system.[24] Such empirical observations would seem to reflect the micro-simulation exercises conducted by Oeppen. These have suggested that, given prevailing birth rates, ages at marriage and ages at death, the maximum 'achievable' density of kinship probably rose from the later eighteenth century, but in absolute terms was still low.[25]

Yet, we should not take these perspectives at face value. Both the generalisations themselves and the evidence used to support them can be misleading. Mean household-size figures for any single community are no more reliable than are the mean ages at first marriage reviewed in chapter seven. Take the example of Appleby where the population was listed as part of the Westmorland census referred to above. The average household size for the parish was 4.91 (393 people in 80 households) and this fits well with the figures advanced by Laslett and others. However, the biggest household was that of the husband-man Joseph Blackett which comprised 12 people including 2 servants and a lodger, while 5 households comprised just 1 person. In all, 31 households had 6 or more members, while 28 had 3 or fewer. Just 21 households fell within the range of 4–5 members.[26] Potentially, this breadth of experiences tells us much more about the nature and role of English domestic units than does the mean for the community. Meanwhile, if we branch out to the wider lessons that might be drawn from the Westmorland census we can begin to see that there *were* important spatial variations in household size and structure even as between different parts of a given region. Figure 8.1 maps the mean household sizes of communities fully or partially covered by the census listing, plus a few more almost contemporaneous listings made for other reasons. The differences between the 'high' mean household sizes of north Westmorland and the 'low' mean sizes of the south of the county are significant, and cannot be explained simply with reference to the size of settlement, underlying demography, socio-economic typology or broad differences in age structure.[27] Rather, these differences probably reflected conscious choices over household size. Some confirmation of this is gained by realising that there were similar spatial variations in household structure, so that larger mean household sizes reflected a greater propensity to take in kin members.[28]

Whether these observations count as evidence of 'systematic' spatial variations is difficult to say. However, we can also point to rather more in the way of socio-economic variation in household sizes and structures than the conventional generalisations allow. Thus, proto-industrial communities during the eighteenth and early nineteenth centuries often boasted mean household sizes well above five people within the framework of usually rapid population growth.[29] One of

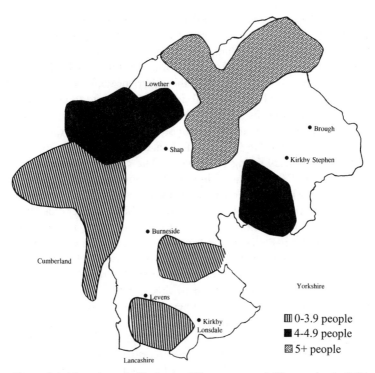

Lowther ●

● Brough

● Shap

● Kirkby Stephen

● Burneside

Cumberland

Yorkshire

● Levens

● Kirkby Lonsdale

Ⅲ 0-3.9 people
■ 4-4.9 people
▨ 5+ people

Lancashire

**Figure 8.1** Mean household size in different parts of Westmorland, 1787

the initial effects of proto-industrial development was to allow more people to live out more of their lives in the locality of their birth, where before they might have had to migrate to find work. This experience, combined with a general but not inevitable tendency for the children of proto-industrial workers to leave the parental household later than children in rural areas, and large numbers of lodgers, underpinned relatively large household size.[30] The mining communities of the Midlands and north could also boast mean household sizes well above five people for similar reasons. Paradoxically, these perspectives fit in rather well with Peter Laslett's own survey of 100 census listings between the seventeenth and nineteenth centuries, which revealed a mean size spectrum running from 3.5 to 7.25 people per household.[31] To the uninvolved eye, this wide spectrum might tell us more about contemporary understanding of domestic life than simple averages.

We need to be equally careful with generalisations on household complexity. The idea that at any point in time English households looked 'simple' is compelling, but for students of the Industrial Revolution the experiences of the minority of households that were complex might reveal more than the experiences of the majority of households upon which historical demographers tend to concentrate. In fact, the complexity of the non-simple households gives students of the Industrial Revolution an important indication of the tangled nature of everyday life in early modern communities. Let us return to the 1787 census listing of Appleby. The central message is clear – in Appleby 73 per cent of households (once we also account for solitary households) were simple in their basic structure. However, we can see that two John Richardsons headed households in the same house. One contained a married couple with a son, plus a cousin and John Richardson's brother, Thomas. The other, headed by what we take to be the elder Richardson, consisted of a married couple, two grown-up sons and two grandchildren. What was the process of negotiation which led to this complex arrangement, and what does it tell us about the inherent flexibility of household arrangements? Table 8.1 reproduces some more examples of the complex household relationships which could wind through a small community like Appleby. These stories represent a minority of household experiences certainly, but we might tentatively suggest that they are evidence that contemporaries made few hard-and-fast or long-term decisions on household size and structure. Rather, they had an underlying willingness to expand the horizons of domestic units, and perhaps an expectation that this goodwill would at some point be called upon. These ideas stand in contradistinction to Peter Laslett's speculative characterisation of an ingrained cultural preference for simple families and households in English society.[32]

Other parts of the general picture also fall victim to a detailed look at the underlying data. It is generally true, for instance, that those of the very highest social status had the largest households, but further down the social scale variations in household size according to status are less compelling. In the Westmorland parish of Kirkby Thore, the 1787 census indicates that Mr Mathew Atkinson, Gentleman, had a household complement of fourteen, including three maids, an apprentice and a gardener. However, Mr Norton, Gentleman, and Mr Richard Cornforth, Gentleman, both had household sizes of just four. This was much smaller than some labourers in the parish, less

**Table 8.1** Complex households in Appleby, 1787

| Names | Relationship | Status | Sex |
|-------|--------------|--------|-----|
| James Harrison | Master | Weaver and grocer | M |
| Mary Harrison | Wife | Grocer | F |
| Jane Jackson | Step-daughter | Keeping dairy | F |
| Betty Harrison | Daughter | Spoolwinder | F |
| Thos Abbot | Journeyman | Weaver | M |
| Ann Harrison | Daughter | Girl | F |
| Wm Jackson[a] | Lodger | Old man | M |
| Edward Idle | Master | Tailor | M |
| Peggy Idle | Wife | Housekeeper | F |
| William Idle | Son | Tailor | M |
| Edward Idle | Son | Tailor | M |
| Geo Idle | Son | Weaver | M |
| Mary Blackett | Granddaughter | Spinster | F |
| Ann Blackett | Granddaughter | Spoolwinder | F |
| Thos Bousfield | Son-in-law | Schoolmaster | M |
| Peggy Bousfield | Wife of above | Spinster | F |
| Jenny Bousfield | Infant | | F |
| John Robinson | Master | Labourer | M |
| Jane Robinson | Mother | Spinster | F |
| Ann Robinson | Sister | Spinster | F |
| Jane Robinson | Niece | Schoolgirl | F |
| Michael Collin | Master | Husbandman | M |
| Betty Abraham | Aunt | Housekeeping | F |
| Mally Collin | Sister | Confined to bed | F |
| Jane Robinson | Servant | Milkmaid | F |
| Robt Hodgson | Lodger | Gentleman | M |

*Source*: Ashcroft, *Vital*, pp. 11–13
*Note*: [a] Presumably the ex-father-in-law of Mary Harrison/Jackson.

than the seven members of Thomas Atkinson's pauper household, and considerably less than the twelve members of the John Brownrigg (Currier) household.[33] Nor do accepted conclusions fit when we turn to the other extreme of the social spectrum. Using census data from Essex in the eighteenth and nineteenth centuries, Thomas Sokoll has been able to show that the idea of small pauper households has been based upon a misreading of treacherous evidence. Censuses of the poor tend to record only the names of direct recipients of poor relief or charity, or at best their immediate family, while others living with these people often escaped the registration process. By placing the poor back into their residential context, Sokoll has been able to show that contrary to established views, pauper households were actually relatively large and complex.[34] Clearly, some rethinking of the link between status and household size might need to be undertaken.

A similar rethink of the barren landscape of kinship might also be required. The established view that English kinship was uniformly shallow when measured over time and area has now begun to give way to a more complex analysis which allows for the development of very dense kinship networks in some places during the Industrial Revolution period, and shallow ones elsewhere.[35] Barry Reay has shown that in the Kent village of Hernhill in 1851, 60 per cent of all households were related to at least one other and that a further 10 per cent of households could claim kin in villages a short distance away.[36] The latter observation fits well with the contention of Mills that parental households in Melbourn, Cambridgeshire, were the focal point for dense kinship networks which could run over the boundaries of the individual community.[37] Nor should we forget convincing evidence that kinship densities in mining and proto-industrial areas firmed up with industrial penetration. In the Lancashire coalfield areas by the late eighteenth century, at least 50 per cent of all households would be related to at least one other within the same community.[38] For the proto-industrial woollen communities to the west of Leeds, the comparable figure was almost 80 per cent by the early nineteenth century.[39] We still lack sufficient studies to discern whether English kinship as a whole was dense or shallow, and whether it became more dense or more shallow over time, but it would be true to say that the earlier conclusions of Laslett suggesting uniformly loose kinship as a basic feature of English demography now have to be regarded with some scepticism.

Clearly, then, we must be cautious in accepting the established generalisations on the form of English households. This said, there can be little doubt that the English family and household system looked 'different' from that in some other areas of Europe. On balance, England did not have the populous households which characterised some European family systems, and which have proved so enduring in popular fiction. Nor did the Industrial Revolution stimulate radical change, on the surface at least. While proto-industrial and mining communities saw household size rise and the frequency of complexity increase, their experiences were not outside the known range for English populations, as the work of Laslett makes perfectly clear. On the face of it, in fact, there is not much in family history for the student to untangle, and making sense of the Industrial Revolution could presumably be a family-free process.[40]

Such a stance would be potentially misleading in three senses. First, English family history has more subtle twists and turns than much of the current historiography allows. We have already started to explore some of the dark corners of family history in this section, but there is also a rather bigger issue to engage with. If we are to truly appreciate contemporary understandings of notions of family and household, and thereby to locate how domestic units interacted with the process of the Industrial Revolution, then it is essential to move away from point-in-time analysis and towards the question of how size and structure varied over the family life-cycle. Moreover, there is a further need to look beyond statistics and to try to understand the language of the family and household, and the nature of the decision-making process which kept households simple or made them complex. Second, even if the broad form of the family and household remained stable, the character of internal family relations might not have. In other words, we must consider the functionality of the domestic unit separately from its form. Finally, it is important to remember that while historical demographers have often talked of the effect of the Industrial Revolution on the family and household, they have hardly ever talked about the way in which the character of local and regional domestic structures could shape the nature of industrial or agrarian change. Let us look at some of these issues, starting with some basic interpretative problems.

### English family history: the twists and the turns

Interpreting the form of the family and household over time and area, and within communities, involves grappling with three thorny interpretative problems. First, while it *may* be true that household and family were small and simple at any point in time, it might also be true that over the life-cycle of most families there would be one or more periods of complexity.[41] It is easy to construct a hypothetical example to illustrate the need for a life-cycle approach. Assume a young couple marry in the parish where they were both born. They raise a number of children but then ill-health and old age begin to take effect on their parents. Subsequently, the marriages of the parental generation break up. The father of the young man comes to live briefly with his son before he remarries. Then the mother of the young woman moves in to take his place. She does not remarry and tarries for a number of years before she dies. In the meantime, the brothers and sisters of the couple are themselves caught up in their own individual and family life-cycles, and during periods of sickness, marriage break-up or economic stress, nieces, nephews and brothers and sisters-in-law briefly pass through the household. As the children of the couple leave home, so they have to take in servants to meet family labour requirements. One of their daughters bears an illegitimate child which then comes to live with the couple, and eventually old age necessitates help from their own children in the form of grandchildren sent to live with grandparents to help relieve the pressure of space in the younger household and the need for labour in the older household. For any one census day there would be a strong likelihood that the historian would see the household as simple, and statistically this is precisely what it was for much of the time. However, the enduring feature of the household would be the number of relatives moving through it, and the fact that it was flexible to needs elsewhere in the kinship network.

Historical demographers and family historians have never denied the possibility that hypothetical examples of this sort could be played out in real life. Laslett, for instance, acknowledged in 1972 that snapshot pictures of the sort provided by census listings give no indication of previous and future complexity (or size) on the part of individual families.[42] However, he also suggested that periods of complexity were confined to a limited number of stages in the house-hold life-cycle, and that we need to make a distinction between permanent co-residence/family extension and the complexity which arises out of short-term visits or crisis boarding by members of the kinship group.[43]

Such comments show how far from centre stage in the conceptuali-sation of the English family and household system the notion of the life-cycle remains. Yet, we have convincing evidence that families and households *were* volatile over the life-cycle, and more volatile than Laslett and others have allowed. For his nineteenth-century Kent villages, Reay was able to reconstruct family life-cycles between cen-suses. He suggested that one-half of all households could be classified as 'complex' at least once in the life-cycle, with a very slight tendency for craftsmen and farmers to experience a higher chance of complexity than labourers. Moreover, he goes further, suggesting that while the period of complexity for labourers was often short, the wider and deeper family economy of other occupations (a theme taken up in chapter nine) facilitated long-term complexity.[44] These figures are very significant indeed. They tie up with the picture of life-cycle complexity drawn by Michael Anderson in his study of nineteenth-century Preston.[45] If in turn we accept the conclusions of Cooper and Donald that up to two-thirds of those who appear in census schedules as unrelated to the head of household (by virtue of being given a title such as 'servant' or 'lodger' and of not sharing the same name) were actually related, then it is clear that the vast majority of households would experience several periods of complexity during the life-cycle.[46]

How these experiences were played out on the ground can best be exemplified with reference once again to the Westmorland census of 1787. Given the detail in this listing, it is possible to link the census data with evidence from tax returns, wills and inventories, diaries and a range of other sources to recreate the general outlines of life-cycle household forms for a few indicative families. These may or may not be representative of all the families living in the area, but this is not the point. As we saw in the last section, in 1787 John Richardson (the elder) of Appleby was living with his wife Mary, his sons James and Thomas, and two of his grandchildren. They were living in the same house as another John Richardson, his wife, a son called John, a cousin and a brother called Thomas. Where does this complexity fit into the overall life-cycle of the household, family and kinship group? The survival of Richardson's notebook, family records and other sources allows us to go some way in constructing an answer to this question. John Richardson (the elder) was the oldest of three sons from the marriage of James and Sarah Richardson. He was married to Mary Atkinson, in 1763. His oldest child, James, was born in 1765 and he was followed by a daughter, Sarah, a further son, Thomas, and two more daughters, Hannah and Elizabeth. Richardson inherited part of his father's 44-acre freehold plot when the father died in 1772. However, the will made John's brothers, John and Thomas (both of whom appear in the other household at the time of the 1787 census), the main beneficiaries of the will in the light of money already given to John over his father's life-cycle. His brother Thomas was obliged to care for their mother during her lifetime. By combining the sources outlined above, it is possible to trace the elder John Richardson's probable household structure from these early years to the census of 1787.

Thus, for the first fourteen years of its existence, the Richardson household had consisted of just a simple nuclear family. In 1777, with family income at a low point, the oldest son was apprenticed to an Appleby waller (Christopher Salkeld) at age twelve. At the same time Richardson took on two servants to help him work land while the other children were in their infancy. One was Andrew Winskill, who was to become the servant of Christopher Salkeld by the time of the 1787 census, and the other was Elizabeth Rudd. The household had grown but not become more complex in the sense of taking in relatives. John Richardson's daughter, Sarah, was sent to be a spinner in the house of William Rudd, the father of Elizabeth, in 1779. The family clearly preferred children to gain experience and contacts elsewhere and take on servants or other relatives in their stead. To this end, a niece, Mary Richardson, came to live with John and his family in 1780. In 1782, James Richardson returned from his apprenticeship and the family rented more land. Andrew Winskill did a direct swap with James and went to work for Christopher Salkeld. Elizabeth Rudd returned to her family in the following year, and was replaced by 'cousin' Ruth Richardson. In 1784, both of the youngest daughters, Hannah and Elizabeth, were sent to live with Thomas Atkinson, Mary's father, after the death of her mother. The niece Mary Richardson left in the same year. By late 1785, John's heavily pregnant oldest daughter Sarah was getting married to John Rudd, a son in the household where she had been learning spinning. The couple removed from Appleby in late 1786, but left their twins to the care of John and Mary for over a year. These were the grandchildren recorded at the time of the 1787 census.

On the eve of the census year, there were three further developments. First, 'cousin' Ruth left the household to live with Thomas Richardson to help him nurse his mother. Second, Hannah and Elizabeth left the home of their grandfather and were sent to their sister, living in Preston Patrick. The grandfather then took Elizabeth Rudd, who had served John and Mary, as a housekeeper, and also her brother John as a servant. Third, John's mother died and his brother Thomas fell into debt to the extent that his goods were distrained in January 1787. With his other brother, John, also in financial straits, all three brothers moved in together with their respective households. This is precisely the situation which the 1787 census recorded.[47] The Richardson story is a long and complex one, but it delivers an important message. For the first sixteen years after marriage, the household remained a simple nuclear unit with or without servants. For the next decade, the household became complex, and at times very complex. A census listing which yields a static account of household size or structure would give no indication of the immense volume of 'person transactions' between households. There was a constant throughflow of relatives, the children of friends and neighbours, and employees, through John Richardson's household. More widely, the whole Richardson kinship group in Appleby seems to have been in constant flux, something which can only be hinted at when considering individual households. The value of a life-cycle approach to *supplement* simple static representations of household size and structure should thus be abundantly clear.

Reconstructing life-cycles in this way is time-consuming, potentially full of errors, and not feasible for most individuals. Moreover, the simple fact that households could go through a number of periods of complexity over the life-cycle does not necessarily undermine the view that not much changed with the Industrial Revolution as far as household and family forms were concerned. The key question is whether periods of complexity became more common or more extended over time, and how contemporary expectations on the issue of household size and structure changed. We can offer no definitive answers here, because there are none. However, there is a logical sense in which we might have expected household instability to become more pronounced over the eighteenth and nineteenth centuries. Agrarian proletarianisation, proto-industrialisation, the development of factory industry and urbanisation were broad processes the effect of which was to intensify the traditional seasonality of agriculture and industry, to bring new swathes of people within the rhythms of the international trade-cycle, and to foster fundamental economic instability amongst the firms and farms which became increasingly responsible for livelihoods during the industrialisation process. Moreover, while death rates fell, ill-health probably intensified during the Industrial Revolution period. For these and a whole host of other reasons, all of the life-cycle stresses and strains which could lead to the break up and formation/reformation of households would have been intensified. Where such processes played themselves out against the backdrop of dense or increasingly dense kinship networks within a locality, it would be reasonable to suppose that households would experience more periods of extension, and that these periods would last longer.

This was certainly the case with the Richardson household, and we could have reproduced several other examples to confirm this point. Moreover, there is at least some evidence that industrial and agrarian change was accompanied by a rising expectation of access to households through co-residence on the part of kin. Speculative letters from distant kin seeking help in the face of life-cycle crises become more common in family collections in the eighteenth century.[48] Pauper narratives from the eighteenth and nineteenth centuries which exemplify a willingness to break up families as a short-term coping mechanism, also provide evidence of an expectation that family and kin would play their part in caring for detached household members.[49] Nor should we forget that it was only from the 1780s that legal pro-formas covering the duties and obligations of families and co-resident kin (particularly the old) were drawn up, probably in response to rising demands for this sort of document. Of course, these are disparate sources of evidence, but we feel that there is a case to be made for the idea that the Industrial Revolution increased household instability, and that in turn families and kinship groups came to expect help in the form of temporary or longer-term co-residence at different points of the life-cycle.[50]

Perhaps one of the reasons why so little stress has been laid upon life-cycle considerations is to be found in the second thorny problem which must be addressed in interpreting the household and family forms suggested by sources such as local censuses – the assumptions which historians believe to have underlain motivations for variation of household size and structure. Historians have been quick to assume that families were rational actors, and more than this that they were rational economic actors. In other words, a household head would decide to take in relatives and other household members if the family could afford to take them in or if taking a person in might increase the resources of the family. By the same token, if the economic circumstances of the household changed, then the first reaction of the head of household might be to eject household members that could no longer be afforded. Of course, this is a crude depiction of a complex topic, but the basic point – that families and household undertook a constant balancing act between resources and mouths to feed and that the need to achieve balance in the short, medium and long term was a vital influence on attitudes towards complexity – is an important one. In turn, if we accept that basic economics lies at the heart of decision making, then the fine line between viability and inviability of the household economy that characterised so many social units during the Industrial Revolution (a feature explored in chapter nine) would have left little room for complex households in English history. And even where imbalances did exist, they could be met easily by taking on, or disposing of, servants and apprentices rather than relatives. These ideas are precisely the ones which underpinned so much of the early writing on household and family structure.

However, this model does not distinguish adequately between conscious changes in household structure and the irrational or involuntary ones imposed by urgent circumstances, guilt or feelings of obligation. The sister who needed to offload children to relatives to avoid the workhouse, the cousins burnt out of their house by one of the frequent fires of the early modern period, the sick mother in need of nursing, and the emotional obligations with which these situations were charged, have no place in the rational model. Yet, one of the effects of the Industrial Revolution was to impose a new sense of risk and powerlessness on social units like the household, and it should not surprise us to see rationality suspended in the face of such problems. Certainly there seems to have been little systematic consideration behind the changing family parameters of the Richardson household. It became complex at times of prosperity, but even after 1787 when the family economy was weak, the complexity remained since Richardson had entered into long-term care obligations for his grandchildren and nieces. At times of economic stress, the Richardsons chose to send their own children to other households and employ servants in their stead. When they took on kin, there was no clear economic logic (in terms of labour demand or payment from the person themselves) in doing so, and it appears that issues of duty and custom outweighed considerations of space, economy and viability. Meanwhile, we might do well to remember that the same processes of industrial and agrarian change that made household heads act 'irrationally' also increased the range of consumer goods, work opportunities and diet, so that to contemporaries the notion of what was viable and what was not may have been very much more obscure than the reasoning of modern historians would suggest. Once again, the lessons on household and family forms to be read from sources such as census returns are not as simple as at first sight they appear.

There is also a need for a cautious approach to historic family forms in a third sense, for the whole language of household, kinship and family is increasingly suspect. As we saw in the opening section of this chapter, Harris suggested, in the early 1980s, that contemporaries understood terms such as 'family' or 'kinship' rather differently from their modern usage.[51] Naomi Tadmor has taken this analysis further, suggesting that all sorts of relationship – master and apprentice, shopkeeper and customer, friend and friend, neighbour and neighbour – could engender obligations and expectations as strong as those based upon blood and marriage and that because of these alternative worlds, contemporaries cast their understanding of family, household and kinship rather wider than we would today. Servants, neighbours and friends could all be termed 'family' in contemporary conventions, while labels such as 'cousin', 'brother' or 'kin' could extend to occupational colleagues and members of the same religious group.[52]

Certainly, contemporary diarists and autobiographers consistently employed seemingly unproblematic terms such as 'kin' to describe a disparate range of social relationships both inside and outside the spatially distinct household unit.[53] If we also acknowledge that where kin did not share a residence they often lived very near each other for substantial portions of their life-cycle, *forming effective extended households* at neighbourhood level, then it is easy to see a situation in which what we can measure – membership of independent spatial family and household units at fixed points in time – need bear no resemblance whatever to contemporary understandings of, and decision making over, household and family forms. The Richardsons had close kinship and friendship ties with substantial numbers of families around them. Indeed, their changing household structure was a means of both creating and confirming these ties, and the vagaries of marriage could overnight transform someone from being conceptually a paid employee or neighbour to being kin. To contemporaries, then, the key point about families and households may have been fluidity and flexibility of form, rather than the inflexibility and insularity that census returns would seem to suggest and that have become the accepted norm of English family history.

Whether these broad conclusions are acceptable or not, it is clear that for the student of the Industrial Revolution stepping beyond ostensibly convincing census figures showing small and simple households is a brave move which poses all sorts of conceptual and linguistic challenges. However, it is also a necessary move. If we are right to suggest that household complexity was rather more common when measured over the life-cycle than at a single point in time, that the frequency and duration of life-cycle complexity increased during the Industrial Revolution, and that the very meaning of terms such as 'small', 'simple' or 'complex' is undermined by contemporary under-standing of notions of kinship, household and family which diverge from our own,[54] then simply quoting figures of mean household size really tells us very little. Instead, we need to understand the family, the household, and family and household forms as processes in which the enduring feature was the number of 'person transactions' between related and unrelated households. This is what contemporaries would have been most aware of. Another of their concerns was likely to have been the related issue of household and family functionality – the degree to which the individuals within families and households were cemented together to provide welfare, child socialisation and emotional support. This is the subject of the next two sections.

### The functionality of the family, 1700–1850

The modern idea of the family under threat has deep historical roots. Contemporaries were consistently worried about the integrity of the family, about the individualism of youth and about weakening inter-generational ties in the Industrial Revolution period. The concern was that the traditional role of the family – providing welfare, socialising children, creating personal reputation and acting as the foundation stone for early modern communities – was being lost in the whirlwind of urbanisation and economic change which had incrementally enveloped England from the mid-eighteenth century. To some contemporaries at least, the family was becoming dysfunc-tional.[55] Historians are split on the issue of how industrial, agrarian and institutional change influenced the internal bonds of the family and its functionality. One school of thought suggests that the internal economic, social and cultural variables that tied families, households and generations together were weakening during the course of the eighteenth century. The family was becoming a collection of individ-uals rather than an entity greater in importance than the sum of its individual parts.

There are five reasons for this point of view. First, in the classic proto-industrial model the ability of young people to earn good wages earlier in the life-cycle than if they were involved in agricultural work apparently fostered a number of tensions within households. Because children were an integral part of the production unit, there was an incentive for parents to try to retain their labour and surplus value for as long as possible. At the same time, wage-earning children were enabled to marry earlier and establish spatially distinct households. They were no longer bound by the uncertainty of inheritance by and large, and so parents lost a major control over the activities of a younger generation. The burgeoning number of lodging houses to be observed in most proto-industrial areas also suggests that young workers could leave the parental household well before marriage.[56] Even where labour could be retained, continental studies of proto-industrial areas suggest forcefully that individualised boarding arrangements rapidly overtook a traditional rural tendency for the young worker to contribute all earnings to the household economy. Little surprise, then, that young proto-industrial workers appear to have engaged heavily in consumption of the most modern foods and fashions, further alienating them from the norms of a more rural society and generating significant intergenerational tensions.[57]

Broad changes in the English agrarian society and economy provide a second reason for suggesting that there was a crisis of integrity amongst Industrial Revolution families. Loss of commons, wastes and traditional resource rights in the rural economy, combined with the impact of enclosure on smallholders, intensified the seasonality of labour demand, created unemployment and altered the family economy of those newly proletarianised.[58] In large parts of the Midlands, south and west, the livelihoods of ordinary rural people were increasingly tied up with the employment policies of a small core of local employers (or distant employers if they lived in 'closed' parishes) who were also responsible for paying the rates and governing the parish through offices of local administration. These were powerful people (men by and large), and the development of the Speenhamland system and other ways of keeping a passive labour pool tied to the land at minimal costs for harvest purposes testifies that this power could be abused. There are, of course, more positive views, but there is now little doubt that enclosure instigated out-migration and emigration, and that it lay at the heart of a fundamental shift in the way in which men and women in the rural economy spent their time. Whereas in 1700 many of the employment tasks of men and women may have been complementary, taking place at the same time during the agrarian year, by 1800, as Snell has convincingly argued, women in the labour market were assigned lesser-status jobs and that this placed peak demand for male and female labour in very different parts of the agrarian year.[59]

What these observations amount to is unclear since the rural family still awaits its historian. However, analysis of contemporary narratives does little to suggest a cohesive rural family system, and some commentators have detected a norm of family conflict to match similar threads of conflict running throughout the wider institutions of rural society.[60] Other evidence supports this idea. Johnston, for instance, has analysed 399 wills made by rural Lincolnshire and Worcestershire labourers between 1700 and 1824 to show that over time it became much more common for wives to be left use of an estate for life, rather than to be given it absolutely.[61] We might read this as evidence of a decline in cohesiveness, more especially if Susan Staves and other commentators are correct to see increasing conflict over bequests between widows/widowers and children, and between children themselves, during the Industrial Revolution period.[62]

Thirdly, a pessimistic view of the coherence of ordinary working families is also underpinned by ingrained perceptions of the impact of urbanisation, particularly in the Midlands and the north. Michael Anderson's important study of mid-nineteenth-century Preston indicates that urban factory workers had a significant chance of experiencing complex households because relatives were absorbed to provide childcare and thus free up women for work in mill employment, but he believes that this experience was the outcome of 'calculative reciprocity'. In other words, families were complex because both parties had something to gain in material and emotional terms. Where gains were more one-sided, presumably there would not be the readiness to foster complex households.[63] Factory workers were a minority of the labour force in Preston and in most other communities elsewhere, but there are other reasons to expect a decline in the coherence and functionality of urban families. Urban space, for instance, came to be increasingly classified along class, age or sex lines, leaving little room for the expression and reinforcement of family unity through family activities.

Moreover, in-filling and the lack of public open spaces until the 1830s meant that a vibrant street culture developed in northern industrial towns, taking entertainment, and even eating, outside the realms of the domestic unit. This was an essentially male preserve.

Women were active in the creation and maintenance of neighbour-hood networks, and these, along with the fact that work largely ceased to be linked to the domestic situation, meant that families spent much less time together than may have been the case in rural society. Indeed, the very dynamism of urban life created a whole series of networks which stood as alternatives to or in conflict with the notion of family duties and family ties. The development of a distinctive youth culture in many urban areas, for instance, provided an alternative to the family for young people seeking an outlet for their material and emotional resources. For the late nineteenth century, outside the period covered by this book, oral history projects are peeling back the veil drawn over the family to reveal a complex spectrum of coherent inward-looking urban families at one end, and dysfunctional collections of individuals at the other. Pessimistic historians would place the bulk of urban families at the latter rather than the former end by the 1850s.

Such chronology fits rather well with a fourth pillar of the pessimistic view of the industrial family. In a classic text, Smelser argued that there was a three-stage transformation in the nature of the industrial family which was tied up with technological development and changes in industrial organisation. During the initial phase of rural industrial development around the mid- to late eighteenth century, new technology could be integrated into domestic production with relative ease. In turn, the effects of such technological change on the internal bonds of the family were minimal, even if women were displaced from traditional earning tasks. During a second stage, from the late eighteenth to the early nineteenth centuries, further technological improvement shifted the locus of work to centralised (rural and urban) production units. While the effect of this on the family was potentially devastating, the fact that whole family production units were transferred to the factory minimised the damage. Man and wife would work together in factory production, their children would do all of the menial jobs, and the family would continue to be paid as a single work unit. However, this stage was in turn superseded by faster and larger-scale production, the substitution of female for male labour and the individual wage. Crucial in this process was the rise of the self-actor and truly automated machinery, which required a raft of non-family labour to service larger-scale machines. The family-unit ethos of factory production broke down, and the training function which had been previously held by parents now passed to an overlooker paid by the owner of the factory. The wages of young people became their own, and long-established intergenerational relationships and behaviourial norms were whittled away to create a much more individualistic culture.[64]

Such conclusions have generated a storm of critical comment. They are seen to have applied only to cotton factories, and in any case there is evidence that cotton factory families were actually more rather than less coherent over time. Moreover, critics have argued that the phase during which technological advances could be contained in the domestic economy was brief, and that the phase where the family unit lay at the heart of factory production was probably non-existent in most areas.[65] We should perhaps not be as quick to judge Smelser's work. Contemporaries, as we have already suggested, were very worried indeed about the state of the early nineteenth century family, and a look at the correspondence columns of most newspapers or magazines will convince students of the Industrial Revolution of the depth of this concern. The Coventry ribbon weaver Joseph Gutteridge may well have reflected the thought of his times when he lamented the moral depravity of many of his workmates and worried about the effect that this had on family and society.[66] No surprise, then, to find so many committees of inquiry into factory and industrial life and their wider implications for institutions like the family, as we saw in chapter three.

Meanwhile, the final reason for taking a pessimistic view of family coherence and functionality during the Industrial Revolution is change in institutional structures, particularly those of welfare and the law. The classic expression of these changes is the new poor law, which had an inbuilt antithesis to the concept of the family. Dependence on communal relief represented individual and family failure, and was greeted by breakup of the domestic unit along sex and age lines. Of course, it is absolutely true that such harsh guidelines were only enforced on the ground for relatively short periods after the new poor law was enacted in 1834, and that in any case most individuals and families continued to be given relief in their own homes rather than in a workhouse where such breakup could take place, but this is not the point. The same 'public' which expressed concern over the integrity of the nineteenth-century family also passed a law which compromised that integrity in the most vulnerable parts of the social spectrum. Other legal changes may have had similar, if unintentional, effects. The factory acts, railway legislation and changes to the public-order framework all had implications for the family. Compulsory purchase of urban sites for railway development increased overcrowding in the poorest parts of urban England, curtailing privacy and fostering tension between family members. The Factory Acts contrived to make children more costly and less economically useful, and the fifty-year gap between the exclusion of younger children from factory work and the decline in working-class fertility which meant that fewer of these children were born must have generated a marked tension between family poverty and child idleness. Meanwhile, one of the effects of new police forces in urban working-class areas was to begin to drive family disputes into the confines of the home rather than their being played out within a neighbourhood context. Inter- and intra-generational family relationships may have been more tense as a result of the loss of communal input to dispute and its resolution.

Whatever happened to the form of the family, then, the evidence that its functional coherence declined during the industrialisation process would seem to be very strong indeed. From the 'traditional' family system of 1700 emerges an increasingly urbanised family system in which key elements of functionality, such as the socialisation of children, increasingly passed to employers, peer groups and others, and in which family members were considerably more individualistic than had been usual in the past. However, there is an alternative, optimistic, view of family coherence during the eighteenth and nineteenth centuries. It is based upon three central contentions. First, the idea that families and households were nowhere near as unified and functional in the 1700s as historians and popular perception have suggested. For many, the concept of the household production unit had either never existed or had declined by the 1700s so that shared economic interests were not necessarily a compelling impetus to family and household unity. In a social sense, church-court records from the seventeenth and early eighteenth centuries provide powerful evidence that families and communities were riven by infidelity and conflicts of all kinds, including tensions between the interests of the family and those of other networks to which individuals might be tied. Narrative evidence also provides a warning against a stylised romantic view of the early family. In the late seventeenth century Roger Lowe of the Lancashire town of Ashton in Makerfield kept a diary which provides substantial evidence of conflict with his 'family' and conflict in the families of the women he courted.[67] The autobiography of William Stout of Lancaster provides an even bigger canvas on which to trace the turmoil of family life between the late seventeenth and early eighteenth centuries. He clashed over issues such as finance, courtship and residence with nephews, nieces, his brother and his mother, and his wider autobiographical commentary traces similar conflict between other families in his kinship network. Ultimately, the fact of kinship kept the families involved together, but this did not mean that we should regard them as 'unified'.[68] Clearly, if these minor examples were duplicated in the wider population, it would be hard to argue for a decline in the unity and functionality of families during the industrialisation process because these features were not there in the first place.

The second component of the optimistic view is the idea that the decline in coherence has been overplayed on the basis of evidence that allows many interpretations. We have already seen, for instance, that wills can support a pessimistic interpretation of family coherence. Yet the general tendency for bequests in wills to become more closely centred on immediate family during the eighteenth century is now well established, and might actually be taken as prima facie evidence of the strength of the family.[69] Certainly Johnston believes that 'feelings of duty, tradition, morality, even love must have powered the concern these married men expressed in their provision for their wives'.[70] And while it is certainly true that wills and bequests could generate conflict between and within families, the fact that many studies point to substantial ante-mortem asset disposal as parents genuinely tried to do what they could to help young couples perhaps more than balances this perspective.[71] Turning from the ambiguity of wills, we should also perhaps recognise that many of the individual developments (urbanisation, agrarian change, etc.) which have been characterised as having a negative impact upon the family could actually be given a rather different spin. Richard Wall's comparison of the age at which children left home in rural and proto-industrial communities, for instance, throws doubt on the idea that wage earning uniformly provided more opportunity for young workers to break away from parents. He found that proto-industrial workers in some areas were likely to leave the parental home later (even if they married earlier) than the children of agricultural labourers. King has suggested similar conclusions for the proto-industrial districts of eighteenth-century West Yorkshire, but also goes further. He notes that in some communities there is clear evidence that proto-industrial development was associated with a strengthening rather than a weakening of parental involvement in the decision-making process of young workers, and that intergenerational co-operation rather than tension was the norm.[72]

The process of urbanisation also had ambiguous effects on the family. It certainly undermined the centrality of the domestic unit to social and cultural life, and yet oral history evidence from the late nineteenth century testifies to the survival in most northern urban areas of the tradition of men and young workers 'tipping up' to wives and mothers and getting an allowance in return.[73] Urban families were also an important reception and integration point for relatives new to towns, with all this implies for coherence.[74] Moreover, while the new poor law was conceptually hostile to families, on the ground we can find considerable evidence that it worked with families to maintain stability and functionality, much as the old poor law had done before it. Against this backdrop, it should come as no surprise to find that autobiographers, diarists and the writers of other narratives provide consistent evidence of the internal strength of the family, even by the mid-nineteenth century. Where family coherence was missing, as was the case with Joseph Gutteridge in nineteenth-century Coventry, tension and dispute were a source of material and emotional misery which had to be addressed through constant attempts at healing rifts and building bridges. The *expectation*, then, may have been of closely integrated families rather than the loose confederation of individuals favoured in a more pessimistic interpretation.

The final component of the more optimistic view is the idea that we simply have too little information to generalise. Whether industrialisation had a positive or negative effect on family coherence and functionality depended in part on the institutional, cultural, land-holding, social and household structures already in place as industrialisation began. It depended too on the nature of the industrialisation process itself, on its speed and on its regional dimensions. These are issues that historians have barely begun to get to grips with. For individual communities we must also avoid thinking of the character of family relationships as 'constant' even for relatively short periods. The coherence of the family and the strength of generational and intergenerational relationships almost certainly varied according to the number of siblings still present in the household, whether parents were in good or bad health, individual feelings of duty and emotional attachment, and the habits of parents. At times we might be able to characterise the integrity of individual families and families in the aggregate as strong, at other times not. Drawing a balance of these short-term experiences to highlight long-term trends is a challenge which has yet to be really convincingly tackled.

This review of the two schools of thought seemingly leaves us back where we started. Contemporary commentators (mostly middle-class) were concerned about the integrity of the family by the start of the nineteenth century. Yet ordinary people who have left records suggest that they expected to have closely integrated families. By and large they often appear to have achieved this expectation, though the strength of the family wavered within and between generations according to a whole range of factors. Historians are still nowhere near reconciling this optimistic and pessimistic evidence. The 'truth' is probably that the Industrial Revolution and all of the social and cultural changes associated with it probably had a subtle and contradictory impact on the meaning of terms such as 'family', 'coherence' and 'functionality' at local, regional and national level. Such conclusions are frustrating (though at least they show how much more potential there is for historical exploration), but we can begin to explore the question of relationships between family and household members during the key phases of the Industrial Revolution by focusing on one particular area of functionality – the role of the family in generating welfare for those in need.

## Welfare and family functionality in England

The idea that English families did not fulfil a welfare role, and may even have been less willing to offer welfare to poor relatives over time, has been an enduring one and would seem to lend support to the pessimistic interpretations outlined in the last section. Peter Laslett's 'nuclear hardship' model suggested that the combination of an English preference for independent residence, the fact that large numbers of people were missing key types of kin (because of death or migration) who might have been expected to offer welfare, and the fact that identifiable periods of need in the welfare life-cycle (for instance old age) coincided with times when other kin were least able to meet welfare needs, meant that

> the potential value of the wider kin network as an insurance against misfortune, a resource which could have been tapped by most people

271

on many occasions, even if it was finally unreliable for their sustained support, seems to have been of little or no significance.[75]

The community (through the poor law), rather than families and wider kinship groupings, provided the main plank of welfare to people at times of life-cycle and other crises.

David Thomson has taken a different line, arguing not that families were *constrained* by demographic or economic circumstance, but that they actively *chose* not to offer welfare to family members and other kin. Vague legal duties for kin to provide welfare to poor relatives were not enforced by town or parish authorities because, according to Thomson, doing so 'could unleash powerful passions and promote dangerous levels of disorder in a lightly policed society'.[76] Poor people thus had to react to the spectre of poverty by varying their household structure to change the balance between consumption and production, by exploring avenues such as charity or (mainly) by turning to the poor law. The evidence for this view is substantial. In a sample of five nineteenth-century census returns Thomson found that one-fifth of elderly widows lived alone, two-fifths headed their own households, and the other two-fifths lived in the households of others. Of this final two-fifths, most were paid a communal pension and made a net economic contribution to the household, rather than being taken in by relatives on a cost-free basis.[77] Richard Wall's analysis of Lichfield, Stoke and the aggregate of 500 other listings suggests that this sort of pattern among old women in particular, and old people collectively, showed remarkably little regional or chronological variation.[78] More generally, the rapid and inexorable rise in both poor-relief bills and the numbers on relief from the 1750s onwards could be taken as prima facie evidence that families were not fulfilling moral and legal obligations to offer welfare to poor relatives of all age groups, not just the old.

Whether kin could not or would not offer help to poor relatives, most contributors to current welfare historiography identify a central role for the old and new poor laws in the individual, communal and national welfare patchwork. The poor law took from wealthier people and the solvent parts of the life-cycle via poor rates, and gave to less wealthy people and to less solvent parts of the individual and family life-cycle via regular pensions and occasional relief, freeing families from their notional welfare role. Such relief could be generous and flexible, and, it has been suggested, came to encompass a large proportion of the most vulnerable elements of society. Contemporary decision making provides some support for this perspective. For the Lancashire town of Garstang, the vestry book records the following series of decisions about an old man called Edmund Leatherbarrow. In 1816, the overseer was 'to enquire what Jno Leatherbarrow will keep his father for'.[79] Whether Edmund Leatherbarrow had any say in this sort of bargain is unclear, though later parts of this story suggest not. The bargain for co-residence was made, but then,

> Mr John Leatherbarrow attended to say he could not afford to keep his father for the 2s a week any longer; he hopes that this committee considering his situation and the age of his father will not think 3s too much to be allowed him for tending his father. Allowed 3s per week.[80]

At the census of the poor of Garstang in 1817, Edmund Leatherbarrow was recorded in his own right as a recipient of three shillings per week, with no indication that this was to pay for houseroom with his son. By 1820 the stresses of co-residence were clearly beginning to show, with the vestry minutes noting that, 'Agreed that Edward Leatherbarrow shall have 4/ per week to himself and 1/ lodging to be paid.'[81]

This sort of detailed bargaining is rarely elaborated in the discussion over residential patterns; the important point is that similar examples could have been drawn from any number of poor-law acounts up and down the country. The example does much to suggest that English families were a relatively loose confederation of individuals by the early nineteenth century. John Leatherbarrow did not offer help voluntarily, and the fact that he regularly approached the vestry for increases in the lodging allowance for his father suggests that he may actually have made a profit out of the arrangement. There are echoes here of the 'calculative reciprocity' with which Preston families approached the question of co-residence in the mid-nineteenth century. Of course, these are minor examples, but a wider reading of poor-law accounts, vestry minutes and pauper letters might on the face of it suggest that families living through the Industrial Revolution lost much of the residual welfare functionality with which they may have entered the eighteenth century. Just as many Industrial Revolution textbooks have become family-free zones, so they have also become peopled by state-welfare junkies in the guise of the deserving and undeserving poor.

However, there are alternative perspectives. David Thomson based his discussion on Bedfordshire parishes, while that of Laslett was more theoretical than empirical. Not everywhere was the poor law as generous as in Bedford, and not everywhere did it encompass such a high proportion of the population. Anne Crowther points out that under both the old and new poor law the level of relief in western, Midlands and northern parishes was frequently so low that families sometimes had no choice but to get involved in the welfare process of their relatives.[82] Pat Thane's work on the welfare strategies of the old supports this viewpoint, suggesting that historians have tended to concentrate on poor relief because this is the most accessible part of the welfare patchwork which individuals had to deploy to cope with a given life-cycle crisis.[83] Certainly where we can trace life-cycles of welfare in some northern communities, it is clear that the poor law contributed less than one-quarter of total welfare needs, and that this contribution was unstable from year to year.[84] Few places, north or south, had consistent welfare policies, and we know little about what entitled someone to relief at the same time as another person was turned down.

The old poor law in particular could be parsimonious, harsh and exclusive in some areas at the same time as it was extremely generous and flexible in others. Periodic economy drives in most areas, however, could throw large numbers of those who had previously been entitled to relief off the communal support list. What happened to them? Other avenues beckoned of course. Charity, crime, or exploitation of commons or woodlands were all coping strategies which we can identify. However, at the heart of many local welfare states must have lain the family and kinship. For some West Riding parishes in the eighteenth and nineteenth centuries we have evidence that those without relatives came to the poor law more often, and earlier, than those with relatives, stayed on it for longer and were more dependent on the meagre income offered by the community.[85] Here, and elsewhere, families did play a welfare role, and a substantial one. This was true even where it was demographically and economically illogical to offer help, reinforcing the point we made earlier about the tendency of historians to erroneously assume rationality in household formation processes.[86] The poor law might help to support this arrangement, but often at levels nowhere near cost. Against this backdrop, it comes as no surprise to find that paupers applying for relief by letter frequently stressed that they had managed to keep off relief thus far, or had kept their relief demands to a minimum, because family and kin had been active in offering help.[87]

Once more, we can offer no definitive proof that families did or did not play an important welfare role, because that proof does not yet exist. We can say, however, that there was a spectrum of experiences. In Bedfordshire and other parishes kin obligations to provide welfare were apparently not met, and the poor law stood at the heart of individual welfare. At the opposite extreme, in places such as Westmorland and the West Riding there is convincing evidence that the poor law played a small or non-existent role in providing resources and that the family and kin stood at the heart of welfare provision. The bulk of families and communities would fall between these two extremes, and the key question is whether the Industrial Revolution and its associated social and cultural changes shunted experiences noticeably in either direction. We think that it did, particularly where we adopt a wide definition of the term 'family' to include the numerous related households that we find grouped around the ostensibly autonomous nuclear family in many areas. The rediscovery of dense English kinship networks, the realisation that life-cycle household complexity probably became more frequent as well as longer lasting, the probability that English families did not become loose federations of distinct individuals by the nineteenth century, and an emerging literature on the complexity of the English welfare patchwork, convince us that rising poor-law expenditure and numbers on relief were not inconsistent with an increased welfare role for the family. As the Industrial Revolution instigated new life-cycle risks and intensified existing ones, it seems likely that dense and functional family and kinship groups were one of the few effective defences which individuals could deploy. There is little doubt that those writing contemporary narratives both expected and received help from family and kin, and this may be the best evidence of all for the point which we are trying to make.

## Conclusion

There are many ways to read a topic marked by a lack of empirical evidence and by inadequate methodologies. However, our interpretation is that the Industrial Revolution had a profound effect on the form and function of English families and households. Current ideas that English families were small and simple, and located within a kinship structure which was very shallow and loose, are not as soundly based as the historiography would have us believe. Within and between regions there were significant variations in household size and structure, and over the life-cycle of the family periods of extension could be frequent and prolonged. By 1800 most families would experience at least one period in which they took kin into their homes. What limited evidence we have suggests that the way in which the Industrial Revolution intensified old risks and introduced new ones placed greater emphasis on the family for contemporaries, and periods of complexity were a more extensive and more expected part of the social landscape in 1850 than had been the case in 1700.

At the same time, that the internal bonds of families and the strength of intergenerational ties were undermined by industrial and agrarian changes is only one potential reading of complex evidence. By the late nineteenth century, oral history projects point forcefully towards extensive kin networks and strong families which had adapted to the changes of the period 1700–1850 with remarkable vigour. If anything, then, family bonds became stronger rather than weaker. As an element in, and an expression of, this sort of streng-thening, we might point to a reinterpretation of the nature of the welfare role of the family. While it is true that in some areas families failed to set a floor to the welfare they would offer their relatives, it is equally true that in many other areas the corollary of increased risk arising out of the Industrial Revolution was an enhanced role for the family and kin in acting as a welfare insurance policy against life-cycle and trade-cycle vagaries. In parishes from the West Riding to Bristol, family and kinship can be shown to be the key element in dictating dependence on relief. Overall, then, we believe that households and families, defined widely to include all relatives living in a community, rather than narrowly with a fixation on spatial household boundaries, became an increasingly important focus for individuals as a response to the industrialisation process. The fundamental change in demography outlined in chapter seven was accompanied by and reinforced important changes in contemporary understanding of the nature and role of household and family.

It would be convenient to finish here, but there is a further point which needs to be made and which was highlighted towards the start of this chapter. For just as industrialisation shaped the outlines and character of the most basic of social units, so the character and flexibility of households, families and kinship shaped the way in which processes of industrial and agrarian change were played out at local and sub-regional level. If we are right to suggest, as we did in chapter two, that the Industrial Revolution must be understood as an agglomeration of regional and sub-regional parts, then this is a potentially important contention. It can be briefly explored by contrasting the nature of the development of textile production under the proto-industrial system around Leeds, Halifax and the Leicestershire township of Shepshed. The woollen industry to the west of Leeds was organised for much of the eighteenth century on the basis of a traditional system of independent clothier production. Here, industrial production was conducted alongside the working of small plots of land in a dual occupation system. Over the eighteenth century, this system was subjected to intense pressure as rapid population growth outstripped the supply of land and forced downward social mobility and proletarianisation. Yet, even by 1806 the representative producer was a man with one or two looms working within a domestic environment. Part of the explanation for the longevity of this system is to be found in the family conditions which we find in the area, and on which proto-industrial structures were partly superimposed. Families were larger and more flexible than those which Laslett seemed to find, and kinship became increasingly dense as proto-industrialisation intensified. Kin groups were important players in the welfare process, and reflected the development of producer dynasties which mediated the expansion of proto-industrialisation. People married early with the expectation that they would receive material help from their families, so that a large and buoyant labour force underpinned industrial production without draining the communal coffers through the poor rates. There was thus little sense in undermining the dual occupation production system which proved so responsive to market needs.[88]

Meanwhile, around Halifax the nascent worsted industry of the 1730s and 1740s had expanded rapidly by the later eighteenth century. Production here was organised along 'putting-out' lines, where individual labouring families worked on the raw materials (and sometimes with the tools) of merchants to produce cloth which the merchant subsequently marketed. Proto-industry in this area was superimposed on an upland family system which had been racked by half a century of population growth resulting in heavy out-migration, limited kinship and families with shallow roots. Subsequently, increased kinship densities, combined with a remarkable set of marriage strategies for labouring families, generated dynasties of weavers, shoemakers and others, and fostered the development of a whole new set of trades in the early nineteenth century. While textile industries elsewhere were going into reverse, the worsted producers around Halifax avoided industrial involution through a flexible and extensive kinship and family system which allowed the diversification of economic interests and the deployment of collective power to prevent merchants whittling away at wage rates for industrial production.[89]

The contrast with the Leicestershire hosiery village of Shepshed is stark. Like the worsted industry, hosiery production was organised along putting-out lines and was superimposed on a weak demographic system. However, in Shepshed proto-industrialisation does not seem to have led to dense kinship networks, and there is no obvious evidence of large or flexible family structures. When faced with industrial decline, individual families worked harder in a process of self-exploitation, and there is no evidence of other defence strategies such as the creation of dynasties or the development of integrated production groups of the sort which we can see in the West Riding. Clearly, family structures were only one influence on the character and longevity of industry in the three places, but the key lesson is that the family could mediate the impact of change in the socio-economic sphere, as well as simply react to it. The character and flexibility of the family economy had a similar dual role, and this is one of the issues explored in the next chapter.

## Notes

1   See M. Anderson, 'The emergence of the modern life-cycle in Britain', *Social History*, 10 (1985) 69–87.
2   P. Laslett and R. Wall (eds), *Household and family in past times* (Cambridge, Cambridge University Press, 1972), pp. 1–90.
3   For an early discussion of these issues, see O. Harris, 'Households and their boundaries', *History Workshop Journal*, 13 (1982) 143–52.
4   M. Abbot, *Life cycles in England 1560–1720: cradle to grave* (London, Longman, 1996), p. 118.
5   Because of the conceptual and terminological difficulties involved in looking at 'families', households will be the preferred level of analysis in this section.
6   For the definitive statement of these general conclusions, see P. Laslett, 'Size and structure of the household in England over three centuries', *Population Studies*, 23 (1969) 199–223.

7 This term is problematic in the sense that it makes no allowance for involuntary restrictions imposed upon family sizes by architectural styles, lease restrictions or the space requirements of domestic production.

8 P. Laslett, *Family life and illicit love in earlier generations* (Cambridge, Cambridge University Press, 1977), pp. 12–49, suggested that only around 12 per cent of all households were extended at any time in the past.

9 R. Wall, 'Characteristics of European family and household systems', *Historical Social Research*, 23 (1998) 50.

10 See R. Wall, 'Mean household size in England from printed sources', in Laslett and Wall (eds), *Household*, pp. 159–203, and R. Wall, 'Regional and temporal variations in English household structure from 1650', in J. Hobcraft and P. Rees (eds), *Regional demographic development* (London, Croom Helm, 1978) pp. 89–116.

11 See R. O'Day, *The family and family relationships, 1500–1900* (Basingstoke, Macmillan, 1994).

12 P. Laslett, 'Mean household size in England since the sixteenth century' in Laslett and Wall (eds), *Household*.

13 What constituted a significant rise or fall is open to individual interpretation. We should remember that even a small change in mean household size could mask fundamental changes in the structure of underlying demography and co-residence. See *ibid.*, pp. 137–8.

14 See R. Wall, 'Leaving home and the process of household formation in pre-industrial England', *Continuity and Change*, 2 (1988) 77–102.

15 Wall, 'Characteristics'.

16 B. Reay, *Microhistories: demography, society and culture in rural England, 1800–1930* (Cambridge, Cambridge University Press, 1996), p. 159.

17 M. Anderson, *Family structure in nineteenth century Lancashire* (Cambridge, Cambridge University Press, 1971), p. 44.

18 See T. Sokoll, 'The household position of elderly widows in poverty: evidence from two English communities in the late eighteenth and early nineteenth centuries', in J. Henderson and R. Wall (eds), *Poor women and children in the European past* (London, Routledge, 1994), pp. 211–15.

19 D. Baker, 'The inhabitants of Cardington in 1782', *Publications of the Bedfordshire Historical Record Society*, 52 (1973). A late seventeenth-century census for the Lancashire town of Bolton suggests that even for earlier periods, and for urban areas, this picture of dominant simple households is equally relevant. See Lancashire Record Office (hereafter LRO), DDKe 2/6/2, Census of Bolton, 1674. We are grateful to Richard Hoyle for bringing this source to our attention.

20 Laslett, 'Mean', has suggested that servants and inmates (lodgers and visitors) were the most fluid part of the English household system, and their presence or absence does much to explain variation in mean household sizes within and between communities. Students should not however think that there was an inevitable relationship between status

and household size. Abbot, *Life cycles*, pp. 116–17, suggests that both life-cycle position and 'external constraints' created important differences in the household sizes of those who belonged to the same upper strata.

21  L. Ashcroft (ed.), *Vital statistics: the Westmorland census of 1787* (Berwick, Curwen Archives Trust, 1992).

22  E. Lord, 'Communities of common interest: the social landscape of south east Surrey 1750–1850', in C. Phythian-Adams (ed.), *Societies, cultures and kinship 1580–1850* (Leicester, Leicester University Press, 1992), pp. 131–99.

23  K. Wrightson, 'Kinship in an English village, Terling, Essex, 1550–1700', in R. M. Smith (ed.), *Land, kinship and life cycle* (Cambridge, Cambridge University Press, 1984), pp. 313–32.

24  W. Coster, *Kinship and inheritance in early modern England: three Yorkshire parishes* (York, Borthwick Institute, 1993).

25  J. E. Smith and J. Oeppen, 'Estimating numbers of kin in historical England using demographic microsimulation', in D. S. Reher and R. S. Schofield (eds), *Old and new methods in historical demography* (Oxford, Oxford University Press, 1993), pp. 280–317.

26  Ashcroft, *Vital*.

27  Sokoll, 'The household', p. 212, suggests that the more a community age structure was weighted towards old people, the more prevalent were solitary and/or complex (smaller and larger) households.

28  See S. A. King, 'Making the most of opportunity: reconstructing the economy of makeshifts in the early modern north', in S. A. King and A. Tomkins (eds), *Coping with the crossroads of life: the economy of makeshifts in early modern England* (Manchester, Manchester University Press, 2001).

29  See S. A. King, 'The English proto-industrial family: old and new perspectives', in *History of the Family* (forthcoming, 2001).

30  Wall, 'Leaving'.

31  Laslett, 'Mean', p. 137.

32  Laslett, 'Introduction', *Household and family*.

33  Ashcroft, *Vital*. These examples do not of course control for life-cycle stage.

34  Sokoll, 'The household', and T. Sokoll, *Household and family among the poor: the case of two Essex communities in the late eighteenth and early nineteenth centuries* (Bochum, Verlaag, 1993).

35  For a 'recent' reiteration of the older view, see P. Laslett, 'Family, kinship and collectivity as systems of support in pre-industrial Europe: a consideration of the nuclear hardship hypothesis', *Continuity and Change*, 3 (1988) 153–75.

36  B. Reay, 'Kinship and the neighbourhood in nineteenth century rural England: the myth of the autonomous nuclear family', *Journal of Family History*, 21 (1996) 87–104.

37  D. R. Mills, 'The residential propinquity of kin in a Cambridgeshire village', *Journal of Historical Geography*, 4 (1978) 265–76.

38  J. Langton, 'People from the pits: the origins of colliers in eighteenth century southwest Lancashire', in D. Siddle (ed.), *Migration, mobility and modernisation in Europe* (Liverpool, Liverpool University Press, 2000), pp. 233–82.

39  See S. A. King, 'Migrants on the margin: mobility, integration and occupations in the West Riding, 1650–1820', *Journal of Historical Geography*, 23 (1997) 284–303.

40  As it has been in some of the key textbooks thus far, though see P. Hudson, *The Industrial Revolution* (London, Arnold, 1992).

41  Equally, over the individual life-cycle a person might find themselves in a wide range of different household situations, even if for much of their life they were firmly embedded into a standard nuclear family. See Wall, 'Characteristics', for interesting methodological advances in this area.

42  Laslett, 'Introduction'.

43  Laslett, 'Mean'.

44  Reay, *Microhistories*. In the early part of this analysis, we were quoting figures from Reay on household complexity *at individual points in time*.

45  Anderson, *Family*.

46  D. Cooper and M. Donald, 'Households and hidden kin in early nineteenth century England: four case studies in suburban Exeter', *Continuity and Change*, 10 (1995) 257–78.

47  See King, 'Making', for a fuller review of the Richardson life-cycle and the processes which underpin its reconstruction.

48  See D. Cressey, 'Kinship and kin interaction in early modern England', *Past and Present*, 113 (1986) 38–69.

49  J. S. Taylor, *Poverty, migration and settlement in the Industrial Revolution: sojourners' narratives* (Palo Alto, SPSS, 1989).

50  Against this backdrop, it seems unlikely that contemporaries distinguished between degrees of co-residence, even if Laslett argues that modern historians should make this distinction.

51  Harris, 'Households'.

52  N. Tadmor, 'The concept of the household-family in eighteenth century England', *Past and Present*, 151 (1996) 111–40.

53  For just two of many examples, see J. E. Crowther and P. A. Crowther (eds), *The diary of Robert Sharp of South Cave: life in a Yorkshire village 1812–1829* (Oxford, Oxford University Press, 1997), and D. Vaisey (ed.), *The diary of Thomas Turner, 1754–1765* (Oxford, Oxford University Press, 1984).

54  On these issues see also R. Trumback, 'Kinship and marriage in early modern France and England: four books', *Annals of Scholarship*, 2 (1981) 113–28.

281

55  J. Gillis, *A world of their own making* (Oxford, Oxford University Press, 1997).

56  See M. Mitteraur, 'Servants and youth', *Continuity and Change*, 5 (1990) 11–38.

57  For a review of this material, and for a challenging reinterpretation, see M. R. Somers, 'The "misteries" of property: relationality, rural indus-trialisation, and community in chartist narratives of political rights', in J. Brewer and S. Staves (eds), *Early modern conceptions of property* (London, Routledge, 1995), pp. 62–92. The classic text on this issue is H. Medick, 'The proto-industrial family economy: the structural function of the household and family during the transition from peasant society to industrial capitalism', *Social History*, 6 (1976/77) 291–316.

58  For a pessimistic interpretation of the effect of enclosure on ordinary people, see J. M. Neeson, *Commoners: common right, enclosure and social change in England 1700–1820* (Cambridge, Cambridge University Press, 1993).

59  K. D. M. Snell, *Annals of the labouring poor: social change and agrarian England 1660–1900* (Cambridge, Cambridge University Press, 1985).

60  See, for instance, B. Bushaway, *By rite: custom, ceremony and community in England 1700–1880* (London, Junction Books, 1982), and J. P. D. Dun-babin, *Rural discontent in nineteenth century Britain* (London, Holmes and Meier, 1975).

61  J. A. Johnston, 'The family and kin of the Lincolnshire labourer in the eighteenth century', *Lincolnshire History and Archaeology*, 14 (1979) 47–52.

62  S. Staves, 'Resentment or resignation? Dividing the spoils among daughters and younger sons', in Brewer and Staves (eds), *Early modern*, pp. 194–218.

63  Anderson, *Family*.

64  N. Smelser, *Social change and the Industrial Revolution: an application of theory to the Lancashire cotton industry 1770–1840* (London, Rout-ledge and Kegan Paul, 1959).

65  M. Anderson, 'Sociological history and the working class family: Smelser revisited', *Social History*, 3 (1976) 317–34, and R. L. Jones, 'N. J. Smelser and the cotton factory family: a reassessment', in N. B. Harte and K. G. Ponting (eds), *Textile history and economic history* (Manchester, Manchester University Press, 1973), pp. 304–19.

66  V. E. Chancellor, *Master and artisan in Victorian England: the diary of William Andrews and the autobiography of Joseph Gutteridge* (London, Evelyn Adams and Mackay, 1969).

67  W. L. Sasche (ed.), *The diary of Roger Lowe of Ashton in Makerfield, Lancashire, 1663–1674* (Wigan, Picks, 1994).

68  J. D. Marshall (ed.), *The autobiography of William Stout of Lancaster, 1665–1725* (Manchester, Manchester University Press, 1969).

69  See J. A. Johnston, 'The probate inventories and wills of a Worcestershire parish 1676–1775', *Midland History*, 1 (1971) 20–33, who argued that just over one-half of all bequests went to either a spouse or a child. However, for an apparent exception to this rule, see R. T. Vann, 'Wills and the family in an English town: Banbury 1550–1800', *Journal of Family History*, 4 (1979) 346–67.

70  J. A. Johnston, 'Family, kin and community in eight Lincolnshire parishes 1567–1800', *Rural History*, 6 (1995) 182.

71  See R. Wall, 'Real property, marriage and children: the evidence from four pre-industrial communities', in R. M. Smith (ed.), *Land, kinship and life-cycle* (Cambridge, Cambridge University Press, 1984), pp. 443–80, and L. Bonfield, 'Normative rules and property transmission: reflections on the link between marriage and inheritance in early modern England', in K. Wrightson et al. (eds), *The world we have gained: histories of population and social structure* (Oxford, Blackwell, 1986), pp. 155–76.

72  S. A. King, 'Calverley und Sowerby: die protoindustrielle entwicklung in zwei gemeinden Yorkshires (1660 bis 1830)', in D. Ebeling and W. Mager (eds), *Proto-industrie in der region* (Bielefeld, Verlaag, 1997), pp. 221–54. Also Wall, 'Leaving'.

73  E. Roberts, *A woman's place: an oral history of working class women 1890–1940* (Oxford, Blackwell, 1985).

74  K. Schurer, 'The role of the family in the process of migration', in C. G. Pooley and I. D. White (eds), *Migrants, emigrants and immigrants: a social history of migration* (London, Routledge, 1991), pp. 106–41.

75  Laslett, *Family*, 166.

76  D. Thomson, 'The welfare of the elderly in the past: a family or community responsibility?', in M. Pelling and R. M. Smith (eds), *Life, death and the elderly: historical perspectives* (London, Routledge, 1991), pp. 194–221.

77  *Ibid.* For an excellent overview of the whole area, see P. Thane, 'Old people and their families in the English past', in M. Daunton (ed.), *Charity, self-interest and welfare in the English past* (London, UCL Press, 1996), pp. 113–38.

78  R. Wall, 'Elderly persons and members of their households in England and Wales from pre-industrial times to the present', in D. Kertzer and P. Laslett (eds), *Aging in the past: demography, society and old age* (Los Angeles, University of California Press, 1995), pp. 81–106.

79  LRO, DDX 325, Garstang vestry minutes, June 1816.

80  *Ibid.*, August 1816.

81  *Ibid.*, September 1820. By July 1821, the allowance had risen to 6s. 6d.

82  M. Crowther, 'Family responsibility and state responsibility in Britain before the welfare state', *Historical Journal*, 25 (1982) 131–45.

83  Thane, 'Old people'.

84 King, 'Making'.
85 S. A. King, 'Reconstructing lives: the poor, the poor law and welfare in Calverley 1650–1820', *Social History*, 22 (1997) 318–38.
86 In this sense, Richard Wall's analysis of the ways in which English families were extended compared to the continent is significant. The variety of relatives found within the English extended household was rather greater than in Europe, suggesting that the English family had a key welfare role in taking in, over the short term, drifting and desperate relatives, while elsewhere extension was part of the process of changing headship of the households concerned. See Wall, 'Characteristics'.
87 See the different contributions to T. Hitchcock, P. King and P. Sharpe (eds), *Chronicling poverty* (Basingstoke, Macmillan, 1996).
88 For more on this issue, see S. A. King, 'English historical demography and the nuptiality conundrum: new perspectives', *Historical Social Research*, 23 (1998) 130–56.
89 For more on this, see P. Hudson and S. A. King, 'A sense of place: industrialising townships in eighteenth century Yorkshire', in R. Leboutte (ed.), *Proto-industrialisation: recent research and new perspectives* (Geneva, Droz, 1996), pp. 181–210.

# CHAPTER NINE

# THE CHANGING ECONOMICS
# OF THE HOUSEHOLD

## Conceptual framework

Previous chapters have taught us important lessons about the general framework within which we must try to understand the economics of the household over the period 1700–1850. National population size increased substantially from 1750, accompanied by a dramatic rise in the size of the urban population and a shift in the locus of population growth to the emerging industrial areas. The form and function of the family changed rather more than it has so far been conventional to allow, reacting to the enhanced life-cycle risks that the Industrial Revolution foisted on to ordinary people.[1] Outside the demographic aspect of ordinary life, integration of regional food and product markets gave families and households access to more regular food supplies at the same time as the number of families with links to the means of food production tumbled from an already relatively low base after the early eighteenth century. Agriculture, domestic service, food processing and trades such as building were key features of the occupational structure in 1851, as they had been in 1700. However, a range of dynamic industries had created distinctive regional economies. Cotton textiles, mining and metalworking (in both rural industrial and factory modes) offered opportunities for those who spent increasing parts of their working lives within these occupations, but such industries also generated a fragile form of capitalism which periodically, during trade downswings, could plunge whole regions into abject need. Moreover, the corollary of industrial expansion in some areas was de-industrialisation in others, dealing a body blow to the diverse household economies of some southern communities in particular. We outlined this process in detail in chapter two. There were also persistent eighteenth- and early nineteenth-century regional differences in wages, even amongst those doing the same job. Agricultural labourers in Lancashire, for instance, earned at least 50 per cent more than their counterparts in Dorset by 1801. We could go on with this sort of listing, but the core point is that the 'average' family economy would have been caught up in a complex process of economic opportunity and economic restriction after 1700.

For some families and individuals this situation offered material opportunity. Higher wages, more regular employment, the utilisation of more of the potential family labour force, the benefits as well as the drawbacks of urban living and the opportunity to begin to invest in human capital beckoned for those individuals and families who were in the right place at the right time. However, material opportunity was balanced by the potential for deep individual and household misery. For those caught up in technological redundancy, for families in high-wage areas where poor budgeting saw household resources spirited away to the ale house, for agricultural labourers stripped of common rights, and for proto-industrial workers whose response to market glut was simply to produce more, a compromised household economy might lead to economic marginality for a prolonged period of the family life-cycle. Understanding how the nature of the household economy changed after 1700 is thus a vital precursor to appreciating how families internalised the economic, social, cultural and institutional changes which together made the Industrial Revolution.[2]

However, this is to start in the middle of a story, and initially students of the Industrial Revolution must understand that 'the household economy' poses some thorny practical and conceptual problems. What do we actually mean by the term 'household economy'?[3] The collective income of household members? The outgoings of the household? The balance in consumption between food and other items? And when we have defined what we mean by 'household economy', should we distinguish the household economies of the urban worker from the rural worker, the kinless from the kin rich, or the migrant from the native? Once these questions have been addressed, then we have to ask the most thorny question of all – how do we reconstruct the different elements of the family economy and measure its strength? Reconstruction is no easy process and so we concentrate on the issue in some depth here. There was no Industrial Revolution equivalent of the Family Expenditure Survey of the post-World War II era and while the household accounts of middling people survive in greater numbers than we had ever realised, the same is not true of farm labourers, factory workers, straw plait workers or others. For these people, the closest approximation to family accounts are to be found in household budgets which were constructed by largely middle-class observers on an often uncertain information basis.[4]

We return to the subject of household budgets later in the chapter. An alternative approach to measuring the household economy is to adopt the tools of those engaged in the standard-of-living debate, using wage rates to approximate household income and the cost of a basket of consumer goods to approximate household outgoings. However, such an approach carries manifest dangers. On the income front, wage rates are treacherous even where we can find surviving information. They usually make no allowance for underemployment or unemployment and they often give little hint about payments in kind or deductions by employers. Concentrating on wage rates also privileges the wage-earning powers of men as against women and children simply because data survival is better for men or because wages went as an aggregated lump to the male head of household where men, women and children worked together. There are good reasons to think that these exclusions will give an unsatisfactory picture of the income side of the household balance sheet. While Horrell and Humphries have suggested that women and children played a lesser part in household earning patterns than was once thought, they have confirmed very strongly that for certain occupations (particularly proto-industrial workers), and for certain parts of the family life-cycle, the earnings of women and children were what made the family economy viable.[5] Nor should we forget that whatever its level, the symbolic significance of 'the wage' changed over time and this is also important in gaining an appreciation of contemporary understandings of the household economy. While debate still continues, there is now a majority consensus that, in so far as they had ever been active in the labour market, women and children were streamed out of the labour force and the best-paying jobs in the nineteenth century by a combination of legal restriction, technological and organisational redundancy, union action and employer–male worker collusion to maintain paternalistic industrial relations.[6] In many areas and for many families, 'wages' increasingly came to mean 'male wages' and 'family economy' increasingly came to be synonymous with the male wage. Concentrating simply on the level of wages misses this key symbolic change which may have had important negative connotations to contemporary observers.

On the outgoings front, the 'average consumer' is a difficult animal to identify at the best of times, more so when there were very real differences in spending patterns and even diet between areas and over time. Crudely put, for most of the eighteenth century northern families ate more diversified basic foods, including several types of brown bread, than their counterparts in the south where the idea of 'fashion foods' (such as white bread and sugared tea) seems to have caught on rather earlier.[7] Even if such differences had not existed, we should not forget that within communities families with the same nominal income might have very different spending patterns depending on the personalities and preferences of the people involved. As social investigators from the late eighteenth century onwards were fond of noting, we can fairly easily locate the thrifty household where everything was done in moderation and place it against the household where adequate wages were drunk away at the ale house, compromising living standards.[8] A further complication stems from the fact that even if we knew what aggregate income and expenditure were at family level, it would be wrong to assume that there was an equal division of family resources between different household members. Men and paying children may well have had a greater claim to food and other resources than would women or younger children.[9]

Clearly, then, reconstructing changes in the diversity and strength of the household economy of ordinary people, however we define 'household economy' in the first place, is a process beset by problems of finding and interpreting evidence and the perennial issue of regional differences. Other interpretative complexities suggest that we would be best advised to drop any aspirations to construct detailed balance sheets or to 'count' the household economy and look for general indicators of economic health or weakness. We saw in chapter eight, for instance, that family and household units were frequently unstable in membership terms, and this instability could forge unseen and perhaps unknowable consequences for the well-being of the family economy at times of life- or trade-cycle crises. Neither budgets nor wage and consumption figures will factor this variable into an assessment of the strength and weakness of family economy. Linked to this point, we should bear in mind that individual families and households were not insulated from related and unrelated families living nearby. Neighbourhood lending and borrowing networks, or the ability to turn to several branches of one's family in the same street, might have made an important difference to contemporary appreciations of the character of their family economy, but source-constrained historians will miss this phenomenon from their assessment. Finally, it is important to note that when historians talk of 'household economy' what they often mean is the household economy at a single point in time. The snapshot picture is of course valuable, but it is likely that contemporaries understood the household economy as a life-cycle phenomenon in which there would be identifiable highs and lows and periods of crisis or comfort. Understanding the household economy, assessing its weakness or strength, and relating the notion of the household economy to our attempts to make sense of the Industrial Revolution, relies at least in part on our ability to understand the intra- and inter-life-cycle connotations of what we observe.[10]

These are important cautions. Bearing them in mind this chapter will sidestep the search for quantitative certainty and definitional precision. Instead, it will seek general indicators of the health of household economies over time and the life-cycle, concentrating in particular on the ability of households to cope with extraordinary circumstances such as illness, unemployment, death of the main wage earner and trade depression. Against this backdrop, creating core generalisations on the strength and width of ordinary household economies between 1700 and 1850 will be the outcome of a three-stage process. First, the chapter will use a number of local sources and local examples to suggest some of the basic household economy experiences which may have more general relevance to the period 1700–1850. Second, it will identify the extremes of the household economy spectrum – the definite losers and the gainers from the Industrial Revolution – to broaden out the discussion and to give two fixed reference points. Finally, the chapter will attempt to reconstruct the family economies which fell between these sets of extreme experiences, using the ability or inability of families to avoid contact with the poor-law system and the wider economy of makeshifts after 1700 as a yardstick against which to judge the economic health of families during the Industrial Revolution. Of course, there are other potential approaches to the issue of household economy, but for the purposes of this chapter in this book, a generalised approach yields the greatest returns.

Characterising the household economy, 1700–1850:
key lessons

There are many sources which directly or indirectly throw light on
the nature of the English family economy. Up to 1705 we might use
the relative size of that group paying, and that group not paying, the
tax on vital events (marriages, baptisms and burials) as a general
indicator of those family economies that contemporaries considered
viable. The relative size of the groups who paid, did not pay, were
late payers of, or were distrained for, local taxes, might also be used
as a general indicator. Poor-law data might fulfil a similar function,
and we return to this issue later in the chapter. There is a sense,
however, in which some very detailed local examples and local sources
can tell us much more about the nature of household economies and
changes in those household economies over time and area than a
wide discussion of tax returns or other data. This is the strategy
which we initially prefer in this chapter.

Our first example is the land and cottage rentals for the Yorkshire
township of Calverley in the mid-eighteenth century, just before
formal enclosure of its commons. These provide data on levels of
rents, types of tenure, the quality of land and housing, and the amount
and value of land taken by those poor people who had encroached
on commons. On the face of it, these seem odd sources to start with
in looking at household economies. However, in the sense that rent
levels, the ability to hold on to land and the quality of cottages were
variables likely to be closely related to the health of individual household economies, they provide an important proxy measure which
could be employed using similar data elsewhere and which might
yield general lessons of some importance.[11] Figure 9.1 sets out the
rental value of the dwellings and landholdings of all of those living
in the village at mid-century.[12] Some of the village cloth-making and
farming elite were clearly very important and must have had strong
and diversified family economies. A survey of the township prior to
the sale of the holdings of the major landowner in 1755 broadly
confirms this perspective, tracing elegant farm buildings and extensive
supplementary interests in fruit growing, spring water, sub-letting
and wool tentering.[13]

By contrast, those making the lowest rental payments (a feature
again confirmed by the survey of 1755) lived in mean houses on and
around the common and waste, or in the lowest-lying and most boggy

parts of the township. These people – disproportionately widows, migrants or those falling down the social scale – must have had weak and unstable family economies, a feature perhaps confirmed by their inability to keep their children alive compared with people in other parts of the parish. If in turn we adopt a threshold figure (say an annual rental of 40s. or less) below which we would expect the family economy of those paying the rental to be chronically weak, we can see that perhaps 11 per cent of households fall within this category. Of course this is misleading. Some of these low-rental families might have been major landowners in another township, or the fact of low rental might be a short-term reaction to extreme circumstances. None-theless, a quick look at the poor-law accounts in the township confirms that there was an association between low rental payments and unstable household economies that required poor-law support. Linking figure 9.1 with family reconstitution evidence for the township suggests very clearly that the people paying the lowest rentals were those hit by life-cycle crises, particularly old age and widowhood, and that the payment of low rents represented a long-term rather than short-term situation for most people.[14]

This detailed local example, then, suggests that households were ill-equipped to deal with life-cycle crises even towards the start of our Industrial Revolution period. The consequences of this experience were not only poor housing and dependence on relief, but also

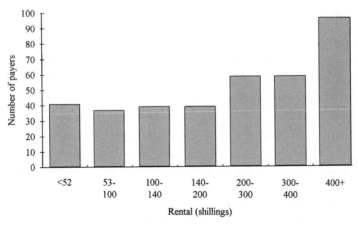

Figure 9.1 Land and cottage rentals in Calverley, *c.* 1750

291

enhanced risks of death and illness. Chronically weak household economies of this sort – one in ten of the total household stock in the mid-eighteenth century – underpinned a wider body of marginal households, and their collective experience must be contrasted with the 20 per cent of households where rental and other data suggest considerable levels of comfort. What this sort of analysis does not allow us to do, of course, is to definitively reconstruct the household forms of those caught up in the chronically weak and unstable family economies. Were these households small and simple? Or were they weak because they were large and extended? These important questions – and the general lessons to be drawn from the local rental data – can be addressed and extended using a second source from Yorkshire.

In 1811, the worsted industry of Halifax was confronting a slump and the income of many industrial workers was under pressure. The response of the local social and industrial elite was to form a committee charged with raising money through private subscription to buy food. By late 1811, their efforts had been remarkably successful, with over £1,200 subscribed. Flour was duly purchased and a record was kept of the individuals who were deemed needy enough to receive it. However the record – in the form of a 'dole' book – went much further than just recording names, noting also the family size of recipients, their trade, their average weekly income (in 'normal' times), their employer and the cause of their need, as well as whether the recipient also got relief from the poor law or other sources. In this sense, it constitutes a rich snapshot source to continue trying to draw key lessons about the strength and depth of household economies.[15] Nonetheless, we must also inject a note of caution. In an industrial area like Halifax there was a diverse range of earning possibilities, not all of which might have been included in these records. Moreover, we are unsure where the information about weekly earnings came from. The occupation and employer of the main recipient is clearly listed in the records and it may be that some combination of enquiry by employers and statements by the recipients explains how these figures were derived. Plainly, both sources of information could be inaccurate, but the entry for John Utley, which reads 'since called upon – 12 shillings earnings', suggests that the relief committee did go to considerable lengths to secure an accurate picture of the state of the family economy of those whom they relieved.

With these caveats in mind, figure 9.2 correlates family size with the normal weekly family earnings recorded in the dole book, allowing us to approach the issue of the character of the household economy with more precision than was possible using rental records. Three important lessons spring immediately from the graph and the source which underpins it. First, we can see that the smallest families, disproportionately those of widows, experienced very low income levels indeed. This is precisely what the rental figure suggested in a general sense for the earlier period. By contrast, the largest families often seem to have been associated with absolutely higher (but not necessarily higher per capita) income levels. We might have expected no less, but a second observation is that even within family groups of the same size and sharing the same basic occupational profile there were marked variations in income experience. Thus, of those families with eight members, more had total weekly earnings of under 4s. than had earnings of over 16s. Both groups were classified as 'needy' by the relief committee, confirming that the strength or weakness of the family economy is not simply a function of income level.

Some individual stories can clarify this point further. Take the labourer Royal Clayton, employed by Mr Hicks of Mytholmroyde, who lived with his wife and six children. Three were under ten and three over, and the combined family income was 27s. 6d. William Thorpe, a labourer in exactly the same family circumstances, had a total weekly income of 21s. 3d. Yet William Dixon, labourer, had three children under the age of ten and four over, but secured a family income of just 14s per week. Such rates were, as we shall see shortly, generous compared with those offered by employment in rural southern England at the same time, highlighting very important regional differences in what contemporaries saw as an adequate and stable household economy. However, the key point is that we must think very carefully about the relationship between family size, income and expenditure in trying to understand how households caught up in the Industrial Revolution process made ends meet.

A third observation is that if we aggregate the family sizes of dole recipients (1,377) and relate them to the Halifax township population in 1811, then we can see that 18 per cent of the population were contained within the boundaries of what contemporaries identified as weak household economies. If in turn we go further and include the family circumstances of those who got poor relief but not doles and those who received other forms of charity but not poor relief,

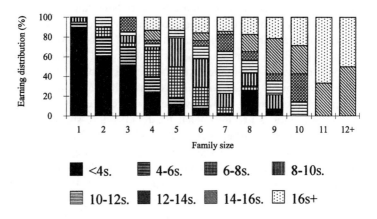

**Figure 9.2** Family size and normal weekly earnings in Halifax, 1811

then fully 22 per cent of the Halifax population might have been contained in weak or unstable household economies.[16] By any stretch of the imagination, this is a significant figure, and a higher figure than that suggested by rental data in Calverley township. This is hardly a valid comparison, of course. The year 1811 was a depression year in the textile industry and Halifax was a much bigger town than Calverley. Nonetheless, as we will see below, the implication that there was a general weakening of household economies over time may not be too far from the truth.

Additional lessons emerge from a more subtle reading of the 1811 dole book. For instance, it confirms that there was a distinctive life-cycle flavour to the viability of the household economy. William Broadbent, a cotton weaver, earned 2s. per week and received a further 2s. per month from the local poor law. The committee noted that 'him and his wife aged' and recorded no children living with them. James Howarth, a cotton weaver, was 'aged and infirm', living with two children over the age of ten, with a collective family income of just 6s. per week. Old age then was a potential hurdle for the ordinary household economy and extensive poor-law evidence suggests that up and down the country the faltering ability to work which old age ushered in left at least one-quarter of all households headed by the old in an economically unviable state.[17]

Other life-cycle stages were equally precarious, as the rental data also imply. The example of widowhood is a good one. For those widows who could follow the business of their husbands, the prospects were good. Indeed, commentators have shown just how important this group was for a healthy local credit network.[18] For those without such resources, remarriage, the generation of a complex household to diversify earning strands or more intensive work patterns were options for limiting damage to the household economy and might be employed particularly where young children remained in the household. In the Halifax sample, such were the experiences of widow Crowther and widow Eastwood. The former, listed as a worsted weaver, lived with two non-related adults, three children over the age of ten, one under the age of ten, and even her half-time wages generated a household income of 12s. per week. Widow Eastwood, a factory worker, lived with her sister, one child under ten, four over ten, and generated a household income of 15s. per week. For others, though, widowhood, especially where combined with old age, could usher in years and years of a fragile household economy periodically supported by the poor law. Widow Bolton, living on her own, received 6s. poor relief per month and apparently had no earnings worth recording. She was seventy-six. Widow Crabtree was 'aged and infirm', had no income from work and was given 4s. per month by the poor law. Widow Crossley was eighty-nine and had one adult child living with her. The child contributed 5s. 6d. to her income, and the parish a further 6s. 6d. per month. Meanwhile, sickness and injury were equally important for the family economy. The labourer Jonas Crowther had a wife and four children under ten in 1811, but he was unable to work because 'he has his leg broken'. His only income was 4s., presumably from the work of his wife. James Mitchill had '3 children insane', while James Pollard was 'cripple on one arm' and thus entirely dependent on the parish and other forms of charity.

The very existence of the dole book also suggests the 'softening' of the household economy which trade downturns could yield. Contemporary commentators were well aware of the debilitating impact of trade depressions and suggested that industrial workers coped with upswings and downswings by investing in goods, clothing and plate during good times which could be liquidated in bad times.[19] This is an inherently appealing observation of coping strategies in the sense that it portrays workers as having an active role in planning their own welfare, but it is also misleading. In some industries, trade

depression, changes in fashion and technical innovation could combine to ensure that family economies were progressively stripped of
domestic comforts, while in other industries and places trade fluctuations were so regular and recovery so slow that workers might not
be able to rebuild a domestic environment and family economy
shattered by a deep recession. Moreover, we need to bear in mind
that trade downturns did not affect all household economies in a
place in the same manner or to the same degree. Those who recorded
the circumstances of the needy in the Halifax survey had seven distinct
grades of worklessness – half work, short of work, little work/em-
ployment, very little work/employment, out of employ/work, very
little work, nearly out of work/employment – and although they did
not always tailor their relief to what we might see as the most extreme
circumstances, the fact that they recorded so many grades suggests
some of the complexities of dealing with the household economy
during times of trade depression.

Once more, local sources have offered potentially far-reaching
lessons. There were clear regional differences in what constituted a
viable household economy. The form of the household provides little
guidance as to the strength of the household economy, but there *were*
distinct parts of the life-cycle when the household economy might be
expected to be chronically weak. By the opening decades of the
nineteenth century it is likely that on average more household economies were chronically weak than had been the case before. Trade
depression (and presumably agrarian depression) could ratchet up the
number of households falling within the 'weak' classification, but
there was no blanket connection between downturn and the weakening of household economies. Turning to a final – and less locality
specific – set of sources, allows us to develop these themes, to
elaborate new ones and to suggest ways in which these key lessons
might be employed to say something more generally about the
strengths and weaknesses of household economies.

Some of the key contributions on the issue of the detailed nature
of the household economy in Industrial Revolution England have
come from those people who have considered household budgets.[20]
In particular, Sarah Horrell and Jane Humphries have used a collection of 1,350 household budgets to make a number of key points
about the strength and diversity of the household economy. The
budgets suggest that the male wage had always lain at the heart of
the English household economy and that there was in an aggregate

sense a consolidation in importance of the male wage as women and children withdrew from the formal labour market. On average the male wage accounted for at least 80 per cent of household resources. Male earning power was more important than average in agricultural and mining areas and less important in outworking or factory families. Even in these trades though, men provided the vast majority of household resources, women provided very few, and children were the most important additional earners.[21] However, if we turn the analysis on its head and use the very few budgets which tell us about life-cycles of contribution, then we can see that women and children had a potentially bigger role to play at certain times of the life-cycle, particularly as men reached advanced middle age and old age. The Halifax dole book implied the same thing. Ultimately, Horrell and Humphries conclude, increasing male wages failed to fully compensate for the falling contribution of women and children to the family budget and for rising prices, so that an increasing percentage of household resources had to be spent on necessities over time. The families of those engaged in mining or trade might have done better than the average, and the households of agricultural labourers some- what worse, but in the aggregate it seems clear that we might characterise the household economy as weak and becoming weaker over time.[22] Again, this is exactly the implication that we can draw from the Halifax dole book.

Such conclusions should not of course be accepted at face value. There are several problems of interpretation to grapple with when using budgets, as we have already suggested. First, recorded household budgets represent the very end of a process of income gathering and expenditure, and we still know relatively little about that process and its exclusions. It is doubtful, for instance, if household budgets really make adequate allowance for the value of gleaning and common rights. The value of gleaning (the right to take crops which have fallen in the field) varied by area, type of crop cultivation and the state of the harvest, but Peter King estimates that this relatively long-lived female and child occupation could augment the household resources of the lowest-income families by at least 10 per cent.[23] Unrestricted access to the full range of common rights (the right to graze animals, take fuel, hunt small animals and take fruit) might also contribute substantially to the nominal money resources of the family if we were to assign them a monetary value, and yet these opportunities are also missing from household budgets.[24]

Second, household budgets are a cumbersome tool to measure a household economy which had to be alive to short-term earning opportunities. To take just one example of the complexity of the issue, it is now established beyond reasonable doubt that women in the textile industry (both outworkers and factory workers) often worked at intervals according to opportunity and the resource needs of the family. In the late eighteenth century, when merchants and manufacturers were attempting to expand their outworking labour force, and in the nineteenth century when labour force turnover in many factories approached 100 per cent a year, the opportunities for short-time and intermittent work were many. Thus in some years women may have made substantial contributions to the household economy and in others – perhaps when the household felt itself to be comfortable – they might make no contribution at all. Nor should we forget, third, that these intermittent female workers had a more complex role in the household economy than is implied by talking just about their earnings. It was, as various historians have reminded us, female networks of lending, borrowing, childcare and food sourcing, which could make the difference between viability or not by making resources go further.[25] There is also a more subtle point to be made. That is, as we have suggested already, the earnings of women and children had a symbolic as well as an economic value which household budgets simply cannot allow for. The presence of female and child earners seems to have been regarded as testimony that families were doing their utmost to generate a stable and comfortable household economy, so that any breakdown of child or female labour contributions could be seen as a justifiable reason for ordinary people to apply for help from the poor law or charity, and could act as a justification for that relief being granted.[26]

These points notwithstanding, we must acknowledge that many of the basic features which Horrell and Humphries highlight – the weakening of the household economy at certain stages of the life-cycle, general pressure on the viability of household economies by the late eighteenth and early nineteenth centuries, the emphasis which trade downturn placed on alternative earning opportunities and the contribution of women and children, and the essential instability of industrial and rural industrial household economies – chime with the lessons which might be drawn from the Halifax dole book. Others of their conclusions 'feel' right. The simplicity and limited resources of the household economy in low-wage agricultural areas such as

Dorset have resonance in some of the narratives which we used in earlier chapters, for instance. Indeed, we can confirm the precarious state of some agricultural household economies by looking at the household budgets constructed by Frederick Eden in his survey of the poor undertaken in the 1790s.[27] For those rural families surveyed outside the crisis year of 1795, the aggregate net shortfall of earnings behind expenditure between 1792 and 1794 was £32 7s. 2d., and this is even including the relatively more viable family economies which seem to have been characteristic of the commercialised agricultural sector in East Anglia.[28] Some of this deficit might be made up from harvest and gleaning income, neither of which were included in Eden's calculations, but there is no escaping the fragility of these rural household economies, just as Horrell and Humphries suggested. Table 9.1 reproduces the Eden figures for the Huntingdonshire township of Buckden, near St Neots, where the fine line between sufficiency and deficit is clearly shown.

These budgets – framed against the backdrop of earnings which had consistently fallen behind inflation – provide powerful confirmation that the Industrial Revolution and its associated changes in agriculture, trade and commerce generated plenty of losers. In turn other household budgets – for instance those of some miners or factory workers – might highlight the fact that there were also distinct gainers from the Industrial Revolution process. It is this spectrum of gain and loss to which we turn in the rest of this chapter as we attempt to draw some more general lessons from the key observations that a consideration of detailed local sources flag up.

## Macro-debates and the family economy: the gainers

Paradoxically, identifying 'gainers' is no easy task. What did the concept of 'gaining' actually mean? Should we measure the gains of individuals or households? For individuals at any point in time, higher earnings, more regular earnings, more stable earnings, a richer and more diverse domestic environment or an ability to participate fully in the more commercialised leisure activities which began to kick in during the nineteenth century might all be taken as evidence that people had 'gained' from the industrialisation process. But did the individual 'gain' when higher earnings were correlated with less regular employment? Whether they did or not, how do we characterise the household where men gained and women lost or where higher

**Table 9.1** Household budgets from Buckden, Huntingdonshire, *c.*1790

| Incomings and outgoings | Family 1, 1792 | Family 1, 1795–96 | Family 2, 1793 | Family 2, 1795–96 | Family 3, 1795 | Family 4, 1795 |
|---|---|---|---|---|---|---|
| Bread and flour | 0-3-10 | 0-2-5 | 0-5-10 | 0-4-11 | 0-2-8 | 0-5-2 |
| Yeast and salt | 0-0-0 | 0-0-2 | 0-0-3 | 0-0-3 | 0-0-3 | 0-0-2 |
| Meat | 0-1-0 | 0-1-5 | 0-0-0 | 0-0-0 | 0-0-10 | 0-0-0 |
| Tea, sugar, butter | 0-0-9 | 0-1-4 | 0-0-9 | 0-1-0 | 0-1-0 | 0-0-11 |
| Soap | 0-0-2 | 0-0-3 | 0-0-2 | 0-0-3 | 0-0-3 | 0-0-5 |
| Candles | 0-0-2 | 0-0-3 | 0-0-2 | 0-0-3 | 0-0-4 | 0-0-3 |
| Cheese | 0-0-4 | 0-0-6 | 0-0-0 | 0-0-0 | 0-0-4 | 0-0-0 |
| Beer | 0-0-3 | 0-0-3 | 0-0-0 | 0-0-0 | 0-0-0 | 0-0-0 |
| Milk | 0-0-0 | 0-0-0 | 0-0-0 | 0-0-0 | 0-0-0 | 0-0-0 |
| Potatoes | 0-0-0 | 0-0-0 | 0-0-0 | 0-0-6 | 0-0-1 | 0-0-8 |
| Thread and cloth | 0-0-1 | 0-0-1 | 0-0-1 | 0-0-2 | 0-0-2 | 0-0-3 |
| Total per year | 16-16-11 | 16-7-2 | 18-13-9 | 18-15-11 | 14-16-10 | 20-3-0 |
| Male earnings (wk) | 0-7-4 | 0-7-4 | 0-7-3 | 0-7-3 | 0-6-3 | 0-8-8 |
| Female earnings (wk) | 0-0-5 | 0-0-5 | 0-1-2 | 0-1-2 | 0-0-11 | 0-1-1 |
| Child earnings (wk) | 0-0-10 | 0-0-10 | 0-0-0 | 0-0-0 | 0-0-0 | 0-1-1 |
| Rent | 2-2-0 | 2-2-0 | 2-7-0 | 2-7-0 | 1-10-0 | 2-0-0 |
| Fuel | 2-3-0 | 2-8-0 | 0-0-0 | 0-0-0 | 1-5-8 | 1-19-4 |
| Shoes | 1-5-0 | 1-10-0 | 1-6-0 | 1-11-6 | 1-9-0 | 1-11-6 |
| Clothes, furniture | 2-18-0 | 3-5-0 | 3-0-0 | 3-11-0 | 1-18-6 | 3-10-0 |
| Unforeseen events | 0-9-0 | 0-9-0 | 1-1-0 | 1-1-0 | 0-7-0 | 1-0-0 |
| Total expenses (yr) | 25-13-11 | 26-1-2 | 26-7-9 | 27-6-5 | 21-7-0 | 30-3-10 |
| Total income (yr) | 22-12-4 | 22-12-4 | 21-17-8 | 21-17-8 | 23-16-8 | 28-5-6 |
| Deficit | 3-1-7 | 3-8-8 | 4-10-1 | 5-8-9 | 0-0-0 | 1-18-4 |
| Surplus | 0-0-0 | 0-0-0 | 0-0-0 | 0-0-0 | 2-9-8 | 0-0-0 |

*Note*:

Family 1 consists of a couple, a sixteen-year-old boy and an infant.

Family 2 consists of a couple and four children.

Family 3 consists of a couple and an infant.

Family 4 consists of a couple and six children.

Figures are expressed in £, s. and d.

*Source*: Eden, *The state*, p. 341. Original calculations.

individual earnings equated directly to higher alcohol consumption? And if we are going to concentrate on households rather than individuals, how do we balance periods of gain or loss over the life-cycle as a whole, as contemporaries may have done? An ideal typical story can bring this issue to life. A couple marry in the mining town of Wigan in the early nineteenth century. The husband is one of those miners who works a consistent week so that on average he earns 35s. per week on piece rates. Notwithstanding the birth of several children, the range and number of household goods increases over the early stages of the family life-cycle. However, as the coal seam becomes harder to work, seasonal layoffs because of flood and slippage increase. At the same time the public health environment of the mining areas deteriorates and the health of the husband begins to suffer. By the time the couple enter their mid-forties family income is falling and the consumption gains of the early part of the life-cycle have to be liquidated. Ultimately they turn to the poor law once the husband has to abandon mining. He may be thought lucky to still be alive after all these years of mining, but did this family 'gain' from the industrialisation process or not?

Even if we can answer this thorny question, how do we then factor into our general analysis of the health of household economies the idea that households could 'gain' as a result of the industrialisation process within the life-cycle limits of the family, or 'gains' could manifest themselves between the generations? An ideal typical example might be a couple who spend their life-cycle engaged in the urban casual trades (a subject to which we return below) and thus have a precarious and unstable family economy but whose children all become skilled workers in the local textile factories. The children may all have lived around and about the parental home and have remitted occasional money payments when their parents were in particular need. The gain here is clearly intergenerational, but to what extent are the parents gainers because of the money they have from their children and the very fact that those children have gone on to achieve prosperity in their own right?

To some extent these problems are intractable. One way of addressing them is to ask who contemporaries thought were gainers from the Industrial Revolution and by inference who were losers. Reading diaries, autobiographies, newspaper and magazine articles, the records of committees of inquiry, letters and other sources suggests that one of the most prominent set of 'gainers' were the skilled spinners of the east Lancashire cotton industry. Their story is an interesting one. After the technical advances of the later eighteenth century, coarse and then fine spinning rapidly became factory processes. Initially, factories demanded the services of highly skilled men, but then spinning became automated and semi-automated, prompting employers to try to substitute women spinners as a way of instilling discipline and reducing wages. The effort was to fail and spinning was confirmed as a high-earning, essentially male, trade in the nineteenth century.[29] For these workers, as well as for those who were connected to factory work in other capacities, household budgets suggest very high earning capacity. Collier sums this situation up very well, concluding that:

> the most important social effect of the factory system was the increase it made possible in the earning power of the family. This increase was greatest in those families which had an adult male employed in a factory but, even where this was not the case, the higher earnings of women and children, who formed the majority of the personnel of the factories, meant a substantial increase in the incomes of the families to which they belonged.[30]

The absolute wage figures are in many cases impressive. The coarse spinners of east Lancashire could comfortably earn twenty shillings per week during the opening decades of the nineteenth century, while in fine spinning earnings of thirty or more shillings weekly were common. Female-headed households could make a comfortable living and short depressions were not sufficient to drag down annual earnings of factory workers to anything like the subsistence wages offered to rural labourers in the south. Table 9.2 uses some of the wage and price material assembled by Collier to put together pseudo-household budgets for five different factory families for the period 1810–19. The weekly surpluses of some families appear modest, but they were nonetheless surpluses. Contemporary commentators were equally sure that these surpluses existed and lamented the fact that they were spent on changed diet and clothing rather than saved or expended on self-improvement. Contemporaries and subsequent historians have also noted the high incidence of friendly societies in factory areas and while the argument about why people joined these societies looks set to continue, the fact is that dense membership did require household surpluses.[31]

Table 9.2 Sample household budgets for five factory families, 1810–19

| Units | Family income (average per week) | Food | Rent | Fuel | Clothing | Other | Surplus/ deficit |
|---|---|---|---|---|---|---|---|
| Family 1 | 43 | 14 | 4 | 7 | 5 | 3 | 10 |
| Family 2 | 31 | 14 | 3 | 5 | 3 | 2 | 4 |
| Family 3 | 23 | 14 | 2 | 4 | 2 | 0 | 1 |
| Family 4 | 35 | 14 | 4 | 5 | 3 | 2 | 7 |
| Family 5 | 48 | 14 | 7 | 7 | 6 | 4 | 10 |

*Notes:*
Family 1 consists of a male fine spinner and two working children.
Family 2 consists of a male coarse spinner and two working children.
Family 3 consists of a woman stretcher and two working children.
Family 4 consists of a male coarse spinner, a working wife and one child.
Family 5 consists of an overlooker and his wife.
Figures represent average values for the entire period and are expressed
in terms of nearest whole shillings.
*Source:* Collier, *The family*, pp. 61–6 and 99.

Competition for factory work (bringing downward pressure on
wage rates) might reduce these potential surpluses over time and
trade-related fluctuations might reduce their real value when measured
over a complete cycle. Employer attempts to pass on the economic
impact of trade fluctuations in the form of time or piece-rate cuts
might also generate vicious conflict and intensive short-term fluidity
in wages.[32] Ultimately, however, these factory workers may have
gained substantially for a significant portion of their own life-cycles
from the development of the industry. Michael Huberman takes this
discussion forward, suggesting that since spinning firms worked on
tight margins, employers increasingly had an interest in recruiting
and retaining a stable labour force with a record of quality work.
This meant high wages in good times but, crucially for the family
economy, it also meant ensuring stable employment patterns. Thus,
at times of downturn, firms would initially keep piece rates up and
try to dispose of the labour contribution of any outworkers. Then
they would often reduce the working week or the level of output,
spreading the pain of recession equally across the whole workforce
instead of a specific section to avoid widespread unemployment. In
the case of longer-term depressions, where layoffs became inevitable,
the records of individual firms suggest that it was the relatively less

productive but more experienced older workers who were kept on in preference to more productive but less experienced younger workers. It is the different variations on these themes deployed by individual firms which explains the variety of descriptions of worklessness in the Halifax survey.[33] However, these observations tell us only part of the story of 'gain' by factory workers, because not only did they spend a significant part of their own life-cycles in accumulation mode, they were also disproportionately likely to see their own children enter the factory or similar gaining occupations. Little wonder, then, that contemporaries identified factory workers as standing at the forefront of the *economic benefits* offered by the Industrial Revolution, whatever they thought of their morals.[34]

The high and steady income offered by factory work did not, of course, lead seamlessly to a strong household economy. We too often assume that all income went into the family pot for communal expenditure, when in fact there were considerable complexities associated with the use of earnings. Men in northern communities sometimes kept drinking money back from the household economy, while children might also be reluctant to give up income. Angus Reach, writing at the very end of the period with which we are concerned, noted the earning details of boys working at one Manchester factory. Some were like the fourteen-year-old who 'Has 3s. a week. Gives it to his mother' or the fourteen-year-old who 'makes 5s. 6d. a week, working ten hours a day, and gives it to his aunt who keeps him', but others were like the sixteen-year-old who apparently kept all of his 6s. for himself.[35] High earnings thus do not necessarily add up to high disposable family income. And, even where families had the same notional disposable income and showed no particular tendency to drink, contemporaries noted very significant differences in the actual disposal of that income between families. Some of this reflected the character of the families concerned. The commentator Frances Howes, touring the factory districts in 1821, contrasted the 'ideal' family which wasted no money on luxury foods, maintained a comfortable domestic environment, and paid money to different clubs and societies as insurance against future risks, with the 'chronic factory family economy' which followed fashion in foods and clothing, paid nothing in future insurance and took too much advantage of credit.[36] Some of the differences in disposal were more involuntary. Reach talked about the domestic environment of factory labour in different parts of Lancashire and concluded that:

A fair proportion of what was deal in Ancoats was mahogany in Hulme. Yet the people of Hulme get no higher wages than the people of Ancoats. The secret is that they live in better built houses and consequently take more pleasure and pride in their dwellings.[37]

The quality of housing stock, then, was seen as an important variable in determining how household resources were disbursed. So was the ability to stay in one's home. Those factory operatives forced by prolonged depression to seek cheaper accommodation not only incurred costs of moving, but also lost the neighbourhood networks and credit reputation which might allow families to make their cash income go further. Whether wives worked also influenced the disposal of income. Where no local relatives could nurse young children, for instance, female factory workers would have to pay others for childcare.[38]

Such problems mean that we must tread warily in talking about the material circumstances of factory workers. Nonetheless, there is convincing evidence that they were one of the gainers of the Industrial Revolution and that even allowing for serious periodic depressions such as in 1826 or 1842 the household economy in which *healthy* factory workers found themselves became stronger over time.[39] Commentators who toured the manufacturing districts during the exceptionally bad depression of 1842 showed very well the consequences of industrial concentration for whole regions when the pain could not be spread widely – bare houses, underfed workers, clothes pawned or sold – but when highlighting these depressing scenes they almost invariably pointed to the absolute and relative comfort of factory workers except in these exceptional times. The fact that so many operatives appear to have shown these contemporary commentators pawnshop tickets for goods which might be redeemed during trade upturn is testimony both to the problems of depression and to the richness of the domestic environment of factory workers before depression.[40]

In turn, factory workers represent just one component of a variety of trades and occupations in which workers appear to have unambiguously benefited from industrial expansion during their own life-cycles, and perhaps also between the generations. Supervisors in factories of all sorts might attract high wages and use these to fashion a comfortable domestic environment. Steam-engine makers, silk weavers, engineers, skilled potters, cabinet makers and many of those engaged in supplying the urban luxury trades also appear to have done well from the Industrial Revolution process. Indeed, as a crude generalisation it might be appropriate to argue that by 1850 the 15–20 per cent of the adult male labour force which fell within the ambit of the slippery categorisation 'labour aristocracy' had been broad gainers. This is not to say that at the individual level gains were consistently made and kept, or that deskilling and other trends did not put these trades under pressure, but simply that the labour aristocracy were the most likely to have felt themselves gainers. If we were to add in those miners who worked a regular week, those engaged in the middle and higher ranks of the burgeoning civil service, some workers in the expanding nineteenth-century transport sector and skilled building workers who managed to remain in regular employment, then it would be possible to suggest that up to 25 per cent of the male adult labour force (and rather less than one-fifth of the total labour force) would have had the opportunity to build a strong and relatively resilient family economy, with the realistic hope that their children might also have a comfortable life-cycle experience.[41]

To this group we might add some proto-industrial workers. As chapter two hinted, places which were to emerge as vibrant proto-industrial economies in the later eighteenth and early nineteenth centuries – such as West Yorkshire or Lancashire – had rich traditions of industrial production, such that the gradual expansion of output associated with regional concentration yielded very considerable initial opportunities for profit at family level, particularly in areas where artisan traditions remained strong. In the area between Bradford and Leeds, for instance, these opportunities for profit found expression in an active land market and the tendency for larger rural industrial producers to buy cottages and land outside their own townships. They also found expression in the rise of co-operative 'company mills', acceleration of consumption, and the movement of people in considerable numbers to take advantage of land opened up for rental and sale by the enclosure movement which really picked up after 1755.[42]

The good times of the early proto-industrial period were not to last. Uncertain international markets, technological redundancy for women in some branches of the textile trades,[43] short-term oversupply of labour and products, and subtle changes in the organisation of production all worked to strip away the economic security of proto-industrial workers, particularly in those areas where putting-out had been the norm from an early date. Yet this does not mean that proto-industrial workers failed to gain. On the problem of unemployment and falling rates the 1806 inquiry into the state of the woollen industry concluded that:

> any other of those adverse shocks to which our foreign trade especially is liable ... has not the effect of throwing a great number of workmen out of employ ... In the domestic system, the loss is spread over a large supersicies; it affects the whole body of the manufacturers; and, though each little master be a sufferer, yet few if any feel the blow so severely as to be altogether ruined. Moreover, it appears in evidence that, in such cases as these, they seldom turn off any of their standing set of journeymen, but keep them at work in hopes of better times.[44]

The gains made by these workers *were* often reversed, especially during the involution of the nineteenth century, and other aspects of the proto-industrial system did take the gloss off these positive features. Joseph Lawson, commentating on the Yorkshire village of Pudsey during the 1820s, concluded, for instance, that, 'It was no uncommon thing too, when the work was done, for weavers to be unable to get paid for some time after, which often caused much disappointment, inconvenience and suffering.'[45]

Interruptions to raw wool and yarn supplies, the need to borrow equipment a weaver lacked, uncertainty over how much finished yarn might be derived from a given amount of wool, faults in finished cloth, theft, fire and a whole range of other features might combine to reduce the profitability of cloth production, even in the best of times. However, by concentrating on the last few decades of the period considered by this book, we risk ignoring the three generations of more stable and profitable family economies that rural industry had initially yielded. In practice, there were definite losers whose experiences tell us much more about the nuts and bolts of family economies in this period and allow us to explore more widely some of the lessons that we distilled from the local sources employed in the last section.

### Macro-debates and the family economy: the losers

The process of identifying 'losers' shares the same conceptual and methodological problems as identifying gainers. How do we measure 'losing'? Those for whom piece rates declined? Those who had to work more hours to maintain aggregate income? Those unable to share in the consumer revolution of the eighteenth and nineteenth centuries? Those excluded from the commercialised leisure practices of the nineteenth century by lack of money? Even if we could answer these questions, identifying 'losers' raises important tensions between the experiences of individuals (which are relatively easy to trace) and the experiences of entire families (which are often very difficult to trace). The two were not the same, and we should beware of assuming that they were. Once again, the solution to these thorny problems is to ask who contemporaries thought were the losers of the Industrial Revolution. Some are ostensibly easy to find, and their plight filled many newspaper inches.

As we saw in chapter three, the cotton handloom weavers enjoyed a brief period of affluence during the last three decades of the eighteenth century when improved spinning technology meant that supply of yarn outstripped the supply of weavers. However, there were few barriers to entry to the weaving profession, and this, associated with the slow improvement and innovations of weaving technology and changes in fashion, meant that from the turn of the nineteenth century individual weavers suffered consistent decline in piece rates and general family earnings. Table 9.3 suggests what happened to the likely disposable income of handloom weavers between 1814 and 1833.[46] Clearly, progressive cuts in rates left many handloom weaving families by the late 1820s in serious economic imbalance. The deficits indicated here could partially be met with the deployment of extra family labour (in terms of both more workers and more hours per worker devoted to weaving within the household economy), and it has been suggested that those handloom weavers who moved to urban areas could make ends meet by deploying women or children in the wider labour – particularly the factory labour – market.[47] However, even if this is true, contemporary commentators were acutely aware of the suffering of the urban handloom weavers and the inability of this group to generate acceptable family economies. The experiences of those handloom weavers who remained in rural areas are more ambiguous. Distance from the main urban centres made them particularly vulnerable to the attempts of putting-out merchants to reduce costs or the size of the labour force, but rural economies offered supplementary earning opportunities in finishing, mining and agricultural trades, while some rural handworkers at least came to specialise in the fine and fancy trades, where the decline of piece rates and employment stability was less marked. Nonetheless, for both sets of weavers, it might be argued, endemic structural poverty generated an essentially unstable and low-level household economy which could last over a whole generation and very probably passed between the generations as well.

**Table 9.3** The likely economic position of handloom weaving families, 1814–33

| Year | Earnings | Family earnings | Rent, fuel etc. | Surplus for food and clothing | Likely surplus/deficit |
|------|----------|-----------------|-----------------|-------------------------------|------------------------|
| 1814 | 14 | 19 | 4 | 15 | 1 |
| 1815 | 12 | 19 | 3 | 16 | 2 |
| 1816 | 9 | 13 | 3 | 10 | −3 |
| 1817 | 7 | 11 | 2 | 9 | −4 |
| 1818 | 9 | 12 | 3 | 9 | −4 |
| 1819 | 10 | 14 | 3 | 11 | −1 |
| 1820 | 9 | 12 | 3 | 9 | −3 |
| 1821 | 9 | 12 | 3 | 9 | −3 |
| 1822 | 9 | 12 | 3 | 9 | −3 |
| 1823 | 10 | 12 | 3 | 9 | −3 |
| 1824 | 10 | 12 | 3 | 9 | −3 |
| 1825 | 9 | 13 | 3 | 10 | −1 |
| 1826 | 7 | 7 | 2 | 5 | −8 |
| 1827 | 7 | 7 | 2 | 5 | −8 |
| 1828 | 7 | 7 | 2 | 5 | −8 |
| 1829 | 6 | 9 | 2 | 7 | −7 |
| 1830 | 5 | 9 | 2 | 7 | −6 |
| 1831 | 5 | 8 | 2 | 6 | −8 |
| 1832 | 5 | 8 | 2 | 6 | −7 |
| 1833 | 5 | 7 | 2 | 5 | −7 |

*Notes*: Figures are expressed in terms of the nearest whole shilling.
*Source*: Collier, *The family*, pp. 84–106.

In 1833 a private survey of thirty-five towns in north Lancashire investigated earnings, family structure and the basic expenditure of cotton handloom weavers, looking specifically at weaving families where income per capita was less than 2s. 6d. per week. This was the line under which contemporaries clearly identified a weak or unstable family economy for the north of England, and it is very significant indeed that the 8,362 families which the investigators found to be under this line comprised 24 per cent of the population of the towns concerned. If we were to exclude from the analysis those families engaged in occupations such as fine and coarse spinning, bleaching, engineering and other trades, then it is likely that almost all of the handloom weaving population of these thirty-five towns would have been below the level at which contemporaries started to speak of adequate household economies. The extent to which handloom weavers had lost from the Industrial Revolution process is shown by the earning and expenditure figures which accompany the survey. The average weekly wage for those who worked in the 8,362 families was 3s. 9d., while the average income per household member was 1s. 10d. Subtracting from this figure the cost of rent, fuel, candles, and wear and tear to handloom equipment left the investigators with a figure of 1s. 3d. per capita, from which handloom weaving families would have to find food, clothing, heating, deductions enforced by employers and the cost of items such as medicine. It is clear that these handloom weaving families could not have made ends meet at the most basic level, suggesting both a heavy dependence on poor relief and a progressive degradation of the handloom weaving family economy.[48] Indeed, letters written by poor handloom weavers back to the place where they had a legal settlement, provides ample testimony to their suffering. One, from a female handloom weaver in 1833, said,

> I am under the necessity to solicit your aid at this time for I am in great distress having no bed to lie on but obliged to lie on the bare ground this gentlemen is a bad case But Gentlemen I hope you will seriously consider my case and allow me a bed and some money I have some money to pay and I want a little money to pay my debt and some while I can set up my looms But Gentlemen I want a pair of stays and a shuttle If I get these things I shall want little of you for I do not like coming to crave your assistance If I can help it now. Gentlemen I have an heart rending case to mention to you the Child and me has not been in a bed this fortnight this is a shocking circumstance the Child is in work but he has not drawn anything yet. Do Gentlemen let humanity have a place in your hearts consider if you were placed in similar circumstances reason this way and let things come home to your hearts how unpleasant it would appear to you and no person is certain but it may be his case if he has riches – riches sometimes make themselves wings and fly away.[49]

Even allowing for poetic licence, there is a clear sense here that the handloom weaver was a loser of the Industrial Revolution. Such testimony is confirmed by Reach whose conversation with one handloom weaver from Ashton under Lyne in 1849 went as follows,

I asked him what were his usual wages ... 'Look here – I'll have to
weave eighty yards of cloth in this piece. It will take me eight or nine
days, and I shall have seven shillings for it. I walked to Manchester
and back to the master's to fetch the yarn, and I shall walk there and
back with the cloth when I am paid'. Here was a journey on foot
amounting to nearly thirty miles, and nine days' work at the loom, for
seven shillings. The family consisted of four. They slept together in the
bed of sacking and rags ... Some of the handloom weavers are better
off because they have sons and daughters who work in the mills; but
taken all together, they are a wretched and hopeless set.[50]

Undoubtedly this picture is overdrawn. Both 1833 and 1849 were
years of depression in the Lancashire cotton industry, and so we
would expect extraordinary stories such as these. Moreover, even by
the 1830s there were unseen strengths to the household economies
of handloom weavers.[51] As we saw in chapter three, many manufacturers still had a demand for handworkers of the best sort and were
willing to pay for them, such that piece rates had stabilised, and even
begun to rise for a time during the trade-cycle upturn of the mid-1830s.
For those who did not specialise in this way, we must make a
distinction between the individual experience of falling piece rates
and more hours of work and the family income which might, where
there was labour diversification, decline by somewhat less than piece
rates and be more stable in the long term. Certainly, at the level of
individual families the strength and stability of family economies
could be dependent on a whole range of variables, such as the type
of cloth produced, the life-cycle stage at which wives gave up work,
and household form and we must use these observations to balance
the stories of woe outlined above. However, we must not take these
caveats too far. A consideration of east Lancashire poor-law accounts
shows that they were dominated by handloom weaving families,
despite their relative unimportance in the overall occupational structure of the region, and that those families showed a remarkable
tendency to pass poverty on to their children. This above all is
testimony to the fact that handloom weavers in Lancashire were
losers from the Industrial Revolution process.[52]

Meanwhile, southern agricultural labourers are often placed in a
similar 'losing' category. The de-industrialisation highlighted in
chapter two stripped away one of the pillars from the household
economy of rural workers in the south, east and west as the eighteenth
century progressed. This, allied with rapid rural population growth,

parliamentary enclosure, changing land use, and attempts to curtail customary rights such as the taking of small animals or fuel from waste and common land, fundamentally compromised the household economies of rural people. The underemployment stemming from the traditional seasonality of agriculture got worse, unemployment became more common, particularly for women, and the wages of those in work remained remarkably sticky in the face of considerable chronological variation in prices and agricultural prosperity. Female wages in particular seem to have been remarkably stable over long periods and across most southern regions.[53] Of course, this picture, like that for the handloom weavers, is overdrawn.[54] Yet, household budgets lay testimony to the precariousness of the lives of rural labourers in the late eighteenth and early nineteenth centuries, as we started to show earlier in this chapter. Arthur Young calculated the earnings of a Norfolk labouring family in 1804 at £26 0s. 6d. (including the earnings from gleaning) but balanced this against rent (£2 10s. 0d.), fuel (£3 1s. 4d.), soap and lighting (£1 8s. 10d.), male clothing (£2 7s. 0d.), female clothing (£1 15s. 0d.), tools (£0 8s. 0d.) and food (£18 19s. 0d.) to show that, even without allowing for extraordinary costs such as furniture, unemployment, illness or inflation, labouring families would have had a shortfall of over £4 in a year which would have to be made up by going without meals or clothing, or via recourse to the poor law.[55] Similarly, as we have already seen, Frederick Eden dwelled extensively on the economic situation of rural labour during the 1790s. For the village of Stogursey in Somerset he calculated the family circumstances of four families and found their collective deficit at the end of the year to be £44 10s. 4d. In the neighbourhood of Northampton, where we would expect there to have been some competition for labour, the deficit of six families between 1792 and 1795 was £27 6s. 8d., still a very substantial amount to find by recourse to welfare.[56]

Settlement examinations, though they may be biased towards the most vulnerable elements of society, provide some confirmation of this quantitative picture. On 19 February 1822, for instance, Thomas Parsloe gave the following testimony to a magistrate in Cheltenham:

Born in Daglingworth. His parents lived there and received relief from the parish officers. He has also heard his mother say she had received relief from Milton in the parish of Shipton. About 13 years ago he married Maria his present wife by whom he has six children ... Previously to his being married he was never hired as a yearly or any other servant, but earned his livelihood as a daily or weekly labourer. About 4 years ago he applied to the parish officers of Milton where he understood his parents were settled, for relief, and about a month afterwards he had one pound and has since had 4/6 weekly.[57]

This is just one example of many that could have been quoted, and it is significant that his parents had bequeathed him poverty, and the wages of an agricultural labourer were not sufficient for him to retain his own independence against the backdrop of several non-working children under the age of ten. Stories like this provide powerful confirmation of Horrell and Humphries' observation that household income was inflexible compared to the risks and crises which washed over rural families during the eighteenth and nineteenth centuries, particularly in rural southern England.[58] In short, agricultural labourers, like handloom weavers, might be characterised as 'losers' *both within and between the generations.*

The examples of handloom weavers and agricultural labourers are familiar, but they might be joined by other 'losers'. The highly seasonal or sweated trades such as straw plaiting, hatting, gloving, tailoring or matchmaking offered little scope for workers to establish a comfortable and resilient family economy. Even where we allow for the fact that many workers in these areas were part of a larger household work unit, they offered little consistent support to the household economy. In urban areas, those engaged in the casual trades were in an equally precarious position. Dock workers employed by the hour or the job lacked either certainty of employment or a respectable wage when work was available. Refuse collectors, box makers, urban slaughtermen and urban general labourers might earn wages measured over a year somewhat below even the handloom weaver, and since the residence of such casual workers needed to be near places of potential employment the families of these workers found themselves concentrated into the lowest rented and most over-crowded part of the urban infrastructure. For these people, concerns over settlement or, if they were Irish, concerns over the attitude of civic leaders to minority groups meant that application for communal relief was uncertain, and contemporary commentators made an ex-plicit link between the scale and remuneration of the urban casual trades and levels of crime in urban areas. We might add to this list the tin and copper miners of Cornwall, the lace makers of Notting-hamshire, the lead miners of Derbyshire, or the gunpowder makers of Westmorland. All suffered unstable and poorly remunerated employment and this underpinned a constricted and unstable household economy which had in turn to be stabilised through crime, relief, charity or resort to kinship help. All showed a disproportionate tendency to bequeath a legacy of poverty to their children.[59] It is difficult to discern what these examples amount to in terms of the number of people tied up in the 'losing' side of the Industrial Revolution balance sheet, but Williamson has suggested that around one-fifth of families were definite 'losers'.[60]

## The family economy, the life-cycle and welfare

It would be a mistake to think that a rough balancing of those who definitely lost and those who definitely gained from the Industrial Revolution process really solves the problem of how to characterise the household economy in England after 1700. If 40 per cent of households can be characterised in the very broadest terms as losers or gainers from the industrialisation process, what happened to the other 60 per cent of household experiences? The ideal-typical losers and gainers that we have talked about so far in this chapter have attracted historical attention because they represent extremes of experience. The experiences of the anonymous majority remain buried in a plethora of sources of the sort which we used in the first part of this chapter and it is by no means certain that we could reconstruct them even if we tried. Important interpretative problems also remain to be systematically tackled. Crucially, for the young handloom weaver entering the trade in the 1780s, twenty years of prosperity might be succeeded by an equal or longer period of pressure on the household economy and dependence on self-exploitation and poor relief. Consumption gains at one stage of the life-cycle might have to be liquidated at another stage, and there might be a downsizing of housing. Similarly, the factory worker who entered mule spinning in his early twenties might experience ten or twenty years of high earnings and a buoyant household economy, but the lung diseases associated with textile production in the factory environment could usher in a subsequent period of depleted or irregular earnings in which, again, the consumption and other gains of a previous part of the life-cycle would have to be realised. The question thus becomes how we should characterise those life-cycles which represent neither definite gain nor definite loss, and more importantly how contemporaries would have characterised them. These sorts of issues are inadequately explored by using general labels such as 'gainers' or 'losers'.

There is, however, an alternative way to approach the question of the experience of the silent majority and to draw more general conclusions about the strength or weakness of the household economy in the aggregate. It lies in looking at whether the household economy was sufficiently strong to prevent large-scale, point-in-time and life-cycle, poverty as it was recognised by the state or charity. With the explosion of poor-law research over the last decade, using this proxy indicator is a rather more attractive proposition than sifting through complex and contradictory material covering individual or community level household economies. Initially, it is easy to see that the omens are not good for our finding a strong household economy amongst the majority of ordinary people. Figure 9.3 shows that poor-law expenditure increased rapidly alongside the Industrial Revolution process, as did the length of relief lists. Some of this rise is illusory. Inflation, the growing costs of administration and the application of settlement laws, and a ratcheting up of what people thought it was 'right' for the poor law to pay for, means that 'real' relief expenditure grew more moderately than these figures suggest. But it still grew. There were considerable intra- and inter-regional variations in the generosity of relief, with southern regular per capita payments under the old poor law roughly three times more generous than those in the north, but in many places more and more men with families were feeding through to the regular relief lists. The 'traditional' poor (the

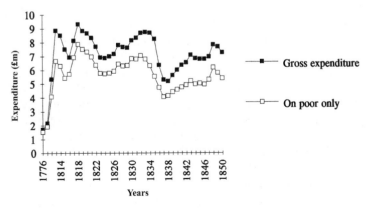

**Figure 9.3** National poor-law expenditure

315

old, the sick and the bereaved) continued also to increase in absolute numbers, but their share of the relief bill fell consistently in many places from the later eighteenth century. In addition to these regular payments, overseers in northern and southern parishes made increasing numbers of small doles to those who needed temporary relief because of trade downturns or an inability to meet lump-sum payments such as rents. Two of the most important lessons from our analysis of the core sources – life-cycle pressure on the household economy and an increasing instability in household economies over time – would seem to have a resonance in these observations.

Figure 9.4 builds upon these observations. It maps the returns, made to parliament by local overseers of the poor, of the proportions of parish or township populations dependent on relief in 1803/4. Now we can begin to see the true implications of rising expenditure. In some southern counties, over one-fifth of the population would have been on relief at any one point. Making a notional allowance for the families of the individuals who received poor relief might take this figure up to 40 per cent or more of the total county population, though there were also important intra-county variations in local experiences.[61] For northern communities these proportions were lower, but there is at least some evidence that were we to include those dependent on charity in this map the proportions might be roughly the same.[62] Of course, 1803/4 is not a particularly good reference point. By this date the poor law in the south was irregularly supplementing wages using Speenhamland-type systems which related relief to the size of families and the cost of bread, while the poor law in the north appears to have been active in subsidising industrial employment. These extraordinary pressures had passed by 1830, but a survey of returns of poor relief published in thirty towns in England during this year suggests that an average of 19 per cent of household heads were to some extent dependent on relief at this date.[63]

There are no comparable national figures for earlier dates, but individual parish accounts suggest that in the 1740s the figures were nearer 7–8 per cent of the local population.[64] The difference between the scale of these point-in-time figures is important, but industrialisation also coincided with an increase in the intensity of dependency. Studies which link full or partial family reconstitution evidence to poor-law accounts have suggested that the poor law was coming to play a larger and larger role in the life-cycle welfare strategies of ordinary families during the eighteenth and early nineteenth centuries.

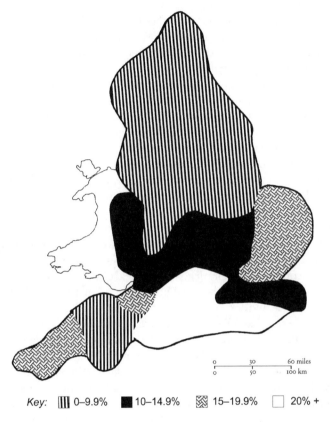

Key:  ▥ 0–9.9%   ■ 10–14.9%   ▨ 15–19.9%   ☐ 20% +

**Figure 9.4** Proportions of county populations on relief, 1803/4

The advent of the new poor law upset this process briefly in the 1830s, but ultimately the trend was re-established towards the end of our period. Thus, in many of the individual studies which inform this perspective, the poor law provided between one-fifth and two-thirds of the total income of poor families by the second decade of the nineteenth century.[65] The implication is that we should be thinking in terms of a growing polarisation in society between the comfortable and the relatively poor, and this is an idea which has considerable resonance in the commentary of contemporary observers. Robert Sharp of South Cave in Yorkshire concluded, for instance, that landlords 'think the poor of almost a different species'.[66]

What implications do these observations have for the way in which we should think about the household economy? To answer this question we must take a conceptual step forward and start to talk once more about life-cycles of dependency and independence. It is clear that for any given village or birth cohort we could (given family reconstitution and adequate poor-law and charity records) classify family life-cycles according to whether they were 'never or rarely' poor, whether they were 'sometimes' poor, whether families were 'often' poor, or whether they were 'always' poor. The exact percentage of a life-cycle a person would have to spend in poverty as recognised by the state or charity in order to be classed as 'always poor' is of course open to debate, but the principle that historians can divide up local populations according to their distinctive poverty experiences is not.[67]

Figure 9.5 links family reconstitution evidence to poor-law accounts and charity data for seven rural or industrial communities in different parts of England, and uses some crude rules of thumb to classify people according to their degree of contact with the poor law.[68] Broadly, those who never received poor relief or charity, or who only received it once and for a short period, are classified as 'never' poor. Those who received relief for more than two-fifths of their total life-cycle fall within the classification 'always' poor, while those who spend up to 15 per cent of their life-cycle in poverty are classified as 'sometimes' poor. Other life-cycles are by default 'often' poor. The graph does not claim that in each year, all of those individuals classified as, say, 'always' poor will be in poverty as measured by the communal relief or charity lists. Rather, it purports to demonstrate how all of the life-cycles in force in a given year might be classified when we view lives in totem. A simple example can help to clarify this point. James Hainsworth lived out his life in the Yorkshire parish of Calverley between 1784 and 1829. He was 'poor' as recorded in poor-law accounts or charity material for 55 per cent of his life, mainly concentrated in his youth, middle and old age. In figure 9.5 his life-cycle would be classified as 'always' poor but in the period 1804 to 1814 he received no poor relief or charity. What we are interested in is much less the detailed poor relief experience of individuals, and much more the way in which the composition of life-cycles along the spectrum of viable to unviable changed in the longer term, and this is precisely what figure 9.5 provides.

Of course, we should not place too much confidence in such exact

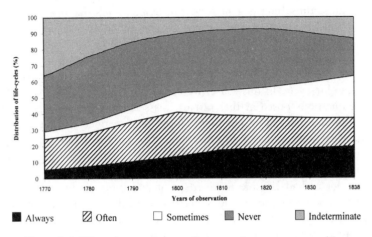

**Figure 9.5** Life-cycle experiences of poverty in seven communities

divisions, but even bearing this caveat in mind the lessons to be drawn are important. We can see that for this small number of communities, there is indeed evidence of growing social polarity in the later eighteenth century. The size of the 'always' and 'often' poor group increased consistently, with a similar increase in the tendency for families to pass on their poverty to children who then also become 'always' or 'often' poor. The size of the 'never' poor group also increased, with the importance of the 'sometimes' poor group dwindling. For these seven communities, then, there was a persistent and linear upward trend in the number of times an average life-cycle would come into contact with charity or poor relief and, for at least 40 per cent of people, an increased period of dependence on each occasion. Overall, where in 1700 perhaps 35 per cent of life-cycles would have needed help from charity or the poor law, and then at very specific times such as old age, sickness or bereavement, by 1820 at least 50 per cent of all life-cycles would come into contact with the welfare framework, and this contact was more likely to be made at times other than life-cycle crisis. There is prima facie evidence here that individual experiences tended in the aggregate towards the 'losing' end of the spectrum of gain and loss which we have used to classify the experiences of family economies so far in this chapter.[69]

Such conclusions apply not only to the 'losers' that we identified earlier in this chapter, but to a range of other groups. Domestic servants, those engaged in food processing, some factory workers, shipbuilders, seamen and others can be found in ever increasing numbers amongst poor-law records, suggesting how risky and tenuous life was for those caught up in the Industrial Revolution process both at times of trade-cycle stress and at numerous indistinguishable points in the life-cycle. In this sense, we can begin to fashion an answer to the questions posed at the start of this section. For the 60 per cent of families that fall into neither a 'loser' nor a 'gainer' category, there are clear indications of an unstable and precarious family economy. For most life-cycles, periods of 'gain' were tempered by periods of loss, and if the poor-law evidence is to be relied upon we can see that losses had become more frequent and more prolonged by the early nineteenth century. It is perhaps for this reason that contemporaries appear to have had little sense of gain or loss within generations, noting only the improvement or not of children as they entered adulthood.

## Conclusion

These observations, even though they are based upon speculative use of limited evidence, present a problem for the usual accounts of the material circumstances of ordinary individuals and families during the Industrial Revolution. There can be little doubt that England, as chapter five suggested, went through a consumer revolution during the eighteenth and nineteenth centuries, a revolution which appears to have put clocks, watches, decent furniture, toys, prints, commercialised leisure and various other 'luxury' items more firmly within the grasp of larger numbers of people.[70] Whether the wider standard of living at individual and family level also increased continues to be debated on the basis of limited evidence, much statistical trickery and an inability to fully reconcile the quantitative and qualitative elements in the living-standards equation. Crudely put, balancing pollution against white bread, tea and sugar will remain at the heart of these disagreements. Nonetheless, the thrust of opinion still favours an upward drift in consumption standards over the long term which was not fully reversed by declining quality of life. Yet, against this picture of improving life quality we must balance the lessons to be drawn from our three-strand analysis – increasing poverty, ever clearer life-cycle patterns of strength and weakness in household economies, chronically weak domestic circumstances amongst households tied into certain occupations, an inability to cope with the pressures on the domestic situation bequeathed by the trade-cycle and household incomes that were increasingly earned by men. Contemporaries were keenly aware of this conundrum as well. Robert Sharp noted, for instance, that 'luxury and want now rule with wide sway'.[71] Such conclusions chime with those of Horrell and Humphries who saw only limited change in living standards at household level, and suggested that any gains may have gone unnoticed because of the severity of nineteenth-century crises and the development of an ever stronger male breadwinner norm. Gains – if gains there were – might also have gone unnoticed because of an ever increasing need to rely on charity and communal welfare, which had important psychological as well as material effects.

Students of the Industrial Revolution must try to reconcile these two sets of perspectives in order to make sense of its impact at the most basic level – that of the household and the household economy. Three points of clarification can help in this reconciliation process. First, general measures of the standard of living deal with individual rather than household experiences. Issues such as the gender earning profile of the family, the distribution of resources between family members, and the different priorities of family as against individual expenditure, are thus masked in the conventional standard-of-living debate. Students must identify and explain trends in family and household income rather than individual income if they are to understand the wider questions of living standards and consumption. The second point of clarification is that consumption, nutritional standards and yardsticks of the quality of life are aggregate indicators. In so far as they measure anything at all, they put together the experiences of those on upswings and downswings in the family life-cycle, long-term gainers and long-term losers, those with very different household forms, and the experiences of those with radically different age profiles and family backgrounds. In order to understand both the household economy and the related issues of consumption and living standards, we must first compare like with like and then understand consumption, quality of life and poverty as cumulative life-cycle experiences where 'gains' (if gains there were) could be dissipated within generational life-cycles such that 'real and irreversible' gains might only become apparent over two or more properly three generational cycles. Third, we can begin to reconcile rising consumption standards but unstable and weak household economies by adopting more precision than some historians towards the divisions within the consuming economy. The gainers of this chapter made very significant and durable advances in both the strength of the family economy and living standards. They partly powered aggregate rises in standard-of-living variables and the wider consumer revolution. By contrast, the always poor never had any gains to make or to lose and they were largely cut off from the consumer revolution. These were the extremes of the living-standards spectrum. To really reconcile the evidence of unstable family economies against rising consumption levels, we must thus understand the cycles of accumulation and dissipation experienced by the 'often' and 'sometimes' poor. On this issue students might make up their own minds by reading contemporary diaries and autobiographies, but the evidence of this chapter suggests very plainly that these key groups saw few durable life-cycle gains.

Such ideas are speculative – what is absolutely certain is that the question of how people made ends meet, or more specifically how many failed or succeeded well in this endeavour, is a keystone to our understanding of what the Industrial Revolution meant to those who lived it. For us, and for many of those who wrote the contemporary narratives that underpin much of our analysis, it is plain that the Industrial Revolution period wrought significant changes on the outlines and dynamism of the household economy and on the background levels of risk and loss that households faced over the life-cycle. In this sense, the period 1700–1850 *was* revolutionary, and the lessons to be drawn from figure 9.5 suggest that many of its consequences were unfortunate. Such experiences must in turn have fed back into the industrialisation process and just as family form and function might shape the intensity and longevity of local industrial or agrarian change, so the nature and strength of the local household economy might also have been instrumental in shaping how the wider institutional, industrial, agrarian and commercial changes after 1700 were played out in individual localities. What is becoming clearer in Part III of this book as a whole is that whatever the aggregate numbers tell us, change – in many areas and for many people revolutionary change – would have been very visible to contemporaries whose lives passed through what we have come to label the Industrial Revolution. The next chapter – on the built environment – develops this notion of the visibility of change in a sphere of everyday life that would have had considerable immediacy to contemporary observers.

## Notes

1 For an overview, see R. O'Day, *The family and family relationships 1500–1900* (Basingstoke, Macmillan, 1994).

2 This chapter does not deal with the household economics of middling and wealthier families. The healthy economic status of these families was a vital component in stimulating a wider consumer revolution in the eighteenth century, and they have been very well covered in other publications. See P. Hudson, *The Industrial Revolution* (London, Arnold, 1992).

3 And of course we saw in chapter eight that even definitions of 'household' are uncertain and variable.

4 On family budgets, see S. Horrell and J. Humphries, 'The origins and expansion of the male breadwinner family: the case of nineteenth century Britain', in A. Janssens (ed.), *The rise and decline of the male bread- winner family* (Cambridge, Cambridge University Press, 1998), pp. 25–64.

5 *Ibid.* Also S. Horrell and J. Humphries, 'The exploitation of little child- ren: child labor and the family economy in the Industrial Revolution', *Explorations in Economic History*, 32 (1995) 485–516.

6 The literature on this issue is considerable. For some examples, see M. Valverde, 'Giving the female a domestic turn: the social, legal and moral regulation of work in British cotton mills 1820–1850', *Journal of Social History*, 21 (1988) 619–34, and E. Jordan, 'The exclusion of women from industry in nineteenth century Britain', *Comparative Studies in Society and History*, 31 (1989) 273–96. Also A. Janssens, 'The rise and decline of the male breadwinner family? An overview of the debate', in Janssens (ed.), *The rise*, pp. 1–24.

7 D. Oddy and D. Mills (eds), *The making of the modern British diet* (London, Croom Helm, 1976).

8 See some of the commentary in J. T. Ward (ed.), *The factory system, volume I: birth and growth* (Newton Abbot, David and Charles, 1970).

9 See S. Nicholas and D. Oxley, 'The living standards of women during the Industrial Revolution 1795–1820', *Economic History Review*, 46 (1993) 723–49.

10 For an initial step in this direction, see Horrell and Humphries, 'The origins'.

11 The sources for the analysis which follows are: West Yorkshire Archive Service Huddersfield (WYASH), 21D88/1, Rental 1715–1779, DD/T/S/A/18, Survey book of Calverley moor, DD/T/E/3, Calverley enclosure award, DD/T/R/B/38, Survey book of farms in Calverley, Sp St 5/9/22, Rental of the Stanhope estate, Sp St 5/9/38, Rental of the Stanhope estate, and T/S/a/17, Field book 1750.

12 Freehold plots and buildings have been given an imputed rental value.

For this process, see P. Hudson and S. A. King, *Industrialisation and everyday life in England 1650–1830* (forthcoming, 2002).

13 Yorkshire Archaeological Society DD12/I/10/7, Survey of the lands of Sir Walter Calverley.

14 For more on this point, see Hudson and King, *Industrialisation*.

15 WYASH, Halifax dole book, 1811.

16 For details on poor relief and charities, and for a deeper analysis of the dole book, see Hudson and King, *Industrialisation*. The family circumstances of charity and poor-law recipients are 'created' simply by assuming that all recipients had the 'national average' family size of 4.5. The precise figures are less important than the broad magnitudes indicated by this calculation.

17 See S. R. Ottoway, 'Providing for the elderly in eighteenth century England', *Continuity and Change*, 13 (1998) 391–418, and R. M. Smith, 'Ageing and well-being in early modern England: pension trends and gender preferences under the English old poor law 1650–1800', in P. Johnson and P. Thane (eds), *Old age from antiquity to post modernity* (London, Routledge, 1998), pp. 64–95.

18 B. Todd, 'The remarrying widow: a stereotype reconsidered', in M. Prior (ed.), *Women in English society 1500–1800* (London, Methuen, 1985), pp. 54–92. Also E. Foyster, 'Marrying the experienced widow in early modern England: the male perspective', in S. Cavallo and L. Warner (eds), *Widowhood in medieval and early modern Europe* (London, Longman, 1999), pp. 108–24.

19 See W. Cooke-Taylor, *Notes of a tour in the manufacturing districts of Lancashire* (New York, Augustus Kelley, 1968 reprint).

20 See S. Horrell and J. Humphries, 'Old questions, new data, and alternative perspectives: families' living standards in the Industrial Revolution', *Journal of Economic History*, 52 (1992) 849–80.

21 In the Halifax dole book, Abraham Naylor, a labourer, was given flour because 'children, no work'. He earned just seven shillings per week without contributions from his children, confirming their importance to the family economy in certain areas. Many of the disputes which arose when overseers exercised their legal right to apprentice the children of the poor were made more severe by the fact that poor families might be losing a key element of the family economy in this process. See M. B. Rose, 'Social policy and business: parish apprenticeship and the early factory system 1780–1834', *Business History*, 31 (1989) 5–32.

22 See Horrell and Humphries, 'The origins'.

23 See P. King, 'Customary rights and women's earnings: the importance of gleaning to the rural labouring poor 1750–1850', *Economic History Review*, 54 (1991), 461–76, and P. King, 'Gleaners, farmers and the failure of legal sanctions 1750–1850', *Past and Present*, 125 (1989) 116–50.

24 J. Humphries, 'Enclosure, common rights and women: the proletariani-

sation of families in the late eighteenth and early nineteenth centuries', *Journal of Economic History*, 50 (1990) 17–42.

25  See, for instance, B. Capp, 'Separate domains? Women and authority in early modern England', in P. Griffiths, A. Fox and S. Hindle (eds), *The experience of authority in early modern England* (Basingstoke, Macmillan, 1996), pp. 117–45.

26  See the posturing in pauper letters highlighted by J. S. Taylor, 'Voices in the crowd: the Kirkby Lonsdale township letters 1809–1836', in T. Hitchcock, P. King and P. Sharpe (eds), *Chronicling poverty: the voices and strategies of the English poor, 1640–1840* (Basingstoke, Macmillan, 1997), pp. 109–26.

27  F. M. Eden, *The state of the poor* (London, Cass, 1969 reprint).

28  The three budgets from Norfolk showed a surplus of £10, so that the real deficit figure for the other counties was very severe indeed at the opening of the 1790s, even before war inflation had really set in.

29  D. Valenze, *The first industrial woman* (Oxford, Oxford University Press, 1995).

30  F. Collier, *The family economy of the working class in the cotton industry 1784–1833* (Manchester, Manchester University Press, 1964), p. 16.

31  For the most recent survey of the literature, see M. Gorsky, 'The growth and distribution of English friendly societies in the early nineteenth century', *Economic History Review*, 51 (1998) 489–511.

32  For a discussion of the influence of employer capital accumulation on the employee household economy, see M. Huberman, *Escape from the market: negotiating work in Lancashire* (Cambridge, Cambridge University Press, 1996).

33  M. Huberman, 'The economic origins of paternalism: Lancashire cotton spinning in the first half of the nineteenth century', *Social History*, 12 (1987) 177–93.

34  This raises the wider problem that 'gain' has to be measured in terms of 'advantage' or 'opportunity' (rather than simply economic outcomes) and thus might encompass imponderables such as access to social mobility. This important caveat should be borne in mind during the following discussion.

35  C. Aspin (ed.), *Manchester and the textile districts in 1849* (Helmshore, Helmshore Local History Society, 1972), pp. 48–9.

36  F. M. Howes, *A tour of the factory districts* (Manchester, Head, 1837 reprint).

37  Aspin (ed.), *Manchester*, p. 4.

38  *Ibid.*, p. 81.

39  Of course, factory work was unhealthy, and in the later stages of a family life-cycle persistent ill-health could ravage the nominal gains from factory work. See J. C. Riley, *Sick not dead: the health of British workingmen during the mortality decline* (Baltimore, Johns Hopkins

University Press, 1997), and the discussion below of life-cycle gains and losses.

40 Cooke-Taylor, *Notes.*

41 See J. Burnett, *Idle hands: the experience of unemployment 1790–1990* (London, Routledge, 1994), and R. Q. Gray, *The aristocracy of labour in nineteenth century Britain 1850–1914* (London, Macmillan, 1981).

42 Hudson and King, *Industrialisation.*

43 In Lancashire, technological change in spinning pushed former female spinners into hand weaving, and so technological redundancy did not equate to unemployment. However, in the sense that this drift of women to weaving underpinned the rapid oversupply of labour to the handloom weaving market, the medium- and long-term impact of technological change was no less fundamental.

44 Parliamentary Papers, *Report from the committee of the woollen manufacture of England, with minutes of evidence and appendix 1806 (268) III* (Shannon, 1968 reprint), p. 10.

45 J. Lawson, *Letters to the young on progress in Pudsey during the last sixty years* (Leeds, J. M. Young, 1886), p. 75.

46 Collier, *The family economy*, p. 99.

47 J. S. Lyons, 'Family response to economic decline: handloom weavers in early nineteenth century Lancashire', *Research in Economic History*, 12 (1989) 45–91.

48 For the return, see Bolton Local Studies Library, ZZ/250/3, Survey of handloom weaving districts.

49 Lancashire Record Office, PR2391/46, 'Letter'. This particular letter illustrates one of the complexities implicit in considering handloom weavers. That is, while some handloom weavers 'lost' as a result of being handloom weavers, others 'lost' as a result of being engaged in other trades and were then obliged to take up handloom weaving in order to avoid absolute dependence on the community.

50 Aspin (ed.), *Manchester*, p. 74.

51 D. Bythell, *The handloom weavers* (Cambridge, Cambridge University Press, 1969), and J. G. Timmins, *The last shift* (Manchester, Manchester University Press, 1993).

52 S. A. King, *Poverty and welfare, 1700–1850: a regional perspective* (Manchester, Manchester University Press, 2000). Handworkers in other branches of the textile industry did not suffer anything like as acutely as cotton handloom weavers, but it is clear from various committees of inquiry that they nonetheless felt themselves to be losers.

53 See P. Sharpe, *Adapting to capitalism: working women in the English economy 1700–1850* (Basingstoke, Macmillan, 1996), and P. Sharpe, 'The women's harvest: straw plaiting and the representation of labouring women's employment 1793–1885', *Rural History*, 5 (1994) 129–42. The northern agricultural regions were caught up less often and less intens-

ively in this vicious spiral because of the competing demands of industry and services in the rural labour market. For some contemporary discussion of this point, see J. E. Crowther and P. A. Crowther (eds), *The diary of Robert Sharp of South Cave: life in a Yorkshire village 1812–1829* (Oxford, Oxford University Press, 1997).

54  Data on heights would appear to show this experience from a different angle, with declining female heights after 1790 pointing towards their marginalisation within the household economy. See Nicholas and Oxley, 'The living standards'. Generalised family budget data conflict with this interpretation, but together the two approaches confirm the limited viability of southern rural family economies.

55  G. E. Mingay (ed.), *Arthur Young and his times* (Basingstoke, Macmillan, 1975), pp. 122–3.

56  Eden, *The state*, pp. 347–50.

57  I. Gray (ed.), *Cheltenham settlement examinations 1815–1826* (Gloucester, Bristol and Gloucestershire Archaeological Society, 1986), p. 58.

58  Horrell and Humphries, 'The origins'.

59  King, *Poverty*.

60  J. G. Williamson, *Did British capitalism breed inequality?* (Boston, Allen and Unwin, 1985).

61  For more on this issue, see King, *Poverty*.

62  *Ibid.*

63  *Ibid.*

64  *Ibid.*

65  See King, *Poverty*, Smith, 'Ageing', and P. Horden and R. M. Smith, 'Introduction', in P. Horden and R. M. Smith (eds), *The locus of care: families, communities, institutions and the provision of welfare since antiquity* (London, Routledge, 1998), pp. 1–20.

66  Crowther and Crowther (eds), *The diary*, p. 57.

67  For more information on how we can link reconstitution and poor law or charity evidence to create 'life-cycles of poverty', and on what sort of categorisations we might employ, see King, *Poverty*.

68  For more on this process and the graph, see King, *Poverty*.

69  In chapter eight we argued that families also came to play a greater role in welfare over time. This position is not incompatible with the interpretations offered here since it was entirely possible for families to turn to both kin and the community for more help when life-cycle patterns of accumulation and dissipation were fundamentally challenged as we argue that they were.

70  C. Shammas, *The pre-industrial consumer in England and America* (Oxford, Clarendon, 1990), and L. Weatherill, *Consumer behaviour and material culture in Britain 1660–1760* (London, Routledge, 1988).

71  Crowther and Crowther (eds), *The diary*, p. 122.

# CHAPTER TEN

# THE BUILT ENVIRONMENT DURING THE INDUSTRIAL REVOLUTION

## Conceptual framework

As discussion in this book has unfolded, we have made a number of references to dramatic changes that were made to the built environment, noting the strong impression they made on contemporaries. Yet, in doing so, we have merely provided instances of the types of developments that were taking place on an extensive scale. Compared with the amount of construction that had occurred in previous times, that undertaken during the Industrial Revolution period was vastly greater. New types of building appeared, and building types that had hitherto been few and far between, including textile factories and cottages specially designed for domestic manufacturing, proliferated. These changes were allied with far-reaching constructional works to underpin transport improvements by road, water and rail. Such developments often generated highly striking and distinctive landscape features, especially in the industrial regions.

The purpose of our final chapter is to examine the extent, nature and causes of this intensifying bout of building activity. In line with our overall approach, we will be particularly concerned with change at regional level and with the attitude of contemporaries towards it. Given space constraints, we will consider the built environment principally in terms of structures above ground level, though we need to be aware that structures below ground level, such as canal and rail tunnels and sewers, also brought a notable and telling element of change to the built environment. For the same reason, we can make only brief mention of the fundamental improvements brought to urban streets by the provision of gas lighting; in 1816 Preston became the first provincial town to acquire this facility and others quickly followed suit.[1] This development would have made a highly significant difference to the safety of pedestrians and road travellers alike.

We begin our discussion by considering changes made to the built environment in general terms. We are concerned with both quantitative and qualitative dimensions. Furthermore, we comment on how the increased levels of building activity were financed. This discussion paves the way for the main part of the chapter, which views these changes in the context of the rural and urban environments in which they took place, especially in the industrial districts. Such an approach facilitates analysis of the ways in which different types of settlement, including industrial colonies and middle-class residential districts, emerged. And in including within this discussion the observations of contemporaries about the changes they saw being made to the built environment, we highlight the differing perspectives they could give as to whether such changes were desirable or not.

## The general perspective

Whilst social and economic change had a wide-ranging impact on the built environment during the Industrial Revolution period, it was particularly evident in relation to housing provision. The doubling of population that occurred in England and Wales during the first half of the nineteenth century, along with the attainment of income levels amongst working-class families that could support regular payment of rent, at least for poor-quality accommodation, meant that the demand for houses rose substantially. At the same time, landowners, attracted by high potential rewards, were willing to make land available for building.[2] The landowners might themselves undertake such necessary development work as marking out building plots and laying down roads, or they might lease land to middlemen who did the work on their behalf.[3] As a result, the national housing stock was much increased. Figures from census evidence suggest that it roughly doubled in England and Wales, rising from about 1.6 million in 1801 to about 3.3 million in 1851.[4] Care is needed with these figures, however, since they are unlikely to be entirely accurate. One problem is that of knowing how the early census compilers defined a house. For instance, would they have consistently counted single houses shared by more than one family as one house or would they sometimes have regarded them as comprising two houses? Additionally, large houses might actually be sub-divided over time, thereby creating houses for the census compilers to count which did not arise from further building.[5] At best, therefore, the census house figures indicate the approximate extent to which new house building oc-curred, though probably they are not too wide of the mark. And we must not forget that considerable additions – which are hard to quantify accurately – were made to the national housing stock during the closing decades of the eighteenth century. Over our period as a whole, therefore, very significant change occurred.

National figures, of course, hide the regional variations that took place in house building activity, as well as variations between rural and urban areas and over time. In fact, higher than average levels of house building took place in the industrial regions, a reflection of the faster rates of population and income growth they experienced. In Liverpool, for instance, census figures suggest that the housing stock increased more than threefold between 1801 and 1851.[6] More-over, population and the housing it required became increasingly urban-orientated, as we saw in chapter seven. The census data on which figures for the proportion of urban to rural dwellers are based may exaggerate somewhat, since the urban enumeration districts extended into the surrounding country districts, thereby including some country dwellers in the urban totals. Even so, the figures reveal a notable change, as we have seen, and one which would be all the more telling if accurate figures were available to make a comparison between the mid-eighteenth and mid-nineteenth centuries.

Much of the new house building was associated with industrial expansion, and the construction of the additional buildings that in-dustry required also had a pronounced impact on the built environment.[7] In some instances, this was because of the sheer scale on which early industrial buildings were constructed – figure 10.1 provides a visual perspective on this point – but it was also because of the extent to which industries grew.[8] In Lancashire, for instance, literally tens of thousands of handloom weavers' cottages were built between the late eighteenth and early nineteenth centuries, accom-modating a huge labour force of around 170,000 people.[9] Additionally, more than a thousand cotton factories had been built in the county by the late 1830s.[10] Since the design of such buildings varied from industry to industry, they helped to give a degree of regional distinc-tiveness to industrial landscapes – a distinctiveness that was the more pronounced according to the degree of dominance that the major industry (or industries) attained.

The requirements of expanding commerce also made their mark on the built environment. The landscape alterations brought by the

**Figure 10.1** Plate-glass works at Ravenhead near St Helens. Built in the
mid-1770s, this works occupied a site of 30 acres, and the casting hall,
inside the building shown, measured 113 yards by 50 yards. Plate
glass was a thick glass used for mirrors, coach windows, etc. and
was formed by rolling into shape on a cast-iron table

construction of roads, canals and railways often proved striking,
especially where aqueducts, viaducts and bridges had to be erected.
Equally notable changes occurred with the provision of docks and
warehouses. By far the most impressive developments were in London,
where the construction of West India Dock and its warehouses (1800–
6) cost £1.2 million and of London Docks (1800–18) as much as £3.25
million.[11] But large-scale expansion of dock facilities also occurred in
Liverpool, especially to handle the rapidly expanding trade in raw
cotton and cotton manufactures. Between 1750 and 1825, some 43
acres of dock were constructed in the town and this was followed by
over a hundred acres more between 1826 and 1850.[12] Dock areas aside,
numerous warehouses were also constructed at canal and riverside
wharves and in town centres. In Manchester, for example, several
were to be found at the termination of the Irwell navigation (in Water
Street); at the Rochdale Canal Company's wharves, off Piccadilly;
and, in far greater numbers, in the city centre, where the warehouse
district spread southwards from the Cannon Street area towards Mos-
ley Street and Portland Street.[13] Using rate-book and trade-directory

evidence, Lloyd-Jones and Lewis have shown that the central business area of Manchester was, in fact, dominated by warehouses. In 1815, no fewer than 1,577 were in use, mainly to meet the needs of the cotton industry.[14] We should note, too, that town centres acquired growing numbers of other types of commercial premises, including banks, insurance offices, produce-exchange buildings and retail outlets.[15]

Commerce and industry apart, the built environment was significantly altered during the Industrial Revolution by the construction of places of worship and of public buildings, including hospitals, charity schools, theatres, town halls, market buildings, workhouses, gaols and court houses. As far as the former are concerned, Chalklin has noted a nationwide increase in church and chapel building between the 1770s and early 1790s. Activity slowed as building costs rose and heavy taxation reduced available funds during the Napoleonic Wars, but a further spurt followed during the 1820s.[16] This pattern of building is well illustrated in the case of Manchester parish, where, following the completion of St George's church in 1798, a period of twenty-two years elapsed without another church being erected, despite the population increasing by some 20,000.[17] Chalklin also notes that much larger nonconformist chapels were being erected during the 1810s and 1820s than previously, including an Independent chapel in Halifax which cost £6,000 in 1819. As to public buildings, he identifies a pronounced rise in their construction during the 1770s, between about the mid-1780s and mid-1790s and in the 1810s and 1820s. Total expenditure on public buildings by the 1820s was running at about a million pounds a year.[18]

In explaining the growth of the number and size of public buildings, Chalklin points to the major developments taking place in English society. For instance, in accounting for the expansion of prison building, we would look towards the growth of the prison reform movement, as well as to population increase, whilst to explain the growing interest in church building, we would highlight the humanitarian movement and the desire for social control. These he sees as basic causes, to which should be added more general influences. Amongst them was the desire to imitate the examples set elsewhere, with larger towns influencing activity in smaller ones; the satisfaction of civic and local pride, especially in constructing town halls and hospitals; and the emergence of townspeople who were sufficiently wealthy to pay for improved amenities.[19] Figure 10.2 shows one of the results of rising wealth and charitable activity.

**Figure 10.2** The former infirmary in Wellington Road South, Stockport. Built in 1832, the infirmary is 21 bays long and has an impressive portico – a centrepiece comprising columns with a pediment above – which in this case projects outwards

So far, we have concentrated on examining the general changes brought to the built environment in quantitative terms. But the changes also had a qualitative dimension. It was characterised by the growing tendency to erect better-constructed and more stylish buildings, upon which contemporaries often heaped lavish praise. One way of viewing this trend is in terms of a quickening of the movement from 'vernacular' buildings to 'polite' buildings. The former were constructed from local materials in plain, locally inspired styles and were designed by amateurs; their functionality was more important than their appearance. The latter were of more ornate appearance, featuring materials and styles from beyond the locality, and were designed by trained architects. Traditionally, polite buildings had been the more important ones, including churches and the houses of leading citizens. But during the Industrial Revolution period, polite features became increasingly evident on buildings of all types, including industrial premises and working-class houses.[20] One of the most obvious manifestations of the change was the erection of brick buildings – or at least of buildings with brick frontages – in districts where stone was the local building material. And in the Pennine areas, where stone often continued to be used, walls were increasingly built using the 'water-shot' technique. This involved laying the outer stones at a slight tilt, so that any moisture penetrating into them tended to drain out. However, since the technique was often confined to the front walls of buildings, it also had a decorative purpose.[21] Other changes included the provision of keystone arches above the front doorways of working-class houses rather than plain stone lintels. That changes to the appearance of buildings often took place using locally available building materials, and that, in terms of adding decorative detail, the changes were often restrained, show we should not overemphasise the degree to which vernacularism was superseded. Nonetheless, the inclusion of polite features even on quite humble buildings became widespread, adding a degree of visual refinement to the built environment which is often overlooked.

One further point to be made regarding the qualitative changes to the built environment concerns the inroads made by revived Gothic (medieval) styles of architecture at the expense of classical (Greek and Roman) styles. Pevsner notes that, for much of our period, Gothic revival was mostly confined to churches and country houses. 'When it was done', he remarks, 'it was done without archaeological scholar-ship or profound conviction.' However, he sees the 1840s as a watershed. It was then that books illustrating original medieval archi-tecture became available in England, from which architects could make accurate copies (see figure 10.3). And further weight was added to the Gothic cause at the time by the polemical writings of Pugin. An ardent supporter of medieval revivalism, he sought to criticise classical architecture on the grounds of its association with paganism. A dedicated Catholic, he believed that all architects should adhere to the old faith and accept its architecture as their inspiration. And the precise style preferred was that of the early decorated, fashionable in the late thirteenth and early fourteenth centuries.[22] However, despite the construction of numerous Gothic revival buildings, classical styles continued to evolve and remained in general favour (see figure 10.4). Both tendencies are evident in the case of Manchester's city-centre warehouses which, by the end of our period, were being built under the influence of Italian rather than Greek models in imitation of their Renaissance forerunners.[23]

Finally in this section, we need to briefly consider the means by which funds were raised to finance the increased building activity, thereby linking with our discussion of investment expenditure in chapter four. Because of the scale of expenditure required, canals

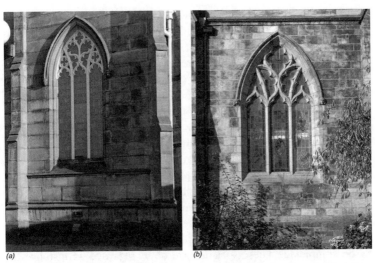

(a)                    (b)

**Figure 10.3** Gothic revival church windows at Preston. The illustrations show church windows either side of the 1840s divide. (*a*) A window at St Peter's church (erected 1822–25) and (*b*) a window at St John's the Divine (erected 1853–55). The latter is a far more exact copy of the decorated style and the form is made from cast iron rather than stone

**Figure 10.4** St Peter's church, St Peter's Gate, Stockport. Classical-style churches, for example, were commonly built, including the example shown here. It dates from 1768 and features a tower with a cap above an octagonal top stage

and railways had to be financed by share flotations, whereas industrial and commercial concerns commonly resorted to family and business contacts and, once successfully established, to profits arising. House builders, too, might rely partly on profits, but they could also draw on funds available from various sources, including advances made by customers, credit granted by builders' merchants, and mortgage loans raised on the security of houses they planned to erect or had partly completed.[24] In some instances, and for a variety of motives, employers would finance the construction of houses for their employees to occupy, particularly in rural districts where house building would not otherwise have taken place.[25] Especially in the Midlands and north, however, terminating building societies were frequently established. The members of these societies paid monthly subscriptions which were used to finance house building – or sometimes house purchase – drawing lots as to who should own the first houses to be completed. These societies are often regarded as instances of self-help, but recent investigation into Yorkshire and Lancashire examples suggests they were essentially a means of providing investment opportunities; the members generally rented out their houses rather than occupying them.[26]

Finance for public buildings, meanwhile, continued to be drawn from various sources. Chalklin's analysis reveals that local justices, both through levying rates and raising loans, played an increasing role.[27] Various sources were also tapped to finance church construction. In some cases special local rates were levied for the purpose and at Blackburn in Lancashire no fewer than three such rates were imposed between 1819 and 1827. The last was voted on by the inhabitants, the five-day contest, not surprisingly, engendering 'much bad feeling and riots'.[28] Local subscriptions might be raised, too, whilst acts of parliament were passed in 1819 and 1824 making £1.5 million available for a programme of church building in rapidly growing urban areas. This was a period when republican sentiment was seen as 'a threat to the constitution', and much could be achieved with regard to social stability, ran the rather optimistic argument, if only a sufficient number of church places could be made available. The Church Building Commission was appointed to oversee the programme, achieving some impressive results. In Lancashire and Cheshire, for example, the erection of 103 churches was facilitated from funds it provided. Even so, in these counties at least, supply was still deemed to have fallen short of demand, as figures provided by the splendidly named Chester Diocesan Society for Promoting the Building of Churches reveal. In 1834, the Society pointed to several towns in Lancashire and Cheshire where the population greatly out-numbered the places available in churches and chapels. For instance, in the town and parish of Wigan, nearly 44,500 people were enumer-ated in 1831, but church and chapel accommodation provided places for only 6,900 of them. And at Dukinfield, in the parish of Stockport, the population of about 14,700 were reported as having 'no church or clergyman whatever'. In an attempt to rectify the situation, the Society sought to establish a fund which would meet up to one-half of the expense incurred in erecting churches, as long as the balance could be raised by local subscription and private resources.[29]

### The development of the built environment in rural areas

The scale on which industry and commerce grew during the Industrial Revolution had a marked impact in rural districts. Numerous indus-trial colonies emerged, associated particularly with mining, textile production and iron working. Where these activities made use of powered machinery, as in iron smelting (to drive furnace bellows), in iron forging (to power trip hammers, as well as rolling and slitting mills) and in textile spinning (to operate preparatory and spinning machinery) the availability of water power was commonly the major locational attraction. Consequently, as evidence derived from early Ordnance Survey maps and field observation so often reveals, river valleys frequently became characterised by series of works' reservoirs and associated buildings. In the Sheffield vicinity, for instance, over a hundred such sites could be found along the river Don and its tributaries, mainly for forging and grinding cutlery and tools.[30] The reservoirs stored water so that its use for turning waterwheels could be better regulated, but they also kept water at a given level as the river continued to fall, enabling powerful overshot and backshot waterwheels to be used.[31] In many instances, previously unoccupied sites were selected, bringing a range of problems for entrepreneurs to resolve, not least the recruitment and housing of labour.

Some entrepreneurs solved these problems by turning to pauper apprentices and in some instances, as in the case of the Gregs' mill at Styal, the pauper apprenticeship system made its mark on the built environment through the provision of houses in which the apprentices lived.[32] But by no means all proprietors of rural textile mills turned to pauper children as a means of meeting their labour needs. Many preferred to employ family working groups and, accordingly, erected family houses, perhaps with other facilities such as schools and reading rooms. The quality of this accommodation varied considerably, with some industrialists building high-quality 'model' housing. Amongst them were Henry and Edmund Ashworth, cotton spinners of Egerton and Bank Top, near Bolton.[33] However, field investigation reveals that whilst the Ashworth cottages were generally of a high standard in constructional terms, they nonetheless varied appreciably in terms of design, size and facilities. Thus, as figure 10.5 suggests, quite a number had a front living room/kitchen and a back kitchen as the downstairs rooms, rather than a separate living room at the front and kitchen at the back.[34] The former type plainly gave less privacy to its inhabitants than the latter. Moreover, the front living room/kitchen was condemned by some contemporaries on the grounds that, in addition to being draughty, it exposed family life to public gaze, since passers-by could see into the front room.[35] The Ashworths also erected two- and three-roomed back-to-backs, of a type similar to those shown in figure 10.6. That they provided housing of varying size and quality reflected their desire, which may not in practice have been attainable, to provide separate sleeping accommodation for children of each sex. It reflected, too, an awareness of the varying amounts of rent their employees could afford or were prepared to pay.[36] And since

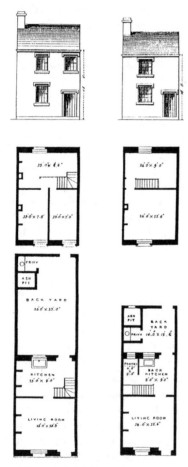

**Figure 10.5** Ashworth cottages

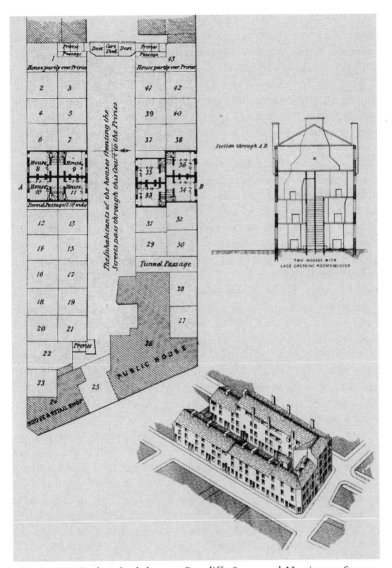

**Figure 10.6** Back-to-back houses, Rancliffe Street and Harrington Street, Nottingham. All the houses had three rooms, one above the other. Each downstairs room would have been used as a living room/kitchen, and the two upper rooms as bedrooms. As the section and elevation drawings reveal, lace-dressing workshops were provided in the upper storey of the houses in the northern block. The houses greatly outnumbered the privies

family earnings would have differed appreciably according to life-cycle stage, there may have been a tendency amongst the Ashworth employees and their families to move from one type of house to another, a situation which may also have applied more generally.

By no means all rural industrial colonies grew up around water-powered sites, even in the textile districts. The remarkable rate at which textile production expanded during the late eighteenth and early nineteenth centuries, coupled with the slow rate at which power-looms came into use, encouraged the formation of numerous colonies of handloom weavers and framework knitters. In many instances, these colonies comprised entirely new settlements. They were characterised by rows of specially designed cottages which had little or no land attached and which, for convenience of access, were sited alongside roads. The workshops in these cottages often contained elongated windows in the front and rear walls, thereby providing good natural light by which the weaver could work. If possible, upper-floor locations were chosen for the workshops, the aim being to minimise any obstruction to light from surrounding buildings or natural features, including trees. In the woollen districts of east Lancashire and West Yorkshire and in the silk districts of Cheshire (centred on Macclesfield) upper-storey loomshops predominated. However, in the Lancashire cotton districts, hand-weavers' loomshops were generally located on the ground floor or in cellars. This was necessary in order to obtain more easily the humid conditions required to weave cottons, especially the finer grades.[37] Figure 10.7 demonstrates these building types.

Rural settlements associated with other occupations also had their distinctive characteristics. For instance, in the 1840s, one observer remarked that the Tyne valley consisted of rows of colliers' cottages interspersed with agricultural villages and the seats of wealthy landlords and capitalists. Generally built by the colliery owners, these cottages were 'all fashioned after nearly the same architectural model', displaying, no doubt, pronounced vernacular qualities. In many cases they were single-storied – as was the case in West Yorkshire, too – though terraces of better-quality cottages were provided for colliery deputies or overmen.[38] From the 1780s, once steam engines had become capable of delivering rotary motion, the process of winding coal from the pit bottom to the surface gradually brought to these settlements the distinctive pulley wheels of the winding shaft head-stocks.[39] Moreover, tramways were increasingly provided to move

(a)

(c)

(b)

**Figure 10.7** Former domestic loomshops. Premises at (*a*) Catherine Street, Macclesfield (upper-storey silk weaving); (*b*) Golcar, Yorkshire (upper-storey wool weaving); and (*c*) Horwich near Bolton (cellar cotton weaving)

341

coal away from pits, especially to link with the growing canal network.[40]

The size to which these rural industrial settlements grew varied considerably. Many were extremely small, comprising a mine or works with no more than a handful of houses or, in the case of hand-weavers' colonies, just a short terrace of houses with workshops. Others, Egerton amongst them, became quite sizeable villages, with several rows of houses, more than one factory and such community facilities as a school, inn and church. We should not forget of course that some of the industrial colonies simply added to existing settlements rather than providing the basis for new communities. Hand-weavers' cottages, for example, might be grouped with a farmstead, perhaps helping to maintain a link between farming and textile production. As William Radcliffe noted, barns and farm outbuildings were increasingly converted into loomshops during the late eighteenth century, a clear indication that the occupational shift was from farming to textile production.[41] This said, it is also important to acknowledge that rural communities were also expanding without the impetus of industry. Thus, new farms continued to be built in the industrial areas during the late eighteenth and early nineteenth centuries, as was the case in northeast Lancashire. Here, new farms appear to have been created mainly on land already farmed rather than on moorland newly enclosed, so that smaller farms became more common. Sarah Pearson suggests that rising demand for food from textile workers raised the profitability of local farming and made small farms on poorer-quality land more economically viable. She notes, too, the growing practice amongst wealthy manufacturers of buying farms to turn them into stylish country residences.[42]

### The development of the built environment in towns

The formation of industrial colonies was also a feature of urban growth and again colonies of both factory and domestic workers emerged. In the case of the former, clustering along canalside locations was common, not only because factory owners could sometimes benefit from their own wharfage facilities, but also because they could use canals to obtain water for their steam-engine boilers and to provide an outlet for the condensed steam from their engines.[43] But too much can be made of the advantages arising from canalside locations, with urban factories also occupying river valley sites, as

**Figure 10.8** Regency mill, Macclesfield. Occupying a roadside location on the town outskirts, the mill has a stylish classical façade with pedimented central bays

well as main road sites. Figure 10.8 provides one example of such siting policy. Moreover, a more general locational influence tended to operate, with industrial colonies emerging on the edges of the built-up areas, or just beyond, the central parts of towns being concerned principally and increasingly with commercial activity, both wholesale and retail. Freetown at Bury and Brookhouse at Blackburn, which John Marshall has analysed, provide useful illustrations of these industrial colonies.[44] So, too, do the hand-weavers' settlements in Preston to which Nigel Morgan has drawn attention. He shows that two main hand-weaving districts emerged in the town, one on the western edge (the Friargate area) and one on the eastern edge (the Horrocks area). Taking the two areas together, he was able to identify over one thousand hand-weavers' cottages, about a quarter of the town's total housing stock in the early nineteenth century.[45] Such developments would have been equally or even more important in other textile towns – Preston had a relatively low proportion of its labour force employed as hand weavers compared with other major Lancashire towns – a matter which awaits much fuller investigation.

To a greater degree than their rural counterparts, urban industrialists relied on steam power, adding an ever-growing number of mill chimneys to the townscape. For the most part, the chimneys were not especially high – forty or fifty feet being common – a reflection of the relatively low boiler capacities that were required to drive early factory steam engines, along with an absence of bye-laws stipulating the minimum height to which factory chimneys should be built. Consequently, mill chimneys tended to be square rather than round or octagonal in cross-section, wind resistance not being seen as a major problem. Such low chimneys tended not to remove the smoke they emitted from the immediate area, however, thereby adding to air pollution. We may also note that windmills continued to provide a conspicuous landscape feature in urban as well as rural environments, finding favour as a cheap power source for corn grinding. Indeed, Butt and Donnachie suggest that it was particularly between 1750 and 1850 that the construction of windmills coincided with peaks of agricultural activity and that, in many northern and western parts of the country, they did not disappear until the late 1800s.[46]

How far industrialists with premises within or close to built-up areas wished (or needed) to provide houses for their workers is debatable. Housing would certainly have been more readily available in towns than in rural areas, as speculative builders took advantage of growing demand. Accordingly, compared with their rural counterparts, urban employers could rely more on their workers finding accommodation for themselves and on others to provide the community facilities their workers required. Even so, employers located in urban industrial areas did provide some housing. Those in Blackburn, for instance, owned 1,588 houses in 1850, though this comprised a small proportion of the total housing stock.[47] Such actions, the extent of which should not be exaggerated, have been seen as expressions of a new employer paternalism which was emerging strongly in Lancashire textile towns during the 1830s and 1840s, perhaps reflecting a genuine and active concern on the part of some employers to promote the moral and intellectual development of their employees and their employees' families. But it is not easy to divorce such a perspective from the need for employers to obtain a hard-working and responsible labour force, over which they could exert a good deal of control.[48]

The industrial settlements that grew up on urban fringes during the closing decades of the eighteenth century and the early decades of the nineteenth did not as a rule extend the physical extent of towns to a very marked degree. Towns certainly came to occupy greater amounts of space, but, even in the mid-nineteenth century, a walk of only around half a mile or so would have been required to pass through all but the biggest of them. Indeed, urban growth during the Industrial Revolution era was dwarfed by that which took place in Victorian and Edwardian times. In explaining such limited spatial growth, it must be noted that the expansion of the built environment also arose through occupying the open spaces that could still be found within urban areas. Many of these spaces comprised long, narrow gardens at the rear of substantial houses built for more prosperous denizens. Such gardens often originated as medieval burgage plots, but, with town expansion, they came increasingly to be seen as development land. In some instances, as Chalklin points out, they might provide plots to erect workshops or warehouses, but more often they were used for building houses. These were often approached by a tunnel through the houses fronting the street and might be constructed on either side of the garden, being separated by a narrow yard. Town-centre building space might also be made available by demolition of older properties and by taking over land that had been used for recreational purposes, such as bowling greens, or for agricultural purposes, including fruit growing or animal grazing.[49]

The formation of urban industrial colonies attracted community buildings of various types, churches, schools and shops amongst them. Such public buildings as town halls, court houses and market halls, however, tended to occupy more central sites since they had to be conveniently located for the townspeople as a whole rather than a section of them. Not infrequently, the more important town-centre buildings, including ancient churches, were rebuilt, opportunity being taken to increase their size and to adopt more fashionable styles. At Blackburn, for example, the medieval parish church was rebuilt between 1819 and 1826, one of the most significant changes being the replacement of a nave that was the same length as the chancel with one that was much longer than the chancel, thereby making far greater space available for the congregation.

## The emergence of middle-class suburbs

A further dimension to consider regarding the development of the built environment in urban areas concerns the provision of housing for the growing number of middle-class families. Many of these families owed their prosperity to success in the professions or as merchants, though, during the eighteenth century, those deriving an appreciable income from industrial activity were becoming much more numerous. Details of the type of houses they were building in the industrial towns during the earlier half of the eighteenth century are far from abundant, but they would have been much more substantial than the norm. Certainly middle-class housing erected at Birmingham between the mid-1740s and about 1780 contained three or four rooms per storey and occupied a street frontage of thirty feet or more.[50]

Fortunately, far more is known about provincial middle-class housing erected during the later eighteenth century, not only because the documentary record, including map evidence, is much fuller, but also because a good deal of it has survived. Such housing usually comprised terraces, often four stories high (including basements) and several bays wide. The houses might front directly on to the street, though they might have sizeable yards or gardens at the rear. Classical in style, but varying in the degree of ornamentation they displayed and in the materials from which they were built, these houses were sometimes located around squares. These had become fashionable in London, since they gave private recreational space for the inhabitants and a more pleasant living environment than in streets. Maurice Beresford has described in detail two such squares on the western fringe of Leeds, the development of which took place from the late 1760s. Commenting on the advantages of their location, he remarks that the houses were 'segregated from the more distasteful aspects of town and yet not too remote from the workplace'.[51] Figure 10.9 provides a visual representation of one such square. From the builders' point of view, houses in squares were expensive in terms of the land required, but had advantage because they were much sought after and could command high prices.[52] The life-styles of families living in these squares was certainly opulent, early Victorian census evidence revealing that they commonly employed several resident servants.

**Figure 10.9** Winckley Square, Preston. Developed during the first half of the nineteenth century, Winckley Square is close to the town centre. The illustration presents a very positive image, but nonetheless indicates an attractive living environment for the better-off

Whilst middle-class terraces built around squares offered a particularly distinctive type of living environment and reflected a move towards residential segregation of social classes in towns, the extent to which they occurred should not be overstated.[53] In many towns they were not constructed and, throughout the Industrial Revolution era, middle-class dwellings might be situated in quite a number of town streets, as trade-directory and census evidence reveal. Thus the twenty-nine Preston attorneys listed in Baines's 1824 directory of Lancashire resided in sixteen streets around the town centre, the only marked concentration being in Fishergate, one of the town's main thoroughfares, where eight of them lived.[54] As Lancashires's leading social and legal centre, Preston may have been home to more middle-class families than was customary in industrial towns at this time. Even so, it was common to find several parts of towns with a distinctly middle-class ethos, especially on the outskirts, offering a striking counterpoint to the squalid housing of which the public-health reformers made so much.

By the early nineteenth century, middle-class town dwellers, especially those in the larger towns, were subject to intensifying pressures on their living space from an expanding commercial sector. The growing need for warehousing and retail space in town centres, and the rising demand for professional services, led to middle-class houses being increasingly converted to commercial use. At the same time, the number of middle-class families grew, raising the demand for high-quality houses. Of course, middle-class families would have formed only a small proportion of any town's population, but they demanded large houses, for which town-centre space was becoming scarce. Accordingly, sites on the fringes of the built-up areas had to be utilised and, in the larger towns, more distinct middle-class suburbs emerged some distance beyond the built-up area. By the late 1840s, for example, such developments could be found in the Buile Hill area, about a mile to the northwest of Salford, and at Higher Broughton and Cheetham, a similar distance to the north of Manchester.

The suburb of Victoria Park, situated about two miles southeast of Manchester town centre, had also emerged. Land for this development was purchased in 1836 and an ornamental park was laid out, with building plots incorporated; by 1844, thirty-three houses were occupied.[55] As in the suburbs to the north of Manchester, the Victoria Park dwellings comprised detached and semi-detached villas set in sizeable gardens instead of the traditional terraces. Such a change, to borrow F. M. L. Thompson's words was 'heralded in the revolutionary plans for the Eyre estate in St. John's Wood [northwest London] in the 1790s', which were implemented from 1815 and became the model for suburban houses.[56] Accordingly, middle-class families could live not only within an exclusive environment, but in one which offered a considerable degree of space and privacy and which was probably a good deal healthier than that in the town. On the other hand, as Thomas Webster and Frances Parkes remarked in 1844, a town residence could be seen as 'superior to any other for social intercourse and varied enjoyment by means of public and private parties, theatres, concerts, balls, public libraries, museums, exhibitions of works of art, with numerous opportunities to acquire general knowledge'.[57] This argument can also be applied to those who built large, out-of-town houses in their own private estates. By 1815, no fewer than forty-five houses of this type had been built to the west of Leeds, most of them dating from the 1780s and 1790s. These houses, Beresford remarks, were not large enough to be 'true country houses', but they were larger and had more outbuildings than those built in the town's squares.[58]

## Contemporary perspectives on the evolving built environment

So far, our discussion has focused on the way that historians have viewed the changes made to the built environment during the Industrial Revolution period. But how did contemporaries regard these changes? Did they see them as generally conferring benefit, perhaps creating not only more visually satisfying environments in which to live, but also more pleasant, perhaps healthier ones as well? Or was their view on the whole more critical? Did they regard the changes as generally disadvantageous, bringing a deterioration in the visual appeal of the built environment as well as leading to more squalid and less healthy living conditions?

In considering these issues, it is necessary to appreciate at the outset that contemporaries expressed widely differing views on these matters. And they did so because they had varying concerns to address. Those wishing to promote public health reform, for instance, tended to highlight the worst features of the built environment, especially insanitary housing. On the other hand, those writing guide books to towns for the most part took a positive stance. Both groups, in fact, were selecting evidence to suit their purpose, and even when both types of comment are available for a town or village, only a very partial impression of the quality of the built environment can be obtained. Furthermore, we cannot assume that the evidence either group adduced is entirely accurate. As ever, we need to check for inconsistencies and to make comparison with other types of evidence that might be available. With regard to the built environment, the study of surviving buildings and other structures – or photographs of them – can often prove highly revealing, even though they are sources which historians all too frequently overlook.

To give some impression of the differing perspectives offered by contemporaries, we have drawn on the type of evidence that is widely available in local publications. We begin with positive impressions given of Rotherham and Birmingham, two industrial towns that might not be immediately thought of as likely to elicit favourable comment from contemporaries. In the case of the former, William White's trade directory of 1837 concedes that the town had a 'dull appearance', but also points out that some of the houses, which were generally constructed of stone, were 'handsomely and substantially built'. More-over, the compiler was decidedly upbeat with regard to both buildings and facilities that could be found in the town. For instance, he reports that the 'parish church is a spacious and handsome Gothic fabric, built in the reign of Edward IV, on the site of a Saxon edifice. It is dedicated to All Saints, and is indisputably one of the finest parochial places of worship in Yorkshire.' Amongst the facilities he could extol were the gas lights, which, from 1833, illuminated the town with 'their brilliant vapour', and the subscription library, which comprised some 2,500 volumes and which was seen as a particularly desirable asset in 'a place where so much provision has been made for affording learning to all classes'.[59]

At Birmingham, a guide book written in 1852 at the very end of our period also makes highly complimentary remarks about major buildings, singling out the town hall, which was erected during the early 1830s in Paradise Street, for particular praise:

> Of the buildings which have been erected by the public spirit of the inhabitants of this town at various periods, and for whatever purpose, the Town Hall is decidedly the most conspicuous and attractive. This splendid edifice ... may be instanced as a remarkable attempt to apply to modern purposes a style of structure which belonged essentially to the Greek temples.[60]

And as if such praise was not enough, J. G. Kohl, who visited Birmingham in 1844, was even more fulsome in his appreciation of the town hall:

> The town hall is a magnificent copy of Greek temple, and may fearlessly be placed by the side of the Glyptothek of Munich, or of the Magdalen Church at Paris. The style is magnificent and purely classical. Within is a hall capable of containing 9000 persons, and said to be the largest room in England.[61]

Favourable comment on the splendour of major buildings is a constant theme within the positive contemporary view, pointing to the desirable effects arising as a result of growing prosperity. More-over, contemporaries often reinforced the positive message by the use of visual images. The engraving of St Peter's church in Preston, published in 1855, provides one example and is reproduced as figure 10.10.[62] The subject chosen is highly edifying and the wholesome image is reinforced by portraying respectable people and fine weather and by including very little detail of the surrounding environment.

**Figure 10.10** St Peter's church, Preston, in the 1850s. The positive image is reinforced by omitting the surroundings and by depicting respectable people and good weather

To illustrate the critical contemporary view on the built environment we can again turn to evidence concerning Rotherham and Birmingham. In large measure, such comment was directed at working-class housing conditions, including the layout of the streets in which such housing was situated. For instance, in 1851, many of the older streets at Rotherham and Kimberworth in Yorkshire, were reported as being 'narrow and crooked', with 'numerous alleys and courts only a few feet wide that admit of little or no ventilation'. In the higher parts of the town, however, the situation was somewhat better 'in the circumstance that the houses stand one above another'.[63]

Streets might also be extremely squalid, both through disrepair and inadequate cleansing. In Edwin Chadwick's famous sanitary report of 1842, for example, it was reported of Birmingham that 'the principal streets are well drained, but this is far from the case with respect to many of the inferior streets, and to many, or rather most, of the courts, which, especially in the old parts of the town, are dirty and neglected, with water stagnating in them'. But the problem was by no means confined to the older parts of town, since the provision of adequate drainage was not enforced when new residential streets were being constructed. 'The want of some regulation in this respect', the report continues

> often causes the accumulation of putrid water in ditches and pools in the immediate vicinity of newly-erected buildings. In some parts of the borough, as at Edgbaston, there are but few public underground sewers, and the water from the houses is discharged into the ditches or gutters by the side of the roads, where it stagnates.[64]

Far more disgusting, though, were the problems arising from insanitary housing. For the most part, removal of excreta was undertaken by means of conservancy systems rather than water-carried systems. The 'state of the art' conservancy system featured the use of an excreta tub which, ideally, was situated in a privy at the bottom of a yard, was used only by one family and was regularly emptied via a back street adjoining the privy. Much less wholesome was the cesspit – a hole dug in the ground and lined with bricks or stone – or a midden – literally a pile of ordure, perhaps contained by walls. The process of emptying cesspits was a matter upon which Robert Rawlinson was moved to comment in his 1849 report on public health conditions at Birmingham. Referring to houses in Hagley Street, he found that at 'Mr. Deykin's, in 1849, a dumb well or cesspool on the premises required to be emptied, and men were engaged to do the work at a cost of £2, but the smell was so bad they required an additional £1, and lastly an additional £1, and a pint of brandy each hour'. Quite understandably, these scavengers were in a strong bargaining position, the alcohol they consumed no doubt helping to dull their senses with regard to the appalling task in hand.[65]

## Accounting for poor-quality housing

The type of evidence we have cited with regard to insanitary houses and streets by no means relates solely to industrial towns or to towns alone; indeed, similar evidence is easy to unearth for rural districts. Despite their shortcomings, the local public health reports published during the early Victorian period reveal that a great many working-class families lived in extremely poor-quality houses, which, as well as lacking adequate sanitation, were often damp, crowded together and of small size in relation to occupancy levels. Why was such housing provided?

One consideration is that, even if there was an overall increase in real wages during the Industrial Revolution period, all too many families did not earn sufficient income to be able to afford good-quality housing. For some families, as we saw in chapter nine, this situation would have been a permanent feature of their lives. For other families low incomes were much more episodic, perhaps occurring during trade depressions, when old age was reached or when obligations to house kin had to be met. Accordingly, there was a substantial demand for cheap accommodation, especially in the form of cellar dwellings and back-to-backs.[66] Such houses were relatively economical in terms of the amount of land they required and, since they adjoined other houses, they saved on the costs of building materials. Accordingly, they could be made available at low rents. But they also encouraged overcrowding because great numbers of them were required as population grew rapidly, because a relatively high number could be provided per acre and because they were frequently built in blocks that were three or four storeys in height.

Adding to the reasons for providing high-density housing was the need for workers to be near their place of work. This was particularly the case with casual labourers, dock workers amongst them, who had to maximise their chances of obtaining any jobs that arose. And this situation was exacerbated as the central business districts of towns expanded, making ever greater demands on space for warehouses and retail premises.[67] Furthermore, that casual workers were amongst the lowest paid in the workforce reinforced the link between high-density housing and housing of low quality. In Rodger's words, 'weak demand for housing ensured mean accommodation'.[68]

The rapidity with which urban populations grew could also place demands on the building industry that proved too severe. As a result, there was a tendency in some towns for average occupancy rates to rise and, therefore, for the likelihood of overcrowding to intensify. Population and housing figures for Bradford borough illustrate the point, though we need to bear in mind our earlier discussion of the problems of how houses were defined.[69] In 1801, the number of persons per house there stood at 4.59, a figure which rose at succeeding censuses to reach 5.31 in 1841. There was a fall to 4.76 in 1851, but this was still a somewhat higher figure than that of 1801. The building industry eventually made inroads into the problem, but it took several decades to do so. At Nottingham, on the other hand, occupancy rates fell from 5.7 people per house in 1801 to 4.1 in 1841, so the argument that the building industry was not always able to keep pace with population increase should not be too strongly pressed.[70]

In addition to the nature and extent of demand, poor-quality housing also resulted from the actions of those who provided houses and the land on which the houses were built. The issue here is partly that some builders were prepared to use inferior materials and labour in order to reduce their building costs and enhance their profits; indeed, the term 'jerry-builder' was in widespread use by the 1830s. And since building costs rose faster than prices in general during the Industrial Revolution era, the incentive to achieve economies remained strong. Furthermore, though both local and national legislation was introduced to provide some regulation on building quality, it did not prove particularly effective, not least because of lax enforcement. As to landowners, the charge made against them is that when they sold rather than leased land for building they lost control over the quality of the housing erected on it.

High-density housing, even where it was associated with back-to-backs and, perhaps, cellar dwellings, need not necessarily have created squalid living conditions. However, we have already seen that in the early Victorian era such housing was generally associated with inadequate water supply and rudimentary sanitation. As the public health reports so vividly demonstrate, the response on the part of local government proved quite inadequate in dealing with the situation. In part, this has been attributed to ignorance about such matters as laying drains and providing adequate foundations for buildings, matters on which experts themselves did not agree. But there was also a lack of co-ordinated effort amongst the proliferating local organisations responsible for public health matters in towns; a resistance to the idea that public health reforms should be imposed on individuals by a centralised authority, especially if private property rights were infringed; and an inadequate legal framework to enforce reform.[71] And this was so despite unprecedented improvements brought to the urban environment by street widening and paving, the construction of new streets and the provision of gas lighting.[72]

## Conclusion

The growth of population, coupled with the expansion of trade and industry had a profound impact on Britain's built environment during the Industrial Revolution period. In urban areas, some outward expansion took place, especially as industrial colonies were formed, though open spaces within built-up areas were also utilised, mainly for housing and commercial premises. For several reasons, including the need to provide cheap housing near to the workplace and the lack of regulation on house building, some exceedingly squalid housing was erected. Whilst the extent to which such housing occurred can be easily exaggerated, there is no doubt that all too many urban families lived in the most deplorable conditions and that, where they relied on unskilled and casual work, they did so for much, if not all, of their lifetimes.

The extent of the built environment also increased in rural areas. It did so partly because of the growing use of water-powered machinery, but also because of the emergence of colonies of handicraft workers, especially in the textile industries, and of workers in extractive industry, particularly coalmining. These colonies might extend existing settlements, sometimes appreciably, but they often comprised entirely new ones. Settlement in rural districts also spread as enclosures of waste land and sub-division of cultivated land led to the creation of new farms. Additionally, there was growing encroachment on the countryside by more opulent urban dwellers. In some instances they built mansions set in extensive private grounds but, in the neighbourhood of larger towns, they also began to occupy suburban estates shared with others.

The increase in the size of the built environment was accompanied by notable changes in its appearance. The vernacular tradition, emphasising local styles and building materials, increasingly gave way to buildings with more pronounced polite features, incorporating styles and building materials that were generally fashionable. This change, a consequence of growing prosperity, was most evident in churches, public buildings and larger houses, though such buildings might still display vernacular characteristics, most obviously in relation to the use of local building materials. Importantly, too, revived medieval styles of architecture increasingly challenged the classical styles that became so fashionable in Britain during the Georgian period. Again, too much can be made of the degree to which change occurred, but its impact was nonetheless real, eventually bringing highly accurate imitations of the styles produced by medieval craftsmen.

Taken together, quantitative and qualitative changes in the built environment would have impacted with force and immediacy on the perceptions of contemporaries. Whether they were rural or urban dwellers, the changing number and style of houses, public buildings, factories and transport channels, allied with physical changes in the landscape wrought by developments such as mining and enclosure, would have been the surest possible sign to those who lived during the period 1700–1850 that 'something' – and more importantly something new and unprecedented – was going on. We are thus back where we started this book – with the contemporary feeling of disjuncture and discontinuity.

## Notes

1  D. Hunt, *A history of Preston* (Preston, Carnegie, 1992), p. 214.

2  C. W. Chalklin, *The provincial towns of Georgian England* (London, Edward Arnold, 1974).

3  *Ibid.*, pp. 57–60.

4  J. Burnett, *A social history of housing, 1815–1970* (London, Methuen, 1983), p. 14.

5  E. Gauldie, *Cruel habitations* (London, Allen and Unwin, 1974), p. 82.

6  J. H. Treble, 'Liverpool working class housing, 1801–1851', in S. D. Chapman (ed.), *The history of working class housing* (Newton Abbot, David and Charles, 1971), pp. 169–71 and 201.

7  See B. Trinder, *The making of the industrial landscape* (London, Dent, 1982), M. Palmer and P. Neaverson, *Industrial landscapes of the east Midlands* (Chichester, Phillimore, 1992), and M. Palmer and P. Neaverson, *Industry in the landscape* (London, Routledge, 1994).

8  See C. Powell, *An economic history of the British building industry, 1815–1979* (London, The Architectural Press, 1980), pp. 13–14. On the value of surveyors' plans in assessing industrial development and the development of the built environment more generally, see D. Crossley, 'The Fairbanks of Sheffield: surveyors' records as a source for the study of regional economic development in the 18th and 19th centuries', *Industrial Archaeology Review*, 19 (1997) 5–20.

9  G. Timmins, *Made in Lancashire* (Manchester, Manchester University Press, 1998), pp. 333–4.

10  E. Butterworth, *A statistical sketch of the County Palatine of Lancaster* (Manchester, Lancashire and Cheshire Antiquarian Society, 1968 reprint),

p. xxvii. The impact of textile mills on the built environment is discussed in E. Jones, *Industrial architecture in Britain 1750–1939* (London, Batsford, 1985), M. Williams, *Cotton mills in greater Manchester* (Preston, Carnegie, 1992), J. Longworth, *The cotton mills of Bolton, 1780–1985* (Bolton, Bolton Museum and Art Gallery, 1986), A. Menuage, 'The cotton mills of the Derbyshire Derwent and its tributaries', *Industrial Archaeology Review*, 17 (1993) 38–61, K. Falconer, 'Mills of the Stroud valley', *Industrial Archaeology Review*, 17 (1993) 62–81, C. Giles and I. Goodall, *Yorkshire textile mills 1770–1930* (London, RCHM, 1992), and A. Calladine and J. Frisker, *East Cheshire textile mills* (London, RCHM, 1993). Work on the landscape impact of other industries includes D. Baker, *The industrial architecture of the Stafforshire Potteries* (London, RHCM, 1991).

11  C. Chalklin, *English counties and public building, 1650–1830* (London, Hambledon, 1998).

12  A. Jarvis, *Liverpool central docks, 1799–1905* (Stroud, Sutton, 1991), and N. Ritchie-Noakes, *Liverpool's historic waterfront* (London, HMSO, 1984), pp. 9–67 and 129–62.

13  See A. Kidd, *Manchester* (Keele, Keele University Press, 1993), p. 24. For early warehouses in Manchester, see S. Chapman, 'The commercial sector', in M. Rose (ed.), *The Lancashire cotton industry* (Preston, LCB, 1996), pp. 63–5, and more generally Jones, *Industrial architecture*, chapters 2–4.

14  R. Lloyd-Jones and M. Lewis, *Manchester and the age of the factory: the business structure of cottonopolis in the Industrial Revolution* (London, Croom Helm, 1987), pp. 44–6.

15  Powell, *Building industry*, pp. 14–15.

16  Chalklin, *Public building*, pp. 17–18.

17  E. Baines, *History, directory and gazetteer of the county palatine of Lancaster, volume 2* (Newton Abbot, David and Charles, 1968 reprint), pp. 127–38.

18  Chalklin, *Public building*, pp. 19–25.

19  *Ibid.*, pp. 24–5.

20  See R. W. Brunskill, *Illustrated handbook of vernacular architecture* (London, Faber, 1971).

21  F. Atkinson, 'Water-shot stonework', *Transactions of the Lancashire and Cheshire Antiquarian Society*, 69 (1959) 141–3.

22  N. Pevsner, *The buildings of England: London I* (London, Penguin, 1973), pp. 98–9, and N. Pevsner, *The buildings of England: south Lancashire* (London, Penguin, 1969), p. 32.

23  Jones, *Industrial architecture*, pp. 85–95.

24  Chalklin, *Provincial towns*, pp. 235–42.

25  See S. Pollard, *The genesis of modern management* (London, Penguin, 1968), pp. 234–6, L. Dewhurst, 'Housing the workforce: a case study of

West Yorkshire', *Industrial Archaeology Review*, 11 (1989) 117–35, and Burnett, *Housing*, pp. 81–5.

26  G. Timmins, 'Early building societies in Lancashire', in S. Jackson (ed.), *Industrial colonies and communities* (Lancaster, CORAL, 1988), pp. 19–24, and M. Beresford, *East end, west end: the face of Leeds during urbanisation 1684–1842* (Leeds, Thoresby Society, 1988), pp. 196–202.

27  Chalklin, *Public building*, especially chapter 3.

28  W. Durham, *Chronological notes on the history of the town and parish of Blackburn* (Blackburn, Bray, 1866), pp. 30–1.

29  *Blackburn Alfred*, 22 January 1834.

30  D. Crossley, J. Cass, N. Flavell and C. Turner, *Water power on the Sheffield rivers* (Sheffield, Sheffield Trades Historical Society, 1989).

31  See R. A. Buchanan, *Industrial archaeology in Britain* (London, Penguin, 1972), pp. 240–8.

32  M. Rose, *The Gregs of Styal* (Quarry Bank Mill, National Trust, 1978).

33  R. Boyson, *The Ashworth cotton enterprise* (Oxford, Clarendon, 1970), particularly chapter 7. Also S. D. Chapman, 'Workers' housing in the cotton factory colonies, 1770–1850', *Textile History*, 7 (1976) 112–39.

34  See Lords Sessional Papers, 1842, xxvi, *Report on the sanitary condition of the labouring population of great Britain, appendices*.

35  See C. Aspin (ed.), *Manchester and the textile districts in 1849* (Helmshore, Helmshore Local History Society, 1972).

36  See G. Timmins, 'Housing quality in rural textile colonies: the Ashworth settlements revisited', *Industrial Archaeology Review*, 22 (2000) 22–37.

37  See G. Timmins, *Handloom weavers' cottages in central Lancashire* (Lancaster, Lancaster University, 1977), G. Timmins, *The last shift* (Manchester, Manchester University Press, 1993), pp. 53–66 and 82–8. Also L. Caffyn, *Workers' housing in West Yorkshire 1750–1920* (London, HMSO, 1986), and C. Giles, 'Housing the loom, 1790–1850: a study of industrial building and mechanisation in a transitional period', *Industrial Archaeology Review*, 16 (1993) 27–9. Also M. Palmer, 'Houses and workplaces: the framework knitters of the east Midlands', *Leicestershire Industrial History Society Bulletin*, 11 (1988) 26–39, and 'Industrial archeaology: continuity and change', *Industrial Archaeology Review*, 16 (1994) 135–56.

38  Trinder, *Industrial landscape*, pp. 187–9, and Caffyn, *Workers' housing*, pp. 28–32.

39  D. Anderson, *The Orrell coalfield, Lancashire, 1740–1850* (Buxton, Moorland, 1975), pp. 61–71.

40  A. R. Griffin, *The British coalmining industry* (Buxton, Moorland, 1977), pp. 133–4.

41  W. Radcliffe, *Origin of the new system of manufacture, commonly called powerloom weaving* (Stockport, Lomax, 1828), p. 65.

42  S. Pearson, *Rural houses of the Lancashire pennines 1560–1760* (London, HMSO, 1985), pp. 124–5.

43  R. N. Holden, 'Water supply for steam-powered textile mills', *Industrial Archaeology Review*, 21 (1999) 41–51.

44  J. D. Marshall, 'Colonisation as a factor in the planting of towns in northwest England', in H. Dyos (ed.), *The study of urban history* (London, Edward Arnold, 1968), pp. 215–30.

45  N. Morgan, *Vanished dwellings* (Preston, Mullion Books, 1990).

46  J. Butt and I. Donnachie, *Industrial archaeology in the British Isles* (London, Elek, 1979), pp. 54–5.

47  D. Beattie, *Blackburn* (Halifax, Ryburn, 1992), pp. 51–2.

48  See P. Joyce, Work, society and politics (London, Harvester, 1980), especially chapters 6 and 7, M. Huberman, 'The economic origins of paternalism: Lancashire cotton spinning in the first half of the nineteenth century', *Social History*, 12 (1987) 177–93. Also M. Rose, P. Taylor and M. Winstanley, 'The economic origins of paternalism: some objections', *Social History*, 14 (1989) 89–98, and M. Huberman, 'The economic origins of paternalism: reply to Rose, Taylor and Winstanley', *Social History*, 14 (1989) 99–103.

49  Chalklin, *Provincial towns*, pp. 66–72. Also G. Firth, *Bradford and the Industrial Revolution* (Halifax, Ryburn, 1990), pp. 174–6, and R. J. Morris, 'Urbanisation', in J. Langton and R. J. Morris (eds), *Atlas of industrialising Britain, 1780–1914* (London, Methuen, 1986), pp. 172–3. Also S. D. Chapman, 'The Robinson mills: proto-industrial precedents', *Industrial Archaeology Review*, 15 (1992) 58–61.

50  Chalklin, *Provincial towns*, p. 196.

51  Beresford, *East end*, ch. 6.

52  See J. Ayres, *Building the Georgian city* (New Haven, Yale University Press, 1998), p. 32.

53  See R. Rodger (ed.), *Housing in urban Britain 1780–1914* (Basingstoke, Macmillan, 1989), pp. 28–9.

54  Baines, *History*, pp. 510–11.

55  M. Spiers, *Victoria Park, Manchester* (Manchester, Chetham Society, 1976), p. 13.

56  F. M. L. Thompson, 'Introduction: the rise of suburbia', in F. M. L. Thompson (ed.), *The rise of suburbia* (Leicester, Leicester University Press, 1982), p. 8.

57  Quoted in D. Rubinstein, *Victorian homes* (Newton Abbot, David and Charles, 1974), p. 27.

58  Beresford, *East end*, pp. 306–32. Also Firth, *Bradford*, p. 177, and G. Timmins, *Blackburn: a pictorial history* (Chichester, Phillimore, 1993), illustrations 28, 29 and 31.

59  W. White, *History, gazetteer and directory of the West Riding of Yorkshire*, I (Sheffield, 1837), pp. 253–8.

60  *A pictorial guide to Birmingham* (Birmingham, 1852), p. 81.

61  J. Kohl, *England and Wales* (Newton Abbott, David and Charles, 1968 reprint), p. 9.

62  See C. Hardwick, *A history of the borough of Preston* (Preston, 1857).

63  W. Lee, *Report of the general board of health on ... the township of Rotherham and Kimberworth* (London, 1851), p. 32

64  *Report on the sanitary condition*, pp. 105–6.

65  R. Rawlinson, *Report of the General Board of Health on ... the township of Birmingham* (London, 1849), p. 121.

66  See Rodger, *Housing*, pp. 31–4, Burnett, *Housing*, pp. 58–61 and 70–6, M. W. Beresford, 'The back to back house in Leeds, 1787–1937', in Chapman, *Working-class housing*, pp. 95–131, and Beresford, *East end*, pp. 421–35.

67  See Rodger, *Housing*, p. 12.

68  *Ibid.*, p. 10.

69  Firth, *Bradford*, p. 184.

70  S. D. Chapman, 'Working-class housing in Nottingham during the Industrial Revolution', in Chapman (ed.), *Working class housing*, p. 155.

71  See Gauldie, *Cruel habitations*, chapters 9 and 10, and Rodger, *Housing*, pp. 26–7.

72  E. L. Jones and M. Falkus, 'Urban improvement and the English economy in the seventeenth and eighteenth centuries', in P. Borsay (ed.), *The eighteenth century town, 1688–1820* (London, Longman, 1990), pp. 128–55.

# CONCLUSION

We started this volume by highlighting the rich and varied tapestry of approaches to the Industrial Revolution. Historians have tried to measure the Industrial Revolution with national numbers such as gross domestic product, factor productivity or industrial output. Sometimes, but not often, they have taken broadly regional approaches. From the 1960s it became common to focus on whether there was an Industrial Revolution, and if so what its character was, using social and cultural variables – demography, family history, labour relations, consumption and gender. And scholars from other disciplines – geography, sociology, anthropology and politics – have also brought their own distinctive talents and approaches to bear on the question of the nature, causes and impact of industrialisation. Yet, the outcome of well over one hundred years of debate has simply been more debate. Scholars have focused on different time periods, different sources, different industries and different regions. The spectrum of opinion still ranges, as it has always done, from those, on the one hand, who perceive a powerful Industrial Revolution occurring sometime between 1700 and 1850 and those, on the other hand, who see nothing spectacularly different about either the eighteenth or nineteenth centuries. For this group, changes are a matter of degree rather than order.

To try to make sense of this debate, we suggested that we ought, as the earliest commentators had done, to focus on the lived experiences of the Industrial Revolution. Contemporaries frequently recorded their *feelings* and their *impressions* about the processes of continuity and change in the eighteenth and nineteenth centuries. In forming these impressions they implicitly adopted a much wider and more fluid definition of their equivalents of terms such as 'change' or 'continuity' than do many modern historians, accounting for a wide range of the social, institutional and cultural variables which went into the melting pot of their everyday lives and those of their peers. Contemporaries also had a very different unit of analysis from that of many modern historians. Rarely did they write about 'the nation' – much of the most penetrating commentary on continuity and change was concerned with the basic socio-economic and cultural fabric of the region, the community or even the individual life-cycle.

Thus, building up from the individual, community and regional roots of the industrialisation process, and making extensive use of contemporary commentary, we have tried to create for the period 1700–1850 a 'big' picture. This is not of course a picture without blemishes, and it is as well to acknowledge some of them right at the outset of our conclusion. Clearly, we have not been able to discuss the full range of cultural, social and economic variables necessary to gain a truly rounded picture of the Industrial Revolution process. We have not discussed directly important issues such as the standard of living or overseas trade. Nor have we said much about transport, changing class structures, the reconfiguration of working-class leisure practices, public health in urban areas, the changing policies of the state, taxation or urban culture. We have not really talked about crime and criminality during the Industrial Revolution, and nor have we considered topics such as Luddism and machine breaking or foreign policy. In part too we have deliberately left out many of the old potatoes of the Industrial Revolution historiography; our aim has not been to provide a comprehensive overview, but to select what we consider to be key variables and to use them to develop students' ideas on *ways of thinking about the Industrial Revolution*. As well as reviewing the historiography, we have tried to dissect it, to highlight its ambiguities and to suggest questions that remain to be answered or have been answered imperfectly. Our aim too has been to foster student research – to use primary sources and contemporary perspectives as a springboard for stimulating a new generation of student dissertations on economic and social-history topics.

There are, though, other blemishes. We have not been able to provide comprehensive regional coverage on any of the subjects that we consider. In part this is because historians are still manufacturing the empirical material for this sort of approach, something that both authors are vigorously engaged in as well. In part too, even a book of this length provides a limited canvas for exploring the rich diversity

362

of regional and local material on different aspects of the industrialisation process that does exist. Our analysis has focused
disproportionately on the north and Midlands, and we have almost
completely ignored London, deliberately given the extent to which it
has coloured Industrial Revolution historiography in the past. Some
of the chapters have a distinctive Lancashire focus. This is something
more than accident or a consequence of limited material. Rather,
such a focus reflects our belief that Lancashire in particular constitutes
a microcosm of the tensions between continuity and change which
were generated and dissipated throughout the country as a whole in
the period 1700–1850. We focus on the county, though not as much
as we could have, because it fills this role and because it offers a
deep pool of historical material with which to work.

Even had we been able to offer a comprehensive regional picture,
a third blemish in our analysis is that any approach which aims to
engage with contemporary views and regional experiences faces distinct source problems. On some issues (such as the landscape and
townscape) the contemporary narratives speak loudly and long, while
on other issues (for instance on sexual matters) they are less instructive.
Whether they appear comprehensive or not, some voices are consistently under-represented – the experiences and perceptions of women,
children and the poor are lost to us too often. And, of course, the
relatively few voices that we have been able to employ in a work of
this length may speak with forked tongues or in ways which are
capable of many different, and sometimes diametrically opposed,
interpretations. There are also *problems of representativeness* – the
key question in adopting what we might label a 'contemporary
approach' becomes which regions, which communities and which
individual life-cycle experiences really encompass the essence of the
Industrial Revolution. Or indeed whether the well-documented
examples at our disposal are anything more than a completely unrep-
resentative sample of the regions, communities and lives that we could
have looked at in a source-rich perfect world.

Nor should we forget *problems of interpretation*. Communities
were criss-crossed by social, economic and cultural sub-groups which
might have complementary or contradictory experiences and which
might interpret exactly the same experiences in very different ways.
'Regions' also provide problems of interpretation. Essentially they
are artificial entities which are difficult to pin down conceptually
and practically, and they could combine communities with radically

different industrialisation experiences. Finally, there are *conceptual problems*. How do we assess an individual narrative to see whether the person experienced 'change' when they never explicitly say so, and how do we characterise individual life-cycles where revolutionary change in one aspect of life could be balanced or more than balanced by fundamental continuity in another aspect of life at the same time or at another point in the life-cycle? How do we allow for the fact that individual life-cycles were not insulated from the families and the communities around them? The experiences and opinions of others may have done as much to shape a particular individual's appreciation of change in the economic, social and cultural fabric as his or her own personal experiences. Risks of death are an excellent case in point. We demonstrated in chapter seven that mortality risks for infants fell consistently in the late eighteenth and early nineteenth centuries, and we further demonstrated that most deaths were concentrated into a range of high-risk, high-mortality families. 'Background risks' of death were thus small, and yet the spectre of infant death haunted the perceptions of many communities and individuals during the Industrial Revolution. In a similar vein, risks of maternal mortality were actually relatively small and yet dread of childbirth because of supposedly high risks of maternal death was profound amongst the middle- and upper-class women who have left records before the later nineteenth century.

We do not deny these potential problems, but nor do we overestimate their impact. While we regret the lack of a distinct gender focus to this work, we have at least taken some pains to include the words, lives and experiences of the poor. If regions are indeed artificial entities, it is clear to us that contemporaries were well aware of where to draw lines on their maps. They talked powerfully and incessantly about 'manufacturing districts', 'pastoral districts', 'commercial districts' and 'arable regions'. They also talked about more subjects than historians have ever allowed. And while there may be biases in the words and thoughts of those who have left us records, there is little evidence to suggest that these were either substantial or systematic. Potentially more important is that we have inserted our own biases by using the words and thoughts of contemporaries who lived in or talked about a restricted number of regions. Lancashire again looms large, but so does Sheffield and West Yorkshire. Can the lessons of contemporary narratives from these areas be extended to other regions given distinctive regional trajectories in the development of an economic infrastructure and the impact of industrialisation on everyday life? There is no answer to a question such as this, but we feel that the narratives we use share one thing in common with each other and with narratives which could have taken their place from other regions, industries or periods. They almost all suggest that contemporaries felt that something significant and, to varying degrees, unparalleled, was 'going on' in the period after 1700. It is for this reason that we talk about an 'Industrial Revolution'. That said, what we offer is an *interpretation*, our interpretation, of the process of the Industrial Revolution based upon one reading of potentially ambiguous evidence. Indeed, this is the most that any of the contributors to the historiography of the Industrial Revolution outlined in chapter one can claim.

What then is our perception of the 'big picture'? How did the period 1700–1850 look 'different' from what had gone before? Take the regional perspective first. As we saw in chapter two the regional concentration of industrial structures had the power to stimulate major changes (positive and negative) in the fabric of everyday life on three levels. First, in those regions where industrial concentration was both substantial and 'permanent' (such as Lancashire), textile workers and others experienced new opportunities for high wages much earlier in the life-cycle than had been the case previously, more trade-related work disruptions, more consumption of food and everyday items, vast increases in urban populations, and fluid labour-market conditions. Their world was one of constant flux, and for them the Industrial Revolution must have been a very immediate phenomenon indeed. Second, in those regions where concentration was more transient (such as in the Leicestershire hosiery industry) opportunities for profit were short-lived and rapidly succeeded by collapsing markets, structural poverty and worsening work conditions. For people living in areas like these, whether directly connected to industrial production or not, the Industrial Revolution also had an immediacy. Finally, regional concentration had an impact, albeit a less dramatic one, on the communities that lost out. The textile workers of East Anglia, the southwest or Northamptonshire, for instance, saw the decline of their traditional occupations and the slow degradation of their household economies and townscapes as regional comparative advantage was brought to bear. While these experiences had deep roots in historical patterns of fluidity in comparative advantage, they were on an unprecedented scale in the period 1700–1850. Textiles led the way in exploiting regional comparative advantage, but iron, coal, metalware, pottery and other industries were also caught up in the wider story of permanent and temporary regional advance and decline.

In Part II of our book we tried to build on this perspective, suggesting that the period 1700–1850 witnessed a very substantial re-orientation of industrial organisation, with the development of domestic outwork, the rapid rise of the manufactory and the factory, and the multiplication of centralised production facilities. All of these organisational forms had been present before 1700, but the pace and scale of their development after 1700 were of a different rank than anything that had gone before. The period also saw fundamental changes in technology. Hand technology was the subject of big new inventions and small productivity-raising modifications; in centralised industries power and chemistry were brought to bear; while in the textile and engineering industries mechanised powered production was very much a reality by 1830. Business finance changed to accommodate these developments. While the extra fixed capital needs of industrialists were generally relatively small, their need for working capital spiralled, and the sources of getting both types of finance changed radically in some regions. The partnership became much more common, and the attorney and the bank became significant features of the regional financial landscape. Investment of this sort underpinned an ever expanding range of consumer and producer goods which had to be marketed in ever more sophisticated ways. And industrial workers had to be fed in ever rising numbers and at ever rising levels. There was an agricultural revolution, widely defined, in the period 1700–1850 which matches in importance the revolution in industry. In short, we think that the English economic infrastructure was transformed after 1700 and that never before had the basic economic changes, viewed from a contemporary perspective, been as fundamental and as widespread as those between 1700 and 1850.

Part III of our book carried this theme forward. We identified a population explosion that coincided with a massive growth in urban living. We also suggested that a historiographical literature on the form and function of the family that has consistently stressed slow and minor change may be incorrect. Using a range of sources and theoretical perspectives we speculated that, in form, families became more unstable in the face of the life-cycle uncertainties generated by the revolution in the economic infrastructure. We also suggested that the same changes may actually have strengthened the internal bonds of the English family system, making it more rather than less functional. One of the major changes that we can identify is a weakening of the household economy. While there were both distinctive losers and distinctive gainers from the revolution of the economic infrastructure, we showed that the key experience was felt by the 60–80 per cent of people whose life-cycles encompassed periods of gain *and* loss. For them, poverty and marginality seem to have been a key experience, in a way that it had not been in the later seventeenth century and would not be in the later nineteenth century. We also looked at the most immediate influence on the lives of individuals living out their lives in the period 1700–1850 – housing. Profound changes in the scale, the quality and the aesthetic of the built environment during the period 1700–1850 were identified. In Part III, then, we tried to create an impression of what the Industrial Revolution looked and felt like and in this sense what is striking is that neither before nor after the period 1700–1850 do contemporary narratives record the same widespread sense of wonder at something big and comprehensive happening as they do in this period. Contemporary commentators might be positive or negative, but the point is that they saw the tension between continuity and change being played out in their life-cycles, between the generations, within their communities and within their regions.

In keeping with the central focus of this book, let us end with three very different individual perspectives. William Rowbottom, from Oldham in Lancashire, kept his diary between the 1780s and 1830s. He made little connection with, or comment on, the wider national picture as opposed to tracing the Industrial Revolution process as it affected his community over his life-cycle. He saw that industrialisation of his locality meant more drownings in the newly built mill ponds, more crime, more poverty, violently fluctuating food prices, the rise of fashionable food, dress and behaviour, and above all more uncertainty for all of those connected with the industrialisation process whatever their social rank. One particular entry in his diary, on 8 September 1793, pointedly illustrates this uncertainty. He noted that:

> The remains of John Smith of Dolstile were interred at Oldham this day. He was one of the oldest Fustian manufacturers in the parish of Oldham and *died poor*.[1]

The workers employed by manufacturers like Smith fared little better. Rowbottom noted on 11 August 1793, for instance, that,

The relentless cruelty exercised by the Fustian masters upon the poor weavers is such that it is exampled in the annals of cruelty, tyranny and oppression for it is nearly an impossibility for weavers to earn the common necessities of life so that a great deal of families are in the most wretched and pitiable situation.[2]

He was clear that industrialisation meant *'dismal times'*, and that whether the economic, social and cultural experience of his contemporaries was positive or negative was very much a lottery. As he suggested:

> The fortunate have years
> And those they choose
> The unfortunate have days
> And those they loose[3]

Other diarists were more outward looking and positive than Rowbottom. Robert Sharp of South Cave in East Yorkshire, for instance, tells us much about his locality and the experiences of the people who lived there in the early nineteenth century, but he was well aware of the wider national canvas upon which his local observations were superimposed. He monitored the development of national transport networks with keen anticipation of being able to send his son fresh produce in London in the expectation that it would not be rotten when it got there. For similar reasons he took an interest in the development of a national postal system. And he had to be in touch with national legislative changes on a whole range of issues such as taxation and weights and measures. His role as a sometime poor-law officer seems to have given him an insight into the regional development of industrial and farming structures – even if he misinterpreted the importance of these developments for the national economy – into the availability of game and into the labour market. In a different way, then, he was as keenly aware of the radical changes going on around him as was Rowbottom.

David Whitehead of Cowpe in Lancashire, meanwhile, was at the heart of the Industrial Revolution process and it is appropriate to finish our book with his story. David Whitehead was born in 1790. He lost his father early on in life, and his mother (who did not remarry) was left to bring up a family of three boys. She was employed as an outworker for the Rossendale putting-out merchants, and made three unsuccessful attempts to get her son David apprenticed to a trade. So he took his life into his own hands, moving from trade to trade in a youth which included hawking in east Lancashire and playing in a band in Wales. He returned home periodically to live with his mother and to pass on his financial support when he had any to give. In 1816, he had accumulated enough money, along with his brothers and a loan from an uncle, to establish a coarse spinning firm. This prospered after a shaky start and it was not long before Whitehead was opening a mill shop in this isolated part of the world. Eventually the firm moved to bigger premises at Waterfoot, near Cowpe, and the workers had to either move or lose their jobs. The brothers went their different ways soon thereafter, so that David became the sole active partner.

The mill went through lean times in the early 1820s and was caught up in the riots of 1826, when workers from other local mills, fearful of their future because of mechanisation, broke windows and forced his workers out on strike. During the mid- and late 1820s he watched his workers become ever poorer both because of their own imprudence and because market conditions obliged him to pare wages to the bone. In better times he lamented their tendency to luxury and their seeming mental block on the concept of saving for the future. However, ultimately he was a paternalistic employer, providing a subsidised shop and education for children, and giving away substantial sums in charity on a regular basis. He endowed the mechanics institute, provided art for the local art gallery, and in 1842 and again in 1848 responded to the dire poverty instigated by trade depression by raising a public subscription. During his lifetime he had moved from a small three-room cottage to a major Victorian town house, and he had seen the landscape transformed from a barren wasteland to a series of industrial valleys with a teeming and mobile population. He had seen his own consumption standards and those of his workers improve and he had made at least three fundamental changes to the structure or location of production, yielding equally fundamental change to the working and domestic lives of his several hundred employees. By the time his diary ends, the railway had begun to forge through Rossendale, opening up the valleys to even more fundamental change. In one generation the Whiteheads were transformed from paupers to princes and were beneficiaries from, and instigators of, a process that had wrought massive changes on the lives of many thousands in their locality.[4] David Whitehead's opportunities, disappointments, aspirations, achievements and reflections tell us more about the nature of the Industrial Revolution and its fundamental character than very many tables or graphs can do. In turn, and perhaps to a lesser degree, there were David Whitehead equivalents throughout industrial, rural and urban England. For us, it is this sort of widely felt experience which locates the period 1700–1850 as a discontinuity.

## Notes

1 A. Peat (ed.), *The most dismal times: William Rowbottom's diary 1787–1799* (Oldham, Oldham Council, 1996), p. 53. Our italics.
2 *Ibid.*, p. 52
3 *Ibid.*, p. 36
4 For the Whitehead material, see Rawtenstall Library, The diary and letterbook of David Whitehead.

# BIBLIOGRAPHY

## Manuscripts

*Lancashire Record Office*
Uncatalogued James Collection, Certificate.
DDX 211, Hodgkinson papers.
DDLi Uncatalogued (192 boxes).
DDB 81/71, Diary.
DDX 115/91, Farming memoranda, 1785–1838.
DDX 325, Garstang vestry minutes.
DDKe 2/6/2, Census of Bolton, 1674.
PR2391/46, Letter.

*Sheffield City Archives*
Stock Book, Sis. 146.
Partnership deed, 1786, Sis. 1.
Scrapbook, Sis. 10.

*West Yorkshire Archive Service, Huddersfield*
21D88/1, Rental 1715–79.
DD/T/S/A/18, Survey book of Calverley moor.
DD/T/E/3, Calverley enclosure award.
DD/T/R/B/38, Survey book of farms in Calverley.
Sp St 5/9/22, Rental of the Stanhope estate.
Sp St 5/9/38, Rental of the Stanhope estate.
T/S/a/17, Field book 1750.
T/S/a/c/17, Halifax dole book, 1811.

*Other repositories*
Bolton Local Studies Library, ZZ/250/3, Survey of handloom weaving districts.
Manchester Central Library, L15/2, Estate papers.
Oxfordshire Record Office, CPZ/15, Otmoor.
Rawtenstall Library, The diary and letterbook of David Whitehead.

Yorkshire Archaeological Society, DD12/I/10/7, Survey of the lands of Sir Walter Calverley.

## Parliamentary papers

*Census of Great Britain, 1851, Population tables II: ages, civil condition, occupation and birth places of the people, volume 1.*
*1842, XV Children's Employment Commission (Mines), ...*
*1843, XIII Second report of the Children's Employment Commission (Trades and Manufactures), ...*
*Report from the committee of the woollen manufacture of England, with minutes of evidence and appendix 1806 (268) III* (Shannon, 1968 reprint).
Lords Sessional Papers, 1842, xxvi, *Report on the sanitary condition of the labouring population of Great Britain.*

## Newspapers

*Blackburn Alfred.*
*Blackburn Mail.*
*Manchester Guardian.*

## Printed sources

*A pictorial guide to Birmingham* (Birmingham, 1852)
Aiken, J., *A description of the country from thirty to forty miles round Manchester* (Newton Abbot, David and Charles, 1968 reprint).
Ashcroft, L., *Vital statistics: the Westmorland census of 1787* (Berwick, Curwen Archives Trust, 1992).
Aspin, C. (ed.), *Manchester and the textile districts in 1849* (Helmshore, Helmshore Local History Society, 1972)
Baines, E., *A history of the cotton manufacture in Great Britain* (London, Cass, 1966 reprint).
Baines, E., *History, directory and gazetteer of the county palatine of Lancaster, volumes 1 and 2* (Newton Abbot, David and Charles, 1968 reprint).
Baines, E., *History, directory and gazetteer of the county of York, volume 1* (Newton Abbot, David and Charles, 1969 reprint).
Baines, E., *The social, educational and religious state of the manufacturing districts with statistical returns* (London, Augustus Kelley, 1969 reprint).
Baker, D., 'The inhabitants of Cardington in 1782', *Publications of the Bedfordshire Historical Record Society*, 52 (1973)
Butterworth, E., *A statistical sketch of the county palatine of Lancaster* (Manchester, Lancashire and Cheshire Antiquarian Society, 1841).
Chancellor, V. E. (ed.), *Master and artisan in Victorian England: the diary*

*of William Andrews and the autobiography of Joseph Gutteridge* (London, Evelyn Adams and Mackay, 1969).

Clark, P., and J. Hosking, *Population estimates of English small towns 1550–1851* (Leicester, Leicester University Press, 1989).

Cobbett, W., *Rural rides* (Dent, Dalglish, 1932).

Colquhoun, P., *A treatise on the wealth, power and resources of the British empire* (London, Cass, 1969 reprint).

Cooke-Taylor, W., *Notes on a tour of the manufacturing districts of Lancashire* (London, Cass, 1968 reprint).

Crosby, A. (ed.), *The family records of Benjamin Shaw, mechanic of Dolphinholme and Preston* (Manchester, Manchester University Press, 1991).

Crowther, J. E., and P. A. Crowther (eds), *The diary of Robert Sharp of South Cave: life in a Yorkshire village 1812–1829* (Oxford, Oxford University Press, 1997).

Cudworth, W., *Round about Bradford* (Queensburn, Mountain Press, 1968 reprint).

Defoe, D., *A tour thro the whole island of Great Britain* (London, Penguin, 1987 reprint).

Dodd, G., *Days at the factories* (New York, Augustus Kelley, 1967 reprint).

Durham, W., *Chronological notes on the history of the town and parish of Blackburn* (Blackburn, Bray, 1866).

Eden, F. M., *An estimate of the number of inhabitants in Great Britain and Ireland* (London, Wright, 1800).

Eden, F. M., *The state of the poor* (London, Cass, 1969 reprint).

Faucher, L., *Manchester in 1844* (London, Cass, 1969 reprint).

Fiske, J. (ed.), *The Oakes diaries: business, politics and the family in Bury St Edmunds 1778–1800* (Woodbridge, Boydell Press, 1990).

Gray, I. (ed.), *Cheltenham settlement examinations 1815–1826* (Gloucester, Bristol and Gloucestershire Archaeological Society, 1986).

Guest, R., *A compendious history of the cotton manufacture* (London, Cass, 1969 reprint).

Hannah, G. (ed.), *The deserted village: the diary of an Oxfordshire rector, James Newton of Nuneham Courtenay 1736–86* (Stroud, Sutton, 1992).

Hardwick, C., *A history of the borough of Preston* (Preston, 1857).

Head, G., *A home tour through the manufacturing districts of England in the summer of 1835* (London, Augustus Kelley, 1968 reprint).

Holland, G. C., *The vital statistics of Sheffield* (London, Robert Tyas, 1843).

Holt, J., *General view of the agriculture of the county of Lancaster* (Newton Abbot, David and Charles, 1969 reprint).

Howes, F. M., *A tour of the factory districts* (Manchester, Head, 1837 reprint).

James, V. E. (ed.), *The autobiography of James Harker, a Dorset labourer* (London, Greenwood Press, 1954).

Kay, J. P., *The moral and physical condition of the working classes* (Manchester, Morton, 1832).

Kay, J. P., *On the nature and training of children in England and Germany* (Manchester, Manchester Statistical Society, 1852).

Kidd, S., *The history of the factory movement* (New York, Augustus Kelley, 1966 reprint).

Kohl, J., *England and Wales* (Newton Abbott, David and Charles, 1968 reprint).

Lawson, J., *Letters to the young on progress in Pudsey during the last sixty years* (Leeds, J. M. Young, 1886).

Lee, W., *Report to the General Board of Health on Reading* (London, 1850).

Lee, W., *Report of the General Board of Health on ... the township of Rotherham and Kimberworth* (London, 1851).

*Lewis's Manchester directory for 1788* (Radcliffe, Richardson, n.d. [1788]).

Malthus, T. R., *An essay on the principle of population* (London, Murray, 1826).

Marshall, J. D. (ed.), *The autobiography of William Stout of Lancaster, 1665–1725* (Manchester, Manchester University Press, 1969).

Marshall, W., *The review and abstract of the county reports to the Board of Agriculture, 1811* (New York, Augustus Kelley, 5 volumes, 1968 reprint).

Nettel, R. (ed.), *Journeys of a German in England in 1782* (London, Cape, 1965).

Parsons, E., *The civil, ecclesiastical, literary, commercial and miscellaneous history of Leeds, Bradford, Wakefield, Dewsbury, Otley and the district within ten miles of Leeds* (Leeds, Hobson, 1834).

*Pawson and Brailsford's illustrated guide to Sheffield* (Sheffield, S. R. Publishers, 1971 reprint).

Peat, A. (ed.) *The most dismal times: William Rowbottom's diary 1787–1799* (Oldham, Oldham Council, 1996).

Pigot and Co., *National commercial directory for 1828–9* (Norwich, Winton, 1995 reprint).

*Pigot and Dean directory for Manchester, Salford, etc. for 1824–5* (Manchester, Pigot and Co., 1825).

Radcliffe, W., *Origin of the new system of manufacture, commonly called powerloom weaving* (Stockport, Lomax, 1828).

Rawlinson, R., *Report of the General Board of Health on ... the township of Birmingham* (London, 1849).

Sasche, W. L. (ed.), *The diary of Roger Lowe of Ashton in Makerfield, Lancashire, 1663–1674* (Wigan, Picks, 1994).

Schmidt, R., *An agricultural journey* (Hanover, Willhelm Back, 1835).

*Slater's royal national classified commercial directory of Lancashire* (Manchester, Slater, 1851).

Vaisey, D. (ed.), *The diary of Thomas Turner, 1754–1765* (Oxford, Oxford University Press, 1984).

White, W., *History and general directory of the borough of Sheffield* (Sheffield, White, 1833).

White, W., *History, gazetteer and directory of the West Riding of Yorkshire, I* (Sheffield, 1837).

F. White & Co., *General directory of the town and county of Newcastle-upon-Tyne and Gateshead* (Sheffield, 1847)

Wood F., and K. Wood, *A Lancashire gentleman: the letters and journals of Richard Hodgkinson 1763–1847* (Stroud, Sutton, 1992).

## Secondary works

Abbot, M., *Life cycles in England 1560–1720: cradle to grave* (London, Longman, 1996).

Adair, R., *Courtship, illegitimacy and marriage in early modern England* (Manchester, Manchester University Press, 1996).

Allen, R. C., 'The two English agricultural revolutions, 1459–1850', in B. M. S. Campbell and M. Overton (eds), *Land, labour and livestock: historical studies in European agricultural productivity* (Manchester, Manchester University Press, 1991).

Allen, R. C., 'Agriculture during the Industrial Revolution', in R. Floud and D. N. McCloskey (eds), *The economic history of Britain since 1700* (Cambridge, Cambridge University Press, 2nd edn, 1994).

Anderson, B. L., 'The attorney and the early capital market in Lancashire', in J. R. Harris (ed.), *Liverpool and Merseyside* (London, Cass, 1969).

Anderson, D., *The Orrell coalfield, Lancashire, 1740–1850* (Buxton, Moorland, 1975).

Anderson, M., *Family structure in nineteenth century Lancashire* (Cambridge, Cambridge University Press, 1972).

Anderson, M., 'Sociological history and the working class family: Smelser revisited', *Social History*, 3 (1976) 317–34.

Anderson, M., 'The emergence of the modern life-cycle in Britain', *Social History*, 10 (1985) 69–87.

Anderson, M., 'What can the mid-Victorian censuses tell us about variations in married women's employment?', *Local Population Studies*, 62 (1999) 9–30.

Archer, J. E., *By a flash and a scare: incendiarism, animal maiming and poaching in East Anglia* (Oxford, Clarendon, 1990).

Ashmore, O., *The industrial archaeology of Lancashire* (Newton Abbot, David and Charles, 1969).

Ashton, T. S., 'The bill of exchange and private banks in Lancashire, 1790–1830', *Economic History Review*, 15 (1945) 25–35.

Ashton, T. S., *The Industrial Revolution 1760–1830* (Oxford, Oxford University Press, 1948).

Aspin, C., *The first industrial society* (Preston, Carnegie, 1995).

Aspin, C., and S. Chapman, *James Hargreaves and the spinning jenny* (Helmshore, Helmshore Local History Society, 1964).

Atkinson, F., 'Water-shot stonework', *Transactions of the Lancashire and Cheshire Antiquarian Society*, 69 (1959) 44–67.

Ayres, J., *Building the Georgian city* (New Haven, Yale University Press, 1998).

Bagwell, P. S., *The transport revolution from 1770* (London, Batsford, 1974).

Baker, D., *The industrial architecture of the Staffordshire Potteries* (London, RHCM, 1991).

Barraclough, K. C., *Steelmaking before Bessemer: volume 2, crucible steel* (London, The Metals Society, 1984).

Beattie, D., *Blackburn* (Halifax, Ryburn, 1992).

Beckett J. V., and J. Heath, 'When was the Industrial Revolution in the east Midlands?', *Midland History*, 13 (1981) 77–94.

Behagg, C., 'Mass production without the factory: craft producers, guns and small firm innovation, 1790–1815', *Business History*, 40 (1998) 1–15.

Beresford, M., *East end, west end: the face of Leeds during urbanisation 1684–1842* (Leeds, Thoresby Society, 1988).

Berg, M., *The age of manufactures: industry, innovation and work in Britain, 1700–1820* (London, Fontana, 1985).

Berg, M., 'Small producer capitalism in eighteenth century England', *Business History*, 35 (1993) 18–39.

Berg, M., 'Factories, workshops and industrial organisation', in R. Floud and D. McCloskey (eds), *The economic history of Britain since 1700, volume 1: 1700–1860* (Cambridge, Cambridge University Press, 1994).

Berg, M., 'Product innovation in core consumer industries in eighteenth-century Britain', in M. Berg and K. Bruland, *Technological revolutions in Europe* (Cheltenham, Edward Elgar Publishing, 1998).

Bettey, J. H., *Dorset* (London, Cass, 1974).

Black, R. A., and C. G. Gilmore, 'Crowding out during Britain's Industrial Revolution', *Journal of Economic History*, 50 (1990) 649–76.

Blaug, M., 'The myth of the old poor law and the making of the new', *Journal of Economic History*, 33 (1963) 151–84.

Bonfield, L., 'Normative rules and property transmission: reflections on the link between marriage and inheritance in early modern England', in K. Wrightson et al. (eds), *The world we have gained: histories of population and social structure* (Oxford, Blackwell, 1986).

Borsay, P. (ed.), *The eighteenth century town, 1688–1820* (London, Longman, 1990).

Boyer, G. R., 'Malthus was right after all: poor relief and birth rates in southeastern England', *Journal of Political Economy*, 97 (1989) 93–114.

Boyer, G. R., *The economic history of the English poor law 1750–1850* (Cambridge, Cambridge University Press, 1990).

Boyson, R., *The Ashworth cotton enterprise* (Oxford, Clarendon, 1970).

Brakensiek, S., 'Agrarian individualism in north-western Germany, 1770–1870', *German History*, 12 (1994) 137–79.

Brandstrom, A., and L. G. Tedebrand (eds), *Society, health and population during the demographic transition* (Umea, Umea University Press, 1986).

Brewer, J., and R. Porter (eds), *Consumption and the world of goods* (London, Routledge, 1993).

Brewer, J., and S. Staves (eds), *Early modern conceptions of property* (London, Routledge, 1995).

Brown, A. V., 'Last phase of the enclosure of Otmoor', *Oxoniensia*, 32 (1967) 35–52.

Brunskill, R. W., *Illustrated handbook of vernacular architecture* (London, Faber, 1971).

Buchanan, R. A., *Industrial archaeology in Britain* (London, Penguin, 1972).

Buchinsky, M., and B. Polak, 'The emergence of a national capital market in England, 1710–1880', *Journal of Economic History*, 53 (1993) 249–84.

Burnett, J., *A social history of housing, 1815–1970* (London, Methuen, 1983).

Burnett, J., *Idle hands: the experience of unemployment 1790–1990* (London, Routledge, 1994).

Bushaway, B., *By rite: custom, ceremony and community in England 1700–1880* (London, Junction Books, 1982).

Butt, J., and I. Donnachie, *Industrial archaeology in the British Isles* (London, Elek, 1979).

Butterworth, E., *A statistical sketch of the County Palatine of Lancaster* (Manchester, Lancashire and Cheshire Antiquarian Society, 1968 reprint).

Bythell, D., *The handloom weavers* (Cambridge, Cambridge University Press, 1969).

Caffyn, L., *Workers' housing in West Yorkshire 1750–1920* (London, HMSO, 1986).

Calladine A., and J. Frisker, *East Cheshire textile mills* (London, RCHM, 1993).

Campbell, B. M. S., and M. Overton (eds), *Land, labour and livestock: historical studies in European agricultural productivity* (Manchester, Manchester University Press, 1991).

Cannadine, D., 'The past and the present in the English Industrial Revolution, 1880–1980', *Past and Present*, 103 (1984) 149–58.

Capp, B., 'Separate domains? Women and authority in early modern England', in P. Griffiths, A. Fox and S. Hindle (eds), *The experience of authority in early modern England* (Basingstoke, Macmillan, 1996).

Caunce, S. A., 'Complexity, community structure and competitive advantage within the Yorkshire woollen industry, *c.* 1700–1850', *Business History*, 32 (1998) 26–43.

Cavallo S., and L. Warner (eds), *Widowhood in medieval and early modern Europe* (London, Longman, 1999).

Chalklin, C. W., *The provincial towns of Georgian England* (London, Edward Arnold, 1974).

Chalklin, C. W., *English counties and public building 1650–1830* (London, Hambledon Press, 1998).

Chambers J. D., and G. E. Mingay, *The agricultural revolution 1750–1880* (London, Batsford, 1966).

Chapman, S. D., *The early factory masters* (Newton Abbot, David and Charles, 1967).

Chapman, S. D., 'Memoirs of two eighteenth century framework knitters', *Textile History*, 1 (1968) 103–18.

Chapman, S. D., 'Fixed capital formation in the British cotton industry, 1770–1815', *Economic History Review*, 23 (1970) 235–66.

Chapman, S. D. (ed.), *The history of working class housing* (Newton Abbot, David and Charles, 1971).

Chapman, S. D., 'Working-class housing in Nottingham during the Industrial Revolution', in S. D. Chapman (ed.), *The history of working class housing* (Newton Abbot, David and Charles, 1971).

Chapman, S. D., 'Industrial capital before the Industrial Revolution: an analysis of the assets of a thousand textile entrepreneurs 1730–50', in N. B. Harte and K. C. Ponting (eds), *Textile history and economic history* (Manchester, Manchester University Press, 1973).

Chapman, S. D., 'Workers' housing in the cotton factory colonies, 1770–1850', *Textile History*, 7 (1976) 112–39.

Chapman, S. D., *The cotton industry in the Industrial Revolution* (London, Macmillan, 1987).

Chapman, S. D., 'The Robinson mills: proto-industrial precedents', *Industrial Archaeology Review*, 15 (1992) 22–38.

Chapman, S. D., *Merchant enterprise in Britain* (Cambridge, Cambridge University Press, 1992).

Chapman, S. D., 'The commercial sector', in M. Rose (ed.), *The Lancashire cotton industry* (Preston, LCB, 1996).

Chartres, J. (ed.), *Agricultural markets and trade 1500–1750* (Cambridge, Cambridge University Press, 1990).

Chartres, J., 'The marketing of agricultural produce, 1640–1750', in J. Chartres (ed.), *Agricultural markets and trade 1500–1750* (Cambridge, Cambridge University Press, 1990).

Church, R., *The history of the British coal industry, volume 3* (Oxford, Clarendon, 1986).

Clapham, J. H., 'The transference of the worsted industry from Norfolk to the West Riding', *Economic Journal*, 20 (1910) 29–48.

Clapham, J. H., *An economic history of modern Britain, volume 1: the early railway age 1820–1850* (Cambridge, Cambridge University Press, 1930).

Clark, G. N., *The idea of the Industrial Revolution* (Glasgow, Brent, 1953).

Clark, G., 'Agriculture and the Industrial Revolution, 1700–1850', in J. Mokyr (ed.), *The British Industrial Revolution: an economic perspective* (Boulder, Col., Westview Press, 1993).

Clark, P., 'Migration in England during the late seventeenth and early eighteenth centuries', *Past and Present*, 85 (1979) 57–90.

Collier, F., *The family economy of the working class in the cotton industry 1784–1833* (Manchester, Manchester University Press, 1964).

Collins, M., *Banks and industrial finance in Britain, 1800–1939* (London, Macmillan, 1991).

Cookson, G., 'Family firms and business networks: textile engineering in Yorkshire, 1780–1830', *Business History*, 39 (1997) 9–12.

Cooper, D., and M. Donald, 'Households and hidden kin in early nineteenth century England: four case studies in suburban Exeter', *Continuity and Change*, 10 (1995) 257–78.

Corfield, P., *The impact of English towns, 1700–1800* (Oxford, Clarendon, 1982).

Coster, W., *Kinship and inheritance in early modern England: three Yorkshire parishes* (York, Borthwick Institute, 1993).

Crafts, N. F. R., *British economic growth during the Industrial Revolution* (Oxford, Clarendon, 1985).

Crafts, N. F. R., 'British economic growth 1700–1850: some difficulties of interpretation', *Explorations in Economic History*, 24 (1987) 245–68.

Crafts, N. F. R., and C. K. Harley, 'Output growth and the British Industrial Revolution: a restatement of the Crafts–Harley view', *Economic History Review*, 45 (1992) 703–30.

Cressey, D., 'Kinship and kin interaction in early modern England', *Past and Present*, 113 (1986) 38–69.

Crossley, D., J. Cass, N. Flavell and C. Turner, *Water power on the Sheffield rivers* (Sheffield, Sheffield Trades Historical Society, 1989).

Crossley, D., 'The Fairbanks of Sheffield: surveyors' records as a source for the study of regional economic development in the 18th and 19th centuries', *Industrial Archaeology Review*, 19 (1997) 5–20.

Crouzet, F., *Capital formation in the Industrial Revolution* (London, Methuen, 1972).

Crouzet, F., *The Victorian economy* (London, Methuen, 1982).

Crowther, M., 'Family responsibility and state responsibility in Britain before the welfare state', *Historical Journal*, 25 (1982) 131–45.

Crump, W. B., *The Leeds woollen industry 1780–1820* (Leeds, Harper, 1931).

Cunningham, H. 'The employment and unemployment of children in England c.1680–1851', *Past and Present* 126 (1990) 115–50.

Daunton, M. J., *Progress and poverty* (Oxford, Oxford University Press, 1995).

Daunton, M. (ed.), *Charity, self-interest and welfare in the English past* (London, UCL Press, 1996).

Davenport-Hines, R. (ed.), *Markets and bagmen* (Aldershot, Gower, 1986).

Davis, R., *The Industrial Revolution and overseas trade* (Leicester, Leicester University Press, 1979).

Day, L., and I. McNeil, *Biographical dictionary of the history of technology* (London, Routledge, 1996).

Deacon, B., 'Proto-regionalisation: the case of Cornwall', *Journal of Regional and Local Studies*, 18 (1998) 1–22.

Deane, P., *The first Industrial Revolution* (Cambridge, Cambridge University Press, 1965).

Deane, P., and W. A. Cole, *British economic growth, 1688–1959* (Cambridge, Cambridge University Press, 1967).

Derry, T., and T. Williams, *A short history of technology* (Oxford, Clarendon, 1960).

de Vries, J., 'The Industrial Revolution and the industrious revolution', *Journal of Economic History*, 54 (1994).

Dewhurst, L., 'Housing the workforce: a case study of West Yorkshire', *Industrial Archaeology Review*, 11 (1989) 117–35.

Dobson, M. J., 'The last hiccup of the old demographic regime: population stagnation and decline in late seventeenth and early eighteenth-century south-east England', *Continuity and Change*, 4 (1989) 395–428.

Dunbabin, J. P. D., *Rural discontent in nineteenth century Britain* (London, Holmes and Meier, 1975).

Dutton, H. I., *The patent system and inventive activity during the Industrial Revolution, 1750–1852* (Manchester, Manchester University Press, 1984).

Eastwood, D., 'Communities, protest and police in early nineteenth-century Oxfordshire: the enclosure of Otmoor reconsidered', *Agricultural History Review*, 44 (1996) 35–46.

Edwards, M. M., *The growth of the British cotton trade, 1780–1815* (Manchester, Manchester University Press, 1967).

Engels, F., *The condition of the working class in England in 1844* (London, CTR, 1991).

Esteban, J. C., 'The rising share of British industrial exports in industrial output, 1700–1851', *Journal of Economic History*, 57 (1997) 879–901.

Everitt, A., 'Country, county and town: patterns of regional evolution in England', *Transactions of the Royal Historical Society*, 29 (1978) 79–107.

Everitt, A., *Landscape and community in England* (London, Hambledon, 1985).

Falconer, K., 'Mills of the Stroud valley', *Industrial Archaeology Review*, 17 (1993) 62–81.

Farnie, D. A., *The English cotton industry and the world market, 1815–1896* (Oxford, Clarendon, 1979).

Feinstein, C. H., 'Capital formation in Great Britain', in P. Mathias and M. M. Postan (eds), *The Cambridge economic history of Europe, VII* (Cambridge, Cambridge University Press, 1978).

Feinstein, C. H., and S. Pollard (eds), *Studies in capital formation in the United Kingdom, 1750–1920* (Oxford, Clarendon, 1988).

Ferdinand, C. Y., 'Selling in the provinces: news and commerce round eighteenth century Salisbury', in J. Brewer and R. Porter (eds), *Consumption and the world of goods* (London, Routledge, 1993).

Field, A. J., 'On the unimportance of machinery', *Explorations in Economic History*, 22 (1985) 378–401.

Firth, G., *Bradford and the Industrial Revolution* (Halifax, Ryburn, 1990).

Flinn, M. W., *Origins of the Industrial Revolution* (London, Longman, 1966).

Flinn, M. W., *The European demographic system 1500–1820* (Brighton, Harvester, 1981).

Floud, R., and D. McCloskey (eds), *The economic history of Britain since 1700, volume 1: 1700–1860* (Cambridge, Cambridge University Press, 1994).

Foster, J., *Class struggle and the Industrial Revolution: early industrial capitalism in three English towns* (London, Macmillan, 1974).

Foyster, E., 'Marrying the experienced widow in early modern England: the male perspective', in S. Cavallo and L. Warner (eds), *Widowhood in medieval and early modern Europe* (London, Longman, 1999).

Galley, C., 'A model of early modern urban demography', *Economic History Review*, 58 (1995) 448–69.

Gauldie, E., *Cruel habitations* (London, Allen and Unwin, 1974).

Gaunt, D., D. Levine and E. Moodie, '*The population history of England 1541–1871*: a review symposium', *Social History*, 8 (1983) 139–68.

Gilboy, E., 'Demand as a factor in the Industrial Revolution', in R. M. Hartwell (ed.), *The causes of the Industrial Revolution* (London, Methuen, 1967).

Giles, C., 'Housing the loom, 1790–1850: a study of industrial building and mechanisation in a transitional period', *Industrial Archaeology Review*, 16 (1993) 1–16.

Giles, C., and I. Goodall, *Yorkshire textile mills 1770–1930* (London, RCHM, 1992).

Gillis, J. R., *A world of their own making* (Oxford, Oxford University Press, 1997).

Glennie, P., *Distinguishing men's trades: occupational sources and debates for pre-census England* (Historical Geography Research Series Number 25, 1990).

Goldstone, J., 'The demographic revolution in England: a reexamination', *Population Studies*, 40 (1986) 5–34.

Goose, N., 'Urban demography in pre-industrial England: what is to be done?', *Urban History*, 21 (1994) 273–84.

Gorsky, M., 'The growth and distribution of English friendly societies in the early nineteenth century', *Economic History Review*, 51 (1998) 489–511.

Gourvish, T. R., 'Railways 1830–70: the formative years', in M. J. Freeman and D. H. Aldcroft (eds), *Transport in Victorian Britain* (Manchester, Manchester University Press, 1988).

Gray, R. Q., *The aristocracy of labour in nineteenth century Britain 1850–1914* (London, Macmillan, 1981).

# Bibliography

Gregory, D., *Regional transformation and Industrial Revolution: a geography of the Yorkshire woollen industry* (London, Macmillan, 1982).

Gregory, D., 'The production of regions in England's Industrial Revolution', *Journal of Historical Geography*, 14 (1988) 50–8.

Griffin, A. R., *The British coalmining industry* (Buxton, Moorland, 1977).

Hajnal, H. J., 'European marriage patterns in perspective,' in D. V. Glass and D. E. C. Eversley (eds), *Population in history* (Cambridge, Cambridge University Press, 1965).

Hajnal, H. J., 'Two kinds of pre-industrial household formation systems', *Population and development Review*, 8 (1981) 449–94.

Hammond, J., and B. Hammond, *The rise of modern industry* (London, Methuen, 1925).

Hardwick, C., *A history of the borough of Preston* (Preston, 1857).

Hardy, A., 'Diagnosis, death and diet: the case of London 1750–1909', *Journal of Interdisciplinary History*, 28 (1988) 387–401.

Harris, J. R. (ed.), *Liverpool and Merseyside* (London, Cass, 1969).

Harris, O., 'Households and their boundaries', *History Workshop Journal*, 13 (1982) 143–52.

Harte, N. B., and K. C. Ponting (eds), *Textile history and economic history* (Manchester, Manchester University Press, 1973).

Hartwell, R. M., *The Industrial Revolution and economic growth* (London, Methuen, 1956).

Hartwell, R. M. (ed.), *The causes of the Industrial Revolution in England* (London, Methuen, 1967).

Heaton, H., *The Yorkshire woollen and worsted industries from earliest times up to the Industrial Revolution* (Oxford, Oxford University Press, 1920).

Heaton, H., 'Introduction', in R. M. Hartwell (ed.), *The causes of the Industrial Revolution in England* (London, Methuen, 1967).

Heim, C. E., and P. Mirowski, 'Interest rates and crowding out during Britain's Industrial Revolution', *Journal of Economic History*, 47 (1987) 434–68.

Henderson, J., and R. Wall (eds), *Poor women and children in the European past* (London, Routledge, 1994).

Hey, D. G., *The rural metalworkers of the Sheffield region: a study of rural industry before the Industrial Revolution* (Leicester, Leicester University Press, 1972).

Hibbert, J., 'Modern practice and conventions in measuring capital formation in the national accounts', in J. P. P. Higgins and S. Pollard (eds), *Aspects of capital investment in Great Britain, 1750–1850* (London, Methuen, 1971).

Higgins, J. P. P., and S. Pollard (eds), *Aspects of capital investment in Great Britain, 1750–1850* (London, Methuen, 1971).

Hill, B., 'The marriage age of women and the demographers', *History Workshop Journal*, 29 (1989) 129–47.

Hill, B., 'Rural–urban migration of women and their employment in towns', *Rural History*, 5 (1994) 185–94.

Hitchcock, T., P. King and P. Sharpe (eds), *Chronicling poverty* (Basingstoke, Macmillan, 1996).

Hobcraft, J., and P. Rees (eds), *Regional demographic development* (London, Croom Helm, 1978).

Holden, R. N., 'Water supply for steam-powered textile mills', *Industrial Archaeology Review*, 21 (1999) 41–51.

Honeyman, K., *Origins of enterprise* (Manchester, Manchester University Press, 1982).

Hoppit, J., *Risk and failure in English business 1700–1800* (Cambridge, Cambridge University Press, 1987).

Horden, P., and R. M. Smith, 'Introduction', in P. Horden and R. M. Smith (eds), *The locus of care: families, communities, institutions and the provision of welfare since antiquity* (London, Routledge, 1998).

Horrell, S., 'Home demand and British industrialisation', *Journal of Economic History*, 56 (1996) 564–82.

Horrell, S., and J. Humphries, 'Old questions, new data, and alternative perspectives: families' living standards in the Industrial Revolution', *Journal of Economic History*, 52 (1992) 849–80.

Horrell, S., and J. Humphries, 'The exploitation of little children: child labor and the family economy in the Industrial Revolution', *Explorations in Economic History*, 32 (1995) 485–516.

Horrell, S., and J. Humphries, 'The origins and expansion of the male breadwinner family: the case of nineteenth century Britain', in A. Janssens (ed.), *The rise and decline of the male breadwinner family* (Cambridge, Cambridge University Press, 1998).

Houston, R., and K. Snell, 'Proto-industrialisation? Cottage industry, social change and the Industrial Revolution', *Historical Journal*, 27 (1984) 473–92.

Huberman, M., 'The economic origins of paternalism: Lancashire cotton spinning in the first half of the nineteenth century', *Social History*, 12 (1987) 177–93.

Huberman, M., 'The economic origins of paternalism: reply to Rose, Taylor and Winstanley', *Social History*, 14 (1989) 99–103.

Huberman, M., *Escape from the market: negotiating work in Lancashire* (Cambridge, Cambridge University Press, 1996).

Huck, P., 'Infant mortality and living standards of English workers during the Industrial Revolution', *Journal of Economic History*, 55 (1995) 528–50.

Hudson, P., *The genesis of industrial capital: a study of the West Riding wool textile industry 1750–1850* (Cambridge, Cambridge University Press, 1986).

Hudson, P. (ed.), *Regions and industries: a perspective on the Industrial Revolution in Britain* (Cambridge, Cambridge University Press, 1989).

Hudson, P., 'The regional perspective', in P. Hudson (ed.), *Regions and industries: a perspective on the Industrial Revolution in Britain* (Cambridge, Cambridge University Press, 1989).

Hudson, P., 'Capital and credit in the West Riding wool textile industry *c.* 1750–1850', in P. Hudson (ed.), *Regions and industries: a perspective on the Industrial Revolution in Britain* (Cambridge, Cambridge University Press, 1989).

Hudson, P., *The Industrial Revolution* (London, Arnold, 1992).

Hudson, P., 'Financing firms, 1700–1850', in M. W. Kirby and M. B. Rose (eds), *Business enterprise in modern Britain* (London, Routledge, 1994).

Hudson, P., and M. Berg, 'Rehabilitating the Industrial Revolution', *Economic History Review*, 45 (1992) 24–50.

Hudson, P., and S. A. King, 'A sense of place: industrialising townships in eighteenth century Yorkshire', in R. Leboutte (ed.), *Proto-industrialisation: recent research and new perspectives* (Geneva, Droz Press, 1996).

Hudson, P., and S. A. King, *Industrialisation and everyday life in England 1650–1830* (forthcoming, 2002).

Humphries, J., 'Enclosure, common rights and women: the proletarianisation of families in the late eighteenth and early nineteenth centuries', *Journal of Economic History*, 50 (1990) 17–42.

Hunt, D., *A history of Preston* (Preston, Carnegie, 1992).

Inglis, B., *Poverty and the Industrial Revolution* (London, Hodder, 1971).

Innes, J., 'The mixed economy of welfare in early modern England: assessments of options from Hale to Malthus (1683–1803)', in M. J. Daunton (ed.), *Charity, self-interest and welfare in the English past* (London, UCL Press, 1996).

Innes, J., and J. Hoppit, *Failed legislation 1660–1800* (London, Hambledon, 1997).

Jackson, R. V., 'Growth and deceleration in English agriculture 1660–1790', *Economic History Review*, 38 (1985) 333–51.

Jackson, R. V., 'Rates of industrial growth during the Industrial Revolution', *Economic History Review*, 45 (1992) 1–23.

Janssens, A. (ed.), *The rise and decline of the male breadwinner family* (Cambridge, Cambridge University Press, 1998).

Janssens, A., 'The rise and decline of the male breadwinner family? An overview of the debate', in A. Janssens (ed.), *The rise and decline of the male breadwinner family* (Cambridge, Cambridge University Press, 1998).

Jarvis, A., *Liverpool central docks, 1799–1905* (Stroud, Sutton, 1991).

Jarvis, C., 'The reconstitution of nineteenth-century rural communities', *Local Population Studies*, 51 (1993) 45–63.

Johnson, P., and P. Thane (eds), *Old age from antiquity to post modernity* (London, Routledge, 1998).

Johnston, J. A., 'The probate inventories and wills of a Worcestershire parish 1676–1775', *Midland History*, 1 (1971) 20–33.

Johnston, J. A., 'The family and kin of the Lincolnshire labourer in the eighteenth century', *Lincolnshire History and Archaeology*, 14 (1979) 47–52.

Johnston, J. A., 'Family, kin and community in eight Lincolnshire parishes 1567–1800', *Rural History*, 6 (1995) 179–92.

Jones, E., *Industrial architecture in Britain 1750–1939* (London, Batsford, 1985).

Jones, S. R. H., 'The origins of the factory system in Great Britain', in M. W. Kirby and M. B. Rose (eds), *Business enterprise in modern Britain* (London, Routledge, 1994).

Jordan, E., 'The exclusion of women from industry in nineteenth century Britain', *Comparative Studies in Society and History*, 31 (1989) 273–96.

Joyce, P., *Work, society and politics* (London, Harvester, 1980).

Kearns, G., 'The urban penalty and the population history of England', in A. Brandstrom and L. G. Tedebrand (eds), *Society, health and population during the demographic transition* (Umea, Umea University Press, 1986).

Kent, D., 'Small businessmen and their credit transactions in early nineteenth century Britain', *Business History*, 36 (1994) 47–64.

Kertzer, D., and P. Laslett (eds), *Aging in the past: demography, society and old age* (Los Angeles, University of California Press, 1995).

Kidd, A., *Manchester* (Keele, Keele University Press, 1993).

King, P., 'Gleaners, farmers and the failure of legal sanctions 1750–1850', *Past and Present*, 125 (1989) 116–50.

King, P., 'Customary rights and women's earnings: the importance of gleaning to the rural labouring poor 1750–1850', *Economic History Review*, 54 (1991) 461–76.

King, S. A., 'The nature and causes of demographic change in an industrialising township' (unpublished Ph.D. thesis, University of Liverpool, 1993).

King, S. A., 'Historical demography, life-cycle reconstruction and family reconstitution: new perspectives', *History and Computing*, 8 (1996) 62–77.

King, S. A., 'Profitable pursuits: rural industry and mortality in the proto-industrial West Riding 1650–1830', *Local Population Studies*, 59 (1997) 26–40.

King, S. A., 'Reconstructing lives: the poor, the poor law and welfare in Calverley 1650–1820', *Social History*, 22 (1997) 318–38.

King, S. A., 'Dying with style: infant death and its context in a rural industrial community', *Social History of Medicine*, 10 (1997) 3–24.

King, S. A., 'Calverley und Sowerby: die protoindustrielle Entwicklung in zwei gemeinden Yorkshire (1660 bis 1830), in D. Ebeling and W. Mayer (eds), *Proto-industrie in der Region* (Bielefeld, Verlaag, 1997).

King, S. A., 'Migrants on the margin: mobility, integration and occupations in the West Riding, 1650–1820', *Journal of Historical Geography*, 23 (1997) 304–26.

King, S. A., 'English historical demography and the nuptiality conundrum: new perspectives', *Historical Social Research*, 23 (1998) 130–56.

King, S. A., 'Chance encounters? Paths to household formation in early modern England', *International Review of Social History*, 44 (1999) 23–46.

King, S. A., *Poverty and welfare in England 1700–1850: a regional perspective* (Manchester, Manchester University Press, 2000).

King, S. A., 'Rethinking the English regions', in S. Brakensiek and A. Flugel (eds), *Regional history in Europe* (Stuttgart, Verlag für Regionalegeschichte, 2000).

King, S. A., 'Migration networks in Lancashire', in D. Ebeling and S. A. King (eds), *Community, locality and life-cycle: migration and mobility in eighteenth and nineteenth century Europe* (forthcoming, 2001).

King, S. A., 'Making the most of opportunity: reconstructing the economy of makeshifts in the early modern north', in S. A. King and A. Tomkins (eds), *Coping with the crossroads of life: the economy of makeshifts in early modern England* (Manchester, Manchester University Press, forthcoming).

King, S. A., 'The English proto-industrial family: old and new perspectives', in *History of the Family* (forthcoming, 2001).

King, S. A., and A. Weaver, 'Lives in many hands: the medical landscape in Lancashire 1700–1830', *Medical History* (forthcoming, 2001).

Kirby, M. W., and M. B. Rose (eds), *Business enterprise in modern Britain* (London, Routledge, 1994).

Knick-Harley, C., 'Reassessing the Industrial Revolution: a macro view', in J. Mokyr (ed.), *The British Industrial Revolution: an economic perspective* (Boulder, Col., Westview Press, 1993).

Knick-Harley, C., 'Cotton textile prices and the Industrial Revolution', *Economic History Review*, 51 (1998) 49–83.

Knodel, J., *Demographic behaviour in the past: a study of 14 German village populations in the eighteenth and nineteenth century* (Cambridge, Cambridge University Press, 1988).

Kussmaul, A., *Servants in husbandry* (Oxford, Oxford University Press, 1981).

Kussmaul, A., *A general view of the rural economy of England 1538–1840* (Cambridge, Cambridge University Press, 1990).

Landers, J., *Death and the metropolis: studies in the demographic history of London 1670–1830* (Cambridge, Cambridge University Press, 1993).

Landes, D., *The unbound prometheus: technological change and industrial development in western Europe from 1750 to the present* (Cambridge, Cambridge University Press, 1968).

Landes, D., 'The fable of the dead horse; or, the Industrial Revolution revisited', in J. Mokyr (ed.), *The British Industrial Revolution: an economic perspective* (Boulder, Col., Westview Press, 1993).

Langton, J., *Geographical change during the Industrial Revolution* (Cambridge, Cambridge University Press, 1979).

Langton, J., 'The Industrial Revolution and the regional geography of England', *Transactions of the Institute of British Geographers*, 9 (1988) 145–67.

Langton, J., 'People from the pits: the origins of colliers in eighteenth century southwest Lancashire', in D. R. Siddle (ed.), *Migration, mobility and modernisation in Europe* (Liverpool, Liverpool University Press, 2000).

Langton, J., and R. J. Morris (eds), *Atlas of industrialising Britain, 1780–1914* (London, Methuen, 1986).

Laslett, P., 'Size and structure of the household in England over three centuries', *Population Studies*, 23 (1969) 199–223.

Laslett, P., 'Mean household size in England since the sixteenth century', in P. Laslett and R. Wall (eds), *Household and family in past times* (Cambridge, Cambridge University Press, 1972).

Laslett, P., *Family life and illicit love in earlier generations* (Cambridge, Cambridge University Press, 1977).

Laslett, P., 'Gregory King, Robert Malthus and the origins of English social reason', *Population Studies*, 39 (1985) 351–62.

Laslett, P., 'Malthus and the development of demographic analysis', *Population Studies*, 41 (1987) 269–81.

Laslett, P., 'Family, kinship and collectivity as systems of support in pre-industrial Europe: a consideration of the nuclear hardship hypothesis', *Continuity and Change*, 3 (1988) 153–75.

Laslett, P., and R. Wall (eds), *Household and family in past times* (Cambridge, Cambridge University Press, 1972).

Laslett, P., K. Oosterveen and R. M. Smith (eds), *Bastardy and its comparative history* (Cambridge, Cambridge University Press, 1981).

Lawton, R., 'Regional population trends in England and Wales, 1750–1971', in J. Hobcraft and P. Rees (eds), *Regional demographic development* (London, Croom Helm, 1978).

Laxton, P., 'Textiles', in J. Langton and R. J. Morris (eds), *Atlas of industrialising Britain, 1780–1914* (London, Methuen, 1986).

Leboutte, R., 'Introduction', in R. Leboutte (ed.), *Proto-industrialisation: recent research and new perspectives* (Geneva, Droz Press, 1996).

Leboutte, R. (ed.), *Proto-industrialisation: recent research and new perspectives* (Geneva, Droz Press, 1996).

Lee, C. H., *British regional employment statistics, 1841–1971* (Cambridge, Cambridge University Press, 1979).

Lehning, J. R., 'Nuptiality and rural industry: families and labor in the French countryside', *Journal of Family History*, 8 (1983) 333–45.

Lemire, B., *Fashion's favourite: the cotton trade and the consumer in Britain 1660–1800* (Oxford, Oxford University Press, 1991).

Levine, D., *Family formation in an age of nascent capitalism* (New York, Academic Press, 1977).

Levine, D., 'For their own reasons: individual marriage decisions and family life', *Journal of Family History*, 7 (1982) 255–64.

Lindert, P., 'English living standards, population growth and Wrigley and Schofield', *Explorations in Economic History*, 20 (1983) 131–55.

Lipson, E., *History of the woollen and worsted industries* (London, Cass, 1921).

Lipson, E., *The economic history of England* (London, Longman, 1934).

Lloyd-Jones, E., and M. Falkus, 'Urban improvement and the English economy in the seventeenth and eighteenth centuries', in P. Borsay (ed.), *The eighteenth century town, 1688–1820* (London, Longman, 1990).

Lloyd-Jones, R., 'N. J. Smelser and the cotton factory family: a reassessment', in N. B. Harte and K. G. Ponting (eds), *Textile history and economic history* (Manchester, Manchester University Press, 1973).

Lloyd-Jones, R., and M. Lewis, *Manchester and the age of the factory: the business structure of cottonopolis in the Industrial Revolution* (London, Croom Helm, 1987).

Longworth, J., *The cotton mills of Bolton, 1780–1985* (Bolton, Bolton Museum and Art Gallery, 1986).

Lord, E., 'Communities of common interest: the social landscape of south east Surrey 1750–1850', in C. Phythian-Adams (ed.), *Societies, cultures and kinship 1580–1850* (Leicester, Leicester University Press, 1992).

Loschky, D., and D. Krier, 'Income and family size in three eighteenth century Lancashire parishes: a reconstitution study', *Journal of Economic History*, 29 (1969) 429–48.

Lyons, J. S., 'Family response to economic decline: handloom weavers in early nineteenth century Lancashire', *Research in Economic History*, 12 (1989) 45–91.

McKendrick, N., 'Josiah Wedgewood: an eighteenth century entrepreneur in salesmanship and marketing techniques', *Economic History Review*, 12 (1959/60) 121–46.

McKendrick, N., J. Brewer and J. Plumb (eds), *The birth of a consumer society* (London, Longman, 1982).

Mackinnon, A., 'Were women present at the demographic transition? Questions from a feminist historian to historical demographers', *Gender and History*, 7 (1995) 222–40.

MacLeod, C., *Inventing the Industrial Revolution* (Cambridge, Cambridge University Press, 1988).

Mantoux, P., *The Industrial Revolution in the eighteenth century: an outline of the beginnings of the modern factory system* (London, Cape, 1961).

Marshall, J. D., 'Colonisation as a factor in the planting of towns in northwest England', in H. Dyos (ed.), *The study of urban history* (London, Edward Arnold, 1968).

Marshall, J. D., 'Proving ground or the creation of regional identity? The origins and problems of regional history in Britain', in P. Swan and D. Foster (eds), *Essays in regional and local history* (Beverley, Hutton Press, 1992).

Mathias, P., *The brewing industry in England 1700–1830* (Cambridge, Cambridge University Press, 1959).

# Bibliography

Mathias, P., *The first industrial nation* (London, Methuen, 1969).

Medick, H., 'The proto-industrial family economy: the structural function of the household and family during the transition from peasant society to industrial capitalism', *Social History*, 6 (1976/77) 291–316.

Menuage, A., 'The cotton mills of the Derbyshire Derwent and its tributaries', *Industrial Archaeology Review*, 17 (1993) 38–61.

Midwinter, E. C., *Social administration in Lancashire, 1830–1860* (Manchester, Manchester University Press, 1969).

Miles, M., 'The money market in the early Industrial Revolution: the evidence from West Yorkshire attorneys, *c.* 1750–1800', *Business History*, 23 (1981).

Miller, G., *Blackburn, the evolution of a cotton town* (Blackburn, THCL Books, 1992).

Mills, D. R., 'The residential propinquity of kin in a Cambridgeshire village', *Journal of Historical Geography*, 4 (1978) 265–76.

Mingay, G. E. (ed.), *Arthur Young and his times* (Basingstoke, Macmillan, 1975).

Mitteraur, M., 'Servants and youth', *Continuity and Change*, 5 (1990) 11–38.

Mokyr, J., *The lever of riches* (Oxford, Oxford University Press, 1990).

Mokyr, J., 'Technological change, 1700–1830', in R. Floud and D. McCloskey (eds), *The economic history of Britain since 1700, volume I: 1700–1860* (Cambridge, Cambridge University Press, 2nd edn, 1994).

Mokyr, J. (ed.), *The British Industrial Revolution: an economic perspective* (Boulder, Col. Westview Press, 1993).

Morgan, N., *Vanished dwellings* (Preston, Mullion Books, 1990).

Morris, R. J., 'Urbanisation', in J. Langton and R. J. Morris (eds), *Atlas of industrialising Britain, 1780–1914* (London, Methuen, 1986).

Neal, L., 'The finance of business during the Industrial Revolution', in R. Floud and D. McCloskey (eds), *The economic history of Britain since 1700* (Cambridge, Cambridge University Press, 1994).

Neeson, J. M., *Commoners: common right, enclosure and social change in England 1700–1820* (Cambridge, Cambridge University Press, 1993).

Nicholas, S., and D. Oxley, 'The living standards of women during the Industrial Revolution 1795–1820', *Economic History Review*, 46 (1993) 723–49.

O'Brien, P. K., 'Agriculture and the home market for English industry 1660–1820', *English Historical Review*, 50 (1985) 773–800.

O'Brien, P. K., and R. Quinalt (eds), *The Industrial Revolution and British society* (Cambridge, Cambridge University Press, 1993).

O'Day, R., *The family and family relationships, 1500–1900* (Basingstoke, Macmillan, 1994).

O'Hara, D., 'Ruled by my friends: aspects of marriage in the diocese of Canterbury *c.* 1540–1570', *Continuity and Change*, 6 (1991) 9–42.

Oddy, D., and D. Mills (eds), *The making of the modern British diet* (London, Croom Helm, 1976).

Ogilvie, S. C., and M. Cerman (eds), *European proto-industrialisation* (Cambridge, Cambridge University Press, 1996).

Ottoway, S. R., 'Providing for the elderly in eighteenth century England', *Continuity and Change*, 13 (1998) 391–418.

Overton, M., 'Estimating crop yields from probate inventories: an example from East Anglia 1585–1735', *Journal of Economic History*, 39 (1979) 363–78.

Overton, M., 'The critical century? The agrarian history of England and Wales 1750–1850', *Agricultural History Review*, 38 (1990) 185–9.

Overton, M., 'Re-estimating crop yields from probate inventories', *Journal of Economic History*, 50 (1990) 931–5.

Overton, M., *The agricultural revolution in England: the transformation of the rural economy* (Cambridge, Cambridge University Press, 1996).

Palmer, M., 'Houses and workplaces: the framework knitters of the east Midlands', *Leicestershire Industrial History Society Bulletin*, 11 (1988) 23–36.

Palmer, M., 'Industrial archaeology; continuity and change', *Industrial Archaeology Review*, 16 (1994) 135–56.

Palmer, M., and P. Neaverson, *Industrial landscapes of the east Midlands* (Chichester, Phillimore, 1992).

Palmer, M., and P. Neaverson, *Industry in the landscape* (London, Routledge, 1994).

Payne, P., *British entrepreneurship in the nineteenth century* (London, Macmillan, 1988).

Pearson, S., *Rural houses of the Lancashire pennines 1560–1760* (London, HMSO, 1985).

Pelling, M., and R. M. Smith (eds), *Life, death and the elderly: historical perspectives* (London, Routledge, 1991).

Perkin, H., *The age of the railway* (Newton Abbot, David and Charles, 1970).

Pevsner, N., *The buildings of England: Yorkshire West Riding* (London, Penguin, 1967).

Pevsner, N., *The buildings of England: south Lancashire* (London, Penguin, 1969).

Pevsner, N., *The buildings of England: London I* (London, Penguin, 1973).

Phillips, C. B., and J. H. Smith, *Lancashire and Cheshire from 1540 AD* (London, Longman, 1994).

Phythian-Adams C. (ed.), *Societies, cultures and kinship 1580–1850* (Leicester, Leicester University Press, 1992).

Pollard, S., *Three centuries of Sheffield steel* (Sheffield, Butt, 1954).

Pollard, S., 'Fixed capital in the Industrial Revolution in Britain', *Journal of Economic History*, 24 (1964) 120–41.

Pollard, S., *The genesis of modern management* (London, Penguin, 1968).

Pollard, S., *Peaceful conquest: the industrialisation of Europe 1760–1970* (Oxford, Oxford University Press, 1981).

Pooley, C., and S. Da Cruz, 'Migration and urbanization in north west England c. 1760–1830', *Social History*, 19 (1994) 339–54.

Pooley, C., and J. Turnbull, *Migration and mobility in Britain since the 18th century* (London, UCL Press, 1998).

Pooley, C., and I. White (eds), *Migrants, emigrants and immigrants* (London, Routledge, 1991).

Pope, R., *Atlas of British social and economic history since 1700* (London, Routledge, 1989).

Porter, S., *Exploring urban history* (London, Batsford, 1990).

Powell, C., *An economic history of the British building industry, 1815–1979* (London, The Architectural Press, 1980).

Randall, A., *Before the Luddites* (Cambridge, Cambridge University Press, 1991).

Razzell P. (ed.), *Essays in English population history* (Chichester, Caliban, 1994).

Reaney, B., *The class struggle in nineteenth century Oxfordshire* (Oxford, Clarendon, 1970).

Reay, B., 'Sexuality in nineteenth-century England: the social context of illegitimacy in rural Kent', *Rural History*, 1 (1990) 219–47.

Reay, B., 'Before the transition: fertility in English villages 1800–1850', *Continuity and Change*, 9 (1993) 91–120.

Reay, B., 'Kinship and the neighbourhood in nineteenth century rural England: the myth of the autonomous nuclear family', *Journal of Family History*, 21 (1996) 87–104.

Reay, B., *Microhistories: demography, society and culture in rural England, 1800–1930* (Cambridge, Cambridge University Press, 1996).

Redford, A., *The economic history of England 1760–1860* (London, Longman, 1931).

Reher, D. S., and R. S. Schofield (eds), *Old and new methods in historical demography* (Oxford, Oxford University Press, 1993).

Reid, D., 'Weddings, weekdays, work and leisure in urban England 1791–1911: the decline of St. Monday revisited', *Past and Present*, 153 (1996) 135–63.

Richards, E., 'The margins of the Industrial Revolution', in P. K. O'Brien and R. Quinalt (eds), *The Industrial Revolution and British society* (Cambridge, Cambridge University Press, 1993).

Richardson, P., 'The structure of capital during the Industrial Revolution revisited: two case studies from the cotton textile industry', *Economic History Review*, 41 (1989) 484–503.

Riley, J. C., 'Working health time: a comparison of pre-industrial, industrial and post-industrial experiences in life and health', *Explorations in Economic History*, 28 (1991) 169–91.

Riley, J. C., *Sick not dead: the health of British workingmen during the mortality decline* (Baltimore, Johns Hopkins University Press, 1997).

Ritchie-Noakes, N., *Liverpool's historic waterfront* (London, HMSO, 1984).

Roberts, E., *A woman's place: an oral history of working class women 1890–1940* (Oxford, Blackwell, 1985).

Rodger, R. (ed.), *Housing in urban Britain 1780–1914* (Basingstoke, Macmillan, 1989).

Rollison, D., 'Exploding England: the dialectics of mobility and settlement in early modern England', *Social History*, 24 (1999) 1–16.

Rose, M. B., *The Gregs of Styal* (Quarry Bank Mill, National Trust, 1978).

Rose, M. B., 'Social policy and business: parish apprenticeship and the early factory system, 1780–1834', *Business History*, 31 (1989) 5–32.

Rose, M. B., 'The family firm in British business, 1780–1914', in M. W. Kirby and M. B. Rose (eds), *Business enterprise in modern Britain* (London, Routledge, 1994).

Rose, M. B. (ed.), *The Lancashire cotton industry* (Preston, Lancashire County Books, 1996).

Rose, M., P. Taylor and M. Winstanley, 'The economic origins of paternalism: some objections', *Social History*, 14 (1989) 89–98.

Rostow, W. W., *The stages of economic growth* (Cambridge, Cambridge University Press, 1991 reprint).

Rowlands, M. B., 'Continuity and change in an industrialising society', in P. Hudson (ed.), *Regions and industries* (Cambridge, Cambridge University Press, 1989).

Royle, E. (ed.), *Issues of regional identity* (Manchester, Manchester University Press, 1998).

Rubinstein, D., *Victorian homes* (Newton Abbot, David and Charles, 1974).

Ruggles, S., 'Migration, marriage and mortality: correcting sources of bias in English family reconstitutions', *Population Studies*, 46 (1992) 507–22.

Schofield, R. S., 'Through a glass darkly: the population history of England as an experiment in history', *Journal of Interdisciplinary History*, 15 (1985) 571–94.

Schofield, R. S., 'British population change 1700–1871', in R. Floud and D. McCloskey (eds), *The economic history of Britain since 1700, volume I* (Cambridge, Cambridge University Press, 1994).

Schurer, K., 'The role of the family in the process of migration', in C. Pooley and I. White (eds), *Migrants, emigrants and immigrants: a social history of migration* (London, Routledge, 1991).

Scola, R., *Feeding the Victorian city: the food supply of Manchester 1770–1870* (Manchester, Manchester University Press, 1992).

Scott, J., and L. Tilly, *Women, work and the family* (New York, Academic Press, 1978).

Seccombe, W., *Weathering the storm: working class families from the Industrial Revolution to the fertility decline* (London, Verso, 1993).

Shammas, C., *The pre-industrial consumer in England and America* (Oxford, Clarendon, 1990).

Sharlin, A., 'Natural decrease in early modern cities: a reconsideration', *Past and Present*, 79 (1978) 126–38.

Sharpe, P., 'The women's harvest: straw plaiting and the representation of labouring women's employment 1793–1885', *Rural History*, 5 (1994) 129–42.

Sharpe, P., *Adapting to capitalism: working women in the English economy 1700–1850* (Basingstoke, Macmillan, 1996)

Smelser, N., *Social change and the Industrial Revolution: an application of theory to the Lancashire cotton industry 1770–1840* (London, Routledge and Kegan Paul, 1959).

Smith, D. J., 'Army clothing contractors and the textile industries in the eighteenth century', *Textile History*, 14 (1983) 153–64.

Smith, J. E., and J. Oeppen, 'Estimating numbers of kin in historical England using demographic microsimulation', in D. S. Reher and R. S. Schofield (eds), *Old and new methods in historical demography* (Oxford, Oxford University Press, 1993).

Smith, R. M., 'Fertility, economy and household formation in England over three centuries', *Population and Development Review*, 7 (1981) 595–622.

Smith, R. M., 'Ageing and well-being in early modern England: pension trends and gender preferences under the English old poor law 1650–1800', in P. Johnson and P. Thane (eds), *Old age from antiquity to post modernity* (London, Routledge, 1998).

Snell, K. D. M., 'Parish registration and the study of labour mobility', *Local Population Studies*, 33 (1984) 29–43.

Snell, K. D. M., *Annals of the labouring poor: social change and agrarian England 1660–1900* (Cambridge, Cambridge University Press, 1985).

Sokoll, T., *Household and family among the poor: the case of two Essex communities in the late eighteenth and early nineteenth centuries* (Bochum, Verlaag, 1993).

Sokoll, T., 'The household position of elderly widows in poverty: evidence from two English communities in the late eighteenth and early nineteenth centuries', in J. Henderson and R. Wall (eds), *Poor women and children in the European past* (London, Routledge, 1994).

Solar, P., 'Poor relief and English economic development before the Industrial Revolution', *Economic History Review*, 58 (1995) 1–22.

Somers, M. R., 'The "misteries" of property: relationality, rural industrialisation, and community in Chartist narratives of political rights', in J. Brewer and S. Staves (eds), *Early modern conceptions of property* (London, Routledge, 1995).

Souden, D., 'Movers and stayers in family reconstitution populations', *Local Population Studies*, 33 (1984) 11–28.

Southall, H., 'The tramping artisan revisits: labour mobility and economic distress in early Victorian England', *Economic History Review*, 44 (1991) 272–91.

Southall H., and E. Garrett, 'Morbidity and mortality among early nineteenth-century engineering workers', *Social History of Medicine*, 4 (1991) 231–52.

Spagnoli, P. G., 'Population history from parish monographs: the problem of local demographic variations', *Journal of Interdisciplinary History*, 7 (1977) 427–52.

Spiers, M., *Victoria Park, Manchester* (Manchester, Chetham Society, 1976).

Stapleton, B., 'Migration in pre-industrial southern England: the example of Odiham', *Southern History*, 10 (1988) 47–93.

Staves, S., 'Resentment or resignation? Dividing the spoils among daughters and younger sons', in J. Brewer and S. Staves (eds), *Early modern conceptions of property* (London, Routledge, 1995).

Stobart, J., 'Geography and industrialisation: the space economy of north-west England 1701–1760', *Transactions of the Institute of British Geographers*, 21 (1996) 681–96.

Styles, J., 'Clothing the north: the supply of non-elite clothing in the eighteenth century north of England', *Textile History*, 16 (1994) 43–68.

Sullivan, R. J., 'England's "age of invention": the acceleration of patent and patentable inventions during the Industrial Revolution', *Explorations in Economic History*, 26 (1989) 424–52

Swan P., and D. Foster (eds), *Essays in regional and local history* (Beverley, Hutton Press, 1992).

Szreter, S., 'The importance of social intervention in Britain's mortality decline 1850–1914', *Social History of Medicine*, 1 (1988) 23–56.

Tadmor, N., 'The concept of the household-family in eighteenth century England', *Past and Present*, 151 (1996) 111–40.

Taylor, G., *The social experience of the Industrial Revolution* (London, Longman, 1959).

Taylor, J. S., *Poverty, migration and settlement in the Industrial Revolution: sojourners' narratives* (Palo Alto, SPSS, 1989).

Taylor, J. S., 'Voices in the crowd: the Kirkby Lonsdale township letters 1809–1836', in T. Hitchcock, P. King and P. Sharpe (eds), *Chronicling poverty: the voices and strategies of the English poor, 1640–1840* (Basingstoke, Macmillan, 1997).

Taylor, A. J., 'Concentration and specialization in the Lancashire cotton industry, 1825–1850', *Economic History Review*, 1 (1949) 114–22.

Taylor, A. J. P. (ed.), *The standard of living in Britain in the Industrial Revolution* (London, Methuen, 1975).

Thane, P., 'Old people and their families in the English past', in M. Daunton (ed.), *Charity, self-interest and welfare in the English past* (London, UCL Press, 1996).

Thirsk, J. (ed.), *The agrarian history of England and Wales, vol. V: regional farming systems; vol. VI: 1640–1750* (Cambridge, Cambridge University Press, 1984 and 1987).

Thirsk, J., *England's agricultural regions and agrarian history 1500–1750* (London, Macmillan, 1987).

Thomson, D., 'The welfare of the elderly in the past: a family or community responsibility?', in M. Pelling and R. M. Smith (eds), *Life, death and the elderly: historical perspectives* (London, Routledge, 1991).

Thompson, E. P., *The making of the English working class* (London, Penguin, 1968).

Thompson, F. M. L., 'Introduction: the rise of suburbia', in F. M. L. Thompson (ed.), *The rise of suburbia* (Leicester, Leicester University Press, 1982).

Thwaites, W., 'Women in the market place: Oxfordshire 1690–1800', *Midland History*, 9 (1984) 43–69.

Timmins, G., 'The commercial development of the Sheffield crucible steel industry' (unpublished M.A. thesis, University of Sheffield, 1976).

Timmins, G., *Handloom weavers' cottages in central Lancashire* (Lancaster, Lancaster University, 1977).

Timmins, G., 'Concentration and integration in the Sheffield crucible steel industry', *Business History*, 24 (1982) 26–44.

Timmins, G., 'Early building societies in Lancashire', in S. Jackson (ed.), *Industrial colonies and communities* (Lancaster, CORAL, 1988).

Timmins, G., *The last shift* (Manchester, Manchester University Press, 1993).

Timmins, G., *Blackburn: a pictorial history* (Chichester, Phillimore, 1993).

Timmins, G., 'Technological change', in M. B. Rose (ed.), *The Lancashire cotton industry* (Preston, Lancashire County Books, 1996).

Timmins, G., *Made in Lancashire* (Manchester, Manchester University Press, 1998).

Timmins, G., 'Housing quality in rural textile colonies: the Ashworth settlements revisited', *Industrial Archaeology Review*, 22 (2000) 22–37.

Todd, B., 'The remarrying widow: a stereotype reconsidered', in M. Prior (ed.), *Women in English society 1500–1800* (London, Methuen, 1985).

Toynbee, A., *The Industrial Revolution* (London, Green and Co., 1894).

Treble, J. H., 'Liverpool working class housing, 1801–1851', in S. D. Chapman (ed.), *The history of working class housing* (Newton Abbot, David and Charles, 1971).

Trinder, B., *The making of the industrial landscape* (London, Dent, 1982).

Trumback, R., 'Kinship and marriage in early modern France and England: four books', *Annals of Scholarship*, 2 (1981) 113–28.

Turner, M. E., J. V. Beckett and B. Afton, *Agricultural rent in England 1690–1914* (Cambridge, Cambridge University Press, 1997).

Tweedale, G., 'English versus American hardware: British marketing techniques and business performance in the USA in the nineteenth and early twentieth centuries', in R. Davenport-Hines (ed.), *Markets and bagmen* (Aldershot, Gower, 1986).

Valenze, D., *The first industrial woman* (Oxford, Oxford University Press, 1995).

Valverde, M., 'Giving the female a domestic turn: the social, legal and moral regulation of work in British cotton mills 1820–1850', *Journal of Social History*, 21 (1988) 619–34.

Van Der Woude, A., A. Hayami and J. De Vries (eds), *Urbanisation in history: a process of dynamic interactions* (Oxford, Oxford University Press, 1991).

Vann, R. T., 'Wills and the family in an English town: Banbury 1550–1800', *Journal of Family History*, 4 (1979) 346–67.

Vickery, A., *The gentleman's daughter* (New Haven, Yale University Press, 1998).

von Tunzelmann, N., *Steam power and British industrialisation to 1860* (Oxford, Clarendon, 1978).

von Tunzelmann, N., 'Coal and steam power', in J. Langton and R. J. Morris (eds), *Atlas of industrialising Britain, 1780–1914* (London, Methuen, 1986).

von Tunzelmann, N., 'Technological and organisational change in industry during the early Industrial Revolution', in P. O'Brien and R. Quinault (eds), *The Industrial Revolution and British society* (Cambridge, Cambridge University Press, 1993).

von Tunzelmann, N., 'Technology in the early nineteenth century', in R. Floud and D. McCloskey (eds), *The economic history of Britain since 1700, volume 1: 1700–1860* (Cambridge, Cambridge University Press, 1994).

von Tunzelmann, N., 'Time-saving technical change: the cotton industry in the Industrial Revolution', *Explorations in Economic History*, 32 (1995) 1–27.

Wadsworth, A. P., and J. de Lacy Mann, *The cotton trade and industrial Lancashire, 1600–1780* (Manchester, Manchester University Press, 1935).

Wall, R., 'Mean household size in England from printed sources', in P. Laslett and R. Wall (eds), *Household and family in past times* (Cambridge, Cambridge University Press, 1972).

Wall, R., 'Regional and temporal variations in English household structure from 1650', in J. Hobcraft and P. Rees (eds), *Regional demographic development* (London, Croom Helm, 1978).

Wall, R., 'Real property, marriage and children: the evidence from four pre-industrial communities', in R. M. Smith (ed.), *Land, kinship and life-cycle* (Cambridge, Cambridge University Press, 1984).

Wall, R., 'Leaving home and the process of household formation in pre-industrial England', *Continuity and Change*, 2 (1988) 77–102.

Wall, R., 'Elderly persons and members of their households in England and Wales from pre-industrial times to the present', in D. Kertzer and P. Laslett (eds), *Aging in the past: demography, society and old age* (Los Angeles, University of California Press, 1995).

Wall, R., 'Characteristics of European family and household systems', *Historical Social Research*, 23 (1998) 44–66.

Walton, J., 'Proto-industrialisation and the first Industrial Revolution: the case of Lancashire', in P. Hudson (ed.), *Regions and industries: a perspective on the Industrial Revolution in Britain* (Cambridge, Cambridge University Press, 1989).

Ward, J. T. (ed.), *The factory system, volume 1: birth and growth* (Newton Abbot, David and Charles, 1970).

Weatherill, L., *Consumer behaviour and material culture in Britain 1660–1760* (London, Routledge, 1988).

Webb, S., and B. Webb, *The history of trade unionism* (London, Green and Co., 1894 reprint).

Weir, D., 'Rather never than late: celibacy and age at marriage in English cohort fertility, 1541–1871', *Journal of Family History*, 9 (1984) 340–54.

Westall, O. M., 'Market strategy and the competitive structure of British general insurance, 1720–1980', *Business History*, 36 (1994) 1–28.

White, P., and R. I. Woods (eds), *The geographical impact of migration* (London, Longman, 1980).

Williams, D., 'Liverpool merchants and the cotton trade 1820–1850', in J. R. Harris (ed.), *Liverpool and Merseyside* (London, Cass, 1969).

Williams, K., *From pauperism to poverty* (London, Routledge and Kegan Paul, 1981).

Williams, M., *Cotton mills in greater Manchester* (Preston, Carnegie, 1992).

Williams N., and G. Mooney, 'Infant mortality in an age of great cities: London and the English provincial cities compared 1840–1910', *Continuity and Change*, 9 (1994) 185–212.

Williamson, J. G., 'Why was British growth so slow during the Industrial Revolution?', *Journal of Economic History*, 44 (1984) 689–712.

Williamson, J. G., *Did British capitalism breed inequality?* (Boston, Allen and Unwin, 1985).

Williamson, J. G., *Coping with city growth during the English Industrial Revolution* (Cambridge, Cambridge University Press, 1990).

Wilson, C., *England's apprenticeship 1603–1763* (London, Longman, 1965).

Wilson, C., 'Natural fertility in pre-industrial England 1600–1799', *Population Studies*, 38 (1984) 225–40.

Wilson, J. F., *British business history, 1720–1994* (Manchester, Manchester University Press, 1995).

Winch, D., *Malthus* (Oxford, Oxford University Press, 1992).

Woods, R. I., and C. Wilson, 'Fertility in England: a long term perspective', *Population Studies*, 45 (1991) 399–415.

Woods, R. I., and N. Shelton, *An atlas of Victorian mortality* (Liverpool, Liverpool University Press, 1997).

Wrightson, K., 'Kinship in an English village, Terling, Essex, 1550–1700', in R. M. Smith (ed.), *Land, kinship and life cycle* (Cambridge, Cambridge University Press, 1984).

# Bibliography

Wrightson, K., and D. Levine, *Poverty and piety in an English village: Terling 1525–1700* (London, Academic Press, 1979).

Wrightson, K., and D. Levine, *The making of an industrial society: Whickham 1560–1765* (Oxford, Oxford University Press, 1991).

Wrightson, K., et al. (eds), *The world we have gained: histories of population and social structure* (Oxford, Blackwell, 1986).

Wrigley, E. A., 'The growth of population in eighteenth century England: a conundrum resolved', *Past and Present*, 98 (1983) 121–50.

Wrigley, E. A., *People, cities and wealth: the transformation of traditional society* (Oxford, Oxford University Press, 1987).

Wrigley, E. A., *Continuity, chance and change: the character of the Industrial Revolution in England* (Cambridge, Cambridge University Press, 1988).

Wrigley, E. A., 'Brake or accelerator? Urban growth and population growth before the Industrial Revolution', in A. Van Der Woude, A. Hayami and J. De Vries (eds), *Urbanisation in history: a process of dynamic interactions* (Oxford, Oxford University Press, 1991).

Wrigley, E. A., 'The effects of migration on the estimation of marriage age in family reconstitution studies', *Population Studies*, 48 (1994) 81–97.

Wrigley, E. A., 'Explaining the rise in marital fertility in England in the long eighteenth century', *Economic History Review*, 51 (1998) 435–64.

Wrigley, E. A. (ed.), *Identifying people in the past* (Cambridge, Cambridge University Press, 1972).

Wrigley E. A., and R. S. Schofield, *The population history of England, 1541–1871* (London, Arnold, 1981).

Wrigley, E. A., and R. S. Schofield, 'English population history from family reconstitution: summary results 1600–1799', *Population Studies*, 37 (1983) 157–84.

Wrigley, E. A., R. S. Davies, J. E. Oeppen and R. S. Schofield, *English population history from family reconstitution 1580–1837* (Cambridge, Cambridge University Press, 1997).

Yasumoto, M., *Industrialisation, urbanisation and demographic change in England* (Nagoya, Nagoya University Press, 1994).

# INDEX

## Index

industrial productivity 80
industrious revolution 28, 59, 151–2
infant mortality 44, 55, 214–17, 221, 234
inheritance 228–30, 264–5, 269
innovation 81–7 passim, 96
inns 142–3, 189, 342
insurance records 109
intergenerational relationships 45, 263, 265, 270, 301, 304–5
invention 79–81, 96
inventories 181
inverse projection 209

keystone arches 334
kinship 55, 102, 119, 125, 128, 225–6, 231, 245–50, 254–61, 269, 271, 274–5
Kussmaul, A. 171, 177, 193

labour aristocracy 306–7
Lancashire 12, 34, 36–7, 41–2, 45, 53–4, 56–9, 78, 85, 90, 109, 127, 149, 167, 180, 195
landscape 36, 46, 186, 189, 198, 330–1
land usage 172–4
Landes, D. 22–3, 26, 29, 81
Laslett, P. 245, 247, 251, 254, 256, 271–2
lending 168
life expectancy 215
Liverpool 15, 73, 140, 149, 192, 216, 330
lodging houses 264
luxury trades 52, 81, 151, 155–6, 305

male breadwinner norm 287, 297–9
Malthus, T. 19, 193, 207
Manchester 14–16, 34, 51, 85, 89, 116, 123, 127–8, 140–2, 148–9, 153, 195, 331, 348
manufactory 49–52
marriage
  ages 43, 213–14, 221–2
  cohorts 214, 232
  motivations 224–5, 227–32 passim
  rates 213
Marshall, W. 164
Mathias, P. 22, 116

mechanisation 49–56 passim, 74–8 passim
medical marketplace 196–7
merchants 15, 116–17, 119, 123–4, 126–7, 145–6, 148–50
microsimulation 249–50
migration 44, 47, 54–5, 207, 222–41 passim
mills 57, 68, 90, 265, 328, 344
Mokyr, J. 26, 28, 80
mortality rates 212, 232

natural increase 220
neighbourhood networks 266, 288–9, 305
Newcastle 115
newspapers 17, 88, 138–41, 144–9 passim, 151, 159, 267, 301

open fields 163
Otmoor 185–9 passim
outworkers 36, 40, 45, 55, 298
Overton, M. 172–3, 181, 185, 191, 198

pamphlets 167
parish registers 208, 213
partnerships 102–8 passim, 114–20 passim, 126–7, 143
patents 80–3, 155
patronage 137–47 passim
pauper
  households 253–4
  letters 310–11
periodisation 5, 21–2
ploughback 118–19, 125–6, 336
polite buildings 333–6
Pollard, S. 105–6, 110
Pooley, C. 222–7 passim
poor law 58, 102, 227–8, 230, 232, 267–8, 273, 291, 311, 315–20 passim
population
  growth 19, 157, 164, 207–12 passim, 235, 277, 329
  regional dimensions 210–11, 216, 235
pottery industry 35–6, 38, 43, 71, 91, 94, 136–45 passim
poverty 4, 10, 21, 23, 45–7, 184, 189–91, 217

401